Michigan Government and You

by Steven L. Thomas

editorial assistance by
Stella McConnell
Elizabeth Pechta

layout by
David McConnell
Timothy Pickell

cover art by Theresa Deeter

cartoons by
Theresa Deeter

Hillsdale Educational Publishers

Made In Michigan

1993-94 Edition

© 1993 Hillsdale Educational Publishers

39 North Street
P.O. Box 245
Hillsdale, Michigan 49242
517-437-3179

02 01 00 99 98 97 96 95 94 93 ——— 10 9 8 7 6 5 4 3 2

Library of Congress Cataloging-in-Publication Data

Thomas, Steven L.
    Michigan government and you / by Steven L. Thomas ; editorial assistance by Stella McConnell, Elizabeth Pechta ; layout by David McConnell, Timothy Pickell ; cover art by Theresa Deeter.
        p.   cm.
    Includes index.
    ISBN 0-910726- 47-7
    1. Michigan--Politics and government.   2. Local government--Michigan.   I. Title.
    JK5816.T48   1992
    320.4774--dc20

                                        91-32794
                                        CIP

Acknowledgments

It is probably assumed that a book such as this is the product of the author alone. Such is not the case. The publisher, in this case David McConnell, is much like a coauthor and his assistance and guidance have been essential to the book's successful completion.

Many other individuals have provided their unique skills along the way. Several experts reviewed each chapter, but of course the author takes complete responsibility for any errors in the thousands of facts presented. It is impossible to list all those who have helped and I trust such individuals will find forgiveness in their hearts. Providing considerable help were County Commissioner Mark Grebner, Circuit Judge Michael Harrison, Representative H. Lynn Jondahl, Vince Leone, District Judge Pam McCabe, Probate Judge Donald Owen, Carmen Seats, Senator William Sederburg, and Clerk Virginia White.

The Okemos School Board must be acknowledged for its vision and patience. Without granting a sabbatical leave, this book would never have been completed. The government students, both at Okemos High School and Michigan State University, assisted as the text was fine tuned. Especially helpful were Jim Lobsinger, Laurie Nelson, Vince Porreca, Patrick Thomas, and Chen Yan.

Future editions of *Michigan Government and You* will benefit from reader suggestions and corrections. Do not hesitate to write or call the publisher or author. Your comments will assist thousands of readers throughout Michigan.

Steven L. Thomas

The publisher expresses gratitude to Stella McConnell for her many hours of proofreading. Special thanks also go to Theresa Deeter, the artist, for completing the illustrations under a tight deadline. Theresa's art adds a bright touch to this publication!

Hillsdale Educational Publishers
39 North Street
P.O. Box 245
Hillsdale, Michigan 49242
517-437-3179

Dedication

I dedicate this book to the following individuals:
My family in apology for the time we missed and will never see again;
My parents for encouraging me by their example to care about others more than myself;
Carmen Seats, an outstanding state worker among thousands of dedicated civil servants who as a group are too often criticized and too little appreciated;
Senator Bill Sederburg and Representative Lynn Jondahl who have served as models of professionalism and integrity for a combined 30 years in one of America's best legislatures.

Steven L. Thomas

CONTENTS

1 GOVERNMENT TOUCHES OUR LIVES   1

2 THE LAWMAKERS   8

3 THE BILL PASSAGE PROCESS   32

4 THE EXECUTIVE BRANCH: THE GOVERNOR   48

5 THE EXECUTIVE BRANCH: THE DEPARTMENTS   62

6 MICHIGAN'S COURT SYSTEM   90

7 FINANCING STATE GOVERNMENT   116

8 MICHIGAN'S COUNTY GOVERNMENT   134

9 TOWNSHIP GOVERNMENT   156

10 CITY & VILLAGE GOVERNMENT   170

11 SCHOOL DISTRICTS & RELATED ISSUES   187

12 LOCAL BUDGETING: TAXES & SPENDING   198

13 VOTING & ELECTIONS IN MICHIGAN   213

14 POLITICAL PARTIES, NOMINATIONS & PRIMARIES   229

15 POLITICAL ACTIVISM   246

Glossary   261

Michigan's Constitution   280

Index   317

1

GOVERNMENT TOUCHES OUR LIVES !
An Introduction

Students often wonder why they should study government at all. Everyone knows governments make laws which have an impact on our lives, but the cause and effect all seem quite remote. One of the aims of this book is to help you know why it is a good idea to study about government, especially those government units which are closest to you— city, school district, township, county, and state. The other main aim is to help you understand how these governments operate so you can deal with them in an effective way.

Here are several examples that show how people and local governments interact. In each case a student is involved.

Case 1. Tina's mother, Mrs. Salas, buys a Michigan lottery ticket every week even though her father says it is no different than gambling. Her mother responds that all state lottery money goes to the public schools and she is helping the cause of education even if she doesn't win. The other day a television program said that, for each dollar going into education from the lottery, a dollar is cut from the amount received from the state's general fund. Mrs. Salas is now confused and wonders if her husband is right. Tina would like to know what to tell her mother.

Case 2.

Jacob Hamtramck's father died suddenly of a heart attack. Of course, the family is emotionally crushed, but even worse they cannot find a will. The family must clear up its financial affairs so they can continue to run Mr. Hamtramck's business. Jacob's mother thinks they made a will many years ago but she has no idea where it is. Meanwhile Jacob read in his government textbook that wills can be left in the county probate court office for safe-keeping. How can he find out if his father put his will there?

2

Case 3. Kimberly's older sister Willa thinks it would be a good idea to start a beauty salon in the spare room of her home. She promises Kimberly she can work in the salon after school to earn extra money. Both sisters are excited about the plan. The room has been remodeled and the salon is ready to open for business, but both young women are in for a shock. A township zoning official learns of the new

salon and calls to say that the township does not allow businesses to be operated in homes. Later they discover that no building permit was issued for the remodeling and Willa could be fined. She has not yet heard from the state Bureau of Occupational and Professional Regulation regarding the operation of a beauty salon without a license; but she will!

Case 4. One afternoon Ryan was walking in the woods near his family's farm in rural Michigan. He spotted some men and women who had instruments and seemed to be surveying the land. He stopped and asked what they were doing and in the course of the conversation he learned the people were gathering

information about potential locations for a low-level radioactive waste dump. When he told his parents they were really shocked. They most certainly did not want a radioactive dump located near their home! Ryan wondered what low-level meant? He wanted to know who could give him the facts about this dump and if there is a way they could stop it from being built?

From these four examples it is obvious that government becomes more interesting when it hits close to home. The evening television news almost always focuses on the federal government and what is happening in Washington, D.C. But the examples above are not talking about federal laws or services provided by the federal government. They all relate to state, county or township government. It will take some patience to unscramble the maze of different units of government which affect us. Before seriously studying state and local government, let's review the basics.

THE BASICS

State Government

The largest and most powerful government in Michigan belongs to the state and is based in our *capital*, Lansing. Much of its activity takes place in the white domed *capitol* building*, but not all of it by any means. Today Michigan's state government is housed in dozens of buildings in Lansing and many in other parts of the state.

The governor is normally thought of as the head of our state government, but he or she shares power with many other officials. Actually the governor is the head of only one of the three main parts of state government, the executive branch. The legislative branch and the judicial branch are the other two parts.

The legislative branch is made up of the house and the senate. These two groups make Michigan's state laws. They each have their own meeting room, or chamber, in the capitol building. Many, but not all, of the legislators also have offices in the capitol.

The judicial branch contains all of the courts of the state. At the top of its ladder is the state supreme court which decides major cases in Michigan. The supreme court also decides if laws made by the legislative branch violate the Michigan *constitution. The state constitution is the rule book which organizes Michigan government and says what it may or may not do.*

There are many other kinds of courts in this branch and most of them have authority over only certain parts of the state. The state court system is divided into various districts depending on the type of court.

One important aspect of state government is raising money to pay for the services it provides. Along with the sales and income taxes, the state runs the lottery which concerns Mrs. Salas in Case 1.

* The word capital spelled with an "al" is the city, while the word capitol spelled with an "o" is the domed building in Lansing. The building is spelled with an "o" just as the word dome has an "o".

4

Several other layers of government exist in every state. Much like the layers of an onion, each one deals with smaller and smaller areas. The next layer below the state is the county.

County Government

Michigan has 83 counties. Look at a map and you can see most of Michigan's counties are squares which are alike in shape and size. Some stand out such as Marquette county which is Michigan's largest. Almost everyone has seen a county courthouse which is the headquarters of county government. Like its name says, this building often is  the place where one or more local courts meet. The probate court in case 2 is probably located in a county courthouse.

One of county government's more important tasks is keeping records about the people who live there. Each county has a clerk who maintains information such as births, deaths and marriages. There is also a *register of deeds* office where the staff registers or keeps track of all sales of homes, buildings, land, etc.

In most cases there is not any single person who is in charge of county government. Counties are run by a board of commissioners who are elected. Usually the more people living in a county the more complex county government becomes. Other important county officials are the sheriff, prosecuting attorney, medical examiner, and road commission. As you can see from this list of people, county government includes many important jobs.

Township Government

While nearly everyone realizes the state is divided into counties, they may not know that each county is divided into even smaller pieces called townships. Townships developed in the days of pioneers and settlers and they weren't government units at first, but square units of land six miles on each side. Later, townships were given governmental powers. Today Michigan has over 1,200 townships but they may not always be the same 6 miles square they were  originally because some have been combined and others subdivided. Each of these is governed by a board of elected officials. Some township boards may do very little and the only contact people have with them is to pay their property taxes to the township treasurer's office. But in townships near rapidly growing cities, there may be lots of activity dealing with *zoning* and other issues which can create heated debates.

The voters in Kimberly and Willa's township probably wanted to control where new businesses opened when they prohibited a beauty shop in Willa's home. This was done with the township zoning law. *Zoning is the division of a city or township into areas which can only be used for specific purposes.* One zone may only be for single family homes while another can include businesses and light industry.

School Districts

The school district is the unit of government which first affects the daily life of almost everyone. Michigan has a patchwork quilt of over 500 school districts.

Each district is governed by an elected board. This board controls most of the policies and practices which take place in the district's schools. They are responsible for paying all the bills and raising money to build new buildings and operate fleets of school buses. They hire a superintendent, principals, teachers, and custodians. They also have the final say over what courses are offered. School boards can find themselves in the middle of controversy when they feel the need to raise more money by increasing the property tax rates or when they must cut programs when there is a shortage of money to pay for everything.

City Government

Most of Michigan's people live in a city and each city has its own government. Even though every city is in a county, usually activities inside the city limits are under the control of the city and not the county or township.

In most cases the leader of city government is the mayor who works with a city council though there are several different types of city government. City councils pass local laws covering zoning, parking fines, changes in streets and parking areas, regulation of apartment buildings, setting the hours certain businesses can be open, and much more.

City government also operates public libraries, police and fire departments, and sewage treatment facilities, among other things.

Village Government

Another kind of local government is the village, which is usually smaller than a city. Simply put, the village form of government is less powerful than the city form. Villages are still under the township government in the township where they are located. Villages usually began their history as small settlements in a farming area.

Perhaps the village started when settlers moved to a four-corners near a blacksmith shop or general store. As the years passed, the residents may have found a need for some extra government services like a police department or a common water system. The residents then applied to the state to form their own village government. Once this was granted, they elected a village president and trustees to run the village.

In recent years one big problem some villages have had to face is the construction of a waste treatment system in order to meet state and federal pollution standards. These systems can cost millions but there may only be a few hundred people to pay the bill.

State Versus Federal Government

Which activities belong to the federal government and which belong to state government? The U.S. Constitution specifically gives certain powers to the federal government and leaves others to the states. For example, it is the federal government which prints money; operates the army, navy, and air force; makes treaties with foreign countries; and decides citizenship requirements. Over the course of American history, practice and court cases have decided whether the states or the federal government can do various other things. It seems the federal government continues to gain power and makes laws concerning more and more things each year. But, in a nutshell, the federal government controls those things which cross state lines or involve all of the states together. Having said this, there are many times when both the states and the federal government have laws in the same area. Both have laws about such things as the minimum wage, highway speeds, and civil rights, for example.

Each state is generally responsible only for those activities which take place inside its borders. Each state may have its own rules about many things unless those rules contradict the spirit of the U.S. Constitution. States can decide at what age people may vote in state elections, they control the educational system, have traffic laws, building codes, decide on fines and prison terms for crimes, build highways, tax people, and so forth.

Just as the federal government is like one big box with all of the state governments operating inside it, so is each state government a large box which holds smaller boxes containing county, township, city and village governments.

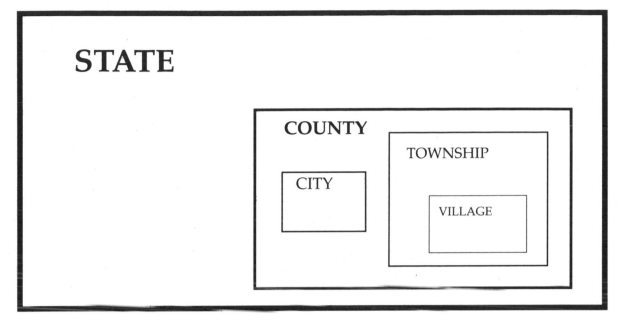

Relationships of Michigan's state and local governments.

Questions

1. What are the three branches of state government?

2. Which branch does the governor head?

3. Which branch contains the state's court system?

4. What does the state constitution do?

5. What is one of county government's more important tasks?

6. Michigan's 83 counties are further divided into over 1,200 of these.

7. Which unit of local government probably affects high school students more than any other?

8. Give an example of a service city government provides.

9. In a few sentences, explain which government activities belong to the states and which to the federal government. In which areas are there overlapping activities?

2

THE LAW MAKERS

Chapter 2 Section 1

The Legislature: Purpose and Organization

Here are the key concepts in this section:

1. The legislature is needed to identify needs, update laws because of a changing society, and to work out compromises.

2. The house and senate are the two parts of Michigan's legislature.

3. Each member of the legislature is elected from a district where he or she lives. Each member is responsible to help with the problems of the people living in that district.

Most people will never run for a seat in the Michigan house or senate, but if you ever want to have an impact on the kind of laws which are made in Michigan, you need to understand what the process is and how it works! The legislature is generally considered the most important part of a democratic government since it makes the laws.

Its members, known as representatives, are elected with the purpose of representing the interests and needs of their *constituents. Constituents are the citizens of each district and they are the people each representative works for. This includes those who are too young to vote along with those who did not vote for the winner.* No other part of state government is as close to the people as the legislature. Legislators are our neighbors; their children often go to the local schools. We tend to see them more than we see other officials. These men and women feel it is their duty to help their constituents and they are more accessible than anyone else in state government.

The Michigan legislature is a highly energetic body. It is considered one of the most professional and one of the best in the United States. Legislators work full time at their jobs and are paid accordingly.

WHY THE LEGISLATURE IS NEEDED

1. We are Too Busy!

We elect people to the Michigan legislature to represent our interests because we are busy with our day-to-day activities. Each session 3,500 to 4,500 bills are introduced, although most of them never become laws. No one working at another job would have the time to keep track of the many things going on at the capitol. There are several other reasons why people need the state legislature.

2. To Identify and Meet Needs

The nine million people in Michigan have different needs and wants. Many Michigan residents need very little from the government and they may even want the government to do less, spend less, and lower state taxes. Others, however, may need or want various services the state can provide. These

services can range from the state's administration of the federally funded social security program and food stamp program, to providing state police, or operating 23 state psychiatric centers and hospitals. These differences can cause legislative conflicts.

3. To Update Laws As Needs and Perceptions Change

Changing needs and perceptions make the legislature necessary. For example, in 1972 the legislators voted by a 4-1 majority to give those 18 years of age and older the right to vote. Previously, a Michigan citizen had to be 21 to vote. But during the Vietnam War many people felt if 18-year-olds could be drafted, they should be allowed to vote.

Also in 1972, Michigan legislators gave 18-year-olds the right to drink alcoholic beverages. But this new law had more unfortunate consequences than the legislators had anticipated. Eighteen and 19-year-olds bought alcoholic beverages for even younger teens and the numbers killed in alcohol-related automobile crashes increased. The legislators changed the legal drinking age back to 21 in 1978. As perceptions are reevaluated, our legislators take action.

4. To Work Out Compromises

Even when people agree on similar needs, they do not always agree on the best approach. For example, many believe the property tax in Michigan is too high. To make any change in the law though, will require legislative compromise because few individuals can agree on exactly what system will be an improvement. Differences of opinion over how to best meet our needs is true for any number of issues.

5. Other Duties and Services

The legislature also imposes taxes and decides how this money will be spent to provide government services. It may propose changes or amendments to the state constitution. It interacts with the executive branch when the senate approves or disapproves the governor's choices to fill appointed positions. There are also some less crucial jobs performed by members of the legislature:

Individual Assistance

When people need help interacting with other aspects of government they often turn to their state legislator. If some state agency is not responding properly to our needs, we may ask our legislator to talk with them. If an older couple needs help with a heating assistance rebate, they could receive guidance from their legislator. Agencies of our government often respond with renewed efforts when a legislator phones them.

Ceremonial Requirements

Legislators are asked to do ceremonial duties. Occasionally, we need someone to cut a ribbon or give a speech. Who better than our state senator? Legislators are in high demand to provide words of wisdom at commencements. One legislator even tells of his involvement in a goat milking contest!

Recognition of Achievements

Another function legislators provide is the passage of *resolutions* honoring those who have done something special. *A resolution is a written expression of the legislature's sentiment.* If the local girls' basketball team wins the state championship, its senator might present the team with a resolution passed by the Michigan senate. The same is often done for a retiring civic leader.

Organization of the Legislature ....

ITS STRUCTURE HAS TWO PARTS—
Michigan's legislative structure is outlined by the state constitution which was modeled after the national constitution. The one important difference is that senatorial districts of state governments cannot be formed on the basis of land areas as the United States Senate is. This change came about after a series of important court cases; one of which began in Michigan in 1959. (See Scholle versus Hare)

Michigan, like every state except Nebraska, has a *bicameral* legislature. *Bicameral means two chambers—a house of representatives and a senate.* Nebraska has a *unicameral* (one-house) legislature. *In a unicameral government the house of representatives and senate are combined.* Michigan considered a unicameral legislature in 1973, but Representative Joe Swallow of Alpena could not get his bill passed.

Why Two Parts? Which System Is Best?
Supporters of the bicameral system argue that emotions will cool down by the time two groups have decided an issue, since in order for a bill to become a law, both the house *and* the senate must pass it individually. Many believe Michigan is likely to have better laws if all 148 legislators, rather than just 38 senators or 110 representatives, give their input.

Those who oppose unicameral legislatures have one other argument. Politicians often need someone to blame for derailed legislation. In the bicameral system a legislator can blame a popular bill's failure on the other house.

If Michigan ever considers a unicameral legislature again, we should take note that some experts say in a unicameral system it is easier to vote for bills that are irresponsible but popular with the public because legislators expect the governor to veto them. Legislators can still look good and rely on the governor's veto to stop the legislation from becoming law. This is especially likely when the majority in the legislature and the governor are from opposing parties.

Questions

1. List five reasons people say we need a professional legislature on the state level.

2. Explain the meaning of the term "bicameral legislature." Does Michigan have one of these?

Chapter 2 Section 2

Districts and Their Importance

Here are the key concepts in this section:

1. District boundaries are changed every 10 years when new census information is available. The redrawing of these boundaries has become a very political process which can have important consequences.

2. Because of key court cases a revolution has taken place in the redrawing of district boundaries all across the nation. Today each district must have close to the same number of people. This concept is known as "one person, one vote"

3. Political parties try to redraw district boundaries to their advantage. This strategy is known as gerrymandering (JERRY mandering).

DISTRICTS

Another important aspect of the legislature's structure is the way the state has been divided into house and senate districts. Michigan has 38 senate districts and 110 house districts. Each of us lives in one state house district and in one state senate district. To provide fair representation for the people of Michigan, the state constitution calls for voters of each district to elect their own legislators. This way people are closer to the person they elect to represent them.

The use of so many small districts allows fairer representation. Minority groups, representing 5, 10, or even 20 percent of the people, might not achieve any representation if there were only a few large districts.

Note that in Michigan the three very urban counties of Wayne, Oakland, and Macomb in the southeastern corner of the state have 43 percent of the population. This great concentration of voters affects Michigan politics in many ways.

How Many Members? What Size of District?

States vary greatly in the size of their legislatures. There is no ideal number of legislators. The goal is to have districts small enough to allow for adequate input from the public, but not so large a group of legislators they are unmanageable.

Michigan has a population of about nine million people. Court interpretations of the state and federal constitutions call for each house district to be of nearly equal size and for each senate district to be of nearly equal size. Since Michigan has 110 districts for its house of representatives and 38 districts for its senators, the average house district has about 80,000 people and the average senate district contains about 240,000 people.

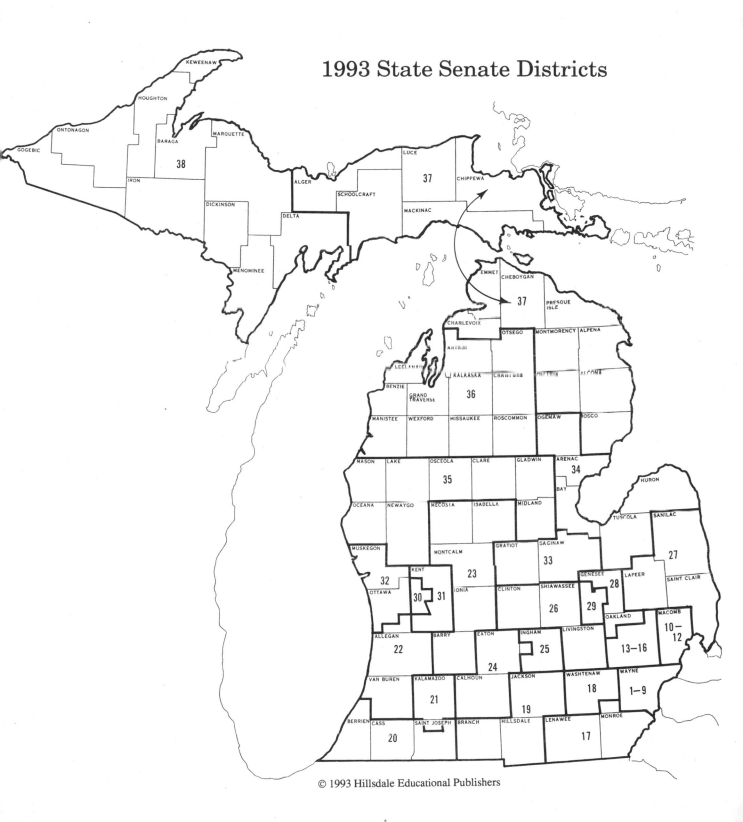

1993 State Senate Districts

© 1993 Hillsdale Educational Publishers

14

1993 State House Districts

Michigan's legislature is fairly average in size. Most state houses range from 100 to 150 members. State senates usually have 30 to 50 members. Alaska has only 20 senators, while Minnesota with 67 has the largest senate.

It might be expected that states with larger populations would have larger numbers of state legislators but this is not true. California, the state with the most people, has 80 members in its *"lower chamber". Tradition says the group with the most members can be called the "lower chamber" while the smaller group, usually known as the senate, can be called the "upper chamber."* On the other hand, the much smaller state of Massachusetts has 400 legislators. This means a Massachusetts house member only represents about 17,000 people compared to a California legislator's 300,000.

Reapportionment

The federal government takes a new census of the population each decade, 1990, 2000, etc. When this information is released, all U.S. and state government districts must be redrawn and new boundaries made to account for population changes.

The changing of these boundaries is called *reapportionment. Reapportionment is the redrawing of legislative districts to equalize their populations.* The law dictates districts are to be as equal in population as possible because in a democracy everyone is legally equal; if one district has a larger number of people than another, each person in the larger district has less representation in government. New districts cannot be drawn in just any manner. They must be *contiguous* (together, not in scattered parts), compact, and should not cut county, city, and township boundaries unless necessary.

In Michigan, the process of reapportioning state house and senate districts is supposed to be carried out by the *Legislative Apportionment Commission.* Deciding these new district boundaries is a very difficult and complex matter. There are an infinite number of possibilities.

Reapportionment Once Ignored

Long ago more people lived in rural areas and as Michigan cities grew, these population shifts were often ignored. Extremely unequal districts resulted. This was probably at its worst in Michigan and the rest of the country after the 1960 census. For example, Michigan's 12th Congressional district in the Upper Peninsula was the least populous in the nation, with only 177,431 residents. At the same time, the 16th district in Wayne County was one of the largest in the United States with 802,994 people. Each district was represented by only one person in Congress. But, Michigan was not the only state where such inequities existed.

The Issue Goes To Court -- Scholle versus Hare

In the late 1950s some people began to feel such unequal districts violated the principles of democracy. Cities had grown rapidly but they did not have any added districts. More and more people were represented by the same number of representatives. Many felt those living in rural districts had more power than they should.

One such person was Gus Scholle, the head of the Michigan AFL-CIO union. The union found it hard to have the kind of laws passed in the Michigan legislature that it wanted because that body was so conservative, especially the senate. The Michigan senate had not been reapportioned since 1925.

In 1959 Mr. Scholle sued Michigan's Secretary of State James Hare and the case went before the state supreme court. Gus Scholle, the *plaintiff, the person making the complaint in court,* said the imbalanced situation violated his rights under the 14th amendment of the U.S. Constitution.

About the same time similar cases were taking place in other states, including a famous one in Tennessee, Baker versus Carr. Charles Baker of that state complained his vote was not as powerful because he lived in a district with a large population. Many districts in Tennessee were smaller than his.

Some of the attorneys in these cases formed a network to share information as their desire was so strong to see better representation take place. Nonetheless, most people thought these cases were foolish and couldn't be won. Michigan's attorney general said if Scholle were victorious it would throw state government into "unprecedented chaos".

In 1960 the state court dismissed Scholle's case, but he did not give up. An appeal was made to the U.S. Supreme Court where the Baker case from Tennessee was already awaiting action. By 1962 the Supreme Court made a decision about Baker versus Carr and it found such apportionment inequities to be unconstitutional. This decision from the highest court in the United States forced all states to provide districts of equal population. Another way to say this is "one-person, one-vote." The Scholle case was sent back to the Michigan supreme court and this time he won. These court cases, Baker versus Carr and Scholle versus Hare, brought about a revolution in the redrawing of legislative districts.

The importance of the reapportionment cases of the 1960s cannot be exaggerated. They resulted in the present situation where most states, including Michigan, are now controlled by the interests of their urban areas. That's where the people are.

Legislative Apportionment Commission

Who is supposed to decide how districts are to be redrawn? This is the job of the legislative apportionment commission. Their work would seem simple enough: take our state's population and divide it by the number of house or senate districts. With the senate, for example, all that is necessary is to make 38 districts of equal population size. The problem is the political parties will try to shape the districts to their own advantage.

The Commission has eight members— four members from each of the two major political parties in Michigan. A new plan is completed only when a majority agrees— and this is the worst part of all. In a group equally divided among political parties, this project is bound to fail. Each party's appointees want to gain more seats for *their party*.

During its life Michigan's commission has never been able to reach a single agreement on redrawing districts! When this happens, the issue may be submitted to the state supreme court. Each political party usually sends its own plan. It is up to the court to decide which of the plans is fairer.

However, supreme court members hardly enter this process with a completely unbiased viewpoint since all of them came to their position by nomination from one party or the other. So the Court is inclined to select the plan presented by the party that supported the majority of the justices. The result is almost always gerrymandering.

Gerrymandering

The drawing of political districts for the purpose of gaining more political power is gerrymandering. It is commonplace in all states. How can one party redraw district boundaries to give their members an advantage? Districts are not uniform and they have concentrations of Democratic voters in some places and concentrations of Republican voters in others.

Those intent on gerrymandering find out where Democrats and Republicans tend to live. If they want to make sure the district is a bit more Democratic, they simply draw district lines excluding a few Republican areas. Then, they add a few Democratic areas. The result is a district consisting of voters more likely to vote Democratic. Both parties gerrymander districts if they are in the position to do so.

Michigan's gerrymandering has become a showcase of maneuvering, infighting, lawsuits, and name-calling. In the last three reapportionments, 1970, 1980, 1990, the commission's plans ended in the Michigan supreme court. In 1982 the court decided to have Bernie Apol, the retired director of the Elections Division of the Secretary of State's office, draft a plan. Apol was highly respected by both political parties and his plan was then adopted.

Political battling reemerged during the 1990 reapportionment and was not resolved until after the 1992 elections.

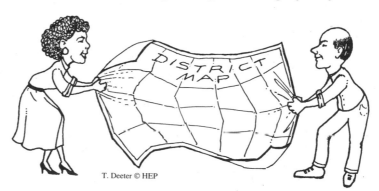

T. Deeter © HEP

Future reapportionment methods are undecided at this time. The court has even said the legislature may reapportion itself. One of the best suggestions came from Senator William Sederburg (Republican-24th District) who wanted to give the problem to one of our brightest, most objective, non-political brains—a computer.

Questions

1. How many members does the Michigan senate have? The Michigan house?

2. At what point in time are state house and senate districts redrawn or revised? What is the name for this process?

3. What principle is involved in deciding how many people are living in each house or senate district? Does each Michigan house district have about the same number of residents? Is a Michigan house district the same size as a senate district? Explain.

4. Study a map of Michigan house and senate districts. Do you believe either map shows signs of gerrymandering? Give an example to support your opinion?

Chapter 2 Section 3

Qualifications, Background, Pay & Benefits

Here are the key concepts in this section:

1. The Michigan legislature meets for a two-year term which is divided into two one-year sessions. Most of the actual house and senate meetings take place on Tuesdays, Wednesdays, and Thursdays.

2. All those who are 21, a registered voter, and not convicted of a felony in the last 20 years may run for the Michigan house or senate.

3. The Michigan legislature has both men and women members, along with a number of blacks and other minorities. Many members were lawyers or teachers before they were elected to office.

4. Being a legislator in Michigan is a full-time job with the house and senate meeting throughout most of the year. The representatives are paid quite well, earning over $45,000 plus other benefits.

EVERY TWO YEARS A NEW LEGISLATURE

Each term of Michigan's state legislature lasts for two years and is given its own unique number starting with the number 1 in 1835. The house and senate members serving during the period 1991-92 are in the 86th legislature; those in 1993-1994 are in the 87th, and so on. Remember, senators are elected for four years so they serve during two legislatures, but representatives only serve during one.

All law making activity must be completed by the end of the term. No bills are carried over from one term to the next. If a bill cannot be passed into law within this two-year period, it is scrapped. They may be introduced as new bills in the next legislature, but they must start all over again.

The finish line is two years away...

T. Deeter © HEP

Sessions

Each term of the legislature is divided into two one-year *sessions*. In Michigan there is no set number of days to meet. The state constitution requires each session to start at 12 noon on the second Wednesday in January. There are occasional *recesses* or breaks for holidays and campaigning, but the session usually continues until the last week of the year when it *adjourns*. Neither the house nor the senate may adjourn without the permission of the other. *Adjourning is the official act of closing a legislative session, but a recess is a temporary break.*

If the legislature has adjourned, the governor may call a special session to consider matters needing immediate attention. In recent years, however, the Michigan legislature has nearly always been in session and special sessions have not been necessary.

Meeting Times

When the house and senate are in session, they normally meet Monday evenings and Tuesday, Wednesday, and Thursday. This is because many of the legislators leave Lansing on Friday to return home for the weekend. If you come to Lansing to visit a session, check with the office of a representative about exact meeting times.

OUR STATE LEGISLATORS

BACKGROUND

The legislature is made up of a variety of professions, ages, races, and both sexes. The number of women in the legislature has slowly increased in the last two decades. In 1993-94 the house had 24 women and the senate had three.

Backgrounds of Members of the Michigan Legislature

MICHIGAN STATE SENATE:

TEACHERS AND EDUCATORS	8	DOCTOR	1
ATTORNEYS	6	FUNERAL DIRECTOR	1
FARMERS	5	PSYCHOLOGIST	1
LEGISLATIVE ASSISTANTS	3	PUBLISHER	1
REAL ESTATE BROKERS	3	STOCKBROKER	1
PUBLIC OFFICIALS	2	U.S. DIPLOMATIC CORPS	1
ACCOUNTANT	1	UNION OFFICIAL	1
BUSINESSMAN	1		
CONSTRUCTION WORKER	1		
COUNTY ROAD COMMISSIONER	1		

MICHIGAN HOUSE OF REPRESENTATIVES:

Teachers and educators	21	Nurses	2
Attorneys	15	Real estate brokers	2
Business women and men	12	Social workers	2
Farmers	8	Baker	1
Legislative assistants	6	Civic volunteer	1
City and county government	5	Construction contractor	1
Manufacturing	5	Court officer	1
Accountants	3	Director of economic development	1
Communications (radio, TV, newspaper)	3	Manager, Secretary of State branch	1
Fiscal analysts	3	Miner	1
Law enforcement	3	Policy associate of education foundation	1
Bankers	2	Political analyst	1
Community planners	2	Resort owner	1
Insurance agents	2	Union official	1
Ministers	2		

Women have been a powerful force in the legislature and state government in general. Governor Blanchard chose Martha Griffiths for his running mate in 1982. In the 1986 and 1990 races for governor, both candidates had female running mates. Connie Binsfeld succeeded Griffiths as lieutenant governor and president of the senate in 1991. Representative Teola Hunter served as speaker pro tem of the house. It is expected the influence of women in the legislative process will continue to grow.

Most legislators are white, but minorities have been powerful for many years. The senate had three minority members in 1993 and the house had 13. Minorities have held the position of house speaker pro tem, floor leader, and several have chaired powerful committees.

Many state legislators are attorneys by profession. Another large group in Michigan consists of former teachers. See the chart with background information about Michigan's legislators.

FULL-TIME (VERSUS PART-TIME) LEGISLATORS

Many state legislatures throughout the United States are given only a few months to do their work. Others only meet once every two years. The Michigan legislature has met each year from January through December since 1969, with occasional recesses. All our legislators are not convinced they are needed in Lansing full time. Occasionally, there have been rumblings of changing to a part-time legislature.

WHY THEY DO IT

The life of a legislator can be very hectic. What would ever cause someone to run for this office? Every two or four years they must defend themselves against criticisms, verbal abuse, name calling, and mud-slinging. Surely, there must be an easier way to make as much money. There are many reasons why people choose such jobs, including the desire to do good for the state and its people. Others want to represent a certain philosophy or point of view, while some are deeply interested in passing certain new laws. The power and prestige is an attraction too.

QUALIFICATIONS, ELECTIONS, AND COMPENSATION

Qualifications

To be a Michigan state senator or representative, a person must be:

A.   21 years of age

B.   A registered Michigan voter

C.   Live in the district

D.   Not convicted of a felony in the last 20 years

Besides these constitutional requirements, the voters establish other criteria they expect a candidate to meet. They generally prefer an individual who is a good public speaker, energetic, personable, and experienced in political matters.

Restrictions of Office

Once elected, a member cannot be appointed to another office within the state or have a business contract with any political subdivision of the state. It should go without saying that an elected official cannot serve in two or more offices at the same time; however, people have tried this on occasion. In 1896 Hazen Pingree tried to be the mayor of Detroit and governor at the same time, until the state supreme court ruled against him.

Each house decides its own rules, judges its own members, and may expel a member by a two-thirds vote. This is occasionally done. Several years ago the house expelled Monte Geralds who had been convicted of embezzlement.

Elections

Both members of the house and senate are elected in the November elections of even-numbered years— 1992, 1994, 1996, etc. (the first Tuesday after the first Monday of the month) The members of the house are elected every two years. Senators are elected at the same time as the governor and have identical terms. In 1994 and 1998, etc. the governor and all state senators will be up for reelection.

Removal and Replacement

Vacancies occur when a legislator resigns, leaves the state permanently, dies, or is recalled. When any of these happen, a replacement is needed quickly. In Michigan, the governor must call for an election within 90 days of the vacancy. If more than one candidate from either party file to run, a run-off primary is required first. The winners of the primaries face each other in the actual election to fill the empty seat. The person with the most votes serves until the next general election.

Sometimes legislators are removed from office. In 1983 Democratic Senators Philip Mastin and David Serotkin were recalled for supporting an increase in the state income tax. It was an important situation for Michigan politics. The two Democrats were replaced by two Republicans, putting the Republicans in control of the state senate. If the change had not taken place, the Democrats would have retained control of both houses.

Salary and Benefits

Today being a legislator in Michigan is a full-time job. This level of activity slowly developed over the years. Legislators receive salaries that allow them to leave their prior careers. The salaries paid Michigan legislators are among the highest in the nation. Recently they were $45,450 with an expense allowance of $8,500. Legislators also are reimbursed for their travelling costs to and from Lansing. They receive funds for lodging while they are in session too. Many legislators room together while they are in Lansing to keep their expenses down.

Legislators from most states receive a much smaller salary. Many are from states with part-time legislatures. Some states simply refuse to pay their elected officials very much. The salary in Idaho is only $4,200 per year!

Legislators serving eight years or more may receive an optional retirement pension once they reach age 55. This amounts to 32 percent of their salary when they retire, but may go as high as 64 percent if they have served 16 years or more. Members must contribute seven percent of their salary into the retirement fund if they want to receive this benefit.

State Officers Compensation Commission

In 1968, the people of Michigan adopted a constitutional amendment that established the *State Officers Compensation Commission* which is appointed by the governor. Every two years it determines the salaries of the governor, lieutenant governor, supreme court justices, court of appeals judges, and legislators. Before this, the legislators determined their own salaries which led to criticism and political maneuvering.

After public hearings and research, the commission makes its recommendation to the legislature. The legislature may accept or reject the recommendations, but may not alter them. The recommendations have been accepted every time.

Legislative Immunity

While representatives are trying to find solutions to important issues they cannot be in constant fear that someone disagreeing with them will have them arrested for a trivial matter. This happened frequently during our colonial days. The U. S. Constitution gives *legislative immunity* to U.S. House and Senate members and the authors of Michigan's state constitution did the same. *Immunity means freedom from arrest or prosecution.*

Michigan legislators are free from arrest regarding civil matters but not criminal charges. The immunity is only during sessions of the legislature plus five days before and five days after. This privilege is occasionally, though rarely, abused. For example, legislators can park wherever they please and break the speed limit occasionally without concern of a ticket. In addition, legislators cannot be questioned in any other place for anything they say in either house.

THE JOURNAL

The public has a right to know what bills the legislature is considering and how legislators voted. Anyone can request a bill from either the House or Senate Documents Room during regular business hours. There is currently no cost for this service. Copies of bills can also be requested through the mail. (Write "House" or "Senate" Document Room, Capitol Building, Lansing, MI 48913.)

Plus, a journal detailing the actions on various bills during the session is kept in both houses. The Journal of the Senate and the Journal of the House of Representatives are both available the next day. Notices of upcoming committee hearings are also included as required by the Open Meetings Act. Nearly all committee meetings are open to the public.

Questions

1. Someday it may be useful for you to know some of the details concerning Michigan's legislature. What is the difference between a term and a session? What days and times are the Michigan house and senate actually meeting?

2. What happens to a bill if it has not been passed by the house and senate before the end of a term?

3. Are any of the following practices illegal? Why or why not? Susan Smith owns a successful construction firm which paves hundreds of miles of state highways each year. Susan is elected to the Michigan senate and continues to operate her company and pave state roads. Becky Brown is a popular mayor of a southeastern Michigan city. She runs for the state house and wins— amazingly she has time to do both jobs.

4. What is the approximate salary of a state legislator? Is the pay different for members of the house and senate? What other money do they receive?

5. Where can you get a written copy of a bill or find out what is happening in the Michigan legislature?

Chapter 2 Section 4

The Operation of the Senate and House

Here are the key concepts in this section:

1. The party which has the most members in the senate or house is the majority party and its members gain much influence.

2. Members of the same political party often meet to discuss strategy and to encourage a united vote on bills.

3. Both the house and senate have key positions which are controlled by the majority party. The president of the senate, majority leader, and speaker of the house can use their powers to control most of the laws which are made.

THE SENATE

How Many and Where
Michigan has 38 state senators, each representing a district of about 240,000 people. Between 1955 and 1964, Michigan had 34 senators and 32 between 1853 and 1954. The state senate meets in the south wing of the capitol building.

Length of Term
The term of office for the senate is four years. Senators are elected at the same time as the governor and other major state-wide officers (1990, 1994, 1998, etc.). These are often referred to as "off-year" elections since the President is not up for election.

There is no limit to the number of terms a senator may serve. Senator DeMaso of Battle Creek retired in 1986 after serving 30 years in the house and senate. Senator Basil Brown served 31 years before leaving the senate in late 1987.

Party Control
Political affiliation is very important in the legislature, as it is at most levels of government. The house or the senate is controlled by the party of the majority of the members. This party decides to a large extent what laws will be passed. Whoever can get 20 votes on any issue in the senate will win.

In almost every case, candidates running for office are associated with a political party. They usually choose one of the two major political parties—the Democrats or the Republicans. All Democrats do not agree on all issues. Nor do

26

all Republicans. It is expected, however, that all Democrats and Republicans will give serious consideration to agreeing with their own party.

The party in control of the senate has changed hands several times in recent years. The people of Michigan continue to send nearly equal numbers of Republicans and Democrats to the state senate. In 1971-74, the voters sent 19 members from each party to the senate.

In case of a tie vote, including votes to determine control, the president of the senate may vote. The Lieutenant Governor is the president of the senate. The Republicans controlled the governor's and lieutenant governor's offices during this period so Lt. Governor James Brickley sided with the Republicans on all tie votes.

In the last 20 years there has been a major change in party affiliation by Michigan's voters and in the party controlling the house and senate. The "one man one vote" court rulings have also played a part in what has been happening. For many years Republicans always controlled the senate. Since the Civil War, Republicans were in charge with only two exceptions both during the Depression—in 1933-34 and 1937-38. From 1919-30 there wasn't a single Democratic senator. Even though the Republicans still have the majority, their margin is much smaller than in past years. For example, 20 Republicans and 18 Democrats were elected to the senate to serve from 1991-1994.

The *majority party* gains power because they control everything which takes place—committee assignments, committee chairmanships, appointments, and the success or failure of proposed legislation. They also control office assignments, out-of-state trips, typewriters, pencils, and other things large and small. *The political party that has at least one more than half of the votes in the house or senate is called the majority party.* They use this power to achieve their own goals and to defeat the goals of the other party.

T. Deeter © HEP

Caucuses — Political Party Meetings of Legislators

Before a new term begins, legislators belonging to the same party within each house will usually meet to elect their officers and to establish their goals. Such a meeting is called a *caucus*. The members will frequently meet in their caucuses throughout the session.

A major reason for meeting is to keep their votes together or to determine strategy. If a party has a slim majority, it cannot have any members "defecting" and voting with the other party. Such meetings are like a football huddle. The leaders want to make sure the team members are all doing what they are expected to be doing. Sometimes there are surprises since all members of a party do not always agree on every issue. One legislator's priorities may not be the same as another's, even within the same political party. If a party is to accomplish its goals, though, it may have to get all its members to agree. There are many ways to do this. Some can be discussed in public. Some cannot. In fact, the only exceptions to the "Open Meetings Act" of 1976, other than labor negotiations and sensitive personnel matters, are the caucuses of the house and senate.

Leadership

Any organization needs leaders to work effectively and efficiently. The senate is no exception, but its leadership centers around the political parties. Each party has its special leaders. The Democrats in the senate have a *minority leader*, a *minority floor leader*, a *minority whip*, several assistant minority whips, and a caucus chairperson. *In this use the word whip means to hold together for united action.* The Republicans have similar positions. The major role of this party leadership is to keep the law-making process on schedule.

Party Leadership for the Senate

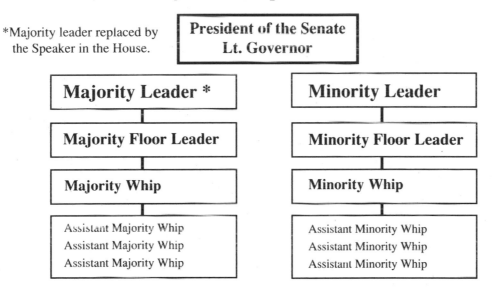

*Majority leader replaced by the Speaker in the House.

**President of the Senate
Lt. Governor**

Majority Leader *	**Minority Leader**
Majority Floor Leader	**Minority Floor Leader**
Majority Whip	**Minority Whip**
Assistant Majority Whip Assistant Majority Whip Assistant Majority Whip	Assistant Minority Whip Assistant Minority Whip Assistant Minority Whip

According to the Michigan constitution the *lieutenant governor* heads the senate where he or she is known as the *president of the senate*. The president of the senate presides over the meetings and votes only in case of ties. Since the lieutenant governor is very busy, they usually let someone else preside much of the time. This particular person is the *president of the senate pro tempore,* or the president pro tem. The president pro tem is selected from the senate majority party to lead "temporarily" while the lieutenant governor is away.

The presiding officer, whether it is the lieutenant governor or the president pro tem, can often be very important, as he or she can decide to hear one speaker rather than another. Of even greater importance is the speed with which they use their *gavel* to strike the podium, known as the "quick gavel". Presiding officers have been known to say "All those in favor say aye...All those opposed...the ayes have it," without giving careful attention to the opposing vote. Followed by an equally quick adjournment, this can be an unbeatable tactic to keep the other side from being heard.

Majority Leader

While the president of the senate is an important position, one which is even more powerful is the senate *majority leader*. This person is chosen by the majority party— the party with the most members. Among the powers and responsibilities of the senate majority leader are the following:

1. Appoints all members to all committees
2. Appoints chairpersons of all committees
3. Assigns all bills to committee
4. Decides who gets what office space
5. Decides who goes on trips and to where
6. Decides the senate staff and budget

In both the house and senate there is a *majority floor leader* who maneuvers legislation and attempts to assure that the majority caucus goals are reached. This person is aided by the assistant majority floor leader. Assisting both are the whips. The position of whip is also found in both chambers. The minority party has a similar organization for its leadership in the house and senate.

THE HOUSE

How Many and Where They Meet

The Michigan House of Representatives meets in the north wing of the state capitol and has 110 members. These are each selected by the 80,000 constituents of his or her house district.

Length of Term

House members serve for two-year terms and there is no limit to the number of terms. Some house members have served for many years. Representative Dominic Jacobetti (Democrat-108th District) is an example of a long serving member of the House. He was first elected in 1954 and was still in office in 1990.

Party Control

Each political party will attempt to elect a majority of 56 or more representatives in the house. Just as in the senate, the majority party controls nearly everything.

Leadership

The organization of the house is almost identical to the senate. The house has its caucus chairpersons, whips, floor leaders, and others needed to move legislation along according to the priorities of each party. The one difference is the position known as the *speaker of the house. The speaker is the presiding officer in the House of Representatives. Because of the vast powers of this position the speaker can control the passage of any bills introduced by either party. Under normal conditions this person is chosen from the majority party in the house.* There is no majority leader in the house.

Speaker of the House

The speaker has historically been the most powerful person in the entire legislature, and is selected by the house members. If the Democrats are in control, as they have been since 1969, they will surely choose one of their own to run things. The decision is initially made in the caucus. The final vote for the speaker's position is taken among the entire membership, not just among the majority party. If members of the majority party argue among themselves and are divided over whom to select, it is conceivable for the minority party candidate to win.

The power of the speaker is hard to imagine by simply reading a list of his or her powers and responsibilities. In practice, the senate majority leader and the house speaker control the passage of any bills introduced during their terms. Following is a list of some of the speaker's powers:

1. Calls the house to order and maintains proper conduct
2. Decides the order of business
3. Appoints all committee members
4. Refers bills to committees
5. Recognizes who speaks
6. Controls the order in which bills appear

7. Answers questions about procedures

8. Appoints most employees of the house

9. Appoints a committee on newspaper correspondents

10. Calls for all votes

11. Votes on all issues before the house (unlike the president of the senate) except appeals of the speaker's decisions

12. Determines when sufficient time to vote has been given

13. Determines the house budget

As with the majority leader of the senate, the speaker usually has someone else preside over the house sessions, while he or she is occupied with guiding and molding legislation.

LEGISLATIVE STAFF

Today, legislators are not alone in doing the job of making our laws. There are hundreds of people who help them. A staff of approximately 500 works in the house and 300 assist in the senate. They usually work in one of the following four areas:

Personal Staff

Typically, representatives will have two staff members and senators will have three. These assistants do many tasks. They answer the phone, draft bills and letters, write speeches, do research, contact constituents, and much more.

Legislative Aides

This group includes those who work in a somewhat non-partisan way for the whole house or senate. The clerk of the house and the secretary of the senate are examples. Included also are *sergeants-at-arms*, clerks, custodians, *pages*, and others. *The sergeant-at-arms keeps order, sees that unauthorized people are kept off the floor of the houses, serves official papers, and controls the heating and lighting. Pages serve as messengers and run various errands for the members.*

Partisan Staff

Many staff people work for the majority and minority leaders. They include speech writers, researchers, analysts, and others.

Committee Staff

Each committee is given a staff person to do clerical duties, as well as assist in the process of amending bills, rewriting bills, and setting agendas. Committee staff members are very helpful as bills move though the various committees.

LEGISLATIVE AGENCIES
Fiscal Agencies

There are a few other agencies which provide valuable assistance to legislators. The senate and house *fiscal agencies* aid the two houses in determining the *fiscal* impact of bills. This means they tell the legislators how much the bills will cost the government and tax payers directly and indirectly. *The term fiscal relates to financial matters when talking about government programs. A fiscal agency is a department which helps keep track of the expenses of programs or changes in the tax laws, etc.*

The Legislative Service Bureau

The *Legislative Service Bureau (LSB) is the organization that actually writes the bills for the legislators. It is a professional organization of experts who put the bills in correct legal language so they can become laws.* Legislators have been known to jot down their ideas for bills on napkins, notepaper, and used envelopes. They may give these ideas to the LSB and then receive back a nicely typed, professional-looking document. Learn more about the Legislative Service Bureau in the next chapter.

This chapter has explained the organization of the house and senate. Another key factor in the law-making process is how an idea for a new law travels through the legislative system. Many things can happen to a bill as it goes through the legislature. Learning about the legislative process is the purpose of our next chapter.

Questions

1. Briefly explain how the party in control of the house or senate gains power because it is in charge.

2. Which meetings concerning the legislature are open to the public and which are not?

3. List at least four important leadership positions in the Michigan house and senate. Which position is considered the most powerful in each chamber?

4. There are many jobs available in the Michigan legislature besides the elected representatives. If you had the option of taking one of the following jobs which would you like to have and why? 1. Personal staff for a senator, 2. fiscal staff for the house, 3. sergeant-at-arms for the house, 4. member of the Legislative Service Bureau.

3

THE BILL PASSAGE PROCESS

Chapter 3 Section 1

Where Bills Come From and How They Become Law

Here are the key concepts in this section:

1. Most ideas for new laws come from lobbyists, departments of state government, or legislators themselves.

2. In a sense, a bill is the name for a law before it is born, before it is passed by the legislature and okayed by the governor.

3. Every bill has a sponsor who is a member of the house or senate and every bill is given a unique number for identification.

4. The detailed wording of each bill is done by the Legislative Service Bureau.

5. The serious development of a bill takes place in one or more committees. Once a bill leaves the committee, few if any changes are made in it.

6. A bill can begin in either the house or senate. Once it has passed through that body, it must also successfully go through the other half of the legislature.

On a bright spring afternoon in April, Senator Ed Fredricks (Republican-23rd District) of Holland dropped a bound stack of papers onto the desk of the secretary of the senate. It was Fredricks' goal to clean up the environment. Five months later, his Wine Cooler Bill (Public Act 235 of 1986) was signed into law by the governor. Wine cooler bottles would soon require a ten cent deposit like many other beverage bottles covered by the original bottle bill passed in 1976.

Senator Fredricks' bill was only one of thousands presented to our state legislators that year. There were even other bills about wine coolers. In addition, they also considered bills to raise the speed limit to 65 on interstate highways, to eliminate state funding of abortions, to make organ transplants easier, and to make it illegal to sell drug paraphernalia. In a typical year Michigan's two legislative chambers will consider some 5,000 bills. Although most fail, many new laws are passed.

SOURCES OF BILLS

Where do the legislators get their ideas for new laws? There are several sources.

Themselves

1.) Their own thoughts provide ideas. Legislators often run for office because of interest in a specific issue. They want to promote new laws about those issues.

Constituents

2.) Constituents provide ideas for new laws. Often ideas do come from individuals, but the most successful ones come from groups with a common interest.

Lobbyists

3.) *Lobbyists* provide a major portion of the ideas for bills. *A Lobbyist is a paid professional who tries to influence public officials and legislators through personal contact.* Lobbyists are paid by individuals and groups who are affected by new laws. They want the legislators to vote in ways that help their clients. Michigan lobbyists must be registered with the secretary of state and provide a record of the money received and spent. Lobbyists often call themselves "legislative agents."

The Government Bureaucracy

4.) Government employees are often closest to the action. They are apt to know what laws need changing, fine tuning, or replacing. Many ideas for new laws come from this group.

HOW A BILL BECOMES A LAW ......A QUICK OUTLINE

It is virtually impossible for 148 legislators to individually read and understand the quantity of bills introduced each year. The committee system breaks that number down and divides responsibility. It also allows legislators to become experts in specific areas. Legislators want to get on committees dealing with issues which interest them the most; although this may not always be possible.

A bill may begin in the house or senate. It is assigned to a committee by either the speaker of the house or the senate majority leader. When it gets to the committee, it may be further assigned to a subcommittee. After discussions and changes, a vote is taken to send the bill to the next step. This is called voting the bill out of committee.

It is then assigned a date to be discussed on the floor by all the members of that house. After debate and amendment, the members vote on the bill. If successful, the bill goes to the other house and the same activities take place there.

If changes are made in the bill in the other house, legislators from both houses form a *conference committee* to "iron out their differences." *A conference committee is made up of six members—two from the majority party and one from the minority party of the house and the senate who work to resolve differences between the house and senate version of the same bill.* If they are successful, the bill then goes back to the house and senate to be reconsidered.

If successful, the bill is sent to the governor. It may be signed into law by the governor or vetoed. The legislators can vote to override a veto if they feel strongly enough about the merits of a bill. The bill would then become law "over" the governor's veto. In a nutshell, that is the process by which bills become laws in Michigan.

BILL SPONSORS

If a legislator cannot find others to support an idea for a bill, it is well to just forget it. A majority of the membership in the houses is necessary to pass a bill. A majority of a committee is necessary to pass the bill out of committee. The obvious key to getting a bill passed is to get enough supporters; so one important early consideration is lining up *co-sponsors* for the bill. *A co-sponsor is one of several legislators who originally backs a bill and adds his or her name to it.*

How does a legislator decide if he or she wants to support a new bill? Since many legislators cannot (or do not) thoroughly read all bills, they rely on the opinions of others to guide them. On the cover page of every bill is a section that lists all the bill's sponsors. One of the first things a person sees when looking at a bill is this important list of names. Many legislators look at this list to decide if they want to support the bill. If they see the name of an experienced legislator whose opinion they value, this may influence them to join the group of supporters.

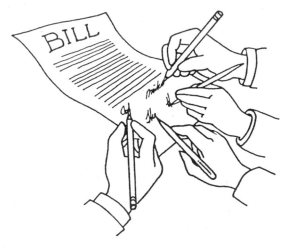

Any group of people working together soon finds it likes and trusts some members of the group more than others. Certain legislators have colleagues who would vote against any bill that legislator sponsored, no matter what issue the bill concerned. Several years ago many conservative legislators refused to vote for any bill sponsored by W. Perry Bullard (D- 53rd), an Ann Arbor legislator, after he attempted to relax marijuana laws, while liberal colleagues supported any bill he proposed.

In getting support for a bill, it may also be necessary to make changes so it is more acceptable to others. The sponsor may have to include or exclude some things to please other key legislators. A lawmaker may have to sacrifice some of his goals at first. However, a patient legislator can often enact most of his or her goals over a period of years.

When the bill is put in final form by the Legislative Service Bureau, a *blueback* draft is given to the major sponsor/author of the bill. *The blueback is a copy of the bill with a larger blue sheet stapled to its back. This blue sheet has lines for the signatures of other sponsors.* The legislator takes this copy around to potential co-sponsors and asks for their signatures. The completed blueback is then introduced by giving it to the clerk of the house or the secretary of the senate who assigns it a number.

Numbering the Bills

With so many bills crossing the legis- lators' desks, it is difficult to keep them organized without a numbering system. For this purpose, legislative bills are numbered in order depending on when the idea for the bill comes to the *Legislative Service Bureau.* Senate bills are usually numbered 1 to 4000. House bills begin at 4001. Thus, a senate bill may be Senate Bill 2089, or S.B. 2089. A House bill may be H.B. 4008. The numbering process starts over with each new term of the legislature.

Legislative Service Bureau

T. Deeter © HEP

In the bill writing process the legislator has help from some important non-legislators known as the Legislative Service Bureau.

It is made up largely of lawyers, research- ers, and writers. Their responsibilities are mainly bill drafting and resolution drafting. They are the people who take an idea given to them in rough form and put it into the proper legal format. Bills are not just ideas. If passed into law, they must conform to the huge mass of laws already on the books. It is unlikely legislators would know the exact form in which to put their ideas. The Legislative Service Bureau does this for them. The bureau also researches what ex- isting laws would have to be changed if the proposed bill is successful.

INTRODUCING THE BILL

Remember, a bill can begin in either the house or the senate. This example starts in the house. To introduce a bill, it is placed in a mahogany box called a hopper. The clerk of the house takes the bill out of the hopper, notes the number of the bill, and reads its title and number aloud to the house members. The clerk would say, "House Bill #5411. A Bill to provide scholarships to high school graduates of this state....." This is called the bill's first reading. Actually, there is not really even a reading of the entire bill. All that is read is the number and title. The state constitution says each bill must be read three times before it can be passed. Court decisions have allowed this requirement to be met by reading the title only.

COMMITTEE ACTION

After the bill is read, the speaker of the house assigns the bill to the committee which deals with the issues in the bill. At this point the bill is still a mass of clay, in a way, waiting to be molded by the committee and others interested in the outcome.

Once a bill leaves committee, it is uncommon for many changes to be made, so the work of the committee is very significant. The better job the committee does, the more likely their bill will be successful. At the committee level the bill is studied and subjected to testimony, analysis, and debate. This is the best time for those who may be affected by the bill to give their opinions. Committees attempt to hear all sides of the issue.

Gathering Information

Committees use several sources of information to guide their work. The most noteworthy are: public hearings, the views of other legislators, lobbyists, trips to gather facts, and questionnaires.

Public hearings may be held, especially if the bill will affect people who live far from the capital. The hearings may be in different cities so more people can participate.

Legislators themselves are another source of information. Even those not on the committee will present their views at this time, especially if they like the bill. If the value of the bill is not made clear in committee, it could be too late later. Members are less tolerant of changes when the bill is before the entire house. They prefer the bill come out of committee in a nice, neat, clean package.

Legislators cannot always get enough information in Lansing. They may need to see a problem first hand— the pollution in a river, to see how people are fighting the drug situation in Miami, to attend a conference of auto makers.

A trip by a lawmaker to gather more information is a junket. These trips are usually taken for good reasons, but some legislators have used them for their own pleasure. This gives junkets a bad name. The majority party leaders in each house decide who goes on junkets.

One more way to find out what people think about a bill is to send them a questionnaire or a survey. This is an easy way for legislators to get answers and compute the responses efficiently.

Outside Contacts—Lobbyists and Special Interest Groups

Not all of the action takes place in the committee. It is during this stage of the bill's progress that special interest groups and lobbyists— those strongly favoring or opposing the bill— make themselves heard. Lobbyists take legislators out to breakfast, lunch, and dinner and invite them to conventions. Lobbyists also testify before committees. Because of all these activities, they are quite successful in getting the votes they want from legislators, but they also help legislators by providing them current information about pending legislation.

What Happens To A Bill In Committee

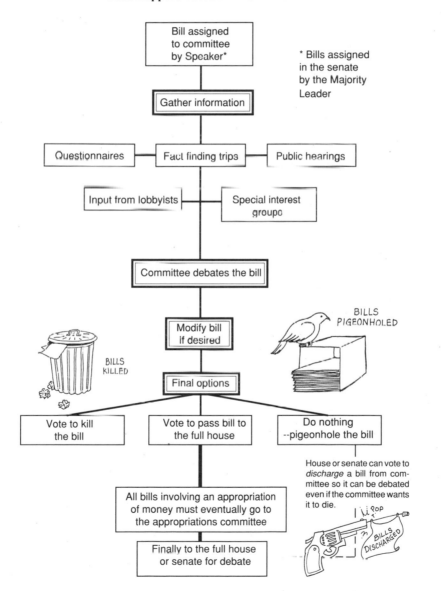

The Committee Completes Its Work

Once the committee members have finished debating and made any desired changes, it is time for them to make a decision on the bill... if they wish. Often they will do nothing. This is what happens to the vast majority of bills. Such bills "die" in committee. Officially, legislators have many options in determining the fate of a bill. The three most obvious choices are:

A. Pass the bill on to the full house.

B. Vote it down (kill it)

C. *Pigeonhole* the bill— do nothing.

To pigeonhole a bill has the same effect as voting against it but legislators don't have to tell constituents how they voted and take a chance of offending them. This is often a plus for the lawmakers. Few bills are voted down.

If the committee members will not let the bill out of committee, it is possible for the full house to vote to *"discharge"* it. *Discharge is a vote taken in the house or senate to move a bill out of its committee to the floor so the entire group can debate it.* This takes a simple majority vote of the entire house, but seldom occurs as it is considered an insult to the committee, especially to the committee chairperson. Because committees are so powerful, one of the commandments for successful legislators is "Never offend thy committee chair!"

CALENDAR

Once a bill is sent to the full house, it must wait its turn. To provide an orderly schedule, the *calendar* has been established. *The calendar is the daily agenda of bills to be discussed.* In the house it is called the "Michigan House Daily Calendar."

In the second reading of the bill it is debated though seldom amended. This is the primary time the full house or senate discusses the proposed law. It then advances to the third reading.

A future date on the Calendar is established for the third reading and final vote. When the day arrives for the third reading, more debate may take place. Few, if any, amendments are made now. When the discussion is at an end, the final vote is taken.

If a bill is thought to be really important, the rules are suspended and the second reading is skipped.

VOTING—*Voice Vote*

Voting is done in one of two ways. If there is little disagreement, a *voice vote* is taken. For this kind of vote, the speaker of the house says, "All those in favor, say 'Aye' (yes). All those opposed say 'Nay' (no)." Whichever side sounds as if it has the most votes wins. This is usually done on amendments and resolutions. If the number of ayes and nays is difficult to determine, the speaker may have a roll call vote. Any member can ask for a roll call and the request is generally granted.

— *Roll Call Vote*

Many years ago, this was done much like calling roll at the beginning of class in school. The clerk of the house would read through all the names. When each legislator's name was called, the legislator would respond with a aye or a nay. It took a long time to go through 110 names, repeating some names occasionally for various reasons.

Now, the roll call is done electronically. The legislators have a box attached to their desks for voting. They may also abstain (not vote) under certain circumstances. The electronic system was installed in the house in 1937 and was one of the first used in the nation. A former clerk of the house once said it reduced the average time for taking the roll from eight minutes to 40 seconds.

Each legislator's vote is shown on a huge, lighted master board in the front of the house of representatives. The senate has a similar arrangement. A "yes" vote shows up as a green light next to the legislator's name. A red light goes on if the vote is "no." Everyone can see how each legislator is voting. When enough time has been granted, the speaker tells the clerk to tally the votes. The votes are then locked in and cannot be changed. The vote is announced and is printed out immediately on paper.

Two-Thirds Vote for Special Cases

In most votes, a simple majority of the house—56 votes—is needed to win. There are a few situations where a greater number of votes is needed. A two-thirds vote is needed in the following cases.

1. Individual grants
2. Amendments to the constitution
3. Changes in the banking laws

Questions

1. Prepare an outline using Roman numerals (I, II, III, IV, etc.) which shows in a simple way how a bill becomes a law in the state legislature. That is to say, goes from introduction to the governor.

2. Why is it important to find the right sponsors and co-sponsors for a bill?

3. How many times does the state constitution say each bill must be read before it can be passed in the house or senate? Are the bills always read completely?

4. If you are vitally interested in a bill which is being considered by the Michigan house or senate, at which point in the process is it best for you to make your opinion known to your representative?

5. After a committee has debated a bill, list the options it has concerning what happens to it next?

6. Suppose you are visiting a session of the state legislature and see a vote taking place. What is the procedure for a roll call vote in the Michigan house? How is the vote recorded and displayed?

7. In your opinion, do the citizens of Michigan learn about key legislation before it is too late to make a real impact in its outcome? Explain your reasoning.

Chapter 3 Section 2

Procedures in the Senate
When House and Senate Versions Differ
The Governor's Options and More

Here are the key concepts in this section:

1. The state senate has procedures which ignore some of the more formal rules used in the house and allow bills to be debated more openly.

2. When house and senate versions of a bill differ, selected members from each group form a conference committee to work things out.

3. Once a bill is passed by the house and senate, the governor normally signs it into law, but there are other options.

4. Ordinary citizens can work to make their own laws through the process called initiative. Initiatives are placed on a statewide ballot for all the people to decide.

5. Committee work is very important in both the house and senate. There are many kinds of committees. The chairperson of each committee is in a powerful position and can often direct which laws are eventually passed.

THE SENATE

Successful house bills go to the senate. Remember, the bill might have begun in the senate; in such a case it would go to the house. Both houses have essentially the same operation.

Once a bill is brought to the senate there is a five-day waiting period. This allows time to reflect on the bill and keeps the legislature from taking hasty action on emotionally charged legislation. The waiting period also gives the public an additional opportunity to speak.

After the five days, the secretary of the senate announces the bill. This is its first reading in the senate. The bill is then assigned to a committee by the majority leader.

When the committee completes its study of the bill, it can send the bill back to the full senate for action. If this occurs, the senate gives it a second reading, also known as putting the bill on *general orders. General orders is the first general discussion of a bill by all the senators and it is roughly the same as the second reading in the house.*

The senate usually considers bills in *committee of the whole.* Under this arrangement, many of the formal rules are ignored and a more open discussion of the bill is allowed. Unlike the house, when the senate is under general orders, there is no recording of senators' votes. In the senate, however, there is a limit on debate. A senator can speak only twice on an issue each day, though a majority of the senators can agree to suspend this rule too.

After this discussion period, the bill is put on the third reading calendar. When that day arrives, the bill is finally voted on. Few, if any, attempts are made to amend it now. The vote is taken much as in the house.

A bill passing the senate, in the same language as the house version, goes to the governor. If the bill has any changes at all, it must go back to the house for re-approval! If the house does not approve of the changes, the house and the senate must work out their differences. This frequently happens with controversial bills and is handled by a conference committee. There may be many conference committees working at the same time— each one hammering out a separate bill.

THE CONFERENCE COMMITTEE

Each has the responsibility of resolving the differences between the houses on a bill. Maybe the house wanted to spend less money on a project than the senate. If the two groups cannot agree on a compromise, the bill will die. Therefore, the work of the conference committees is very important. An agreement must include at least two members from each house. It is possible the conference committee will change the bill more than either house wants. The two houses have the option of voting the new version down, but the conference committee bill is usually adopted because it is too late in the session to start all over again.

The newly worded conference committee report is sent to the two houses upon completion. It first goes to the house where it began, then to the other house. It can be debated but cannot be changed. If both houses adopt the compromise, the bill is sent to the governor.

THE GOVERNOR

The governor has 14 days to act on a bill once it reaches his desk. The time is measured in hours and minutes from the moment it arrives. The governor has four options to choose from in those 14 days:

1. Sign the bill.

2. Veto the bill.

The bill is then returned to the house of origin with the governor's objections.

3. Not sign the bill.

If the legislature is in session, the bill is returned to the house of origin with the governor's objections. It is treated as if it were a veto. If the legislature is not in session, the bill does not become law. This has the same effect as a veto.

T. Deeter © HEP

4. Line item veto.

Another powerful option the governor has is the line item veto. The governor may veto a money line in a budget bill and still sign the remaining parts of the appropriation into law.

OVERRIDE

If the legislature can achieve a two-thirds vote in each house to override the veto, the bill will become law. However, this occurs infrequently in Michigan.

PUTTING THE LAWS INTO EFFECT

A bill does not usually become law immediately. It normally goes into effect 90 days after the close of the session, which could be nearly two years later. If the legislators feel the new law is needed right away, it can be given *immediate effect*. This action requires a two-thirds vote of each house and then the bill becomes law on an agreed-upon date.

DIFFERENT KINDS OF BILLS
Public bills

Of the hundreds of bills considered in a legislative session, most are *public bills. Public bills are those passed for the entire state and affect everyone in the same way.* Bills to provide rules for hunting, new speed limits, or aid to the poor are examples of public bills.

Private Bills

Private bills are those which have a definite effect on one person, company, or organization. If someone had a bad auto accident and it can be determined the state was at fault in some way, the state legislature may provide compensation to the individual. They would do so in a bill—a *private bill.* Very few private bills are passed by the legislature.

HOW VOTERS CAN MAKE LAWS

The people hope their elected officials will carry out their desires, but the political process breaks down sometimes. The Michigan constitution allows voters to take matters into their own hands. They can initiate legislation and even *petition* for constitutional amendments. The legislature may also refer their proposals back to the people for input. The voters use these powers at nearly every election, either locally or statewide. *A petition is a formal written request by the people to the government. It must follow a certain format and be signed by a minimum number of voters.*

INITIATIVE

One of the most powerful rights we have in America is the right to "petition the government for a redress of grievances." One way to do this at the state level is to use the *initiative* procedure. *An initiative is a proposed law written by a group of people which is placed on the statewide ballot.*

The process is made sufficiently difficult so we generally will rely on our elected officials. Ideally only those issues which a majority of Michigan's voters strongly support should be placed on the ballot and only then if the legislature has shown its unwillingness to pass the needed laws.

To assure that a large number of citizens are truly concerned about the proposed law, the constitution requires eight percent of those voting for all candidates for governor in the last election to sign petitions. This means about 200,000 signatures must be acquired. The wording of the law to be passed, and the validity of the signatures are then checked by the Secretary of State's office for verification.

Those interested in the initiative have nearly unlimited time to gather signatures, but only the ones acquired within the last 180 days before filing will count. If enough signatures are received, the legislature is given 40 days to enact the proposed law. It may not change or amend it in any way. If the legislature does not pass it in time, the proposal goes on the ballot at the next general election. The legislature may also place a proposal of its own on the ballot, addressing the problem in a different way. When there are two or more proposals on the ballot, the one receiving the most votes wins, providing it has over 50% of the total.

REFERENDUM

A referendum means to give the voters a chance to accept or reject a law proposed by the legislature—to refer the law to the voters. There are two situations which could involve this process.

1.)   There can be a law which has gone through the legislative process successfully, but which a group of voters finds quite objectionable. By using the referendum procedure they can ask all the voters to accept or reject what the legislature has already passed. Of course it is their hope it will be rejected.

2.)   The second situation is when the legislature has a law it would like to pass but would rather give the voters a direct voice in the process. Laws falling in this category may be "too hot to handle" for the legislature, as they don't want to be blamed by the voters for making the wrong decision. The proposal becomes law if a majority of the voters approve it at the next general election.

There are strict rules which must be followed in the referendum process. One of the most important is there cannot be a referendum on a law that deals with appropriations for state government or concerns a funding deficit. In recent years the state supreme court has used this wording in a broad way to stop some referendum attempts.

Also a petition for a referendum requires about 120,000 names—that is, signatures in excess of five percent of the people voting for governor in the last election. The signatures need to be received within 90 days once the legislative session ends.

If the voters approve and the proposal is successful, it becomes law 10 days after the vote has been declared official. Laws which result from the initiative process may not be vetoed, amended, or repealed by the governor. They can be changed or repealed by a majority vote of the people or a three-fourths vote of the legislature.

CONSTITUTIONAL AMENDMENT

A similar process is used to change or amend the state constitution, except that it requires signatures from 10 percent of the people voting for governor in the last election. If successful, the new proposal becomes part of Michigan's constitution and the legislature may not alter or stop it in any way.

Nowhere is our representative democracy more obvious than in the legislative branch. The people vote for the legislators of their choice. They can lobby

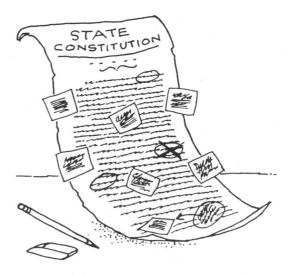

them for new laws. They can pass laws themselves or try to throw out laws the legislature passed if they do not like them. If people do not approve of a legislator's actions, they can refuse to re-elect or can even recall the legislator.

The people really can control their government. When it is not working as it should, the majority can change it. We are given the tools we need, but we must use those tools to be effective.

THE COMMITTEE SYSTEM

STANDING COMMITTEES

There are many kinds of committees in the house and senate. The same sort of issues are considered nearly every year. For this reason, *standing committees* exist. *These are committees that "stand" or continue throughout the term and for all practical purposes are permanent from term to term.*

The House

The house has more standing committees because there are nearly three times as many members. Of the 33 standing committees in the house, the most important are: appropriations, taxation, and judiciary.

The Appropriations Committee determines how much money will be spent and how.

The Taxation Committee determines all laws regarding taxes. It was the Taxation Committee, for example, that recommended raising Michigan's income taxes in 1983 when there was a budget shortage. The same committee recommended lowering taxes in 1986 when the economic situation improved.

The Judiciary Committee considers most of the important legislation concerning crime and the courts.

The Senate

The senate has about 14 committees. The committees in the senate cover the same topics as in the house, although some areas are combined. The Appropriations, Taxation and Judiciary Committees are as important in the senate as they are in the house.

Subcommittees

To smooth the bill passage process, some committees are broken down into subcommittees. This way members handle fewer bills and can be more expert in what they are doing. Senate Appropriations has many subcommittees and one is the Higher Education Subcommittee which controls the state money provided for colleges.

AD HOC COMMITTEES

There are many legislative problems that require attention for a short period of time. These situations are often handled by *ad hoc committees. The expression "ad hoc" means "for a time"; therefore, ad hoc committees are temporary.* Both houses have several and they serve a variety of purposes. Two examples are the Select Committee on the Future of Higher Education and the Select Committee on Health Care Cost Containment.

JOINT COMMITTEES

Agreement between the house and senate is crucial. There are many reasons for the two houses to work together. One way of coordinating activities is to form *joint committees. A joint committee is one which includes members of both houses brought together to solve a specific problem.* The legislature has recently had a joint committee on aging, and another for administrative rules.

COMMITTEE LEADERSHIP

Committees are powerful forces in the law making process. The *committee chairpersons* are especially powerful. They have much control over the passage of bills through their committees. For example, if they don't like a bill it may never be placed on the agenda. If it is never placed on the agenda, it may never be discussed, and may "die in committee."

The speaker of the house and the majority leader in the senate usually know what the various committee chairpersons think about legislation. They take this into consideration when they assign bills to committee. They also make sure the committee chairpersons know what they think about various issues.

Political Party Affiliation

The selection of committee chairpersons is crucial and this is done by the leader of their house. Party affiliation is the first guideline. Majority party members hold all standing committee and subcommittee chair positions. *Seniority, the length of time in office,* is the second most important criteria. The legislators with greatest seniority (from the majority party) serve as chairs of nearly every committee.

Seniority

It makes some sense to have the most experienced legislators as heads of committees. They should have a greater sense of the "history" of the problems facing the committee. However, as one state staffer commented, "It's the 'good old boy' network. We use it because senior members use their knowledge of inner workings to give themselves what they want first." Of course, today the network has more than just good old boys, as many women are involved in key positions of the legislature.

Questions

1. Suppose the Michigan house passes a bill to provide $500,000 for speakers to visit schools and talk about drug abuse. The senate also passes the same bill but thinks $250,000 a year is enough for this purpose. What has to happen before this bill can go to the governor? What will happen if the house and senate cannot agree on the amount of money to be spent?

2. Take the above example. Finally, the house and senate agree on an amount to be spent, but decide that drug abuse is such an important topic the amount is raised to $10,000,000 or $18,600 for each school district in Michigan. The governor says the idea is good but there is not enough money for such a project. What three options does the governor have?

3. Suppose the group, "Parents Against Drugs In Schools," is tired of waiting for the Michigan legislature to provide speakers to schools to speak out against drugs. This group is convinced that if all school students had to listen to five anti-drug speakers each year, the use of illegal drugs would fall dramatically. They want to begin an initiative drive for the state government to spend $10,000,000 a year for this project. Explain what they would have to do for a successful initiative in Michigan.

4. What does the term referendum mean?

5. The committee to which a bill is assigned can be very important. Who in the house and who in the senate is responsible for assigning bills to their respective committees?

6. Explain the meaning of the following terms: subcommittee, ad hoc committee, and seniority. How is a joint committee different from a conference committee?

4

THE EXECUTIVE BRANCH: THE GOVERNOR

Chapter 4 Section 1

Background and Responsibilities

Here are the key concepts in this section:

1. The power of Michigan's governors has increased over the years.

2. Michigan's governors serve four-year terms with a limit of two terms served. (The limitation is the result of proposal B from November, 1992.)

3. In Michigan a candidate for governor must be at least 30 years old and have been a registered voter in the state for the last four years.

4. If the governor leaves office or dies during the term, the lieutenant governor is the first to fill the position followed by the secretary of state and then the attorney general if the others are not available.

The governor is the most important political figure we elect in Michigan's government. Governors have the greatest powers and the most varied responsibilities of all the elected officials in a state. Former Governor G. Mennen Williams said it best in his book *A Governor's Notes:* "It was my opinion that the office of governor, with the exception of the presidency, was without equal in the land. As a matter of fact, it had been my ambition to be governor of Michigan since my college days."

In recent years, Michigan governors have been relatively popular and with few exceptions been reelected for as long as they want to stay in office. In his election for a second term in 1986, Governor James Blanchard received the highest percentage of votes cast for any governor since the 1920s (68 percent). Governor William Milliken served a record 14 years (1969-82). Not too long before, G. Mennen Williams was elected governor six times (1949-60) when terms were only two years long. In fact, only two incumbent governors have lost reelections since 1948 (James Blanchard in 1990 and John B. Swainson in 1962). Compare this with Oklahoma where voters have attempted to recall their governors on five different occasions, with two tries being successful.

Background

When the United States was first established, the people blamed the previous English governors for much of their troubles. They felt the states would be more successful if the governors were kept weak. Typically the governors had one-year terms of office, no appointive powers, and little influence in law making.

As citizens realized their states needed stronger leadership, the office of governor slowly gained status and power. By the time Michigan became the 26th state in 1837, it was more common to have two-year terms. So, Michigan provided for a two-year term in the first three state constitutions. Though the office was given few powers initially, its influence kept growing. With the adoption of our fourth constitution in 1963, Michigan's governors were among the strongest in the country.

Term of Office

Michigan's governors serve four-year terms. The four-year term is now the standard throughout the United States. Only three states continue a two-year term— New Hampshire, Rhode Island, and Vermont. Over half the states now limit the number of terms the governor can serve, including Michigan. For example, Kentucky, Mississippi, New Mexico, and Virginia have a limit of one term. Some other states have a two-term limit or forbid the governor from serving more than two terms in a row.

Qualifications

Who can become governor? The constitutional qualifications for governor of Michigan are not difficult to meet. A candidate must be at least 30 years old and have been a registered voter in the state for the last four years. A candidate cannot run for governor if convicted of a felony or a breach of the public trust in the last 20 years. The age requirement is common; 37 states have a minimum age of 30.

These are the formal qualifications for governor found in the state's constitution, but the voters place additional unwritten requirements on the candidates as well. Preferred candidates are usually 40 to 50 years of age, politically experienced, and lawyers. They tend to be personable, articulate, and viewed as strong, creative leaders.

Election

The successful candidate for governor in Michigan must first win nomination by a political party in the August primary and then win the November general election. At one time candidates for governor found their elections overshadowed by the tremendous attention given presidential campaigns. To keep this from occurring, the election was moved to the even-numbered years when the presidential election is not held (1994, 1998, 2002).

Salary and Benefits

The governor of Michigan is compensated in several ways. In 1994 the governor received about $112,000 in salary. The salary is determined by the State Officers Compensation Commission every four years. The legislature is able to vote against the commission's proposals, but has seldom chosen to deny any of the recommendations including its own legislative salary increases.

The following table shows how the Michigan governors' salaries have changed over the years.

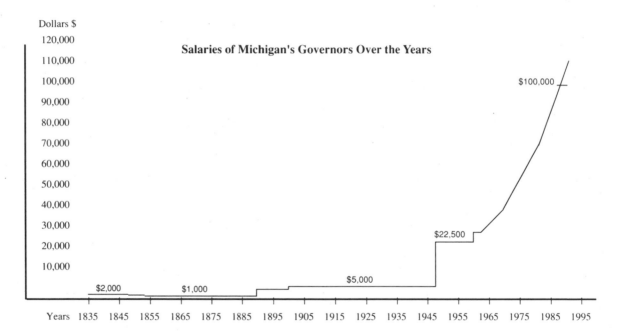

In addition, the governor has the use of a mansion, a large house on Mackinac Island, a chauffeured limousine, bodyguards, an office complex, a pension, and an expense account of some $30,000 per year for entertaining and doing business. The governor may also have an *office holder's account, which is an expense account containing donations from supporters and lobbyists which can be spent on expenses associated with the responsibilities of the office.* Former Governor Blanchard spent all but $6.39 of the $557,126 in his account during a single year. These expenses included $21,000 for Christmas cards, and many other items the government does not feel it should pay for and the governor alone could never afford.

Some states provide even more compensation than Michigan. Most provide less. Salary is not always based on a state's wealth or population. New York usually has the highest governor's salary, but California, which is larger and has more people, pays only half as much.

Filling a Vacancy

Occasionally a governor dies, resigns, or is forced to leave office. Four Michigan governors have resigned. An example is George Romney who joined President Nixon's administration as Secretary of Housing and Urban Development (HUD) in 1969. Only one Michigan governor has died in office— Frank Fitzgerald in 1939. The other ways the office can be vacated are by recall or impeachment, but neither has ever occurred in Michigan.

A vacancy in the governor's office can be quite a problem, but Michigan's constitution spells out how the office will be filled in an orderly fashion. The lieutenant governor is the first to succeed to the position followed by the secretary of state and then the attorney general.

It's possible a Michigan governor could become unable to perform his or her duties. The state constitution allows a majority of the state supreme court to determine if such a disability exists. This is done upon the request of the president pro tempore of the senate and the speaker of the house. If the supreme court feels a disability exists, the lieutenant governor would become governor— at least temporarily. The supreme court could later determine the disability to have ended, permitting the governor to resume the office.

Questions

1. What is the governor's term of office and how often can a Michigan governor be reelected?

2. List the constitutional requirements to be governor and explain the unwritten requirements voters have added. Which of these unwritten requirements do you believe is the most important?

3. Specifically, when are Michigan's governors elected? When are the candidates nominated and by whom?

4. Tell three ways the governor of Michigan is compensated.

5. Which officials would take the governor's place if he or she could not continue in office? Who would be first, second, and third?

Chapter 4   Section 2

Duties and Powers of the Governor

Here are the key concepts in this section:

1. The governor is the head of the executive branch, but some of the governor's powers also involve the legislative and judicial branches.

2. The governor gains power from the ability to appoint and fill the leadership positions in many areas of state government.

3. The major expense of state government is related to the executive branch, so the governor is responsible for the preparation of the state budget each year.

4. A major power of the governor is the ability to stop bills from becoming law by vetoing them. He or she also has the power to veto specific parts of a bill by using what is known as the "line item veto."

5. On special occasions the governor can interact with the judicial system. For example, the governor can free convicted prisoners, reduce or delay their punishment, etc.

The laws of the state of Michigan are enforced by the executive branch of government. The governor as head of this branch is given the responsibility to make sure the laws enacted by the legislature are put into effect and obeyed. This huge job cannot be done by one person; approximately 55,000 employees are there to help.

While the office of governor has many powers to carry out the executive functions, ultimate success depends on the support of the voters and the governor's personality and style.

The formal powers of the governor can be divided into three broad areas—executive, legislative, and judicial.

Executive Powers

There are four categories of executive powers the governor possesses— the power to appoint officials, the power to control the executive branch, the power to plan the budget, and the power to command Michigan's National Guard.

Appoints Important Leaders

The governor directly appoints the leaders for 11 of the 19 state departments and also appoints the controlling personnel in many state agencies. The controlling boards of 10 of Michigan's 13 public colleges and universities are also appointed by the governor. Altogether, he or she has the opportunity to appoint over 100 different individuals every year. Each of these appointees feels a great commitment to the governor and they tend to support the governor's goals. They often campaign for the governor and provide funds for reelection.

Controls the Executive Branch

The governor cannot hire or fire the majority of the employees of this branch because they are selected by the Department of Civil Service (see chapter 5) but he or she does fill the most powerful positions— those who are the bosses— through the appointment process. And these appointed leaders can be removed at any time. They are the ones responsible for setting the goals and priorities of the executive branch departments.

The Budget

The vast majority of the expenses of state government are in the executive branch— in the departments of social services, education, corrections, etc. As the chief administrator overseeing most of these departments, the governor is responsible for the development of the annual budget for the state. The governor, with the help of the Department of Management and Budget, proposes a multibillion dollar budget each January, but planning of this budget begins 13 to 14 months earlier. Because of this connection with the budget, the governor has tremendous influence over state programs and determination over which issues will be considered important and which problems will be solved.

The governor can't directly introduce legislation, including budget bills. So, the senior committee members from the governor's political party on the Appropriations Committees in the house and senate introduce the bills for the governor. No single document is submitted; about 12-14 different budget bills are introduced covering all of the expenditures of the state. The budget goes through the usual legislative process and the entire budget is generally not adopted until the end of the session in December— almost 12 months later!

Military Powers

Each state has a militia. Together, these militias make up the national guard for the United States. The governor is the commander-in-chief of the Michigan national guard and can activate it for emergencies, although this is seldom done. The most widely publicized activity the Michigan guard has had was in response to the Detroit riots of 1943 and 1967. Elements of the national guard were called into action by President Bush during the 1990-1991 Iraq conflict to support the regular army overseas. When the guard is used within Michigan, the governor directs its activities through the appointed commander, the Adjutant General.

Legislative Powers

Besides being the chief executive for the state, the governor has major legislative influence. This would seem strange at first glance since the governor is not even in the legislative branch of government. The governor can control legislation in at least five ways— by encouraging the introduction of legislation, using the veto, personal persuasion, calling special sessions of the legislature, and public speeches.

Introduction of Legislation

One of the largest sources of ideas for new laws is the executive branch, including the governor. Each department in this branch is responsible for important activities requiring money or legislative approval. The governor and the department heads present their ideas for bills through various legislators at the appropriate time.

The governor also has assistants who follow bills through the legislature. When things do not go as planned, the assistant informs the governor so problems can be ironed out.

The Veto

The greatest single legislative power of the governor is the *veto. The word veto means "to stop." When the governor uses this power, a bill passed by the legislature is stopped and does not become law.* The legislature can override a veto if two-thirds of its members will vote to do so. Practically speaking, the legislature must put together bills the governor will accept unless there are at least 74 votes in the house and 26 votes in the senate prepared to override a veto.

Even when the legislature has enough support on the initial vote, many legislators will change their minds when a vote to override comes, because they are not willing to vote against the governor. This is especially true if the governor is from the same political party. The mere threat of a veto may be sufficient to change the content of a bill. In Michigan, only one veto override has been successful in the last several years. In recent years, one of the most frequently vetoed bills was the legislature's attempt to stop public funding of abortions.

Line Item Veto

An additional power the governor has is the *line item veto*. This is another form of the veto and allows the governor to stop a "line" in a budget bill. Nearly every state governor has this power; without it, the governor's influence would be much less during the budget process. Usually, a budget bill passed by the legislature is for millions or even billions of dollars. If there are items buried in a large bill that the governor opposes, it is troublesome to veto the entire bill just to get at one expenditure, although it is done occasionally anyway.

The line item veto allows the governor to pass the majority of the bill about which there is no argument, yet remove items considered disagreeable. After the governor and the leaders of the legislature meet to discuss the vetoed sections, they may be changed and passed separately with the governor's support. There is often intense politicking during these negotiations as legislators try to protect their "pet" projects. Again, this special type of veto only applies to budget bills.

Persuasion

The governor is by far the most powerful politician in state government. He or she is able to make many things "happen" that otherwise would not. This power can be used to influence people to do many things. In 1983, when Governor Blanchard needed one more vote for the income tax increase he proposed, he invited a maverick Republican to meet with him to discuss support of the bill. The senator visited with the governor and rode in the governor's helicopter. The next day, he became the only Republican in the state senate to support the income tax increase. It passed by a vote of 20-18.

Special Sessions

The governor is also given the authority to call the legislature back for a special session to deal with an emergency situation or a problem that deserves immediate attention. This power is used by governors in some states, but is seldom used in Michigan because the legislature is in session nearly all year long anyway. The governor cannot call the legislature back to session if it is already in session.

The last special session of the Michigan legislature was in 1967 when Governor Romney called the legislature back to discuss open housing. No bill succeeded in passing both houses during that session.

Michigan's legislature, don't forget, is a full-time body that usually meets from the first week in January until late in December, with a few breaks. The calling of special sessions, however, is a very effective maneuver in other states.

Speeches and Messages

Another way the governor influences legislators is by setting the agenda for the legislature. This is done through the governor's public comments about important issues. It is also possible to communicate directly with the legislature; sessions are occasionally interrupted so a message from the governor can be read aloud.

In addition, the governor may ask to speak directly to either house or a joint session of the houses. This takes place at least once a year in the governor's *State of the State* message in January. *The State of the State speech is similar to the president's annual State of the Union address. It is a blueprint of the governor's plans for the upcoming year.* The successes of the last year and proposals for solving remaining problems are summarized. Recent failures may be emphasized if the governor is newly elected. An expanded version of the speech is published and distributed. By providing the legislature with these speeches and other messages throughout the year, the governor makes it very apparent what the chief executive's goals and intentions are on the important issues.

Judicial Powers

In addition to these executive and legislative powers, the governor has certain other powers that can best be described as judicial. They involve mercy for persons who have been accused or convicted of committing a crime. If a Michigan governor feels a convicted person has not been treated fairly or has been punished enough, there are several options available including reprieves, commutations, and pardons. The governor also has certain powers over parole and extradition. The meanings of these terms are given below. Any governor must be careful in using these powers because public opinion is usually against the criminal.

Reprieve

The governor can alter the sentence of a convicted criminal by granting a *reprieve. A reprieve is the delay of punishment.* This might be done if the criminal's parent is dying and it is felt the parent should have the company of the son or daughter, or it may be done to allow a college student to complete the semester's classes, or for many other reasons. No reprieves have been granted in recent years.

Commutation

The governor can commute the sentence of a convicted prisoner. A *commutation is a reduction of the penalty to one which is less severe.* It is possible the governor and others feel the criminal was given a sentence too severe for the crime; if so, the governor has the power to change it. A common use of the commutation power in Michigan has been in the reduction of the sentence of a person convicted of first degree murder. In such a case, the sentence in Michigan is mandatory life imprisonment. A person convicted of first degree murder can only be released by the governor's act of a commutation. Different governors over the years have had varying attitudes about such situations. For example, Governor Blanchard only granted one commutation.

Pardon

The most significant change in punishment is a *pardon. A pardon is the forgiving and releasing of a criminal from punishment.* This is seldom done and only when it appears the verdict was incorrect or when an inmate has done some heroic act which suggests he or she deserves immediate release. Very few pardons have been issued in recent years and only for individuals who have been particularly disadvantaged. Some of these cases have dealt with citizens of totalitarian countries who faced deportation back to that country if convicted.

Reprieves, commutations and pardons are only used in unusual circumstances. More frequently seen are paroles and extraditions.

Parole— This is an executive branch function even though the governor is not directly involved in paroles.

After a criminal has been in prison for a period of time, it is possible to be given a *parole, which is an early release from prison.* The Department of Corrections has a parole board which decides whether or not eligible inmates will get their parole. The governor doesn't actually get involved with the paroling of prisoners. The Corrections Department, under the governor's authority, makes this decision. Few of the 18,000 prisoners in Michigan serve their maximum sentences. For example, over 6,000 prisoners were paroled during 1984 and many will remain on probation for some time after their parole. Michigan had over 30,000 felony probationers in 1984.

Extradition

Another power of the governor is to issue an order for *extradition. Extradition means to send a person accused of a crime in another state or country back to that location for trial or to have someone living elsewhere brought back to Michigan for trial.* If a suspected criminal has fled to Michigan to avoid capture, the governor of the state where the crime was committed may ask the governor of Michigan to return the person. Or, if a suspect in a Michigan crime has left the state, our governor may ask another state's governor to return the suspect to Michigan.

Michigan's police officers have no authority to simply drive into Indiana, for example, and arrest a suspect. Permission must be granted to do this. The normal procedure is for the local police to make an arrest and have the officers from out of state come pick up the prisoner. Extradition is usually granted. However, it is sometimes refused in unusual situations where there are serious doubts about the fairness of the charges or if the alleged crime occurred many years ago.

Early Release

Crime has steadily increased in Michigan, resulting in overcrowded jails and prisons. Crowded prisons can cause many problems, so in 1981 the state passed a law called the *Emergency Powers Act*. This forced the governor to shorten or commute all sentences by 90 days for those prisoners convicted of non-violent crimes— if the prison population had been over capacity for at least 30 days. Due to the limited space at that time, the population was frequently over the maximum. This resulted in the governor releasing hundreds of prisoners early. The process occurred nine times. After two people were murdered in 1985 by convicts on early release, Governor James Blanchard refused to continue the practice.

Questions

1. Give several examples of important powers Michigan's governor has and explain in your opinion why each is important. Include at least one power from each of the following areas: executive, legislative and judicial.

2. Which branch of state government spends the bulk of the budget and who prepares the state budget each year?

3. For a long time the President of the United States has complained he should have the line item veto as many governors have. What is the line item veto and why is it important for any chief executive to have this power?

4. Which of the following are true and which are false?
    a.   The governor cannot introduce legislation directly into the legislature; a member of the house or senate must do this for the governor.
    b.   The governor is not allowed the opportunity to speak before the state house or senate while it is in session.
    c.   If the governor vetoes a bill, then the legislature can override the veto if a minimum of 3/4 of the members of the house and senate vote to do so.
    d.   Michigan governors often call special sessions of the legislature, especially later in the year after the members have gone home.

5. Explain the meanings of reprieve, commutation, pardon, and extradition. Be sure to mention who uses these powers.

Chapter 4   Section 3

The Governor's Office— Its Organization
The Lieutenant Governor

Here are the key concepts in this section:

1. The governor has a large staff to help with various jobs. The efficiency of this staff is an important part of his or her success while in office.

2. The lieutenant governor is next in line should something happen to the governor and is also the presiding officer of the state senate.

3. Ceremonial duties such as handing out awards or serving on commissions are often given to the lieutenant governor.

The governor has a large staff to help with the various tasks required of a state's chief executive. Much like the president's White House staff, the governor needs many talented individuals to write speeches and press releases, respond to inquiries, draft legislation, deal with the press, and suggest qualified people for the many leadership positions each governor will appoint during his or her term in office.

Every governor organizes the executive office in a somewhat different manner, emphasizing one area over another and delegating responsibilities to a different degree. One governor might just assign people to problems when they surface, while another may plan ahead and start the term by assigning a special person to handle only particular events when they occur.

A typical governor's executive office staff will usually have the following sections:

1. Press relations
2. Legislative *liaison*
3. Legal
4. Appointments coordination
5. Communications
6. Scheduling
7. Executive departments liaison*

Liaison means to form a close bond or connection— so a person assigned to legislative liaison is responsible to keep in close contact with the legislature.

In addition, the governor will have several staff members overseeing the office activities in areas that are important at the moment— economic development, higher education, hazardous waste disposal, the environment, etc.

The selection of the executive office staff is very important to the eventual success or failure of the governor's programs and hopes for reelection.

Republican Governor Milliken's staff (1969-1982) and its department heads included several Democrats. His administration was somewhat unique in having assistants from the competing political party.

Governor Blanchard (1983-1990) had been in the U.S. Congress just prior to becoming governor and brought many of his staff in from Washington, D. C. Their initial unfamiliarity with the inner workings of Michigan state government caused problems for this governor and contributed to his early unpopularity.

To provide an idea of all of the individuals who are needed to make the governor's office function smoothly, Governor Engler's staff consists of about 60 people working in several key areas. These include a chief of staff, director of state affairs, counsel for executive organization, director of communications, a policy division, legal staff, legislative liaison, and those working with appointments, correspondence, scheduling, community affairs, and computer operations.

THE LIEUTENANT GOVERNOR

Whenever the governor travels outside the state, the lieutenant governor is temporarily in charge. A governor may also leave office permanently to accept another position or for other reasons. This occurred when Governor Romney (1963-1969) left Michigan in 1969 for a post in President Nixon's administration. When the office of governor is left vacant because of death, recall, resignation, or any other reason, there must be a way to fill the position quickly. This is one important reason we have a lieutenant governor.

QUALIFICATIONS, TERM, AND ELECTION

Since the lieutenant governor may replace the governor if necessary, the qualifications for office are the same. Both must be at least 30 years of age and must have been registered voters in Michigan for the four years previous to their election.

The Michigan governor and lieutenant governor are elected as a "team" in the November general election, much like the national president and vice-president. Most states have lieutenant governors and over half are elected together. In the other states the voters have the opportunity of choosing the "teammates" separately and can even choose candidates from competing political parties.

In Michigan, candidates for governor have almost total control over the choice of their running mates. The constitution requires political parties to meet in conventions soon after the August primary election to nominate their candidates for lieutenant governor. The candidate for governor meets with supporters and decides who would make the best running mate; although, technically the party convention delegates make the decision.

POWERS AND DUTIES

The constitution gives the lieutenant governor the responsibility to serve as president and presiding officer of the state senate. This role has proved important for two main reasons. First of all, the lieutenant governor recognizes

or ignores speakers in the senate. And perhaps more important, he or she votes when there is a tie in the senate. Tie votes have occurred more frequently with senators closely divided between the Republicans and Democrats. When there was an equal number of Republicans and Democrats as in 1974, Lieutenant Governor James Brickley used his tie-breaking vote to organize the senate. He placed control of the senate in the hands of his fellow Republicans, allowing them to become the majority party!

Because the lieutenant governor's duties are so few, the governor gives him or her numerous tasks to fulfill, especially ceremonial duties, handing out awards, etc. The lieutenant governor also chairs various commissions and committees, such as the Michigan division of the American Bicentennial Commission.

Questions

1. Outline how you would organize your staff if you were elected governor. Where would you find the necessary qualified individuals?

2. In many states the governor and lieutenant governor are elected separately. What is the practice in Michigan?

3. Explain how the lieutenant governor can be a valuable aid to his or her party while serving as president of the senate.

5

THE EXECUTIVE BRANCH: THE DEPARTMENTS

Chapter 5   Section 1

Purpose and Background

Here are the key concepts in this section:

1. Geography, population concentration, economics, and cultural backgrounds are all important factors which determine what people demand of their government.

2. Major services provided for the people of Michigan by the executive branch include education, the state police, national guard, licensing of important professions, state health department, and much more.

3. This branch is divided into 18 separate departments.

Michigan is the eighth largest state with a population of roughly 9 million people. Industry, agriculture, and tourism provide jobs for the workers. Michigan leads the nation in the number of state parks and recreation areas.

Many factors determine the type of needs people have and what they want their government to do for them. Geography, population concentration, economics, and cultural backgrounds are all important.

Among the states Michigan is unique in several ways. Two particularly outstanding aspects are its economic reliance on the auto industry and its geographic location in the center of the vast Great Lakes.

Geography has provided Michigan with more freshwater shoreline than any other state and it is the only state divided into two parts by water. The St. Lawrence Seaway connects the Great Lakes and the Atlantic Ocean allowing ships from other nations to transport imports and exports. Michigan is fifth among the states in the value of exports to other nations. Detroit is the largest shipping center on the Great Lakes. The locks at Sault Ste. Marie handle more ships than the Panama Canal.

The people of Michigan are not evenly distributed throughout the state with most living in the southern third of the Lower Peninsula. In fact, just three counties have 43 percent of the whole population. They are Wayne, Oakland, and Macomb. This is a very great concentration of people. Comparing this combined population to the number of people living in some states is interesting. Taken individually, thirty-six states have smaller populations than this three-county area! Obviously, these counties influence much of what happens in Michigan.

The Populations of Michigan's Largest Counties

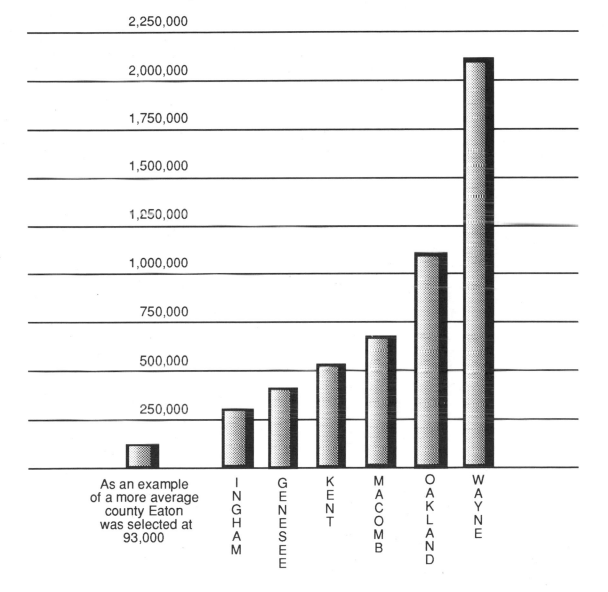

The state's businesses have been built around the auto industry for close to 90 years. Nearly one third of all the cars and trucks made in the United States come from Michigan and about 333,000 workers have jobs with the big three auto makers. In addition, numerous factories produce car and truck parts. The United Auto Workers union is one of the most powerful labor organizations in the country and has significant clout with state and local government.

Michigan's cultural background is diverse with a mixture of over 20 ethnic groups. The largest groups are German, English, African, Polish, Irish, and Dutch. There are more Arabic people living in and around Dearborn than anywhere else in the United States. The different beliefs and desires of these groups affect our government.

It is through the departments of the executive branch that many of the people's needs are met. Some of the most powerful units of state government are contained in the executive branch. Most people expect someone will keep expressways repaired, someone will check to be sure their hamburger does not contain anything but beef, someone will ensure drug dealers are kept in prison, and someone will notify the public if pollution is found in local water supplies. These tasks do not happen by themselves. All of these things are done by departments in the executive branch— involving some 60,000 civil service employees!

Prior to the 1963 constitution, Michigan had over 120 different agencies and departments in the executive branch. Because of the confusion which took place, the 1963 constitution mandated that these agencies, and all others, be placed in one of no more than 20 departments.

Questions

1. Name four key elements which help determine what kinds of services people want from their government.

2. What are the two particularly outstanding aspects which make Michigan unique among the states?

3. In which three counties is Michigan's population concentrated? Tell which section of the state contains these counties.

Chapter 5   Section 2

Departments Headed by Elected Officials

Here are the key concepts in this section:

1. The attorney general is a very powerful position in Michigan government and is elected every four years. This official has broad legal powers.

2. The secretary of state is an important elected official. He or she is second in line to replace the governor should this be necessary.

3. In Michigan, education is governed by both state and local school boards. Members of the state board of education are elected by the people.

APPOINTMENT PROCEDURE

Each department has someone who is in charge— a department head. There are a number of different ways department heads can be selected. Michigan uses four different methods: direct election, selection by an elected board, direct appointment by the governor, and selection by a commission which is appointed by the governor.

Directly Elected Officials

Michigan elects two department heads—the attorney general and the secretary of state. Both are nominated at party conventions in August and elected for four-year terms along with the governor and the state senate.

Elected Board

In only one department, the Department of Education, power rests with an elected board. The State Board of Education is a partisan body of eight members, serving eight-year terms, two of whom are elected statewide every two years in the general election. As a group they choose the state superintendent of public instruction who carries out the policies of the board.

Appointed Department Heads

Ten departments have directors appointed by the governor, but the senate does have the right to disapprove any appointee within 60 session days. The appointed department heads serve as long as the governor wishes. This arrangement is most similar to the selection process for the national cabinet. Departments using this process are Commerce, Labor, Management and Budget, Mental Health, Military Affairs, Public Health, State Police, Social Services, Transportation, and Treasury.

66

Through Appointed Commissions

Five departments are run by commissions whose members are appointed by the governor with automatic approval unless the state senate rejects the appointment within 60 session days. The commissions oversee the departments, much like the Department of Education, and choose the department head. The Civil Rights Commission (eight members) and the Civil Service Commission (four members) were created through the constitution, while the Departments of Agriculture (five members), Corrections (six members), and Natural Resources (seven members) were created by law in 1965. In all cases, the commissions have a specific number of political party positions available.

Unlike the national level where the U.S. Senate actually votes to approve a presidential appointment, the Michigan constitution provides for automatic approval unless the state senate rejects the nomination within 60 days of the appointment. Rejection of appointees is rare.

Additionally, the governor has power of removal. The governor may investigate any public office in the state and may remove any executive official, even those who are elected, for gross neglect of duty or for corrupt conduct in office.

Although the state constitution allows 20 departments, the legislature has been very reluctant to create that 20th department. The agency that came closest to achieving department status is the Energy Administration created in 1976. Until 1991 the number of departments had not changed since Public Act 380 created the present departments in 1965. In 1991 the Department of Licensing and Regulation was absorbed into the Department of Commerce—reducing the number of executive branch departments to 18.

THE ELECTED HEADS AND BOARDS

Many people believe the heads of some departments are so important that these officials are elected directly. State-wide ballots contain the names of those running for attorney general, secretary of state, and the board of education.

Attorney General
— *lawyer for the state and top law enforcement officer* —

The office of *attorney general* traces its origins to English history. The attorney general was the chief legal representative of the king. It was his duty to represent the crown in civil and criminal matters in the courts. The position in Michigan is very similar. The office of attorney general was created in our first constitution of 1835. The constitution does not list all the duties and powers of the office; this is left to the legislature and to the discretion of the attorney general.

The attorney general is the state's chief legal officer and its top law enforcement officer. It is the duty of this official to both prosecute and defend cases pertaining to the public interest of the citizens of Michigan. The attorney general can intervene in any lawsuit where it is felt the interests of the people of the state are involved. The attorney general advises county prosecuting attorneys and may supervise them if necessary. The attorney general has the power to investigate criminal activity, establish grand juries, and investigate complaints for the removal of public officials and election fraud.

The attorney general has a staff of over 200 assistant attorneys who specialize in many areas. One of the assistants is the *solicitor general* who handles appeals in the state supreme court, the Federal Circuit Court of Appeals, and the U.S. Supreme Court. Another position in the department is the *public administrator* who investigates estate matters. Here are some of the other divisions in the department:

- Education
- Consumer Protection
- Civil Rights
- Commerce
- Transportation
- Environmental Protection

Department of State
— in charge of voting, driving and other things relating to cars, and preserving the state's history —

The *secretary of state* is one of Michigan's most important elected officials. This office holder is next in line to become governor if the governor and lieutenant governor cannot perform their duties. Citizens usually first come into contact with the secretary of state's office as they approach the legal driving age of 16 and go to one of the many offices to fill out forms and take the driving tests. License plates for automobiles, motorcycles, motor scooters, and other vehicles are available as well. Also, 18-year-olds and others can register to vote at all sites. The secretary of state has a variety of responsibilities. These are the most significant:

1. Registers motor vehicles, watercraft, snowmobiles, and off-road vehicles.
2. Licenses Michigan car and truck drivers.
3. Serves as state supervisor and coordinator of elections, including providing over 200 voter registration sites, examination of petitions for ballot proposals, and distributes information on ballot issues and voting procedures to voters.

4. Responsible for preservation of Michigan history— operates the state historical museums, publishes the *Michigan History* magazine, and directs the Michigan historic sites and centennial farm programs.
5. Serves as keeper of the Great Seal of Michigan.
6. Registers lobbyists, trademarks, financial statements, and railroad leases.
7. Licenses auto repair facilities and mechanics
8. Regulates private driver-training schools.

The Michigan Historical Museum complex which represents the Department of State's responsibility to preserve Michigan's history. Photo courtesy of the Michigan Department of State.

THE ELECTED BOARD - BOARD OF EDUCATION
— oversees schools and education in Michigan—

There is one elected board in Michigan: the *State Board of Education* with eight members. This state board carries out its responsibilities through the *Department of Education*. The department supervises education in Michigan.

The state board appoints an individual to serve as the *state superintendent of public instruction*. This person carries out the decisions of the board and serves as long as the board wishes.

The department assists the state board in providing statewide educational leadership, advising the legislature on the financial needs of the state's schools, certifying teachers, and administering the state aid programs to schools. It also provides some coordination of higher education, especially with community colleges, except in areas where those duties are the responsibility of that institution's elected or appointed board of trustees.

Michigan has long been considered a leader in education. In 1828, we were the first state to establish the office of State Superintendent of Public Instruction. Michigan has over 3,000 public schools and over 1,000 private schools. We have a public school enrollment of over 1.5 million students and about 80,000 public school teachers. Michigan also has one of the finest systems of higher education in the country with some 500,000 students attending our 44 public and 56 private colleges and universities, including 29 community colleges.

The Department of Education and the superintendent of public instruction are responsible for the following duties and many others:

1. Provision of general supervision of all public schools.
2. Distribution of state aid funds to school districts.
3. Collection and maintenance of school statistics, particularly school enrollment information.
4. Examinations and audits of the official records of school districts.
5. Determination of the requirements for licenses and certificates for teachers.

The Department of Education ensures equal educational opportunities for all of Michigan's students and formulates the general goals in each subject area, such as science. Photo courtesy of the Michigan Department of Education.

The eight members of the board of education serve for 8-year terms, which is longer than most terms for elected officials in Michigan.

Questions

1. How many departments in the executive branch are allowed in our current state constitution?

2. Explain the four different ways Michigan chooses its department heads in the executive branch.

3. The heads of which departments are directly elected in Michigan?

4. How many members are on the state Board of Education and what is the length of their terms? How is the Superintendent of Public Instruction chosen?

5. Name the officials responsible for the following duties:
   A. Certifies auto mechanics in the state.
   B. Distributes state aid to local school districts.
   C. Operates the state historical museum in Lansing.
   D. Advises and supervises all county prosecuting attorneys.
   E. Determines the qualifications of teachers.
   F. Represents the state of Michigan in important legal cases.

Chapter 5   Section 3

Executive Departments With Appointed Heads

Here are the key concepts in this section:

1. Most department heads in the executive branch (10 out of 18) are appointed by the governor.

2. The state senate has the power to veto any appointment the governor might make for a department head.

3. The departments in this section affect nearly every aspect of life in Michigan. For example, the Department of Commerce oversees business activity and its Bureau of Occupational and Professional Regulation, formerly the Department of Licensing and Regulation, controls those working in dozens of professions. While the Department of Labor looks out for the health and safety of workers.

The governor appoints 10 of the 18 department heads. These appointees serve at the governor's pleasure. When a new governor takes office, several of these department heads lose their jobs. Sometimes they remain to serve under several governors, even those of a different political party.

Department of Commerce
— oversees and encourages business activity in Michigan including tourism —

The major purpose of the *Department of Commerce* is to encourage business and economic development in Michigan. It also has regulatory and consumer protection responsibilities. Commerce is one of the departments that was created under the 1963 constitution in an attempt to reduce the over 120 agencies in state government.

The Commerce Department's primary mission is to maintain a healthy economy and protect the consumer in those industries regulated by the department. It also has the goal of assuring good jobs for Michigan's citizens. Among other responsibilities, the Department of Commerce does the following:

1.   Encourages and assists businesses which desire to begin operations or expand in Michigan.
2.   Encourages tourism and travel in Michigan.
3.   Regulates credit companies, finance companies, and small loan companies.

4. Seeks to assure the financial stability of Michigan's banks.
5. Enforces maximum interest rates that can be charged for such things as auto loans.
6. Regulates the distribution and sale of alcoholic beverages within the state
7. Encourages international trade.
8. Regulates all telephone, electric, and gas companies and sets the rates for these utilities through the *Public Service Commission*— a group of three individuals each appointed for a six-year term by the governor.
9. Develops the state's energy plans and administers programs related to energy conservation.

This department has now taken over the duties of the former Department of Licensing and Regulation— see description which follows.

Department of Labor
— helps the workers of the state —

The *Department of Labor* promotes full employment and the welfare and safety of the workers of the state. It attempts to provide a work environment that sees quick and workable solutions to labor disputes and the enforcement of state laws regarding youth employment, minimum and prevailing wages, and other wage claims. The department also provides certain services such as boiler and

The Michigan Department of Labor includes the Governor's Office for Job Training which helps retrain workers for new high technology jobs. Photo courtesy David Trumpie/ Michigan Department of Labor.

elevator inspections, home weatherization, and programs for the blind and deaf.

One important role the Department of Labor plays is assistance to young workers. This is most noticeable in the Michigan Youth Corps, which began in 1983. Since then the Youth Corps has employed over 100,000 18- to 21-year-olds in hundreds of work projects.

The following agencies work within the Labor Department:

Michigan Youth Corps
Workers' Compensation Appeals Board
Michigan Employment Security Commission
Insurance Funds Administration
Employment Training
Workers' Disability Compensation
Barrier Free Design Board

Department of Licensing and Regulation
(Now the Bureau of Occupational and Professional Regulation— a division of the Department of Commerce)
— *oversees and licenses occupations where the public could be harmed by poor practices —*

The *Bureau of Occupational and Professional Regulation* regulates 40 different professions throughout the state of Michigan and licenses some 600,000 individuals who practice in those professions. The bureau has regulatory authority in three key areas: the health professions, commercial services, and the insurance industry.

Why is it important for, say, a beautician to be licensed? In the example at the start of the book Willa felt she was qualified to do the job. However, what if she used a new styling formula on a customer's hair and it became brittle and began to fall out? The customer would certainly be mad and perhaps permanently disfigured. The tests beauticians take for their licenses could avoid this sort of problem.

It is difficult for the consumer to be sufficiently knowledgeable regarding the skills and training or education of various professionals, such as physicians, beauticians, dentists, optometrists, veterinarians, and real estate agents. If these and many other professions were not regulated, it is likely some unqualified individuals would attempt to present themselves as qualified practitioners and the public could be at risk. The mission of the Bureau of Occupational and Professional Regulation is to protect the public's health, safety, and welfare.

Some of the other professions regulated by the bureau include the following:

Accountants-- Architects-- Barbers-- Carnival ride owners
Engineers-- Hearing aid dealers-- Marriage counselors
Pharmacists

Over 300 citizens serve on various boards and task forces within this bureau overseeing these professions and their activities. Most are members of the profession they regulate. Each member is appointed by the governor with the consent of the state senate.

Department of Management and Budget
— helps manage state government, keeps state financial records, prepares the state budget each year —

The most important function of the *Department of Management and Budget*, or *DMB* as it is commonly called, is the development of the annual state budget. The department also presents the budget to the legislature and oversees the budget as the departments receive and spend money according to the provisions of the document. Another major task for the department is the management of the state's many facilities and resources. In doing these tasks, and others, DMB provides considerable financial record keeping for the governor and the entire state government. While these tasks are very important, the department also is involved with the following jobs:

1. Oversees the distribution of federal and state funds for local projects providing educational, medical, economic, legal, housing, and recreational services to the elderly.
2. Does accounting for all state agencies, including the design, review, and control of accounting methods used.
3. Provides budgetary controls and generates financial statements, including the annual summary of all state activities and the spending of all state funds.
4. Provides compensation to victims of crime (not to exceed $15,000) through the Crime Victims Compensation Board.
5. Provides assistance in the construction of state facilities such as office buildings and prisons.
6. Provides consultants to other government departments when they need management advice.
7. Provides centralized support services such as printing, microfilming, and storage through the Office Services Division. They produce the *Michigan Manual*, a yearly overview of Michigan and the people involved.
8. Operates and maintains state-run buildings, grounds, and parking facilities and provides tours of the state capitol through the Property Management Division.
9. Does all central purchasing of supplies, materials, equipment, and services used by state agencies.
10. Purchases, operates, and maintains state-owned vehicles and operates the central fleet of motor vehicles used by the state.

In addition to these services that would logically fall within a department such as DMB, it has also been assigned a number of other responsibilities which you might not expect to be in this department. We list only a few to give you an idea of the breadth of the activities:

1. Michigan Council for the Arts
2. Child Abuse and Neglect Prevention Board
3. Office of Criminal Justice
4. Commission on Indian Affairs
5. Bureau of Retirement Systems
6. Commission on Spanish Speaking Affairs
7. Toxic Substance Control Commission
8. Veterans' Affairs
9. Women's Commission

Bureau of the State Lottery- a unit of DMB

Another agency that receives considerable media attention and is a part of DMB is the *Bureau of the State Lottery*. The Michigan state lottery is one of the most successful in the nation. It was voted into law by a 2-1 margin on the 1972 statewide ballot. It's ballot success was due in large part to the belief that all lottery profits would be used for K-12 education. Hundreds of millions of dollars have indeed been transferred to the department of education and by law, all lottery profits do now go to the state school aid fund. But it wasn't until 1980 that all lottery profits were actually earmarked to go solely for education.

However, most people assumed state legislators would keep the budget for education nearly the same as before the lottery began and that lottery profits would be an added bonus. This has not been the case. Since 1980 as lottery profits have increased, legislators have cut the percentage of the general fund budget for education nearly every year. Because of this trend, Michigan's TOTAL spending on education, including lottery money, was nearly the same for at least five years.

This is a complex slight-of-hand. All lottery profits do go to education, but it can be argued this has not done much to help the cause of education because other sources have been reduced at the same time!

Department of Mental Health
— provides aid to those with mental problems —

The *Department of Mental Health* is responsible for the treatment of mental illness, for the promotion of research into the causes and prevention of mental diseases and for the development of a statewide mental health program. The department also has facilities for the treatment of mental illness and developmental disabilities.

The Department of Mental Health operates regional psychiatric hospitals in Pontiac, Detroit, Kalamazoo, Northville, Traverse City, and Ypsilanti. It operates special psychiatric hospitals in Detroit, Ann Arbor, and Westland. There are five regional centers for developmental disabilities in Mt. Clemens, Mt. Pleasant, Muskegon, Oakdale, and Southgate. And the department has several other agencies throughout the state.

Many facilities have been closed or have had their staffs reduced considerably in recent years due to a change in the philosophy about the treatment of those served by the department. This philosophy argues that those who are mentally or emotionally ill, but pose no serious threat to society or themselves, should not be held in institutions but should be released in an attempt to live normal lives. Many individuals are now in local group homes or live with their families or by themselves. Many others, whose behavior has gotten them in trouble with the law, now spend much of their time in and out of county jails and the prison system.

Military Affairs
— *manages the army and air national guard for Michigan* —

The *Department of Military Affairs* maintains the state's armed forces, currently about 16,000 men and women. Each state is required to have a national guard with the primary purpose of providing combat-ready soldiers to assist the U.S. Army and Air Force such as the United Nations actions against Iraq. It is the national guard's secondary purpose to be prepared to assist when the governor calls for their help in a natural disaster or significant civil unrest within Michigan.

The governor serves as the commander-in-chief of the national guard and an *adjutant general* serves as the commanding officer. The state is responsible for the management of the unit and the physical maintenance of state and federal facilities, including 56 armories, two air bases, and four training sites.

The goal of the National Guard is to help people whether in the area of national defense, state emergency, or community assistance. The Guard may help clean up a city or town after a tornado or flood. Photo courtesy of the Michigan Department of Militiary Affairs.

The largest national guard facilities in Michigan are at Camp Grayling in the central Lower Peninsula and Selfridge Field air base near Mt. Clemens in the southeast corner of the state. There are two other air bases near Alpena and Battle Creek.

Since the major role of the national guard is to assist the regular military forces of the United States, the federal government provides 95% of the money needed for its operations or approximately $200 million a year.

Questions

1. You are writing a term paper and need to know the salaries of several Michigan public officials. Which department might you contact to find all of this information at one time?

2. Suppose you are the mayor of a small town in Michigan and your town is in desperate need of new industry and more jobs. Which department of the executive branch could you turn to for information and assistance?

3. Name five professions which come under the control of the Bureau of Occupational and Professional Regulation. Choose one of these professions, other than beautician, and give an example how the public could be harmed if the profession was not regulated.

4. As a high school student you have just been hired to work at a fast food restaurant but you think the wages and hours they set may be illegal. Which department can help you and provide the answers?

5. What is the current philosophy about the treatment of the mentally ill and why has this reduced the number of state mental hospitals?

6. Why does the federal government pay for most of the budget of the department of military affairs?

Chapter 5   Section 4

Departments With Appointed Heads— Continued

Here are the key concepts in this section:

1. The Department of Public Health works to keep Michiganians safe from disease whether it is an epidemic or bacteria in a public swimming pool.

2. The Department of Social Services operates Michigan's welfare system including medicaid and ADC payments.

3. The Department of State Police and the Department of Transportation help keep motorists safe on Michigan's highways.

4. The Department of the Treasury manages the state's money, collects its taxes, and invests its employee retirement funds.

Department of Public Health
— protects Michigan's people from dangerous diseases —

The *Department of Public Health* is responsible for the protection of the health of the citizens of Michigan. Its primary goals include the prevention of disease and the promotion of good health. It regulates nursing homes and licenses hospitals. There is a radiation advisory board as a part of this department.

The Department of Public Health has regional offices throughout the state and works in cooperation with local governments to promote the health of the citizens. The Department consists of these agencies:

1.   Bureau of Environmental and Occupational Health (Coordinates inspection of water supplies, mobile home parks, campgrounds, food service establishments, public swimming pools, migrant labor camps, and school sanitation.)
2.   Bureau of Health Facilities (Approves rules for licensing health facilities.)
3.   Center For Health Promotion
4.   Office of Substance Abuse Services
5.   Bureau of Community Services (Identifies health problems and sets priorities to address them working through local health departments.)
6.   Bureau of Laboratory and Epidemiological Services (This bureau tests for diseases and makes vaccines for some diseases. During the Iraq conflict its lab was the only one in the U.S. to produce a type of anti-germ warfare vaccine.)

Department of Social Services
— provides aid, generally known as welfare, for needy people, —

The *Department of Social Services* provides financial and medical assistance to the people of the state who are not able to provide for themselves as determined by state and federal agencies. These services are provided to a great extent through county social service departments.

Services and assistance include the following:

1. Financial aid to families with dependent children.
2. Inspection and approval of county medical facilities.
3. Medical assistance to low income individuals.
4. Administration of the food stamp program (state and federal money).
5. Administration of general assistance funds (state money).
6. Adult home care services, protective services, adult placement services, health, housing, transportation, and educational services.
7. Licenses for private child care agencies, child-placing agencies, summer camps for children, day care centers, and nursery schools.
8. Other programs for children, the care, training, and treatment of neglected and delinquent children committed to the department as wards of the state. Services for these children include counseling, adoption, foster care, and the operation of group homes.

Other services include child support collections on behalf of ADC (Aid to Dependent Children) and non-ADC families; investigation of welfare fraud; day care for low income families, employment, training, and educational programs for most public assistance recipients; and housing projects to help low income individuals find safe and adequate housing.

Department of State Police
— operates over 60 state police posts whose troopers patrol state and county roads- also investigates organized crime and more —

The *Department of State Police* was established in 1917 during World War I. Then known as the State Troops, the organization was to provide internal security against the possible dangers of spies and sabotage, labor agitation and unrest, and military draft dodging. It has been reorganized several times, most recently in 1965.

State police officers may exercise all of the powers of a sheriff regarding the laws of the state. It is their duty to discover and prevent crime. They also aid in the protection of life on the public highways. Officers serve and execute criminal and civil process papers when they are issued by the governor or the attorney general. Statewide services are provided around the clock through 69 state police posts.

The department has a number of specialized units for auto theft, narcotics, arson, child abuse, organized and specialized crime, tracking dogs, and drug detection. The state police also has divers for underwater recovery, units for hostage negotiation, aircraft support, and the governor's security.

The department has responsibility for emergency preparedness planning for civil defense in case of natural or man-made disaster and handles state and federal grant money for disaster victims. The department also inspects all school buses to be sure they are safe.

The State Police is an efficient crime fighting organization with several specialized units which cover everything from canine tracking to laboratory analysis of crime scenes. Photo courtesy of the Michigan Department of State Police.

Department of Transportation
— maintains and builds major highways in Michigan, as well as managing all other types of transportation including air travel —

Probably the most well-used service provided by state government is the state highway system. The state *Department of Transportation* is responsible for the construction, improvement, and maintenance of the 9,500 miles of Interstate, U.S., and M-numbered state highways throughout Michigan. It also administers state programs dealing with all other kinds of transportation, including air travel, bus, and rail. In some cases it gives technical assistance to county road commissions and other local transportation agencies.

Laws passed in 1975 and 1978 broadened the department's powers. It was previously concerned only with highways. This was motivated by the energy crisis of that time and the increased use of mass transit. The new laws require the department to oversee all areas of transportation policy.

The Department of Transportation receives its direction from the six-member *Transportation Commission* appointed by the governor for three-year terms. This is the only department in state government which has a commission that does not appoint the director of the department. The commission can appoint a director only if the governor does not.

An interesting aspect of the commission is the requirement that it be equally divided between Republicans and Democrats. This could cause some difficulties because they could be divided along party lines (3-3) and be equally split on important decisions. But department history has shown that such division is rare.

Road construction is done every summer and has become very expensive over the years. In 1909, Wayne County built the first mile of concrete highway in the world on Woodward Avenue in Detroit. The cost was $13,537, including $1,000 in state funds. A similar mile of interstate highway today typically costs $2.5 million. In the city, the cost averages over $10 million a mile and has been as much as $35 million when built through the heart of a major city. Just purchasing the right-of-way in a city can average $7 million per mile.

Highway Trivia:

1. The department maintains nearly 300,000 road signs.

2. The longest highway in Michigan is the 395 mile-long I-75 which begins at the Ohio border and goes across the Straits of Mackinac to the Canadian border at Sault Ste. Marie.

3. The shortest highway is only four-tenths of a mile long. It is M-209 in Leelanau County and connects M-109 with Glen Haven.

4. The most heavily traveled highway is the Ford Freeway (I-94) in Detroit which carries 140,000 vehicles a day, followed closely by the John Lodge (US-10) and the Southfield Freeway (M-39), both in metropolitan Detroit. Outside the Detroit area, the most heavily traveled is 28th Street (M-11) in Grand Rapids.

5. Michigan has one highway not used by motor vehicles, except in emergencies. M-185 is the 7.5 mile blacktopped road circling Mackinac Island.

6. Michigan is one of only three large industrial states that has no toll roads. The others are California and Missouri.

Most roads in Michigan are maintained by local governments. Actually, the state's 9,500 miles represent only about eight percent of the 117,000 miles of roads in Michigan. However, state highways carry about half of the total traffic. Currently it is estimated over 70 billion miles are driven each year by cars and trucks in the state— compared with 33 billion miles in 1960.

The department has a work force of about 4,000 employees, including some 550 civil engineers, to design, build, and maintain the state's highways. To be sure new highways do not cause environmental problems, the department also employs biologists, geologists, and others to develop environmental impact studies. Foresters work on roadside development and maintenance.

Department of the Treasury
— takes care of the state's money and collects state taxes —

The *Department of the Treasury* is the chief financial agency for the state and the primary advisor to the governor on state fiscal matters. The department is responsible for managing the state's cash. This includes investing excess money and arranging any necessary borrowing.

The department also administers most of the state's tax laws, including the income tax on individuals (currently 4.6%), sales and use taxes (4%), taxes on gasoline (15 cents per gallon) and diesel fuel, the single business tax, cigarette taxes, and the inheritance tax.

Regarding the income tax, Michigan is one of only four states which have flat rate taxes. All other states with income taxes have graduated scales with those having higher incomes paying a larger percentage.

The department manages the retirement system for state employees which is worth billions of dollars and issues over 20 million checks every year in payment of bills received by the state. The department receives and pays out all federal grants. The governor appoints a *state treasurer* to head the department.

Questions

1. You live in the country and have your own water well. Suddenly the water develops a strange taste and everyone in your family feels sick. Which department in the executive branch would you contact for assistance?

2. You live close to the Michigan-Indiana border. Your parents rent a mobile home to a man who receives public assistance checks from Michigan. You notice the renter is gone for days at a time and you inquire where he is. A member of your community says that your renter actually lives with his family in Indiana but uses the address of the mobile home so he can collect money from the state of Michigan. Do you consider this to be welfare fraud? Explain your reasoning. If you decide to report this man which department would you contact?

3. Your local newspaper reports the robbery of a bank in your city and that tracking dogs were used to locate the robber who had escaped on foot. Which department would have most likely supplied the tracking dog team?

4. List four types of transportation supervised by the Department of Transportation. Since interstate highways are a part of the federal highway system, who is responsible for their maintenance?

5. Once you have a full-time job you will pay state income tax to which executive branch department? What is the current rate for state income tax?

Chapter 5   Section 5

Executive Departments With Appointed Commissions

Here are the key concepts in this section:

1. Michigan is a world leader in the production of several agricultural products and the Department of Agriculture works to help farmers in the state.

2. The Department of Civil Rights helps Michigan's people overcome discrimination while the Department of Civil Service regulates the employment of all non-elected and non-appointed state government employees.

3. The Department of Corrections runs the state prison system and faces a difficult problem due to a rapid growth in the number of inmates.

4. Michigan's state parks, fishing, hunting, and environmental problems are all handled by the Department of Natural Resources (DNR).

Important Commissions
Five departments get their direction from the governor through appointed commissions. They are the Departments of Agriculture, Civil Service, Civil Rights, Corrections, and Natural Resources.

Department of Agriculture

Farming land is one of Michigan's most important resources. Agriculture is one of the big three industries in Michigan—automobiles and tourism are the other two. Michigan produces over 60 different foods and crops with a combined annual value of about $3 billion dollars. Farmers buy goods and services from many others generating income for more people— producers of equipment, fertilizer, irrigation systems, transportation workers, etc. All are part of the state's huge agribusiness network.

Hundreds of thousands of acres of Michigan land are under cultivation. Well-known products are corn, wheat, beans, and apples, but there are many others. As a matter of fact, Michigan produces a greater variety of crops than any other state except California.

The *Department of Agriculture* assists farmers in many ways. A major role is to help them produce high-quality crops and then promote the sale of those crops to markets throughout the world.

The department is also particularly interested in protecting the public from disease and unsanitary conditions in connection with food production and handling. There are many consumer protection laws which relate to food, and the department is the major enforcement agency. Areas of concern include farm produce storage, dairy product quality, inspection of animal health, control of pests and diseases, and the inspection of perishable fruits and vegetables.

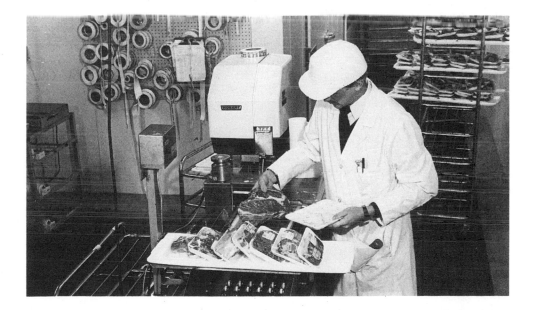

A Department of Agriculture inspector looks over a meat packing operation to check for cleanliness and to certify all proper precedures are being used. Photo courtesy of the Michigan Department of Agriculture.

The department is directed by the *Agriculture Commission*, a group of five individuals; no more than three of whom can be from the same political party. They are appointed by the governor and serve four-year terms.

84

The following is an indication of the importance of several crops produced in this state. Large quantities are sold to other states and to several other nations.

MICHIGAN'S NATIONAL RANK FOR VARIOUS CROPS

1st
blueberries
cucumbers (pickling)
Navy beans
plantation Christmas trees
red tart cherries

2nd
bedding plants
purple plums

3rd
apples
asparagus
carrots
celery
mushrooms
sweet cherries
tomatoes (processing)
veal

Everyone loves Michigan apples which are well-known across the nation. Photo courtesy of the Michigan Tourist Council.

Department of Civil Rights
— works to protect people against many kinds of discrimination and prejudice concerning jobs, education, and housing —

Most societies have prejudice in one form or another. Unfortunately, this seems to be human nature. We especially seem to act this way with regard to another's religion, race, and ethnic background. It is common to show prejudice in other areas as well, such as age, sex, marital status, height, weight, arrest record, and physical handicap.

In 1963 the *Civil Rights Department* was established in Michigan to investigate alleged discrimination against any person because of religion, race, color, or national origin. The department is run by an eight-member *Civil Rights Commission* appointed by the governor for four-year terms. No more than four members can be from any one political party. The commission selects a director to run the department and carry out its decisions.

More recent legislation has added other areas to the "protected categories" including sex discrimination. The department investigates discrimination in the areas of employment, housing, education, public accommodation, and public service. The department also seeks to protect equal opportunity and treatment through *affirmative action programs* which are designed to increase the number of "protected individuals" (minorities, handicapped, etc.) in the work force. The concept behind affirmative action is to reverse the loss of jobs due to years of discrimination.

The Department of Civil Rights helps the handicapped and sees they have access to all types of buildings.

Civil Service Department
— works to find qualified workers for state government jobs and sets standards for the employees and jobs alike —

Years ago, newly elected officials got their campaign workers and supporters government jobs. Previous workers were fired and replaced with friends; qualifications were of little concern. The public suffered as a result of inexperienced and unqualified workers. A move to change this situation took place in Michigan during the 1930s. The legislature established the civil service system in 1938. It quickly became the focus of political maneuvering and most of the sections of the act were repealed the next year. Then the public organized a petition drive which successfully put a constitutional amendment on the ballot through the initiative process and civil service finally became a part of the constitution. The powers of the *Department of Civil Service* remain much the same.

It is run by the *Civil Service Commission*, four persons appointed by the governor for eight-year terms. The terms of office are purposely kept long to make it less likely that one governor will control the commission. It is politically balanced with two Republicans and two Democrats. They select a full-time director.

It is the responsibility of this department to regulate all conditions of employment for the more than 55,000 state civil service employees. All interested persons must qualify on a standardized civil service test in order to be considered for a state job. Public notification is given when there are vacancies. These notices include the place, day, and time where a civil service examination is to be given to applicants.

These examinations are given at several locations in the state. Tests are sent to examiners in sealed packages and only opened when the test begins. After the test is given, all papers are accounted for and returned to the department in Lansing for grading. The scores of the applicants determine their rank on an employment list which is used by all departments. For example, those applicants scoring within a range (known as the bandwidth) of 90 to 100 would be the first to be considered for job openings.

The department also determines the rate of pay for each civil service position in the state. This is done after an analysis of the tasks involved in the job, the educational background and experience needed, and many other factors. This analysis results in a job "classification" relative to others in state government.

Department of Corrections
— operates the state prison system —

Three police officers are assassinated in Inkster. A paperboy is killed while out collecting his newspaper money. A mother is raped while walking home from a restaurant. Three murderers escape from Jackson Prison. Unfortunately, this is not unusual in Michigan, or in most of the United States. All these crimes, and many more, occurred during one week.

When juries or judges find individuals guilty of crimes, they are often sent to one of the more than 30 adult felony correctional facilities in the state. It is the role of the *Department of Corrections* to protect the public by holding individuals who have been convicted of serious crimes. There are facilities for serious offenders and there are also medium and minimum security arrangements. The department also has "half-way" houses allowing prisoners, who will soon be back in society, a chance to be prepared for their eventual release.

The department is run by the *Corrections Commission*, created in 1953 and reorganized in 1965. The five commission members are appointed by the governor and serve four-year terms. No more than three may be from any one political party. The commission selects the director of the department and sets its policy.

The department also has a five-member, full-time *parole board* whose duty it is to determine when a prisoner may be released. Few prisoners serve their "maximum" sentence; most are released much earlier for a variety of reasons. The average prisoner in Michigan stays only two and a half years.

Michigan prisons have been overcrowded for several years, resulting in many prisoners being given early parole. In a recent twelve-month period about 4,000 prisoners were paroled. The experience is not always successful. One study of parolees shows 26.7 percent returned to prison during the parole period. And these are people who are released early because the parole board feels they have a *good chance* of "making it".

Many other convicted felons are not sent to prison at all, but are kept in their community under the watchful eye of counselors. These individuals are on *probation*. They are not considered dangerous and are allowed to live reasonably normal lives. They are encouraged to get a job and their probation officer (counselor) is responsible for helping them see the benefits of running their lives within the law.

Most of us will be affected by crime in some way in our lifetime. Unfortunately, the chances of a woman being raped, of our home being burglarized, or of being mugged or beaten in the streets is all too high. We all have our opinions of who commits crimes and what we should do with the offenders. The following are some interesting facts about prisons and prisoners in Michigan:

1. The number of people held in Michigan's prisons continues to grow each year and recently numbered over 30,000 but is estimated to reach 50,000 by 1993 or 1994. In 1970 it was 8,800. Roughly 1 out of every 22 inmates is a woman.

2. The racial composition of the prisoners changes somewhat over time, but not dramatically. It is about 56% black, 41% white, 1.2% Spanish/American, the rest being Native American, oriental, etc.

3. It cost about $21,000 a year to keep an inmate in prison or $58.00 a day. Most of the cost is in salaries for prison staff.

4. The department of corrections is opposed to capital punishment. They are not convinced there is any reliable evidence that it deters others from similar crimes.

5. About 34 percent of paroled prisoners will return to prison at some time in the future.

6. The department's budget is over $500 million annually.

Prison inmates have committed a variety of serious offenses; while those convicted of misdemeanors often stay in county jails for up to one year instead of being assigned to a state prison. The following chart provides some idea of the kinds of crimes committed by inmates.

For the 7,521 persons sentenced to prison in a recent year.

- 824 committed larceny or attempted larceny of a building. (10.96%)
- 1,389 were convicted of burglary or attempted burglary. (18.47%)
- 837 were convicted of armed robbery or attempted armed robbery. (11.13%)
- 855 committed criminal sexual conduct or attempted criminal sexual conduct. (11.37%)
- 426 were convicted of receiving or attempting to receive stolen property. (5.66%)
- 599 were convicted of the sale, distribution, manufacturing or possession of controlled substances or the attempt to do so. (7.96%)
- 218 were convicted of carrying or attempting to carry a concealed weapon. (2.90%)
- 193 came for second degree murder (2.57%)
- 96 came for first degree murder. (1.28%)
- the remaining inmates were guilty of other crimes. (About 28%)

Despite the state's best efforts, criminal activity has been increasing, and not just in large cities. Judges try to reduce crime by giving criminals stiffer sentences which increases the number of people spending time in our prisons. New programs have been developed to rehabilitate inmates, yet a third of them return to prison. The citizens want criminals off the streets but are often unwilling to pay for more prisons. When money is available for new prisons, no one wants them built near their town.

The Department of Natural Resources
— responsible for Michigan's state parks, regulates hunting and fishing, monitors toxic waste and environmental problems —

Anyone involved with hunting, fishing, boating, or camping should be familiar with the *Department of Natural Resources*. Conservation of Michigan's natural resources and the protection of its environment is the DNR's goal. They also provide recreational opportunities to the people of Michigan and visiting tourists. The Michigan DNR has been a national leader in many of its programs. It has nearly 3,000 employees and a budget of almost $300 million, some of which comes directly from public fees.

Some people consider the DNR to be one of the most powerful of all departments of state government because of their wide range of responsibilities.

The seven members of the *Natural Resources Commission* are appointed by the governor for four-year terms. Not more than four of the members can be from the same political party. The commission appoints the director of the department.

Some of the duties and powers of the department include the following:

1. Acquaint the public with the need for conservation.
2. Provide the public with hunting and fishing licenses.
3. Provide game for hunters and fish enthusiasts by restocking fish and game.
4. Care for Michigan's state forests.
5. Grow seedlings for replanting.
6. Prevent and put out forest fires.
7. Care for the historic sites in the Mackinac Straits area.
8. Care for Michigan's state parks and recreation areas.
9. Investigate Michigan's water resources.
10. Promote the tourist industry.
11. Study the shoreline and develop programs for erosion protection.
12. Review plans, license facilities, and enforce standards of solid and chemical waste disposal.
13. Regulate development on Michigan's wetland areas.

Michigan's Executive Branch and Its Structure

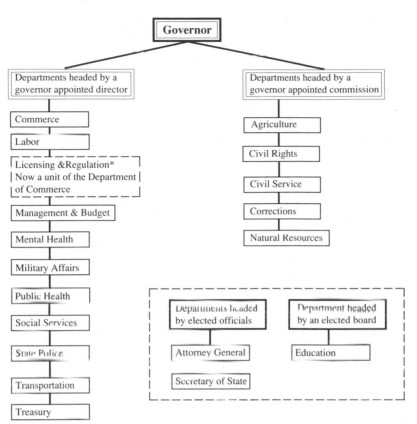

Questions

1. What is the difference between the departments of Civil Service and Civil Rights?

2. The Department of Corrections faces many problems. List at least three of them and give your own ideas how they may be solved.

3. If you saw a large tanker truck parked along a highway with oil pouring from its valve, which department should you try to contact?

4. Name the different departments which are responsible for each of the following: protection and regulation of wetlands, examinations for those wanting jobs with state government, regulation toxic waste in Michigan, inspection of dairy farms, and operation of affirmative action programs with employers.

5. In your opinion, which executive branch department is the most powerful? Provide at least three reasons to back up your belief.

6

MICHIGAN 'S COURT SYSTEM

Chapter 6   Section 1

Purpose & Background

Here are the key concepts in this section:

1. Society has laws to protect its people.

2. Courts apply the law when considering criminal cases and cases involving disputes between people.

3. Courts decide guilt or innocence and set punishments.

4. Our court system is based on the system used in England.

James is 16 years old. His case is real but his name has been changed. He isn't as well-groomed as others his age. His clothes are not as stylish as some and he doesn't appear friendly. Most girls probably would not delight mom and dad if they brought him home and introduced him to the family.

Actually, James is not like a lot of his peers. Right now he is staying at the county juvenile detention facility. In the last five years, James has committed over 20 crimes. Four times he was caught for trespassing, but that is tame for James. He also has charges against him that include arson, assault and battery, breaking and entering a motor vehicle, larceny, aggravated assault, carrying a concealed weapon, felonious assault with a rifle, and more. James is not typical, but his situation isn't as unusual as we would like to think.

Young people like James get involved in the courts of Michigan every day, more specifically the probate courts. Michigan probate courts handle about 35,000 offenses by *juveniles* every year. *According to the law juveniles are young people under the age of 17*. In fact, over 3 million cases a year are filed for all of Michigan's courts to consider. This means, on the average, one out of every three people in Michigan had some contact with the courts last year. At the same time, most citizens do not really know what the courts do. This chapter intends to help you better understand that process.

WHY THE COURTS ARE NEEDED

A Society of Laws

No society will last long without rules. The United States is a civilized nation where control and power is not in the hands of those who are physically stronger than others. It is a nation where the laws are made by an elected government.

The legal system in Michigan and throughout the country involves all three branches of the government. The legislature makes the laws. The laws are enforced through units of the executive branch, the state police being one example. Finally, the courts interpret and apply the law as they seek to settle disputes and decide guilt or innocence.

Criminal and Civil Cases

Courts handle two kinds of cases— criminal and non criminal. Non criminal cases are called civil suits. A *civil suit is a lawsuit brought by one person against another.* People in civil suits have not broken any laws but they are involved in a dispute with someone else, often seeking payment because of damages caused by the other party.

The person starting the civil suit, the *plaintiff,* wants the other, the *defendant*, to do something. Both the plaintiff and the defendant must hire their own attorneys for the case. The government does not supply attorneys for civil lawsuits.

For example, an automobile manufacturer was sued by an individual whose car transmission jumped from "park" into "drive" causing damage to the car and garage. The manufacturer was found responsible and had to pay damages.

A *criminal action* is brought against someone alleged to have broken the law. Such a case is started by the state or local government through the county prosecutor's office. Crimes range from smoking in an elevator to mass murder. Various punishments are designed to fit the severity of the crime within the limits set up by the legislature.

The victim of the crime is called the complaining witness. In both civil and criminal cases the person defending against the charges is called the defendant. If the crime is serious, the court may provide an attorney to the defendant if he or she cannot afford one.

THE FUNCTION OF COURTS

Courts Determine Guilt or Innocence

In criminal cases, the courts determine the guilt or innocence of the individual. This is done usually through the testimony of witnesses to the crime and the use of whatever evidence is presented by the prosecutor. If the evidence is found to prove the defendant's guilt "beyond a reasonable doubt", the individual may be found guilty. In actual practice most criminal cases do not go to trial. The defendant pleads guilty before the judge, often to a lesser charge.

Courts Decide Punishment

If the defendant pleads or is found guilty in minor criminal cases, the judge will usually make a decision immediately. In more serious criminal cases, Michigan law requires the judge receive a pre-sentence report in order to study the person's background. It may take a few weeks for the report to arrive. The report contains information on the individual's marital status, criminal history, past employment, possible school and drug problems, etc.

Judges are allowed to work within a range of sentences set up by the state legislature. There is a book with sentencing guidelines to help them make a decision. While deciding the severity of the sentence, judges take into account the history of the person committing the crime and all the particulars of the case.

Courts Decide What Laws Mean

Michigan's supreme court and its court of appeals have the responsibility to interpret what laws mean. Often one group of attorneys or judges believe a law means one thing while another group believes it means something else. In many such cases the higher courts must choose the correct meaning. They must be certain our laws agree with the state constitution and are properly applied.

ORIGINS OF MICHIGAN'S COURTS— England

About 850 years ago a system of courts and judges began in England. The king at that time wanted to have uniform procedures and sentences throughout the land. Records were kept about each case and later referred to in similar cases. The use of evidence and juries to decide guilt or innocence began.

Ideas Brought to America

The English colonists brought these laws and procedures with them to America. At first, Michigan's law was influenced by French traditions because of our many French settlers, but these influences were displaced as more settlers arrived here from New England.

Today, every state's justice system, except Louisiana's which kept its French influence, is based in large part on the English system of justice. Our present system of justice borrowed much from the English including the system of judges and juries, and the use of evidence in trials. One of the most basic ideas we borrowed is the individual is considered innocent until proven guilty, and the burden of proof is with the accuser.

Questions

1. About how many cases are filed in Michigan courts each year?

2. What are the functions of courts?

3. What is the difference between a civil and criminal case?

4. What is the difference between the plaintiff and the defendant?

5. What concepts and practices has the American system of justice borrowed from the English system?

6. The manager of the Detroit Tigers decides to sue the person who sold him a box of defective baseballs. What type of case is he starting? Who will be the plaintiff? Can the manager expect the court to provide him with an attorney at no cost? Why or why not?

Chapter 6   Section 2

Organization of Michigan's Courts

Here are the key concepts in this section:

1. Michigan's courts are divided into two groups: trial courts and appeals courts.

2. The district courts handle the most cases and affect the most people.

3. Michigan also has several courts which specialize in certain kinds of cases. The probate court is one example. It deals with legal matters concerning children, among other things.

TRIAL COURTS

Do you know which courts you would deal with if you didn't agree with a speeding ticket, if your wife told you she is getting a divorce, or a relative needed placement in a mental institution?

To begin with, the courts of Michigan fall into two major groups. They are either *trial courts* or *appellate courts*.

As might be expected, *trial courts are the courts where trials take place.* This is where traffic violations are heard and murder and rape cases are tried. These are the courts you read about most in the newspapers. Trial courts in Michigan are made up of the circuit courts, probate courts, district courts, recorders court in Wayne county, plus the few municipal courts. It is at this level in the judicial system that cases almost always begin. These courts are the most interesting to the average person. It is possible you have even visited a trial court. We will look at these courts first.

However, when things don't go as expected and a defendant loses his or her case in a trial court, the next step may be to make an appeal in an appellate court such as Michigan's supreme court. *Appellate courts are those where appeals are heard concerning decisions from the trial courts.*

District Court
— traffic cases, minor criminal cases, preliminary work for serious criminal cases —

District courts are the newest part of the state's court system and were created in 1968. District courts replace a collection of small courts including justices of the peace. There are about 250 district judges in the state of Michigan serving in about 100 different districts. Nearly 90% of the trial court cases heard in a year are handled by the district courts. Most are minor and about 75% of the court's work is traffic related and only 10% is criminal.

District courts handle both civil and criminal cases, but they only consider less serious criminal cases and civil suits of $10,000 or less. Less serious criminal cases are called *misdemeanors. A misdemeanor is usually a criminal offense punishable by a sentence of up to one year in a county jail. Most sentences are for 90 days or less. A felony is a criminal offense punishable by one year or more in the state prison system. Circuit courts hear felony cases. Crimes involving $100 or more are felonies.*

Another major part of the district court's job is to do the preliminary work for more serious cases which go on to the circuit court. As a part of this work district courts conduct *arraignments* for individuals accused of felonies. *An arraignment is a judicial proceeding where charges are brought against the individual, at which time he or she enters a plea of guilty or not guilty.* The amount of bail can also be set .

A person who has robbed a gas station would be accused of a felony and tried in the circuit court, but is given an opportunity at the arraignment to hear the charges, some of the evidence, and can plead guilty or not guilty to the crime. The individual is presumed innocent until the prosecutor can prove otherwise and the case is sent up to the circuit court for trial if the district judge believes there is enough evidence. Since an individual is guaranteed the right to hear the charges against him in a timely manner, arraignments are heard very quickly, usually the next day court is in session.

District courts will also hear *preliminary examinations*, usually within 12 days of an alleged crime. *Preliminary examinations are held for the purpose of determining two things - if a crime has been committed and if there is enough evidence (probable cause) to believe the person being held is responsible.* If the case is a felony, the individual is bound over (sent) to circuit court for trial.

The district courts are considered the "people's court" because they handle so many cases. Many grievances we have against others may not be very serious, but they are still important to us.

The Michigan Court System

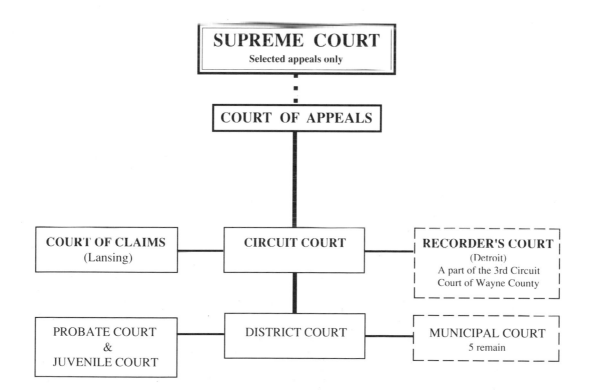

Small Claims Court— A Unit of the District Court

If you were to buy 20 cassette tapes from someone in school, for example, and at home you found that the tapes were not the ones you had agreed to, you would be angry. The obvious next step is to confront the person. If this accomplishes nothing, you may take the person to court. The difficulty in the matter is that the tapes may have cost you $100, but taking the individual to court often costs hundreds or even thousands of dollars due to attorneys' fees and other costs. It would not be practical to bring civil charges against the person knowing the legal expenses involved. A typical reaction is to be vengeful. To avoid such a situation of frustration, Michigan has established a *small claims division* in the district courts.

A small claims court is one where claims up to $1500 may be brought. To keep costs down, there are no attorneys for either side and no jury. Also the decision of the judge cannot be appealed. You can take someone to small claims court for only a few dollars. Often, district courts will hire a magistrate, a non-judge individual, to handle many less serious crimes and civil suits to expedite the case load and save money. Usually cases in the small claims courts are completed in an hour or less. The television show "People's Court" portrays a small claims court.

Only 3% to 4 % of the work in district court is small claims cases. Perhaps one reason the process is not more popular is that BOTH parties must agree in order for a case to go to small claims court.

[See application form for small claims court on the next page.]

Probate Court

— juvenile delinquents, child abuse, adoptions, wills, estates, guardianships, commitment of the mentally ill —

Probate court is one of the most diverse and interesting courts in Michigan's judicial network. The probate court is considered a trial court even though it does not often have trials in the way most people think of them. It is involved with "probating" or resolving the wills of those who have died, committing the mentally ill to mental hospitals, adoptions, child abuse and neglect, and secret marriages. The word probate means to prove a document, such as a will, is authentic. But one of the court's most important responsibilities is in the area of juvenile delinquency. This is such a major part of the probate court, it is often referred to as "the juvenile court."

The young man mentioned earlier (James) sees a lot of the probate court. However, when he turns 17, he is no longer considered a juvenile. If he is charged with some of the same crimes then, he will be tried in a district or circuit court as an adult. Instead of being sent to a juvenile facility aimed at rehabilitation, he will go to one of the state's adult prisons. The probate court is hoping to get

Application Form For Small Claims Court

Approved, SCAO

This form is available from
Target Information Management, Inc.
Mich.: (800) 862-9301 ● USA: (800) 325-4329

Original - Court
1st copy - Defendant

2nd copy - Return
3rd copy - Plaintiff

STATE OF MICHIGAN JUDICIAL DISTRICT	AFFIDAVIT AND CLAIM Small Claims	CASE NO.

Court address

Court telephone no.

SEE INSTRUCTIONS ON BACK OF PLAINTIFF AND DEFENDANT COPIES

1. _____
Plaintiff name

Address

City, state, zip

2. _____
Defendant name

Address

City, state, zip

The undersigned being duly sworn says:

NOTICE OF HEARING

FOR COURT USE ONLY

3. Plaintiff and defendant must be in court:

Day   Date

_____ m.
Time

☐ The court address above _____

☐ _____

_____ Fee paid: $ _____
Process server's name

4. I have knowledge or belief as to all facts stated on this form and am: (check one)
☐ the plaintiff.   ☐ a partner   ☐ a full time employee of the plaintiff.

5. Plaintiff is: (check one)   ☐ an individual   ☐ a partnership   ☐ a corporation   ☐ a sole proprietor

doing business as: _____
Name of business   Complete address

6. Defendant is: (check one) ☐ an individual   ☐ a business: _____
Name of business and complete address

7. Date(s) claim arose: _____   8. Amount of money claimed: $ _____

9. Reasons for claim: _____

_____

_____

_____

_____

10. PLAINTIFF ACKNOWLEDGES: The claim is limited to $1,500.00 by law, and plaintiff gives up the rights to (a) recover more than this limit, (b) an attorney, (c) a jury trial, and (d) appeal the judge's decision.

11. I believe that the defendant is not in the military service, is not mentally incompetent and is 18 years or older.

12. _____
Plaintiff/Agent signature   Date

Subscribed and sworn to before me on _____ , _____ County, Michigan.
                                           Date

My commission expires: _____   Signature: _____
                        Date   Deputy Clerk/Notary Public

DCS 84   (4/87)   **AFFIDAVIT AND CLAIM, SMALL CLAIMS**   MCR 4.302 MCL 600.8401; MSA 27A.8401 et seq.

COURT

98

James to change his behavior before that occurs. Depending on the individual and the crime, the defendant can be charged as an adult at the age of 15 or 16.

There is a probate court in almost every county but eight rural counties have combined to form four probate courts: Alger and Schoolcraft , Emmet and Charlevoix, Osceola and Mecosta, and Clare and Gladwin counties. Most courts have only one probate judge. A few of the more populous counties have several. For example, Kalamazoo, Macomb, and Genesee counties have three each, Kent and Oakland have four each, and Wayne County has eight probate judges. Probate judges are elected in non-partisan elections and serve terms of six years. Non-partisan means the judge runs as neither Democrat, Republican, nor any other party.

Circuit Court
— serious criminal cases, divorce, civil cases over $10,000 —

The trial court handling the most serious cases in Michigan is the *circuit court*. It is the highest court most people are ever involved with. The circuit court is a court of general jurisdiction and has power over all matters not specifically prohibited by law or specifically given to another court. Besides the serious criminal matters, divorces and larger civil cases, this court handles some serious misdemeanors, injunctions, appeals from the district court, some probate court cases, and administrative tribunal (executive branch agency) matters.

The circuit court gets its name from the pioneer days when a single judge would travel from town to town to hold court. The judge would follow his "circuit" on a regular schedule.

Most counties have at least one circuit court judge, or often more. A few counties with small populations share a judge. Check your county on the map of circuit court districts.

Nearly half of this court's workload is related to divorce and domestic relations with the rest divided almost equally between criminal and civil matters.

[See the map of Michigan's circuit court districts on the next page.]

Michigan's Circuit Court Districts

Most districts are made up of one county except those with lower populations, then counties are grouped together to make a single district.

Legend (note that some counties are combined into one district)

1 - Top number is Circuit Court District

(3) - Bottom is number of Judges

Friend of the Court Office
— a support unit for domestic problems —

With the tremendous increase in divorces in recent years, many people have had contact with another part of the circuit court— the friend of the court office. This office, which began in 1983, helps set up child support and visitation rights for divorced parents. A divorced father who lost his job would report to the friend of the court office so his child support could be adjusted. Divorced parents would be asked to come to the friend of the court if one parent complained the other was not allowing them the child visitation rights they had agreed to. Grandparents may also deal with this office so they can continue contact with their grandchildren if the parents are divorced.

THE APPELLATE COURTS
— courts which rule on appeals made concerning decisions already made in a lower court —

In the United States, we have a tremendous interest in providing individuals with the fullest degree of freedom and rights. Even after all the guarantees provided in the Bill of Rights are given to a defendant in court, the constitution still provides the opportunity to take the argument further. Individuals are allowed to *appeal* their cases to a higher court once, as a matter of right. Although most appeals are to the court of appeals in Michigan, district court cases may be appealed to the circuit court. This is also true of some probate courts and *administrative tribunal* cases. *Administrative tribunals are bodies which are not actually courts but are set up in a similar style. The Tax Tribunal, Workers' Compensation Appeal Board, and the Employment Security Commission are examples.*

Michigan has two appellate courts: the court of appeals and the supreme court. In criminal cases the appellant (the person doing the appealing) is entitled to one appeal and may appeal further only if there is a substantial reason for pursuing the appeal. That is to say there must be an allegation that some part of the case was handled improperly in order to appeal.

Illegal gathering of evidence, prejudice or error on the part of the judge, prejudice or misconduct on the part of the jury, or a challenge to the constitutionality of the law are possible reasons to appeal a case. The appeals process normally begins in the court of appeals (except cases appealed from district court and some probate court cases, which go to the circuit court).

Judicial Appeals Process in Michigan

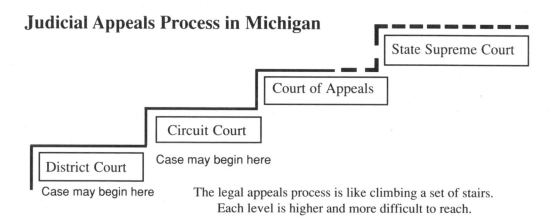

State Supreme Court

Court of Appeals

Circuit Court

Case may begin here

District Court

Case may begin here

The legal appeals process is like climbing a set of stairs.
Each level is higher and more difficult to reach.

The Court of Appeals
— the final stop for all criminal and civil cases tried under state law with the rare exception of those heard by the Michigan Supreme Court —

The *court of appeals* began with the adoption of the 1963 constitution. Previously, appeals went directly to the supreme court. The supreme court, however, sits as one court with seven justices and could not give appropriate consideration to the many cases appealed to it. The court of appeals, then, was created as an "intermediate" court to take some of the load off the supreme court. Presently, the court of appeals hears all criminal appeals presented to it and only those civil appeals it agrees to hear, while the supreme court hears only those cases it chooses to hear.

The court of appeals' requirement to hear all criminal cases that are appealed to it as a matter of right has caused a tremendous increase in its case load. The case load has increased from 1,235 in its first year (1965) to 11,000 more recently. That is an increase of nearly 900% and has caused the legislature to increase the number of judges in the court of appeals from 9 to 24. Still, on the average each judge must deal with over 400 cases a year!

The court of appeals operates differently than any of the other courts in Michigan. It has 24 judges. Eight are elected from each of three different state districts of approximately equal population. As you can see from the map, district I includes Wayne, Washtenaw, and Livingston Counties. District II is several other counties in southeast Michigan and District III is the rest of the state.

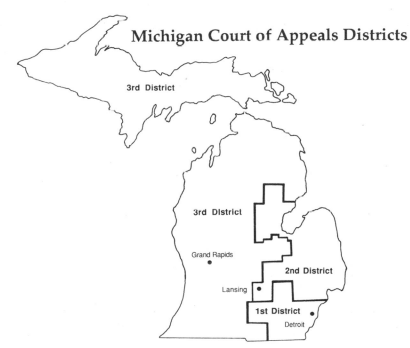

Michigan Court of Appeals Districts

This map shows Michign's three Court of Appeals districts. It is interesting that each district has approximately the same number of people even though the sizes vary greatly.

A panel of three judges always hears each appeals case. Two of these judges are from the court of appeals and the third is a circuit court judge who temporarily joins the court of appeals. This process allows circuit court judges throughout the state to gain experience in the area of appeals. The three-judge panels hear cases in four locations: Lansing, Detroit, Grand Rapids, and occasionally in Marquette. The three-judge panels are rotated so they are not made up of the same three judges for more than a few weeks at a time. This is an attempt to provide uniformity of decisions throughout the state. Appeals court hearings are held the first week of every month, except in the summer.

The appellate procedure for hearing cases is similar in both the supreme court and the court of appeals. It is not like the trial court procedure. It does not last very long and the only people involved in the hearing are the judges and the attorneys for each side in the dispute. There are no juries or witnesses. Both parties present their cases in written form before the hearing. These written statements of each side's position are called *briefs*. They are far from "brief" however, as these statements can be 20-50 pages long. Additionally, both sides present their positions orally during which the judges can ask questions of the attorneys to clarify any unclear points in the arguments. The entire process is over in just a few minutes. The panel usually hears several cases each day.

At a later time, the three judges discuss each of the cases, make their decision by a majority vote, and assign one of the judges to write the decision of the court. The decision of the appeals court is final except in those cases that are successfully appealed to the supreme court. The supreme court does not have to hear a case and only does so when important legal issues are in question. If a majority of the supreme court justices desire to hear the case, however, the case will be heard.

The Michigan Supreme Court
— The last word in legal matters relating to Michigan law. This court chooses the cases it hears —

The supreme court is the highest appellate court in the state. It is the court of last appeal unless national law is being considered. The supreme court hears cases during the first week of every month, except during the summer. It has control over all the courts in Michigan, establishes rules for them and considers complaints about any of the courts or their judges. It has similar control over all attorneys practicing in Michigan.

The Michigan supreme court consists of seven justices. (Supreme court members are called justices, while at all other levels they are called judges.) They are selected in a manner unique to Michigan and described in the next section.

Like the appeals court, the supreme court does not have trials like those you often see on television, but rather holds hearings where both sides present their positions. The presentation is very similar to the appeals court. The justices hear the attorneys present their case, ask a few questions, and do not discuss the matter again in public until they present their decision.

The justices talk over each of the cases among themselves and then make their decision by a majority vote. At that point they assign one of the justices to write the decision of the court and its reasons for the decision, but those who disagreed with the majority may also write their opinions. The justices do not seek public input and do not get much public input. They are not supposed to base their decision on public opinion but on their interpretation of the law.

The state supreme court has about 3,000 cases appealed to it each year. Our society is turning to the courts as a way of solving more and more problems each year and this is true in Michigan also.

The growth in the supreme court's work reflects this new attitude about legal matters. Nearly 25% of all the cases filed in the entire history of this court were in the last ten years! Approximately half of the cases are civil matters. The other half are criminal cases. The court cannot possibly hear that many cases in a year, so they choose to consider only those of great importance or those where they may differ with the decision of the court of appeals. They may hear only 1 in 20 or 1 in 25 cases appealed each year. In the cases they do not consider, the decision of the appeals court is final.

SPECIAL COURTS

There are a few special courts in Michigan that serve important purposes. They are limited in the kinds of cases presented to them. They are explained on the following pages.

Court of Claims
— where cases against the state of Michigan are heard —

A state may not be sued unless it agrees to the suit. You can imagine how this could be a problem. The state could, conceivably, never agree to be sued no matter how worthy the case. Michigan feels the state cannot be "above the law" and allows individuals and businesses to sue it in certain situations. Financial claims against the state are heard in the *court of claims*. A woman could claim, for example, that the Department of Highways and Transportation surveyed land incorrectly and built a highway through her land for which she demands some payment. To simplify the administration of the court, there actually is no separate court of claims in a physical sense. Court of claims cases are considered in Lansing by one of the sitting circuit court judges from Ingham County.

Detroit Recorders Court
— criminal cases within Detroit's city limits —

Detroit's size makes it quite different from any other city in Michigan. To handle this unique situation, the state legislature established a *Recorder's Court* in Detroit. It is much like the circuit court in criminal matters and handles felony criminal cases within the Detroit city limits.

Municipal Courts
— five courts from the old system still used in the Detroit area —

The 1963 Constitution brought many changes to the Michigan judicial organization. One big change is that district courts replaced justices of the peace who had previously handled minor crimes and civil cases and *Municipal courts* which many cities had prior to the 1963 Constitution. Similar to district courts, they were to be phased out and replaced by district courts, but five still remain in East Detroit and the Grosse Pointes. They mostly deal with traffic problems and minor crimes.

The Case Loads for Michigan's Courts

Number of Cases Filed in Each Type of Michigan Court For a Typical Year*

District Court	2,985,519
Circuit Court	218,804
Probate Court	68,675
—juvenile court div.	42,096
Municipal Courts	35,759
Court of Appeals	10,951
Supreme Court	2,809

*Not all cases filed actually go to trial. This is especially true for the Supreme Court.

When there is serious trouble what happens?

You go to a rock concert which happens to be outside the city limits for your 18th birthday. Before you realize what is happening you get into a fight and break a bottle over someone's head. The other person is taken to the hospital and you are arrested. What sequence of events will normally happen next?

1. You are taken by a sheriff's deputy to the county jail, fingerprinted and booked. You use your free phone call to tell your parents what happened but they are not sympathetic. They told you not to go out with those friends in the first place.

2. You are transported to district court (usually within 24 hours) and an arraignment takes place where you hear the specific charges against you; your rights are explained and you can plead guilty or not guilty. Also the amount of bail is given usually following a schedule depending on the crime.

When you hear the county prosecutor, a strict law and order person, charge you with "assault with intent to do great bodily harm less than murder" and that you could spend up to 10 years in state prison and pay a $5,000 fine, you faint. When you wake up, you decide to spend your life savings of $1,000 hiring an attorney and paying a 10% cash bond so you can leave jail.

3. Within the next 12 days you go back to district court for a preliminary examination.

4. After the preliminary examination, the judge decides there is enough evidence to charge you with the crime and you are bound over to circuit court for trial.

Questions

1. List all of Michigan's courts and tell which are trial courts and which are appeals courts.

2. List the types of cases heard in the probate court.

3. Some civil cases go to district court and others to circuit court. What amount of money triggers the switch from a district to circuit court?

4. In general, explain how Michigan's supreme court works and the kind of cases it hears.

5. Define these terms: misdemeanor, felony, preliminary examination, arraignment, brief, and bound over.

6. What are the good and bad points of using the small claims court instead of a higher court? How does small claims procedure differ from the procedure in district or circuit court?

7. If you are involved in a divorce and have young children, which court will you be involved with and which special office of that court will you eventually need to see?

Chapter 6 Section 3

State Versus Federal Courts
Paying for the Court System

Here are the key concepts in this section:

1. In general, Michigan courts try cases concerning state laws and federal courts try cases concerning national laws.

2. Sometimes the state and federal court systems overlap.

3. It costs about $350 million a year to operate Michigan's courts. Cities and counties pay the majority of this cost.

THE RELATIONSHIP BETWEEN FEDERAL & STATE COURTS

The United States has two major court systems. At the national level there is the federal court network. Each of the states has its own system of courts as well. There is some overlapping, but for the most part the two levels of courts consider different issues— much like the national and state legislatures consider different issues.

The federal court system hears cases resulting from claims of violations of U.S. constitutional rights, national laws, and federal administrative rules. The Michigan court system considers cases which have more of a local impact, situations which involve people within the state, things pertaining to Michigan's laws, the state constitution, and state administrative rules. Some issues can be considered in either court system. For example, it is a violation of both federal and state laws to rob a bank or kidnap an individual.

Sometimes the same act may be a violation of quite different state and national laws. An example took place in 1984 when a father and son beat a Chinese-American man, Vincent Chin, to death in Detroit just days before his marriage. The pair thought the man was Japanese. They were upset because Japanese auto manufacturers were increasing car sales and local auto workers were losing their jobs. The racial prejudice of the two led to an exchange of words, then a fight and, later that night, the murder of the man with a baseball bat.

Because of certain circumstances, the circuit court judge found the men guilty of the murder, but only gave them a suspended sentence. The men were free to go. Considerable outrage followed. Nothing could be done to change the circuit court's decision because *the constitution forbids trying (or sentencing) an individual twice for the same crime.* This is referred to as *double jeopardy.*

So, the federal prosecutor tried the father and son successfully in federal court for having "violated the civil rights" of the Chinese-American, a violation of federal law. They were sentenced to prison for several years. But a subsequent appeal by the men to the federal court of appeals was successful and they were released again.

The following lists show a comparison of the kinds of cases heard at the state and national levels:

COMPARISON OF STATE AND FEDERAL COURTS

TYPICAL *STATE* COURT CASES

1. Divorce
2. Disturbing the peace
3. Robbery
4. Assault and battery
5. State income tax fraud
6. Murder
7. Traffic violations
8. Hunting and fishing regulation violations
9. Operating a business without a license
10. Arson
11. Inheritance
12. Juvenile crime
13. Suits against the state
14. Violation of another's civil rights under Michigan law
15. Possession or sale of drugs

TYPICAL *FEDERAL* COURT CASES

1. Counterfeiting
2. Misuse of the postal service
3. Bank robbery
4. Violation of another's civil rights under U.S. Constitution
5. Federal tax fraud
6. Treason
7. Any case in which the U.S. Government is involved
8. Killing an "endangered species" animal
9. Any case involving two or more states— Some years ago Michigan and Ohio had a dispute over their exact border under Lake Erie and this case went to federal court.
10. Crimes committed by aliens
11. Immigration law violations
12. Drug trafficking and racketeering
13. Indian treaty enforcement

PAYING FOR THE COURTS

The state courts are an important part of the democratic process. They are also very expensive to operate. Judges are some of the highest paid individuals in government. Besides the judges' salaries, there is the expense of courtrooms and assistants. There are over 8,000 court employees in Michigan and nearly 600 judges.

The court system is required by the state government. Many of their functions and rules of operation are decided by two groups— the state legislature and the supreme court. The state's courts are under the supervision of the *state court administrator*. In turn the administrator works under the direction of the state supreme court in Lansing. It is the administrator's job to prepare budget estimates on the cost of running the courts, keep statistical information, examine the calendars of cases in the courts, and to make recommendations for improvements in the running of the court system.

The state government pays part of the costs of maintaining the courts, spending over $30 million annually. Even though the state helps pay for the court system, the cities and counties have the greatest share of the expense with roughly $325 million annually.

Our system of justice is very expensive. About half the local government budget is used for the law enforcement system. This includes the police, sheriff, jail, prosecutor, the courts and their staffs.

The courts do have ways to bring in money on their own but this is limited to certain fines and even then much of this money goes to other units of government, like the public libraries. Courts can assess "court costs" to some degree, but this is not a great source of funds either.

Questions

1. Give an example of overlap in the state and federal court system.

2. Compare and contrast the types of cases heard by the state and federal court systems. Provide some examples of each.

3. What is the approximate yearly cost of running Michigan's court system and who pays the largest part?

4. What does the state court administrator do? Who is in charge of the administrator?

Chapter 6   Section 4

Judges and Juries

Here are the key concepts in this section:

1. Michigan judges are elected, but vacancies are filled by appointment from the governor.

2. Officially, Michigan judges are not affiliated with a political party (non-partisan).

3. Judges are very powerful and the way they are chosen is important to many people. Several methods could be used.

4. Judges have a special advantage in elections since their position is printed on the ballot.

5. In many cases, guilt or innocence is decided by ordinary individuals who sit on juries. This is an important responsibility of citizenship

THE SELECTION OF JUDGES

Michigan's Method - Judges Are Elected

Michigan has nearly 600 judges handling over 3 million cases each year. Because judges hold so much power in our legal system, many people are vitally concerned with the method by which they are chosen. Michigan's judges are elected in the non-partisan section of the election ballot during the general election held every two years. (Ballots are divided into three parts: partisan offices, non-partisan offices, and issues to be considered by the voters.) You will also see contests between many judge candidates in the August primary, with the exception of supreme court candidates who are nominated at political party conventions or by petition.

It is hard for the judges to be truly non-partisan. Attorneys who consider running for a judgeship have usually had some previous campaign experience helping a candidate in a partisan race or running for partisan office themselves. Most candidates for judgeships think of themselves as either Republicans or Democrats. Occasionally, political parties will even help judicial candidates in their campaigns. So, it is difficult to have wholly non-partisan candidates available for non-partisan elections but Michigan tries.

Terms

All judges serve for six-year terms, except supreme court justices who serve eight-year terms. However, the qualifications are the same for any position. Candidates for judge must be qualified voters, licensed to practice law in Michigan, and under 70 years of age at the time of the election. They must also have not been convicted of a felony in the 20 years prior to their election.

Supreme Court Justices

Supreme court justices must receive sufficient political party support to be nominated at the party's state convention, usually held in late August or early September. Recently, however, some candidates "invented" political parties to nominate them for supreme court positions. Justice Charles L. Levin first did this in 1972 and won. This "self-nominating" has resulted in a confusingly large number of candidates for the office— 24 in a recent year. Recent legislation requires these individuals to gather signatures on petitions to be nominated. The successful nominees are then placed on the non-partisan section of the ballot for the regular November election. The result is that the candidates nearly always have close partisan (political party) connections, yet are not elected as Republicans or Democrats, etc. Most voters do not pay very close attention to party conventions, so when they vote in the November elections they do not know which party nominated the candidates.

Two of the seven supreme court justices are elected every general election year, except when the seventh is elected alone. Eight of the 24 appeals court judges are also up for reelection every general election year.

How Do They Get Started?

This description of the election process for Michigan judges implies that all of Michigan's judges are elected. Most judges actually begin their judicial careers by appointment from the governor. This occurs because the constitution requires the governor to appoint replacements for judges who resign or retire before their term is completed. This occurs frequently and allows the governor to appoint whomever he or she wishes. Once a judge is in office, it is unusual for the judge to lose an election. The appointment is usually a lifetime job.

A Special Advantage

Incumbents to any office are often reelected. But there is an additional advantage for Michigan judges because the incumbents are actually indicated on the ballot! No other elective office in the state is given this advantage. After the judge's name on the ballot, their office is listed. For example, the ballot does not just say "Jane Doe," it says "Jane Doe, Judge of Probate." This tells the entire electorate that this particular individual is the incumbent. Since the electorate has so many

people to vote for, and cannot really know all they should about all the candidates, they generally vote for incumbents. Many voters would not know the candidate was the incumbent without this statement and it must be assumed judicial incumbents benefit from this constitutional requirement. This listing on the ballot is required by the state constitution, because the judges have no political party affiliation to guide the voter when voting and there are strict campaign limitations on judicial elections.

How SHOULD Judges be Chosen?

Judges are unlike any other officeholder. They make extremely important and very personal decisions. The courts are often deciding cases between private individuals, as in a divorce, and public input is of little value. Their decision-making process is done in private. In all the trial courts, decisions are made by the judges and juries alone. Judges are put on a pedestal unlike any other elected official, which partially comes from an aura of authority that surrounds judges. They wear black robes, often have beautiful wood panelled courtrooms, sit elevated behind expensive desks, and are treated with great respect in their courtrooms.

Since judges are so powerful and usually stay in office for many years, it is very important to have a selection process that provides us with qualified, competent judges. There are probably only three ways to select judges in a democracy. They can be elected, appointed, or a combination of these two can be used. Michigan, theoretically, elects its judges. In practice, you have seen how this isn't exactly the case.

At present, 14 states elect their judges by non-partisan ballot, 10 by partisan ballot, and seven states appoint their judges. The remaining 19 have a "merit" selection process. Michigan's judge selection process is considered good by most, but it is not perfect. It is important to know some alternatives because from time to time they may be proposed to the voters of the state. The Missouri Plan, based on merit, is the most widely-used alternative.

Michigan's Merit Plan

Both the election and appointment processes have their good and bad points. A combination of these two methods is used in the *Missouri Plan*, named after the state that popularized the idea in 1940. Nearly half the states use the Missouri Plan for the selection of some of their judges, but few use it for all their judges.

The Missouri Plan involves a three-step process:

1. A committee submits names to the governor.

2. The governor appoints one of the nominees.

3. At the next general election (provided at least a year has passed) the people vote to keep the judge for a full term.

Governors Milliken and Blanchard recognized the strength of a merit system and adapted it to our situation. When a judgeship is available, individuals write to the governor and indicate an interest. The governor then gives the names to a committee of the Michigan State Bar (the lawyers' professional association).

Each candidate completes a long questionnaire and is interviewed. The committee sends the governor their assessment of each candidate. They are ranked:

1) Very highly qualified   2) Highly qualified
3) Qualified   4) Not qualified
5) Not qualified for lack of experience

This process is based on "merit" and is as close to the Missouri Plan as we can go without a constitutional amendment.

Complaints Against Judges

Most state and national judges are well-qualified and do a good job. A few do not. Where there are problems, it may be necessary to remove a judge. In Michigan, a judge <u>may not</u> be removed by the recall process like other Michigan elected officials. They may be voted out of office, of course, and several judges who have shown a lack of proper behavior have lost their reelection bids. But often the public is not in a position to easily discover behavior unbecoming a judge. So Michigan established a nine-member *Judicial Tenure Commission* in 1968 to review complaints concerning judges.

The Judicial Tenure Commission's goal is to "promote the integrity of the judicial process and preserve public confidence in the courts. It strives to hold judges accountable for their misconduct...." After the commission receives a complaint, it has the power, after a hearing, to recommend to the supreme court that a judge be:

1) Publicly criticized, known as being *censured*
2) Suspended with or without salary
3) Retired or removed from office.

The commission may act in response to the following types of misconduct:

1. Conviction of a felony
2. Persistent failure to perform duties
3. Habitual intemperance (appearing in court under the influence of alcohol)
4. Conduct that is clearly prejudicial (favoring one side during a case)
5. Persistent incompetence or neglect in the performance of judicial duties

A judge may also be removed from office if physical or mental problems keep him or her from doing the job for a long period of time. Breaking a leg, for example, does not usually result in an extended disability, but loss of speech due to a stroke probably would.

Anyone may file a grievance against a judge. Since the commission's formation, over 4,000 grievances have been filed, many by people unhappy with the results of their cases. Most grievances do not hold up after an investigation. Of 503 requests for investigation received by the commission in a recent 18-month period, only 12 resulted in action against judges and judicial candidates. Remember, Michigan has nearly 600 judges handling over 3 million cases annually.

THE JURY SYSTEM

The outcome of most civil and criminal cases is determined by a jury. It is possible for the parties involved to declare a jury unnecessary. Then the judge will decide the issue alone. Like most other states, Michigan has two different jury types.

Petit Jury

A *petit jury* is more common and is used in all trials which have juries. *In circuit court criminal cases, the petit jury consists of 12 individuals and six in civil matters. They hear the evidence and determine which side is correct. District and probate courts have six-member petit juries for both criminal and civil cases.*

It is the head juror (or foreman) of the petit jury who says, "We find the defendant guilty or not guilty of...." Petit juries also can decide the amount of money to be awarded in a civil suit, such as malpractice cases.

This is one reason malpractice and other insurance rates have skyrocketed in recent years. Juries can be easily convinced by attorneys that victims deserve huge sums of money. The attorneys are motivated to ask for larger settlements in part because their fee is based on a percentage of the settlement, usually one third plus expenses. They may of course also feel motivated by their responsibility to help the victim.

Jury Selection

The theory behind using a jury is that a group of randomly-selected individuals should be able to determine the truth in a case, be it a criminal or civil case. The selection of jurors in a county is drawn from lists of those with driver's licenses or Michigan I.D. cards. The jurors used to be chosen from voter registration lists. The new list is so broad as to include nearly everyone in the county. Its intent is to involve everyone in the judicial process and have juries which are a cross-section of the whole society.

Some potential jurors—physicians, college students, and mothers with babies— attempt to avoid serving as jurors because they feel it would be a burden on them, but counties are becoming less willing to allow this, especially where there is a "one day, one trial" or similar system.

Lawyers will also attempt to excuse certain potential jurors from serving or to look for certain types of people on the jury in hopes of a favorable decision. Lawyers can do this through the use of a *peremptory challenge*. Under this technique, *prospective jurors can be dismissed for no stated reason at all*. An attorney may try to get a few economically poor jurors, for example, if the attorney is defending someone accused of breaking into a wealthy stockbroker's home. Lawyers on both sides are allowed the same number of challenges and that number is usually quite small, three to five, though it could be 12 for a criminal case involving life imprisonment.

Grand Jury

The least common type of jury is the *grand jury*. It is not at all like the trial jury which decides guilt or innocence. Grand juries are used to investigate criminal activity.

It is a group of citizens brought together by the county prosecutor or the state attorney general to determine if there is sufficient evidence against someone to bring charges against them.

Grand juries are used to investigate major drug operations, organized crime, crooked government officials or contractors, and other complex crimes. The Michigan grand jury usually numbers between 13-17 members. The term of service for the jurors is six months, renewable for an additional six months. Occasionally, a judge will serve as a one-person grand jury. The grand jury is rarely used now.

Juries— Is There a Better Way?

There are some alternatives to the traditional jury system. Some innovative methods are being used already. Several courts in Michigan now use a one-day, one-trial or one-week, one-trial jury plan. In such a situation, the potential jurors must come to or call the court to see if they will be needed each day. If a juror is not chosen to serve that day, his or her jury duty is over. If chosen, the responsibility lasts as long as the trial. Thus the "one day, one trial" name. Such plans attempt to address the problem of requiring potential jurors to be available for as long as a month at a time.

Some individuals in the court system suggest that what is needed is a more professional jury. They suggest we should have full-time jurors who know their responsibilities, know the law, know people, and are able to filter the truth from all the testimony in a trial. However, serving on a jury is a unique opportunity which goes to the roots of our democracy. It should be viewed as an interesting opportunity to become involved.

IN SUMMARY

The courts are probably the most highly regarded unit of government. They must be. Without a system of laws and rules enforced fairly, there would be no respect for the system. The result would be the reduction of our society to anarchy where only the strong would rule. The courts give "law and order" to our democracy.

Questions

1. About how many judges does Michigan have and how are they selected?

2. What is the term of office for Michigan judges?

3. What age limits are placed on Michigan judges?

4. What other possible methods are there to select judges? Pick a method and explain why you think that method is best.

5. What are some reasons people use to avoid serving on a jury? In your opinion which of these excuses is valid? What is your personal belief about the importance of serving on a jury if requested to do so? Is jury duty an option or a requirement of citizenship?

6. What is a peremptory challenge? What might an attorney be trying to accomplish by using a peremptory challenge?

7. What does a grand jury do?

8. What is the purpose of the judicial tenure commission? What does it mean if this commission is considering "censure"?

7

FINANCING STATE GOVERNMENT

Chapter 7   Section 1

Where the Money Comes From

Here are the key concepts in this section:

1. Michigan's constitution requires that state government have a balanced budget each year.

2. Once each state paid its own bills but today the federal government provides about 20% of the state's revenue. These payments usually have restrictions related to them.

3. There are many sources of income for the state but the biggest is the state income tax which brings in about 30% of the total. The next largest source of revenue is the sales tax and third is the single business tax.

How to Pay For State Government?

The Michigan state government spends billions of dollars every year on services for its residents. Which services are provided and how the government gets money to pay for them is a source of constant debate within the government itself and among the people of the state. There seems to be an endless list of demands for very limited dollars.

Where did it all go?

This debate reached high levels during 1983 and again in 1991. At both times the state's economy was in recession. In the early 1980s car sales had slowed and many workers were unemployed. This resulted in more demands on government with fewer dollars from taxes and fees to meet those demands. Government expenses were cut, but could not be cut enough. Taxes were finally raised, but many people did not agree this increase was necessary.

When Governor Engler replaced Governor Blanchard in 1991, a similar situation existed. Governor Engler decided to make huge spending cuts instead of raising taxes to balance the budget. One governor was Republican and the other a Democrat— each used a different approach to the same problem.

Although demonstrated more dramatically during these two times, the task of balancing revenues and expenses goes on continuously. This chapter provides an explanation of this process and some of the controversies surrounding it.

Because our state constitution requires a balanced budget, the amount of money spent cannot be more than the amount coming into the state treasury. If legislators want to provide more services, they must find more money. They can be quite creative in doing this by obtaining money from both federal and state sources.

FEDERAL SOURCES— *about 20% of state revenue*

Federal aid to the states has been available since our nation was founded. In the beginning, states received land grants which encouraged their development including the financing of state colleges.

Federal Activity Increased

Federal assistance to the states was limited for a long time as the federal government itself didn't have much money for its own needs. As late as 1927 federal assistance averaged two percent of state spending but by the 1990s the federal share was over 20 percent. Federal help dramatically increased in the 1960s when it attempted to solve many problems it felt states were not taking care of well enough. President Johnson's "Great Society" was a major factor in this change. President Nixon's "New Federalism" continued sending money to the states. Then during the 1980s, a growing national debt and other factors changed attitudes about the federal role in helping states. Funding has decreased in recent years.

T. Deeter © HEP

Where Most Federal Money Is Spent

Federal dollars provide for many things, but most goes to the following:

1. Housing assistance to low income families

2. Medicaid

3. Highway construction and maintenance

4. Services to the unemployed and welfare programs

5. Services for the disabled

Kinds of Aid

Today federal assistance is provided in two forms: grants-in-aid, and block grants. A once popular third form, called revenue sharing, has been discontinued.

Grants-in-aid are federal funds used for specific purposes designated by federal law. Highway construction is a major use of this assistance. Several social service or welfare programs also fit in this category. Rules for using grant-in-aid are very strict and the state has little, if any, say in how this money is spent.

More welcomed by the states are *block grants*. They have fewer restrictions on how the money can be spent. Community Development Block Grants aimed at assistance for the cities are typical programs in this category. Other major programs have been the Law Enforcement Assistance Act which provided money for a variety of programs, and CETA (the Comprehensive Employment and Training Act) which provided training to the unemployed so they could learn new job skills. Block grants must be used for the specified purpose but allow the states to decide how the money should be spent.

Federal Strings

The federal government wants to be sure money provided state or local governments is spent as intended. At times, a few local governments and states misspent money, or misinterpreted how the money was supposed to be spent. This caused Congress to watch the process more closely, which is done in two ways.

Congress will provide specific conditions in the bill and in order to receive the money the conditions must be met. As an example, an area must have a specified level of crime or poverty to qualify for the program.

Federal laws may also require spending for only specific purposes and Congress may require that certain programs be created if other federal funding is to continue. This method was used in the early 1980s to require that states lower speed limits to 55 in a national attempt to save fuel. States that didn't comply with the mandate and enforce the new speed law lost their share of billions of dollars for highway construction and maintenance. This requirement was removed in 1989 so states could set their own speed limits once more.

Although federal aid to the states seems to be falling, a substantial portion of Michigan's state and local revenues still come from Washington. Political pressures on Washington are likely to keep this aid coming for some time.

STATE SOURCES OF REVENUES

The federal government is helpful, but state and local governments rely mostly on their own sources of revenues. There are over three dozen different taxes used by the state or by local governments in Michigan. Some bring in only small amounts of money. On the other hand state income taxes, state sales taxes, and local property taxes bring in billions of dollars each year.

How Many Pay?

Michigan has over nine million people, but not all of them pay taxes. Some are too young and others are retired with only small incomes. The state has only about 4.1 million job holders to shoulder the major burden of paying for govern

ment. A number of people pay taxes but the amount, while significant to them, is not large. High school and college students and others with part time jobs are in this group. Besides those with full time jobs, there are very few others who pay to support state government.

Looking at the situation in another way, each group of seven employed people supports two and one third school students plus one person on welfare!

The State Income Tax— *almost 30% of state revenue*

Michigan did not have a state income tax until 1967. The rate has been 4.6 percent in recent years with the exception of a brief period when Governor Blanchard raised it to balance the budget in the mid-1980s. The rate is the same regardless of income.

The tax is not graduated like the federal income tax, which has higher rates for higher incomes. A graduated tax is called *progressive* since most people

120

STATE GOVERNMENT NEEDS ITS SHARE

STATE

YOUR PAYCHECK

think it is fairer to tax those with larger incomes at a higher rate. Michigan is only one of five states with a flat rate income tax. The other 36 states with income taxes use the graduated system. In Michigan a graduated income tax was voted on in 1968, 1972, and 1976, but was turned down each time.

Help For Those With Low Incomes

A flat rate tax, like Michigan's, is considered *regressive* because those with less income pay a larger portion of their available money for the tax. Over the years legislators have eased the burden on lower income individuals in several ways.

Like the national income tax, the state tax law allows several exemptions and credits which permit those who qualify to lower their *taxable income*— the portion of income which is taxed. Each family member is allowed an *exemption* or deduction of $2,100 or more. Similar exemptions go to those over 64 years of age and for disabled individuals.

In addition to exemptions, the state also allows *tax credits* that have the same effect of lowering taxes. Tax credits may change over time as legislators vary their views on what is important. Credits have included city income taxes, donations to Michigan public universities and colleges, and to our public libraries. Home heating costs are also allowed as credits for certain individuals.

One of the more interesting and significant credits is for property taxes. This credit is often called the *circuit breaker* because like a breaker in an electric circuit it protects people who might have to sell their home and find a less expensive one because they cannot afford the property taxes. This may happen to someone who is retired but has a home in a town with rapidly increasing home values. The circuit breaker allows people who pay high property taxes but have relatively low incomes to receive a credit on their state income taxes. (The credit is equal to 60 percent of property taxes in excess of 3.5 percent of household income for most individuals. This is more thoroughly explained in Chapter 11.) The correct and full name of the circuit breaker is the Homestead Property Tax Credit.

The result of these exemptions and credits is a lower rate of income tax for some individuals, which can be much less than 4.6 percent.

AVERAGE MICHIGAN STATE REVENUE BY SOURCE

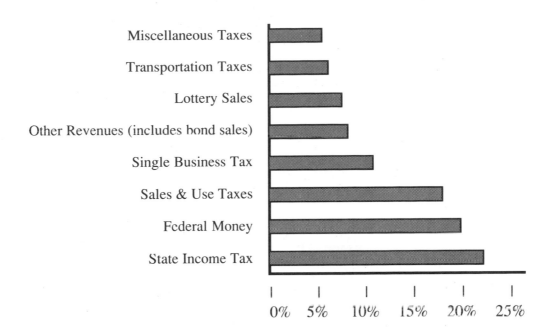

Miscellaneous Taxes
Transportation Taxes
Lottery Sales
Other Revenues (includes bond sales)
Single Business Tax
Sales & Use Taxes
Federal Money
State Income Tax

0%   5%   10%   15%   20%   25%

Sales Tax — about 15 % of state revenue

The state *sales tax* began in the 1930s. Currently it is a four percent tax on most purchases. The voters eliminated the sales tax on food (groceries) and prescription drugs in 1974 and replaced the lost revenue with an increase in the income tax from 3.9 percent to 4.6 percent. Most people hardly notice state sales tax when buying inexpensive items like cassette tapes, but for large purchases like cars and boats it can be hundreds of dollars. For example, it is $600 on a $15,000 car.

How sales taxes are used is designated by law. For several years 60 percent has gone to public schools; 15 percent has gone to cities, villages, and townships; and 25 percent has gone to the state general fund. These percentages can be changed by constitutional amendment.

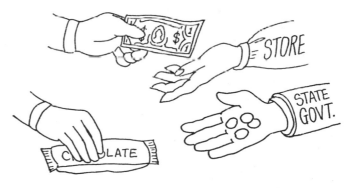

Use Taxes and License Fees— *about 16% of state revenue*

Some feel a fair way to pay for government is to have those who use a service pay for that service— a *use tax is one paid by the user, the person who gets the benefit*. It makes sense, then, to have those who drive on Michigan's roads and highways pay for the costs of building and maintaining these roads. So, every gallon of gasoline includes a tax of fifteen cents. The more a person drives and uses the roads the more tax is paid. Such use taxes also exist on aircraft fuel, diesel fuel, propane gas as a motor fuel, marine fuel, telephones, and other items including state park admission, hunting and fishing licenses. Every year owners of motor vehicles are also required to pay a fee for vehicle registration.

There are other state taxes, some of these are common knowledge but others are quite obscure. Several valuable items have a specific tax instead of property tax applied to them. For example, there is a one cent per pound tax on the weight of all aircraft. Boats are taxed according to their length. Mobile homes are taxed at $3.00 per month.

If you park at an airport parking facility you are paying a rather hefty 30 percent of your parking fee for a state tax. If you stay in one of Michigan's motels or hotels you may pay an additional tax ranging from 1.5 percent up to 6 percent. The higher tax rates are collected from hotels with more than 160 rooms. Those who bet at horse races ante up 4.5 percent on each bet.

If you are in the business of removing valuable resources from Michigan's land, the state charges you a tax based on the value of material you extract. There is a 6.6 percent tax on oil, 5 percent on natural gas, up to 1.1 percent on iron ore, and 10 percent on the value of timber cut from commercial forests.

The state also collects special taxes on many consumer items including cigarettes (25¢ per pack), and various amounts for beer, wine, and liquor.

If you sell your home or any other real estate, the state wants 55¢ per $500 value. This works out to $82.50 on a $75,000 house.

Business Taxes— *about 15% of state revenue*

Before 1975, Michigan had a variety of business taxes that brought in many dollars... and many complaints from the businesses being taxed. Legislators generally have an easier time increasing taxes on businesses than on voters. Being the easier route, this resulted in a complex arrangement of business taxes. After much complaining and politicking, the legislature eliminated 11 business

taxes and replaced them with the *single business tax* in 1975.

It is often referred to as a *value added tax. That is to say, it is a tax on the value a business adds to the product it makes to sell.* The tax is paid on all business expenses— including wages, rent, raw materials, equipment purchased, and other costs of operation. The single business tax rate is 2.35 percent.

This newer tax is thought of as a positive change by some, but certain business people still complain because the tax is based on expenses and not profits. Businesses which do not make a profit must continue to pay the tax. This is especially tough for new small businesses with little extra money.

There is an Unemployment Compensation Tax which is used to provide income to laid-off workers. All businesses must pay this tax too. It is collected even if a business has never laid off any workers!

Besides these taxes on all Michigan businesses, certain businesses pay additional taxes. Oil and gas companies are taxed on crude oil and natural gas extracted from Michigan land. Insurance companies pay a tax on insurance premiums received from Michigan residents.

Inheritance Tax— *about 1% of state revenue*

Individuals who have died, or more accurately the estates of individuals who have died, must pay state inheritance taxes. The amount of the tax depends on the value of the estate and if the deceased has willed it to direct relatives— wife, husband, parents, children— the rate is lower. If it goes to someone else they pay a higher percentage.

Questions

1. List the five most important ways federal aid to Michigan is used.

2. Explain the meaning of the terms "block grant" and "grants in aid."

3. What is the current rate for the state sales tax and the state income tax? Give an example of a common type of item which is sales tax free.

4. Why is it said Michigan's income tax is regressive? Are most state income taxes regressive or progressive?

5. Give three examples of a "use tax" found in Michigan.

6. In your own opinion do you think Michigan should rely on federal aid as much as it does now? What are the positive and negative factors which are associated with aid from the federal government? Give clear answers and use examples when possible.

Chapter 7   Section 2

Other Ways For the State to Raise Money
&
The Headlee Amendment— A Limit On Taxes

Here are the key concepts in this section:

1. Michigan raises money in other ways besides taxation. One way is with the state lottery.

2. Sometimes the state has short-term cash flow problems and has to borrow money. The state may also use long-term borrowing for big projects.

3. In the 1970s there was great frustration with rising tax payments caused by inflation. Because of this frustration, the Headlee Amendment was added to the state constitution. It places limits on new state programs, property taxes, and the percentage of personal income which can be taken by state government.

NON-TAX REVENUE

The State Lottery— *about 4% of state revenue*

One fairly new, very successful, and quite popular source of revenue is the state *lottery*. In 1972 the voters removed the constitutional barrier to a lottery and the state initiated it shortly thereafter. Many voters supported the lottery because they thought it was to provide all its "profits" to education. There is still

some confusion among the electorate about this matter and many are convinced the lottery revenues do not go to education. All the profits do go to education— about 40 percent of the roughly $1.2 billion worth of tickets sold. Some argue, schools actually get no more money in the end than they would without a lottery. Regardless of how the lottery is viewed, it does give state government significant new revenue that would otherwise be unavailable.

Borrowing

Occasionally the state must borrow money, especially when it needs large amounts for a major project. Under such circumstances the state is allowed to borrow, but there are many restrictions on how much can be borrowed. The state cannot get into the predicament that the federal government is in with its nearly incomprehensible debt. Michigan, remember, is constitutionally forbidden to have an unbalanced budget. It must have money to pay for all its expenses.

Short-term Borrowing

Sometimes the state has a "cash-flow problem." The needed funds will come soon, but are not immediately available. When these situations come up, short-term borrowing is allowed. For example, if it is time to pay the annual aid to public schools, the state may not have enough money at that particular moment. It will need a loan for a few weeks or months until revenues come in.

Long-term Borrowing

Long-term borrowing, for a period longer than the 12-month fiscal year, is allowed under limited circumstances. Two-thirds of the state house and the state senate are required to vote and then place such an item on the next general election ballot. At that time a majority of the voters must approve the request.

In the last 30 years or so about half of these bonding requests have passed and about half have failed.

Successful requests have included money to build public recreational facilities, as well as money for environmental protection and cleanup. Both passed in 1988. Unsuccessful requests include funds to build housing for low-income individuals in 1968 and a 1974 request for public transportation money.

STATE BORROWING

T. Deeter © HEP

Selling Bonds to Pay For Projects

When a unit of government needs a large amount of money for a a big project, one of the common ways to get the money is by selling bonds. What is a bond? A bond is a type of loan which pays interest. The bond itself is a piece of paper that says the government has borrowed money and will pay it all back at a set time in the future. These bonds are usually bought by people and organizations who want the interest payments. A retirement fund may buy bonds from state government and use the interest to pay its retirees' monthly checks. As a result of using bonds, government is not limited to borrowing money from a bank as most individuals are.

126

Use of bonds has advantages for both the buyer and the seller. Government benefits by selling bonds because it gets all of the money it needs at one time and usually pays less interest than it would if it borrowed the money from a bank. Those who buy bonds usually receive more interest than they would from a bank account and are reasonably certain they will get their money back when it comes due.

Revenue Bonds

Another form of borrowing is *limited obligation indebtedness*, which is debt paid by revenues from the project. The cost of a loan to build a college dorm paid for by fees from students living in that dorm is one example.

THE HEADLEE AMMENDMENT— A Tax Limitation

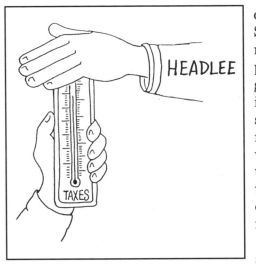

The decade of the 1970s was a time of rapidly rising prices and high inflation. State and local governments benefited as revenue from income tax, sales tax, and property tax went up each year. Local governments, in particular, were receiving huge increases in revenues due to skyrocketing home values. Property tax revenue increased automatically with no voter approval. Few governments returned the increased tax revenues by lowering tax rates; they just spent the extra money on a variety of projects they felt were important.

Throughout the nation citizen groups sought tax relief, particularly concerning property taxes. In Michigan a constitutional amendment was passed in 1978 which is known as the Headlee Amendment because one of its authors was Richard Headlee, who later ran for governor in 1982. This amendment affects both state and local financing in several ways. Its effect on local government is discussed in Chapters 11 and 12, but the following are its limitations on state government:

1. It limits state government spending to 9.44 percent of the total state personal income (not counting federal money received by the state). It provides for refunds if this percentage is exceeded by more than one percent. (This has happened at least twice.)

2. It requires the state government to pay the same percentage of the costs of local governments that it did in 1978-79. This is about 42 percent of the state budget.

3. It requires the state government to pay for any new programs it demands of local governments.

The Headlee amendment also places a maximum rate for local property taxes and tries to limit the growth of property taxes to the rate of inflation.

How could the Headlee amendment affect you as a student? Let us suppose the state board of education felt every high school student should be required to have a course in home pollution prevention. Since the board is a part of state government, the state would have to pay for the cost of this course throughout Michigan. Due to part 3 of the amendment there would be no additional expenses for the local school districts.

Questions

1. Lotteries are becoming more and more popular as a way for state governments to raise money. In your opinion what are the negative and positive aspects of using lotteries for this purpose? Is it important to your answer that about 60 percent of lottery sales go to pay expenses?

2. Television news often mentions the staggering federal debt. Does the state of Michigan have a staggering debt? Why or why not? Does the state ever owe money?

3. What are some sources of "non-tax revenue" for state government?

4. What is a bond and how does the state use bonds to raise money?

5. Explain how the Headlee amendment tries to control the following: Spending by state government. New programs which would have to be paid for by local government. Property tax increases. Do you think this constitutional amendment was a good idea?

Chapter 7   Section 3

How State Government Spends Its Money
&
Planning the State Budget

Here are the key concepts in this section:

1. State government spends money on many programs but education and welfare are the two largest parts of the budget. Together these two items make up about half of the total.

2. Society's goals and economic conditions cause spending priorities to change over time and so does the amount of revenue available to pay for state programs.

3. The annual state budget is one of the most important documents produced by Michigan's government. It takes many months to plan and is full of compromises.

4. The state has a "rainy day fund" which is like a bank account to use when the economy slows down and revenues fall.

PRIORITIES

To provide various services each year, the state of Michigan, not counting local government, spends nearly $2,000 for every man, woman and child living within its borders . This ranks Michigan about 20th in spending among the 50 states. The majority of the money goes to the two largest budget items— education (about 30%) and welfare (nearly 20%). For many years education and welfare had nearly equal budgets but now education is ahead.

Michigan's spending on its different programs does not always rank 20th. Compared to other states, it has different priorities for various needs. The state obviously has a high priority for the poor because welfare expenses once ranked third highest in the nation (Michigan has almost 700,000 people on welfare.) Although Michigan's schools are thought to be among the best in the nation, the state has a much lower comparative priority when it comes to actually putting money into education. The state recently ranked 38th in the school aid category. For one of the next biggest budget items— transportation, including highways— Michigan came in even lower at 42nd.

The state spends $15 billion to 16 billion a year on various programs. The decision to spend for some things and not others is part of the budget-making process. This involves many people in government, most notably the Department of Management and Budget, the governor, and the legislature. In many ways the decisions are political ones. These decisions are also based on economic realities, the willingness of the people to tax themselves, tradition, and many other factors. Let's look more closely at how Michigan spends its tax revenues.

GIVE AND TAKE— UPS AND DOWNS

Spending choices by state officials are difficult ones. Because Michigan must have a balanced budget, there is only a certain amount of money available to spend. Voters are reluctant to raise taxes and typically feel the government can find the money if it will just cut unnecessary programs and be more efficient. Since new taxes are the exception rather than the rule, government has learned to adjust its desires to the money available.

Of course, the money available is not constant. In most years it increases, especially if the national economy is doing well, Michigan's cars are selling, and there are no major agricultural disasters. But recent history shows the economy isn't always so lucky. Economic slowdowns do happen and programs are cut.

Political support for programs changes and there are times when some programs are cut so others can be increased. As an example, in one recent year the budget had overall spending increases of about three percent, but not all programs received three percent increases. K-12 education increased nearly five percent; the Department of Natural Resources responsible for the environment received a seven percent increase; and the Department of Corrections had a 10 percent increase. The concern many people voiced about the lack of good prisons and the interest in cleaning up the environment were factors in those larger increases.

SHARING FINANCIAL RESPONSIBILITY

Until recently, most government units paid their own bills. This dramatically changed beginning in the 1960s. Now each unit depends to some extent on money coming from others. Local schools currently receive a major share of their budget from state government and sometimes a fair amount from the federal government too. Some experts feel that the three levels should contribute approximately equal portions to the education of America's students. This has not happened; and in this particular area local governments have a greater financial burden than the state or national governments. See the chart below.

SPENDING ON PROGRAMS IN MICHIGAN

Service	Percent Financed by:		
	U.S.	State	Local
Education	8	40	52
Public Welfare	50	40	10
Health & Hospitals	7	47	16
Highways	22	59	19
Other	22	45	33

These figures are for the entire state. If we looked at individual communities, there may be more dramatic differences. Education in the community of Okemos, for example, has a federal share of 0.6 percent. The state share is about 1.6 percent while local property taxes pay for 97.8 percent of education costs in this school district.

THE BUDGET-MAKING PROCESS

The annual budget is the closest thing available to a written report of state government's priorities. If any single document tells the public the intentions of state government, it is the completed budget. It is usually considered the most important document produced by the government in Lansing. It includes dozens of compromises and takes months to complete.

Fiscal Projections

The Michigan *fiscal year* covers the 12-month period from October 1 to September 30. *This means that for planning and spending purposes, the new year for state government does not start in January but in October.*

Since budget planning starts months before the budget year begins, it is necessary to make projections well into the future. These "guesstimates" are usually a bit liberal since it is much easier later to spend excess money than to make budget cuts.

An assessment of the future economic outlook is done by the Department of Management and Budget (DMB). It receives assistance from the Department of the Treasury, among many others.

Departments Present Budgets

Nearly a year before the budget is adopted, the state departments are sent information on expected revenues and department spending limitations. Based on these directions, the heads of the departments develop their individual budget requests and return them to the Department of Management and Budget. In case revenues are not as expected, the DMB may also require the departments plan budgets with increases or decreases of various amounts (i.e. 0%, 3%, or 6%, etc.). The DMB, the governor, and others develop their overall budget from this department information.

In January the budget is presented to the legislature as a complete package. But when legislative action begins, it is divided into several appropriations bills. These are submitted by legislators in either the house or the senate. Half the bills are started in the senate and half in the house the first year. The next year the bills are switched and those started in the senate are now begun in the house and vice versa. All the bills must pass both houses, of course, to be successful.

In the Legislature

The budget bills are treated much like other bills and are sent to the appropriations committees where they are further assigned to the various subcommittees. Occasionally, some of the budget bills are sent to other standing committees for their suggestions and recommendations. In the legislature, the bills are looked over very carefully. Legislators might not agree with the governor's assessment of Michigan's economic future.

Compromises

Legislators have their own ideas about the state budget and where money should be spent. If they want to make changes in the budget they must find enough support from other legislators to successfully achieve their goals. There is a fair amount of "vote trading" which takes place— one legislator promising to trade a yes vote for another bill for a yes vote on his bill. This compromising and "trading of votes" is to be expected and is part of most every law-making process.

Because the budget bills are so important, they take a long time to complete. They are usually not finished until the last minute. In fact, the budget is occasionally not completed before the new budget year begins, causing problems for some departments. More than one state paycheck has been held up when last minute agreements were not finished on schedule.

If the legislature passes an appropriation the governor dislikes, it is common for the item to be deleted with a "line item veto." The legislature can override the veto with a two-thirds vote, but this is rare.

Total State Spending for a Recent Year by Department

Department	Amount	Department	Amount
Dept. of Agriculture	$54,000,100	Dept. of Licensing & Regulation	$26,165,500
Dept. of Attorney General	$35,956,400	Dept. of Mgmt. & Budget	$1,234,909,500
Dept. of Civil Rights	$12,231,300	Dept. of Mental Health	$1,202,313,000
Dept. of Civil Service	$27,902,900	Dept. of Military Affairs	$25,665,500
Dept. of Commerce	$306,176,400	Dept. of Natural Resources	$272,960,100
Dept. of Corrections	$695,889,300	Dept. of Public Health	$351,902,500
Dept. of Education	$571,469,600	School Employees' Retirement	$268,414,000
Higher Education:		Dept. of Social Services	$4,495,542,300
Community Colleges	$207,490,469	Dept. of State	$117,458,200
State Colleges & Universities	$1,153,065,577	Dept. of State Police	$229,624,600
School Aid	$2,550,634,000	Dept. of Transportation	$1,535,382,800
Executive Office	$4,027,300	Dept. of Treasury	$133,921,900
Judiciary	$150,428,900	Debt Service	$73,001,400
Dept. of Labor	413,621,300	Capital Outlay	$347,046,500
Legislature	$80,164,000	**TOTAL**	**$16,608,282,046**
Library of Michigan	$30,916,700		

These figures are planned expeditures for 1990 taken from the *Executive Budget.* They include $ 3-4 billion received from the federal government. Much of this federal money is used for progams in the social services area, which explains why the budget totals for social services and education are nearly equal as shown here but are not equal in other presentations of the state budget which do not include federal money.

132

Budget Oversight and Stabilization

After the new fiscal year starts in October and the new budget is in effect, the legislature and the governor continue to closely follow its progress. If revenues rise or fall, increases or decreases in department spending may follow. The governor can propose supplemental spending bills or budget cuts whenever appropriate.

The Rainy Day Fund

To protect against huge decreases in revenues, the state started the *Budget Stabilization Fund* in 1977. Sometimes called the "rainy day fund," it saves money from good financial years to help balance the budget when bad economic times hit the state. It acts as an emergency bank account if the state faces tough times.

T. Deeter © HEP

Money Is Added When—
Personal income in Michigan grows more than two percent above the rate the previous year. When this happens an amount of money goes into the fund based on a formula. (The previous year's General Fund/ General Purpose revenue times the percentage above 2 percent.)

Money Is Withdrawn When—
1.   The growth rate of personal income is lower than the previous year.

This occurred almost immediately in 1980 and 1981 and nearly used up all of the money in the fund! The amount which can be used to help balance the budget also comes from a formula. (The percentage of decline in personal income times the previous year's general fund/general purpose revenue.)

2.   If the average unemployment rate goes above eight percent for any quarter (three months) of the fiscal year, then a total of 2.5 percent of the fund can be released quarterly to pay for programs providing more jobs. Public works

projects are an example. This occurred in 1985, 1986, and 1987 and the money was used to build new prisons and for summer youth programs. (If unemployment goes over 12 percent up to 5 percent can be used.)

3.   The legislature votes by a two-thirds margin in each house that the money is needed for an economic emergency.

Two times when large amounts were taken from the fund were $260 million in fiscal year 1979-80 and about $300 million in 1990-91. Large additions were made in 1977-78, 1978-79, and 1984-85. By 1991 the rainy day fund had about $150 million which could be used to help balance the state's budget.

Questions

1. Give an overview of how state spending is currently divided. If you were Michigan's governor, would you recommend changes in these percentages? Give good reasons for your answer.

2. What document is the closest thing available to a written statement of the state government's priorities for a given year?

3. Which department makes an estimate of future economic conditions as a part of planning the annual budget? What happens if its estimate is wrong? What steps can state government take to keep programs running smoothly when a mistake is made in the forecast?

4. What has to happen so the rainy day fund can be used? Does the fact Michigan has such a fund tell you something about the ability of government to control spending?

8

MICHIGAN'S COUNTY GOVERNMENT
—the largest unit of local government—

Chapter 8 Section 1

Background to Counties

Here are the key concepts in this section:

1. Michigan has 83 counties and each of these has a county seat— the city where the county courthouse is located. The courthouse can be considered the headquarters of county government.

2. Counties provide several important services not done by any other unit of state or local government.

3. The idea of counties came from England long ago, but today the legal basis for counties is spelled out in the state constitution.

4. All of Michigan's counties operate in much the same way following rules laid out by the state.

What Counties Mean To Us!

Everyone in Michigan lives in one of the state's 83 counties. Counties are the largest subdivision of government below the state level. As you look at a map you see many of Michigan's counties are about the same size and shape; however, there are dramatic exceptions. Michigan's counties were developed with the idea they would each contain 16 townships. This is why they are often similar in shape and size.

Each county has a *county seat* which may be thought of as the capital of the county. This is where the county courthouse is located and the courthouse can be considered the headquarters of county government. As explained in chapter one, the name courthouse comes from the fact that usually one or more courts are located in this building.

Besides operating courts, what else does county government do? Other aspects of the law enforcement and legal system are important too. The prosecuting attorney's office is a part of county government and so is the sheriff's department which provides law enforcement for all parts of the county except for cities. Those convicted of minor crimes serve their sentences in the county jail.

Another of county government's more important tasks is keeping records about the people who live there. Each county has a clerk who maintains information such as births, deaths and marriages. There is also a register of deeds office which registers or keeps track of all sales of homes, buildings, land, etc.

A third key area of county government is the maintenance of hundreds of miles of roads within that county. The county road commission may have to build new bridges, re-pave highways, clear roads of snow in the winter and cut brush and tall grass away from the right-of-way in the summer. A huge amount of money is needed to pay for these services.

Counties provide certain medical services too. They may have mental health facilities or a hospital for the aged. Another important county official is the medical examiner.

Only county government provides some of these services. The sheriff, prosecutor, register of deeds, and medical examiner are unique to the county.

Whether counties have a similar size and shape or not, they all operate in much the same way. A county can be thought of as an extension of state government. Each county does a number of things which state government would need to do if it weren't for counties. Both the law enforcement and record keeping functions are examples.

Why Do We Have Counties? Their Origins—

The idea of county government in the United States can be traced back to England where the land area was divided into "shires." English shires performed many of the same functions as our American counties do today. Massachusetts had counties as early as 1643. Today, every state in the U.S. has counties with the exception of Rhode Island and Connecticut. Connecticut discontinued the use of counties in 1960. Rhode Island is so small it never found them practical. Louisiana calls them "parishes" and Alaska calls similar units "boroughs."

Michigan's county history goes back to the Northwest Ordinance, a law passed by the national government in 1796. This established the Northwest Territories, in what is now the geographical area we refer to as the Midwest. The territories were further divided into counties. It also established the procedure by which new counties could be set up and governed.

One of the early ones was Wayne County. At that time Wayne County included all of what is now Michigan, plus parts of Indiana, Illinois, Ohio, and Wisconsin! Eventually, Wayne County was divided into several counties. Wayne took on its present form in 1815. It took nearly another century for Michigan's 83 counties to evolve into what we recognize today, ending in 1891 with Dickinson County.

Even though the concept of counties began long ago they are still a useful unit of local government. They provide services for a convenient and manageable area. County government is close enough to the people for the average person to have a voice in what is happening.

The legal basis for counties in Michigan is spelled out in the state constitution, starting with the first state constitution of 1835. Counties operate under laws passed by state government, so their procedures are uniform and with rare exceptions they cannot make their own rules.

Michigan County Development in the Early Years

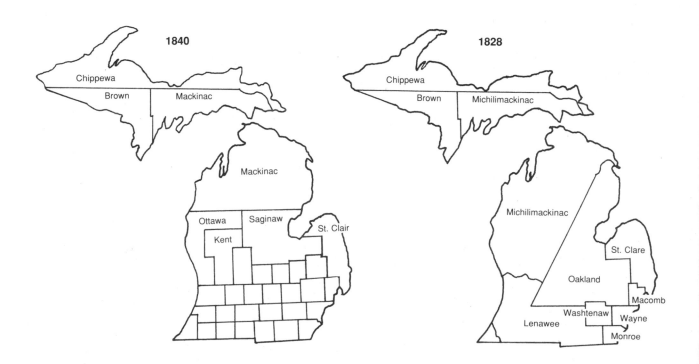

Counties Get Their Shapes

It all began before most pioneers had even arrived. Survey teams traveled on horseback cutting their way through brush and forest, crossing rivers and streams to map out the territory of Michigan. These rugged surveyors mapped out township after township. Townships were surveyed to be six miles square, and 16 went into the typical county making it 24 miles on a side or 576 square miles. Michigan's irregular coastline and the desire of some counties to have more townships or fewer townships caused the exceptions we see today.

Counties were not all laid out at the same time. The pace of development quickened after Congress passed a law in 1825. This law explained how county officials (except judges) were to be elected.

Although Michigan's counties all operate in much the same way and provide the same basic services, there are differences. Marquette is the largest in size with 1,829 square miles and is six times as large as the smallest, Benzie, with 316 square miles. Wayne County is the largest in population with about 2.1 million residents, while Keweenaw has the smallest population with about 1,700. Obviously, the problems of government in Wayne County are much different than those in Keweenaw or Benzie County. Besides differences in population, counties have different ethnic makeups, different industries or agriculture, different access to transportation (highways, or Great Lakes ports, etc.).

Questions

1. What is the county seat of your county?

2. Name three services provided only by county government.

3. Where did the idea of county government come from and why do we continue to have county government today?

4. Why are many of Michigan's counties about the same size and shape?

5. Is it possible for each county to make its own government procedures to fit its own needs as times and problems change? Why or why not?

Chapter 8 Section 2

Who Runs A County?

Here are the key concepts in this section:

1. In all but three of Michigan's counties the board of commissioners are in charge of county government. The other three counties have county executives who share that responsibility.

2. Counties are divided into districts and each district elects one commissioner.

3. In most counties the chairperson of the board of commissioners takes the lead in directing county government. But usually no single person is in charge of all areas.

4. Controlling the county budget is one of the commission's greatest powers.

5. Counties do not actually make laws as the state legislature does.

In most cases there is not any single person who is in charge of county government. Counties are run by a board of commissioners who are elected. This board decides how the county is run and could be considered the legislative branch of county government.

In 1973, the state legislature passed a law allowing counties to provide for an elected or appointed chief executive. A few counties have used this option, so in these cases a single person does have a really powerful role in county government.

However, most of the time no single person is in charge of county government, though the board chairperson is the most powerful commissioner, and in the absence of a county executive, will have influence over many county decisions.

THE BOARD OF COMMISSIONERS

It is not entirely accurate to refer to the *board of commissioners* as the county's legislature because counties are not actually able to pass laws. Unlike a true legislature, a county cannot adopt a law making certain conduct illegal, unless it receives the governor's approval, and such ordinances are quite unusual. These matters are generally left to the level of government above the county (the state) or the level below (townships, cities, and villages). The board spends much of its time watching over the other county officials in an administrative way.

Number of Commissioners

Regulations require the number of commissioners to vary with the population of the county. The commissions can legally range in size from 5 to 35 members, with five being used for the counties having the least people. Currently our largest county boards of commissioners have 27 members; those being in Macomb and Oakland counties. Wayne county is unique because even though it has the largest population of all it only uses 15 commissioners. This limit was set by its county charter.

Districts

Each county is divided into as many districts as there are commissioners. The districts are redrawn after each census so they will be equal in population. This work is done by an apportionment commission consisting of the county clerk, prosecutor, treasurer, and the chairpersons of the two major political parties in the county. Needless to say, it is important for Republicans and Democrats to control at least two of the three county positions (clerk, prosecutor, treasurer) so the panel can draw districts that favor their side. The reapportionment process also sets the number of commissioners for the county, within the limits allowed by state law.

Term of Office and Qualifications

Commissioners are elected on a partisan (political party) ballot for a term of two years. Candidates are nominated at the primary election in August and elected in the November general election of even numbered years. They can serve as many terms as the voters allow and can be removed from office through the recall process if the voters choose. To qualify, a candidate must merely be a registered voter in the district.

Vacancies

If a commissioner leaves office with less than one year of his or her term remaining, a new commissioner is appointed by the remaining commissioners. If one year or more of the term remains, an election must be held. Elections can take several months, so the board may appoint someone to serve until a replacement has been elected.

Compensation

Commissioners control the finances of the county, so they usually decide their own salaries as well. Salaries vary throughout the state. In smaller counties, the position may require less time and commissioners handling smaller budgets usually are not willing to give themselves high salaries. In Wayne County, the job is considered full time with a salary to match, private office, large travel allowance, and more.

ORGANIZATION AND POWERS OF THE COMMISSION

Organization

All boards have a chairperson and a vice-chairperson. The work on smaller boards may be done by the entire group working together with more relaxed rules in what is known as a committee of the whole. Larger counties divide their tasks into various *standing committees*, committees of a more permanent status. A county's standing committees might include the following:

Administrative services

Public safety

Human resources

Personnel

Finance

In addition, the board may have various ad hoc committees to handle other concerns. These are temporary committees. A county may have a special committee to look into rearranging health services, or to consider the feasibility of adding to the number of judges, or for any other purpose.

The board will have a number of other committees and authorities as well. Many of these directly control a county agency and are somewhat independent of county government. Many have non-commissioner members on them. People interested in serving on such commissions can generally find out how to apply by calling the commissioner from their district. It is an excellent way to get involved in government. Some of the commissions that counties typically have available are listed below. Their names give you some idea of the jobs they do:

Airport Authority
Arts Commission
Board of Public Works
Commission on Hunger and Nutrition
Economic Development Commission
Equal Opportunity Commission
Library Board
Parks Commission
Road Commission
Social Services Board
Women's Commission
Zoning Board of Appeals

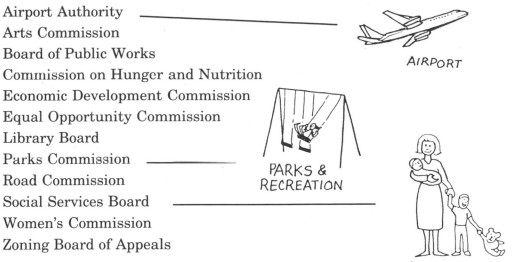

AIRPORT

PARKS & RECREATION

SOCIAL SERVICES

Commission Powers

The county board of commissioners does have some legislative and executive power. These are the most significant:

a. Budget—   Deciding how to spend the county's money and the tax rate
              needed to pay these costs
b. Appointment- Placing qualified people in various county positions
c. Resolutions— Making official decisions on many county matters
d. Oversight—   Watching over county government agencies

1. Budget

The greatest power of the county board of commissioners is control over the budget. Not only does it set spending in areas for which it is directly responsible, it also determines the budget for nearly everyone else in county government. It decides the sheriff's budget, the prosecutor's budget, the budget for the courts, and more. It can raise or lower taxes as necessary, within certain limits. It can also put millage issues on the ballot, asking voters to authorize additional taxes for specific programs. Most county commissioners oversee the spending of millions of dollars a year.

2. Appointments

Another significant power commissioners have is the ability to appoint dozens of people to boards and commissions. These positions may include department heads as well as members of the public to the numerous commissions referred to earlier. The infusion of citizens into the government process through various boards and commissions provides expertise and citizen input at little or no additional cost to the taxpayers. The power to appoint can also be beneficial to those doing the appointing. Those appointed often desire to show their gratitude to those controlling the appointing process, especially at election time. The majority party in each county usually controls the process.

3. Resolutions & Ordinances

County boards can pass resolutions and (with the governor's approval) adopt ordinances (pass laws). These must relate to only county matters. They can't interfere with other local governments or conflict with the state constitution. For example, ordinances may be about animal control, fees for various services, or the establishment of new county programs.

4. Watching Over County Government

Another power commissioners have is reviewing what the rest of county government is doing. As an example, the sheriff, elected on his or her own merits, must still come to appropriate committees of the board for approval to do most things. If the prosecutor wants to add assistant prosecutors, the commissioners must approve the cost. In doing so they question the prosecutor to decide if the assistants are necessary. If a complaint is received that the animal control department is abusing animals, the commissioners may investigate. If they don't like what they see, they can usually correct the situation. They are able to provide assistance or cause considerable misery to any county department head or elected official. The board can remove most non-elected officials. Even elected officials who owe their jobs to the voters may be reluctant to tangle with the county commissioners.

Questions

1. How long is a county commissioner's term? How many times can he or she be elected to this office?

2. List the four significant powers the board of county commissioners have and briefly explain each one.

3. On rare occasions the board of commissioners can pass a law called a county ordinance. Who must approve an ordinance before it can go into effect?

4. Write a short essay comparing and contrasting county government to state government. For example, do they each have what could be called a capital, a legislature, a governor, etc.?

Chapter 8 Section 3

Elected Department Heads

Here are the key concepts in this section:

1. Besides the county board of commissioners, each county elects several important officials.

2. Each of these officials is elected for a four-year term during a presidential election year.

3. The sheriff and the prosecuting attorney are two of these elected officials and they are usually among the most powerful positions in county government.

4. The county clerk and register of deeds are two other elected county officials and they help with the vast record keeping duties of each county.

Most Michigan counties have five or six elected department heads. All have an elected sheriff, prosecutor, and treasurer. The clerk and register of deeds may be elected separately or combined into one position. Most counties have elected drain commissioners. A few have elected road commissioners or surveyors.

It is a continuing debate whether these officials should be elected or appointed. The state government, for example, appoints most of its equivalent officials. The national government appoints all department heads. Nearly all cities appoint equivalent positions as well. The argument in favor of continuing their election is it gives the voters the opportunity to choose.

The problem is voters have only a limited amount of time to become knowledgeable about several candidates, and don't usually find county candidates in the news enough to know much about them. This results in votes for candidates for reasons that have nothing to do with their qualifications. That means voters may be putting people into office and keeping them there when more qualified individuals are available. It's difficult to know which approach is best; both have merit. If positions are elected, the people have more voice in the government. If someone else chooses them, the people are giving up that power. Government scholars say it is generally best to elect policy makers such as county commissioners and to appoint managers, such as clerks and the register of deeds, etc. The choice would be easier if Americans paid more attention to what our elected officials do and if more people exercised their privilege to vote.

Qualifications, Elections, and More

The qualifications for these elected officials are generally the same as for county commissioners. They must be registered voters in the county. The prosecutor must also be an attorney. They are all elected for four-year terms at the same time as the national president. Partisan ballots are used. Nominations take place in the August primary and the final vote is the November general election. They can be removed by the governor or by a recall election. In case they vacate their office for any other reason, their replacements are appointed by other elected officials.

A committee of the clerk, prosecutor, and senior probate judge fills vacancies in the offices of treasurer, register of deeds, drain commissioner, and sheriff. Probably because of their involvement in the courts, vacancies in the offices of clerk and prosecutor are filled by the circuit court judge(s).

THE PROSECUTING ATTORNEY

Each county in Michigan has a prosecutor. This is one of the most powerful positions in local government. It is the job of the prosecutor to decide if there is enough evidence against an alleged criminal to bring charges. The sheriff will often not arrest an individual unless a previous conference with the prosecutor indicates the person can be convicted. If insufficient evidence is available, it is best to wait and attempt to gather it. We often hear law enforcement officers say they "do not have enough evidence to prosecute." They may say this even when they are certain who committed a particular crime. If the evidence is not adequate to convince a jury "beyond reasonable doubt," the case against the guilty party may end in an *acquittal.* (*An acquittal is a dismissal of the charges.*) And the criminal may go free. The sheriff and the prosecutor must use care in these matters because they are sensitive to what the public will think of their decisions. Not only do they want to rid the streets of criminals, but they also want to be re-elected.

Prosecutors in smaller counties may personally handle each case that goes before a judge. Many assistant prosecutors help in the larger counties.

Prosecutors have much leeway in handling the job. Some have set up innovative programs to deal with first offenders, allowing them to pay back the victim and do community work instead of receiving a jail term. At the other extreme, the prosecutor may have a program aimed at serious repeat offenders to make sure the cases against them are brought to trial as quickly as possible.

In some smaller counties, the prosecutor also serves as legal counsel and advisor to the board of commissioners and to the other units of county government. The prosecutor is the chief law enforcement officer of the county and usually the highest paid county official.

THE SHERIFF

The county sheriff's power is nearly as great as the prosecutor's. It is probably the oldest position in American government and the office goes back in history long before the beginning of this country. It dates back to Anglo-Saxon times in England. At that time, in each shire, there was a person known as the shire reeve, who

was appointed by the king, and directly responsible to him. It was the reeve's responsibility to collect the king's taxes, enforce the laws, and oversee the king's government. It is from this early, usually disliked English official, that our sheriff evolved.

The sheriff is responsible for law enforcement activities throughout the county, except where other local governments (usually cities) have chosen to provide their own police protection. The sheriff's duties include patrolling roads, enforcing the laws, arresting those believed to have committed crimes, and holding these individuals before, during, and after their trial (if they are found guilty). The county jail is a very important responsibility of the sheriff. The state police have assumed many of the traditional responsibilities of the sheriff in some counties. The existence of so many law enforcement groups— the state police, county sheriff, township and city police, metro narcotics squads, and others— can cause *jurisdictional questions. A jurisdictional question is when something happens and it is hard to decide who is responsible for taking care of the problem.* Often, a city boundary line is a road. Which department is responsible for handling an accident, then, in the middle of the road, or at an intersection? Some people are even confused about whom they should call for help. Look in the front of your phone book and notice the numerous emergency phone numbers. Considering your address, should you call the city police or the county sheriff if you need help at your home?

THE TREASURER

The treasurer is responsible for all money paid to the county, keeping it in a safe place, preferably a high-interest bearing bank account. All county bills are paid by the treasurer. If taxes on a piece of property (home, business, farm, etc.) go unpaid for three years, the treasurer can sell the property at an auction to collect them. This office may

keep other information on property for tax purposes, including information on why each piece is assessed at the value it is. The treasurer has other financial duties as well.

CLERK

The *county clerk* is a record keeper. The clerk's responsibilities include recording births, marriages, divorces, and deaths. Other records kept involve corporations, partnerships, and a list of people who have been given permits for

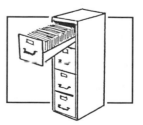

concealed weapons. This person is also the clerk of the circuit court and keeps all its official records. In addition, the clerk keeps the minutes and records for the county board of commissioners, and, in some counties, handles the board's correspondence.

One of the most important duties of the clerk is to oversee all elections within the county. Clerks see that potential candidates follow proper procedures in running for office, including reporting their campaign donations and expenses. The county clerk does this in cooperation with the clerks of townships, cities, villages, school boards, and the secretary of state. Many county clerks serve for 20, 30, even 40 or more years. One Ingham County clerk recently completed 48 years of service before losing an election.

REGISTER OF DEEDS

The register of *deeds* is the other record keeper in county government. *A deed is an official document concerning property ownership and location.* In some counties, the register of deeds and the clerk are combined into one office. This especially makes sense in smaller counties because their responsibilities are quite similar and there may not be a need for two full-time officers. Sixteen counties have combined these offices.

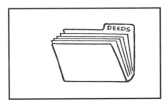

One of the ways we protect the right to buy, own, and sell property is keeping track of the true owners. It is important to keep accurate records of property sales, transfers, *mortgages* and *tax liens* (leens). *A mortgage is a legal document between a bank and those who borrowed money to buy a house or other property. The mortgage says if the borrower does not pay back the money as they say, the bank can sell the property to get their money back!. A lien is a claim against the property for payment of overdue taxes.* All of these things are recorded by the register of deeds. The register also keeps *plats* (*A plat is a detailed map of property boundaries.*) and has other duties regarding land ownership.

If you are interested in buying property, the register of deeds in the county where it is located will help you discover the rightful owner, see the legal description of the property to learn where its boundaries are, and see if any right-of-ways cross the property— for a railroad or electric utility, etc. The register of deeds will also be able to help you find out if the property is mortgaged or not. The treasurer's office can help you discover if back taxes are owed. You can also learn what the annual property tax bill is and how the bill has been calculated. Do not automatically assume the person offering to sell a house is the owner; they could be renting it or still owe money to a bank for it.

DRAIN COMMISSIONER

Of the six county-wide offices usually elected in county government, the drain commissioner is the only one not required by the state constitution. It is statutory. That means it was created by a state law, not the state constitution.

Although the law does not require each county to have a drain commissioner, 72 of the 83 counties do. The other 11 counties have someone else, usually the road commission, handle drainage problems.

Drain commissioners should be fairly expert in their field, yet the law does not require any extra qualifications for the job. You just have to defeat your opponents in a partisan election. It is not unusual to have office-holders with little or no background in drains.

Drainage problems are usually worse in the more developed counties with larger populations. As you might guess, water doesn't easily penetrate roofs, roads, and parking lots. Yet, all the water from heavy rains or quickly melting snow must go somewhere. Citizens don't want water in their basements or streets. A major job of drain commissioners is to determine what areas might have flooding problems.

The work of a county drain commissioner is often not very pleasant. Photo courtesy of George Griffiths.

People may petition the drain commissioner to take specific action to build, repair, replace, or remove a drain. If enough signatures are received, the drain commissioner will make plans to do the requested work, determine who will benefit from the improvement, and arrive at a cost.

Unlike many government services, drain work is charged directly to those who benefit. They pay for the work through a tax assessment. A drainage board of three individuals then investigates the need, the project, the cost, and the assessment and determines the accuracy of the project plan. A public hearing takes place for comments from the affected individuals. If everything appears appropriate, the project begins. Drain assessments become liens against the property. The drain commissioner can assume considerable power because of the ability to assess the costs of drain work against a person's property. Some assessments can run into the thousands of dollars!

Questions

1. What problems do voters face in electing county officials?

2. Who is the only elected county official who must have a specific qualification in order to run for office?

3. Who is responsible for operating the county jail?

4. If you own property and refuse to pay property taxes on it, which county official has the right to sell the land and pay the back taxes?

5. Suppose your former wife told you she has remarried and wants to take your sons with her to her new home out of state. Which county office would you ask to see if she had actually remarried?

6. You see a house marked "for sale by owner" and contact the man inside. You need a larger home and this place is perfect and at a bargain price. He says if you give him $1,000 down you can sign the papers that day and move in next week. Which county office should you visit first and what questions should you ask?

7. You own a small restaurant near one of the county's nicest golf courses and business is good. But you face one problem, every time it rains water runs off the road and nearly fills the basement where you store your supplies. Which county official should you contact? Should you expect county government to fix this problem without any cost to you because the water comes from a county road?

The work of the county road commission never ends.

Chapter 8 Section 4

Appointed Department Heads
Also County Courts

Here are the key concepts in this section:

1. Besides the elected county officials, there are several appointed ones who head departments or serve on important boards.

2. Most money for state welfare programs goes through each county's social services board. This board acts as a pipeline for state money to reach those who are in need.

3. County government helps in other areas of public safety. Three examples are medical examiner, animal control, and emergency services.

4. Counties and the state work together to operate the trial level courts in Michigan.

THE ROAD COMMISSION

Each county in Michigan has a three-member road commission. They can either be elected or appointed. Road commissioners serve six-year *staggered terms. In this case a staggered term means one road commissioner is elected or appointed every two years.* This gives more continuity than if all three road commissioners were appointed or elected at the same time.

The major responsibility of the road commission is to build and repair the county roads. This is a big job as it includes roads in all townships. They also approve new streets in subdivisions, clear snow, and may designate "natural beauty roads." An average county may easily have 1,000 to 1,500 miles of roads within its jurisdiction. In addition, some counties may have special contracts with the state Department of Transportation to maintain selected state roads and highways within the county. The road commission receives its funds from the state. The major sources of revenue are the fuel tax and license fees.

Often counties have parks and recreational areas which they maintain and develop. They may have park boards to supervise these operations.

Human Development Departments

Many counties have health and community mental health departments. Millions of state dollars are funnelled through the counties to provide these services to residents.

In addition, every county has a *social services board*. Most state welfare programs and the money for them are provided to individuals through the social services board which oversees the operation. The board has three members, two appointed by the county commissioners and the third appointed by the governor, all for three-year terms. They may also be responsible for the administration of a county nursing home or other similar facilities.

Some counties have a hospital board to administer a county hospital. Others have library boards to oversee the library system or veteran's affairs boards to aid in the administration of many state and federal programs aimed at assisting veterans.

MISCELLANEOUS PUBLIC SAFETY

Medical Examiner

Another way counties provide protection for their residents is through the appointment of a medical examiner. Once this was an elected position and the person holding it was called the coroner.

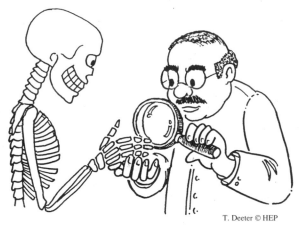

T. Deeter © HEP

Suspicious deaths are investigated by the medical examiner. This is an important part of the criminal justice system. If a medical examiner is not careful, a murder could be called an accidental death and a criminal go on to commit other crimes.

In one Michigan county a young woman was brought to a hospital. Her husband said she fell off her horse and hit her head. The medical examiner then ruled the case an accidental death. Meanwhile the husband tried to collect a large amount of life insurance. But through the insistence of her parents, the case was reopened and a dangerous muscle relaxant discovered in the woman's body.

Animal Control

Most counties have an animal control department responsible for keeping the county safe from stray dogs and other animals. This department may license dogs, carry out a dog census, and recommend the county board of commissioners reimburse residents if they have livestock killed by dogs.

Members of this department may catch stray dogs or track down the owners of dogs which run in packs, endangering wildlife and people.

All counties have regulations about keeping dogs on the owner's property and not allowing them to run loose, having dogs and other pets vaccinated for rabies and other serious diseases.

Emergency Services

Several counties have emergency service organizations which may consist of paramedics and/or ambulances. This is becoming more important in many parts of the state as private ambulance services run by funeral homes continue to go out of business.

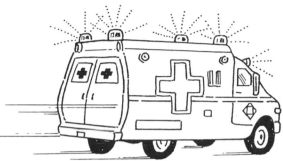

In most counties emergency services include disaster planning and sometimes issuing weather alerts for tornados and the like. Plans are made for several types of disaster such as nuclear accident, toxic chemical spill, enemy attack, and natural disaster. Without an emergency management system in place, it may be difficult or impossible for a county to receive state or federal aid if a disaster takes place. County emergency services departments are coordinated through the Emergency Management Division of the State Police.

One indication of the increased responsibilities of county government is the growth in county employees in the last three decades— increasing from 700,000 to 2,000,000 nationwide. Meanwhile the numbers of national and state employees have been stable.

COUNTY COURTS

The county and the state cooperatively run most of the courts in Michigan. The exceptions are the top two state courts— the Supreme Court and the Appeals Courts— and the district courts operated by larger cities. The counties, however, have a lot to do with the operation of circuit, probate, and county district courts. The county assumes most of the costs for these "trial level" courts, approves most of their programs, hires most of their employees, and oversees much of the work of the courts. But the courts are more independent and often have more to say about their finances and operation than other county offices. See the chapter on the Michigan court system for more details.

Questions

1. Your county has an old but beautiful covered wooden bridge. Over the years vandals and the weather have caused the bridge to deteriorate. Some residents want the bridge replaced by a new modern one while others hope to repair and keep it as an historic landmark. Who has the power to make the decision on the fate of this bridge?

152

2. You are interested in becoming involved in local government and your name has been suggested as a member of the county board of social services. What activities does this board oversee?

3. If you saw several dogs attacking a deer in a field, which county department might you contact?

4. Who operates the ambulance service in the area where you live? What is its phone number?

5. Name the three types of courts operated under the umbrella of county government.

Chapter 8 Section 5

Other Options for County Organization

Here are the key concepts in this section:

1. Eighty of Michigan's counties operate in exactly the same way. The state government has passed laws which allow two other options.

2. Bay and Oakland Counties use one of these options known by the rather odd title "Optional Unified Form."

3. Wayne County voted to accept another of these options called "Home Rule." Currently it is the only county using this option.

4. Counties using either of these options have the right to elect or appoint a county executive to manage county government— much as a mayor or city manager would.

Michigan's 83 Counties

Three Michigan counties have systems that do not rely solely on the board of commissioners. They are organized in what is called the *modified commission* form— of which there are two types. The main difficulties with the traditional organization are the lack of one county leader (like a city mayor) and the division of power and responsibility among the several elected department heads. The two modified commission options attempt to deal with these problems.

THE OPTIONAL UNIFIED FORM

In 1973, the state legislature passed a law allowing counties to elect or appoint a single chief executive. This is called the *Optional Unified Plan*. The county board of commissioners may ask the voters to adopt the plan or the people

may put the issue on the ballot through the initiative process. Several counties have considered the move and three have placed the option on the ballot. Two actually adopted the plan: Oakland County in 1975 and Bay County in 1979. Both chose elected county executives.

Under the plan, an appointed executive may be chosen by the board of commissioners and serve at the pleasure of the board. Or, an elected executive can run on a partisan ballot and serve a four-year term, putting the executive on an equal or better footing with the other elected department heads.

The elected executive, for the most part, has the powers the board of commissioners had under the old system. The elected executive can veto board proposals, and use the line item veto in appropriation matters. The board can override vetoes with a two-thirds vote. The board of commissioners, however, maintains the authority to appoint members to the numerous other boards and commissions.

In summary, the optional unified plan provides for another elected full-time executive, but that's about all. None of the powers of the other elected department heads can be altered. More effective change would be seen if the elected executive could appoint some of the department heads, like the clerk, register of deeds, drain commissioner, and treasurer, but this would require a state constitutional amendment and is very unlikely.

THE HOME RULE OPTION

The constitution allows the voters to establish a *home rule* county. Cities have a similar option. *In this case home rule allows the people of a county to decide for themselves how they want to be "ruled" or organized politically. In order to have home rule the county must adopt a charter.* The process is somewhat complicated.

The county board of commissioners, or the people through the initiative process, can place on the ballot the question of drafting a *charter* for the county. *A charter is a written plan of local government organization similar to a constitution.* If the voters approve, they would elect a charter commission made up of individuals chosen from districts. The charter commission would draft a charter for the county and send it to the governor for approval. If the governor approves, it goes to the people to be voted on at an election.

A charter may not change the other elected officials' departments and the officials are still elected. In counties with populations under 1.5 million, the chief executive must be elected. Wayne County is the only example of a charter county in Michigan. Wayne County's charter was approved in 1980. In 1982 William Lucas was selected as Wayne County's first executive.

The potential power and influence of elected county executives is great. Two of the three county executives ran in the Republican primary for governor in 1986 (Dan Murphy of Oakland County and William Lucas of Wayne County). Large city mayors and these three county executives are among the most significant political officials in the state. As such they are naturals to run for governor or other high offices.

It is apparent why only three counties have chosen these options. While they do provide for an elected "chief executive," not enough of what needs correcting in county government is changed. The problems of division of power and responsibility among several elected department heads remain.

Questions

1. What is one key reason some counties have chosen to use the optional unified form or the home rule form of county government?

2. Do the voters of a county have to approve either of these options or can the board of commissioners decide to make the change on their own?

3. Which county government option causes the voters to approve a county charter? What can a county charter be compared to?

4. Name the Michigan counties which operate under the two optional forms of county government.

5. Do you personally believe either the optional unified form or the home rule form of county government offer any significant benefits over the regular system? Do they have any drawbacks to the older system? Please explain your reasoning.

9

TOWNSHIP GOVERNMENT

Chapter 9   Section 1

Introduction and Elected Officials

Here are the key concepts in this section:

1. This is one of the first forms of local government. Its concept was brought to the United States from England and had its beginnings in Michigan during pioneer days.

2. The entire state was surveyed using townships as the basic unit of land measurement. Later many of the same townships were given names and used as boundaries for this type of local government.

3. Most townships are run by a small number of elected officials, including a supervisor, a clerk, a treasurer, and at least two trustees. Together these officials are called the township board.

4. The township hall is the meeting place for official business. It can be considered the headquarters for township government.

Imagine three men standing in a huddle in the middle of a large field. One is the township supervisor. All of the men are pointing and talking excitedly at times. What are they talking about? Fences. It may seem a rather boring topic,

but it surely isn't to them. "I don't care how much it supposedly benefits me," says one. "I shouldn't have to pay half the cost of Bogner's fence. That cost is his problem." Mr. Bogner did not agree. "The fence," he says, "will keep my animals off your crops. You've been complaining to me for years about the problem, and now I'm suggesting a solution that benefits us both. You should pay your share too." They are both right, to a degree. The present situation is a problem for both of them, and the fence will be a benefit to both of them.

The meeting and conversation in the field was one of the oldest services of township government. The township supervisor was serving as a "fence-viewer." The job of fence viewers, usually township supervisors or trustees, is to resolve disagreements between landowners when one of them decides to build a fence. Building fences around 60, 80, or 300 acres can be very expensive. The fence might be the idea of one of the landowners, but it really does benefit all the adjoining property owners. It certainly isn't fair to have farmer Bogner pay the entire cost, and he won't. The job of the fence viewer is to determine the amount of benefit the other landowners will receive. They, then, pay that portion of the bill.

Township government has come a long way since the time fence viewing was considered a key part of the job! Now township officials spend much more of their time and energies on bigger problems. Townships may provide police and fire protection, make land use decisions, develop parks, and provide many of the other services found in larger cities. In fact, many townships have as many people as some cities. Clinton Township in Macomb County is Michigan's largest township in population with over 85,000 residents. Waterford township has over 66,000. Redford Township has a population of about 54,000.

Many people feel township governments are able to have close ties with the residents. Townships cover 96.5 percent of the land area of Michigan. Cities and villages make up the remaining 3.5 percent. Some 3.6 million Michigan residents live in townships which are a viable, vital part of Michigan government. In fact, the only people who don't live in townships are those living inside the boundaries of cities.

Today more and more people are finding township government means something to them after buying a house with a few acres and a big lawn and moving from the city into the country. They discover they may no longer have all the services city government provided as they face a new kind of government with its own special structure.

ORIGINS OF TOWNSHIP GOVERNMENT

ENGLAND

Like counties, townships trace their existence to England during the Anglo-Saxon times. The word town comes from the Anglo-Saxon word "tun." Ship comes from the word "scipe" meaning "the bounds of." So the word township means the "boundary of the town." Life in those days wasn't as safe as today. The small populated areas in England were continuously under the threat of attack by foreigners. The king's army was not able to defend them on a moment's notice, so the towns were expected to defend themselves. And organizing defenses resulted in the first township government. Later, the township added other functions and became an official part of government in England.

158

PIONEERS FROM NEW ENGLAND BRING THE IDEA HERE

When the early settlers from England established their own local government here in America it was natural for them to make use of this familiar system. Townships were especially popular in New England and the idea spread

to Michigan as many New England pioneers moved here. When the state was surveyed in the late 1820s and 1830s the township was the basic unit of survey work— a square, six miles on each side— for a total of 36 square miles. Soon our whole state was mapped out in the grid pattern of townships which we still have today.

This map shows townships in two Michigan counties and gives an idea of their layout across the state. Townships in some counties are not as uniform as these.

Springport	Tompkins	Rives	Henrietta	Waterloo
Parma	Sandstone	Blackman JACK-SON	Leoni	
Concord	Spring Arbor	Summit		Grass Lake
			Napoleon	Norvell
Pulaski	Hanover	Liberty	Columbia	

Jackson County

Burdell	Sherman	Highland	Marion
Le Roy	Rose Lake	Hartwick	Middle Branch
Lincoln	Cedar	Osceola	Sylvan
Richmond	Hersey	Evart	Orient

Osceola County

THE DEVELOPMENT OF TOWNSHIPS

When people talk about townships they may be referring to just an area of land which was surveyed as a township. On the other hand, they may be referring to a specific township unit of government. So, there are actually two categories of townships. One is the *geographic township*— the ones rugged surveyors set up long ago. The other is the *political township*. Their boundaries are often, but not always, the same. This book deals with political townships for the most part. First, however, you should know how the townships are physically laid out.

GEOGRAPHIC OR CONGRESSIONAL TOWNSHIPS

Geographic townships are also known as *congressional townships* because Congress first authorized their survey to provide settlers and the government an accurate method of determining land descriptions and ownership. Since they are a unit of land survey they are sometimes also called *survey townships*. The entire Northwest Territory (Michigan, Ohio, Indiana, Illinois, Wisconsin, and part of Minnesota) was surveyed using townships as a key part of that process.

Each township generally contains 36 sections and each section is a square mile (640 acres). When pioneers moved into Michigan, land was generally sold in blocks of 40, 80, 160, or 320 acres. It was extremely important to describe these parcels accurately and geographic townships were a helpful part of the process.

Congressional or Geographic Townships
(each is 6 miles square)

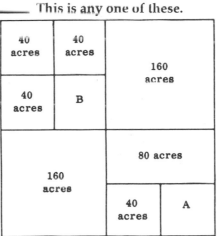

This is any one of these.

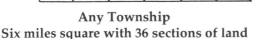

Any Township	A section of land
Six miles square with 36 sections of land	One mile square with 640 acres of land

To get a more personal idea of what we are describing, look up the deed to the property where you live or to a relative's property. It will tell exactly in which of Michigan's over 1200 townships the property is located and specifically where in that township to find it. The register of deeds keeps the records of the deeds to all property in your county. These records go back to the first land sales following treaties with the Native American tribes in your area. It is interesting to note that some of the very early deeds were signed by the President of the United States.

POLITICAL TOWNSHIPS

As more and more people came to Michigan, the need for government increased. They needed the services government can provide, such as land surveying, law enforcement, roads and bridges. But no local government existed to help them. In 1827, the territorial legislature responded and created a legal procedure for citizens to organize a political township following the boundaries of the congressional townships. These political townships became the local units of government in Michigan. As they were organized, names like Zilwaukee, Wheatfield, and Fruitport were given to them until all were named. The survey townships have no individual names, but are just numbered according to their location.

Today, the political townships may have the exact boundaries of geographic townships or they may be a part of one township or a combination of two or three. Political townships provide us with many services— protecting us from fire and crime, protecting us from unsafe or inappropriate building construction, holding our elections, and much more.

TOWNSHIP ORGANIZATION

Almost all of our over 1,240 townships are organized in the same way. The few dozen exceptions are generally seen in the more populated ones. This similarity of organization is unusual as there is a large variety of townships. Michigan townships range in population from Pte. Aux Barques in Huron County with only 15 residents and Grand Island Township in Alger County with 21 individuals to Clinton and Waterford townships each with over 60,000 people. However, most have in the range of 1,500 to 2,500 residents.

While nearly every township is exactly the same size in land area, there are exceptions. The largest in land area is McMillan in Luce County with 382,377 acres, and the smallest is Novi Township in Oakland County with only 300 acres.

WHO GOVERNS THE TOWNSHIP— THE TOWNSHIP BOARD

Some Basics

Township officials include a treasurer and a clerk. There is also a *township supervisor* who serves much like a city mayor. All three serve as department heads or administrators. These three officials combine with two or four *township trustees* who together make up the township's legislative body known as the *township board*. This board then has either five or seven officials who vote at board meetings and run the township.

The trustees are usually part-time positions. They are the "pure" legislators of the board. Most smaller townships have two trustees. If the township has over 5,000 people or 3,000 registered voters, the township board can choose to increase the number of trustees to four. All charter townships have four trustees. They have a special form of township government discussed later.

Most townships have a building or hall which serves as a meeting place and may have an office or two for the officials. If the courthouse can be considered the headquarters for county government, then the township hall is usually the nerve center of township government. These halls are commonly used by township residents as voting places for all elections whether it be for the President or local school board members. On occasion they may be rented for other community events.

Elections

All five (or seven) township board members are elected at the same time in partisan elections for four-year terms. The election coincides with the presidential election rather than with the election of Michigan's governor. In most townships, one of the two major political parties has controlled the board for years. Do you know which party controls your township, or a township near you?

Politically active individuals often run for township offices as the first step in their political careers because the legal qualifications are minimal. Potential candidates must be registered voters in the township. The candidates all run in *"at-large" elections*, meaning the township isn't broken into districts or wards. So each candidate represents the entire township and must be elected by a majority of its voters.

Vacancies

Board vacancies must be filled by the township board within 15 days. If this is not done, the governor must call a special election. Vacancies created by recall are filled only through a special election.

Compensation

The compensation received by township officials is determined by the voters at the annual township meeting. Or the board may choose to set its own salary or establish a compensation commission to do this. This is usually done only every four years since elected officials' salaries in Michigan may not be increased or decreased during their term of office. Compensation received by township trustees may vary from a few hundred dollars a year to several thousand in the larger townships. There is a wide variation in the salaries paid elected administrators as some are full-time while others serve only part time.

THE ELECTED ADMINISTRATORS

The three elected administrators have unique positions. With the exception of some mayors, they are the only ones in Michigan government who serve in distinctly legislative and executive branch positions at the same time. (Mayors in most council-manager forms of city government serve both as mayor and as a voting member of the council.) In fact, it is unconstitutional for others— county clerks, state department heads, state representatives, etc.—to do this. Township government is unique. It makes sense at this local level to have the township board organized this way.

The Supervisor

The supervisor is the chief executive officer of the township and is more powerful within the township than most city mayors are within their cities. This person serves as chair of the board at all meetings, appoints individuals to various boards and commissions in cooperation with other board members, and is looked to for political leadership in the township.

Unless other arrangements are made, the supervisor is the assessor of all property in the township. Property assessments are the basis for property taxes, and property taxes can be painfully visible to the citizen. The supervisor, with the clerk, transacts all legal business for the township and oversees the enforcement of township ordinances. Ordinances may include a curfew, parking violations, gun control, and many others.

The office of supervisor may be a full-time or part-time position depending on the demands of the office and the assistance available. Other duties may include being on the township elections commission and chair of the township board of health.

Many charter townships employ a professional to help the supervisor. This is the *township superintendent* or manager who has the education and experience to know how to aid the supervisor and the board. An arrangement of this type, similar to a council-manager form of city government, is considered the ideal organization for local government by many scholars.

The Clerk

The clerk must perform a number of tasks and duties for the township, most of them clerical. This person is secretary to the board, keeps many records for the township, and runs the elections within the township. It is an important and responsible position which is often a full-time job even in small townships. Additional tasks include the following:

1. Chairs the elections commission and the canvassing board.
2. Keeps all township board minutes and the minutes of most other township government groups.
3. Conducts all elections and keeps a list of the township's registered voters.
4. Keeps a duplicate record of the township's financial information (to check the treasurer's work).
5. Keeps a record of all township ordinances.

To save on expenses in the rural townships, some clerks worked out of their homes or farm kitchens. Today more of them work at the township office.

The Treasurer

The treasurer looks after the township's money. Property taxes and fees are paid to this person who is expected to keep the money in a high-interest account until it is needed to pay the township's bills. Additional responsibilities include the following:

1. Serves as a member of the township's elections commission, except in charter townships.
2. Prepares a list of people who haven't paid their property taxes (called a *delinquent tax roll*) and submits it to the county treasurer who puts the property up for sale at a public auction if the person is over three years behind in paying.
3. Invests the township's money.

OTHER ELECTED OFFICIALS

Up to four constables may be elected for terms of four years. Townships were required to elect at least one constable until 1976, although their function is generally duplicated by the county sheriff. In some townships they are quite helpful as they may arrest individuals for committing misdemeanors in their presence and for traffic violations. They also serve various court documents and legal papers.

Townships may elect park commissioners if there is a township park or library board members for a library. Either board has six members who serve six-year staggered terms.

Questions

1. Approximately how many Michiganians live in townships? Explain how townships vary in population from one to another.

2. Explain why there are two basic types of townships and what each type means. Include the different names used for each type in your answer.

3. How many members does a township board have and what does population have to do with this number?

4. Show what you have learned about townships by writing the minutes of an imaginary board meeting. Mention different officials and what they do and what problems the board is facing, etc.

Chapter 9   Section 2

Appointed Officials, Other Employees, and Services

Here are the key concepts in this section:

1. If a township has a large population, its elected administration may need the help of several appointed professional assistants including a superintendent to manage township business.

2. Many important questions focusing on land, its use and taxation, involve township government. These issues can become very sensitive and lead to emotional debate among the residents.

3. Township government is usually relatively simple and the services it provides quite limited. But in areas with rapidly growing populations there are pressures to do more for the people. In order to meet such demands, townships have to increase their powers and the ability to raise tax money. A growing option is to become a "charter" township.

APPOINTED OFFICIALS

There are many traditional township duties performed by personnel other than elected officials. Also, some townships provide additional services that were never considered a few years ago. This is especially true in the townships with larger populations. For example, some townships have public works departments, solid waste disposal sites, cemeteries, and parks. A few provide assistance to needy individuals, help residents improve their properties, and provide other services uncommon until recently in township government. All of these require additional employees.

The Township Superintendent

Many townships, especially charter townships, hire a full-time professional to run the township on a day-to-day basis. This is particularly helpful when the supervisor is part-time and there is much work to be done.

Most local government specialists feel the various demands on larger townships require a person who has been professionally prepared for the job. Many universities offer degrees in public administration. These programs teach prospective managers what they need to know about finances, employee relations, and state and federal programs that assist local governments. A typical supervisor may be elected more for political skills than for detailed knowledge a superintendent should have. The combination of a politically savvy supervisor and township board with a professionally trained superintendent is hard to beat. Such managers are also common in many cities and villages.

The Township Assessor

Every township is required to *assess* (determine) the value of all real estate as well as certain other property for purposes of developing the *tax rolls* (the list of all taxable property) for the township. This information is also used by the schools, the villages, the county, and the state.

First, all units of local government decide how much money is needed to provide the basic services. Next, they analyze the tax base using the assessed value of the property in their jurisdiction. Finally, the voters are asked to approve the taxes which will bring in the needed revenues.

The township assessor is the person given the task of determining the property values. The supervisor may do this if he or she has had the proper training. In any case, they must follow rules and standards from the state government in doing the task.

Land Use Control —
The Planning Commission and Zoning Board of Appeals

One of the greatest powers of local governments is the right to decide what property owners may do with their property. Townships with rapid growth need to establish *zoning laws* to protect neighboring property owners. *Zoning laws are comprehensive plans indicating what kinds of businesses and housing are*

allowed in each part of the township or city. They establish where the township's residents are willing to allow apartment houses, gas stations, grocery stores, shopping malls, and research parks. They regulate where single family homes are most appropriate and where apartment complexes are allowed.

The planning director will develop these plans. The plans will probably be sent to the *planning commission* for its analysis and a public hearing and then to the board of trustees for final approval. In many suburban townships, land use is the hottest political issue considered by them.

Occasionally, property owners come to the planning commission or the board for a "rezoning" of their property. For instance, someone may want to open an insurance agency in a house located in a residential area. The property would have to be rezoned for residential business. This might be granted, depending on the need for the change, the reasonableness of the change, and the attitude of neighbors.

There is also a *zoning board of appeals*. It receives requests to allow exceptions to the zoning map or to zoning rules and ordinances. A person who wants to enlarge a garage, for instance, may find that the finished structure is too close to the property line, according to a township ordinance. The ordinance was designed to guarantee uniformity and some assurance that one neighbor will not infringe on the rights of another. The zoning board of appeals may allow a va*riance* (exception) to the ordinance for the garage addition if it isn't too severe and if the neighbor agrees. These kinds of problems can be very sensitive issues. Land use ordinances and zoning boards resolve many potentially hostile situations.

Engineer, Public Works Director and Others

Townships may have a number of other employees. Many townships, especially those developing rapidly, will have one person or more to manage this development and growth. The township may hire an engineer to lay out the locations of utilities like water and sewer, or for other engineering work.

If the township, by itself or with neighboring municipalities, develops a water and sewer plant, it will probably establish a special purpose authority to do so. Similar to a drainage district or any other special purpose government, an authority may borrow money for such a facility, build it, and collect user fees to pay for its continuing operation.

THE ANNUAL MEETING
A Disappearing Event

When local governments were first organized in New England, citizens were reluctant to give up their direct say in government decisions. They gave elected officials the authority to carry out the wishes of the people, but they wanted to be sure the officials knew what these wishes were. To assure citizen input, they required an annual meeting be held. This "town meeting" was the purest form of democracy possible. Communities gathered together on the Saturday preceding the first Monday in April of each year to hold their annual meeting.

At these meetings, citizens proposed ways of resolving township problems. They were all given a chance to speak and then they voted, usually by voice vote. Most important was the decision on how to spend the taxpayers' monies. They established salaries, decided on building projects, and heard any complaints.

The meetings were special events which could last all day with occasional breaks for food brought in by the township residents.

The annual meeting still takes place in a few townships in Michigan, but it isn't the affair it was many years ago. The great majority of business is handled by the board as the need arises.

CHARTER TOWNSHIP ORGANIZATION
More Powers and More Revenue

As townships grew, especially those near larger cities, the role of their government changed. People wanted police and fire protection and other services usually provided by cities, but townships were severely limited in the amount of taxes they could receive from the property owners. It is often true that a township can barely receive enough in taxes to pay for its own garbage collection, much less offer other services to its residents.

In response to this need, in 1947 the state legislature passed the Charter Township Act. This law allows townships of 2,000 or more residents to legally become a charter township. The procedure can be started either when the citizens petition the board (the initiative process) or by a simple vote of the board if the population is over 5,000. If the board votes to become a charter township, but some of the people do not want it, they may ask for a reversal of this action by petitioning the township to "refer" the question back to them at an election. This vote would be called a referendum.

Charter townships don't really have their own unique charters as cities do. Rather, the charter act is the charter for all townships choosing this option.

Its major changes include a requirement for four trustees instead of two, taxing powers of up to five mills without a vote of the people, and another five mills with voter approval. This compares to the one mill tax allowed for a general law township. The act also offers the opportunity for the selection of a township superintendent, as described earlier, and it gives townships some additional powers. There are over 100 charter townships in Michigan now, and the number continues to increase.

ADDITIONAL ACTIVITIES IN LARGER TOWNSHIPS

Most townships carry out only traditional powers, but others have responded to the increasing demands of growing populations. Many of these demands are in conflict with one another. New residents who have moved out to the country from the city may want the services and conveniences of a city in a country setting. That can conflict with the desires of those who were already there and who don't feel change is necessary. Those who moved to the country for the beauty, the solitude, and the larger backyards don't always consider some of the other aspects of country life. Sidewalks are not usually found along country roads. They soon discover living near farm animals and fields that receive fertilizer is different than they expected.

When a township reaches the size of a city, the people may expect the same services a city provides. And the concentration of people may require more services as crime and ambulance calls increase. So, in spite of conflicts, many townships have taken on new untraditional responsibilities.

Public Safety

One of the demands of residents is adequate police and fire protection. The sheriff is usually expected to provide police protection, but the sheriff's officers are spread throughout the whole county and may be far away when needed. So some townships have established their own police force. Most townships have fire protection as well, though it can range from a sophisticated full-time department to a totally volunteer department with old equipment. Police and fire protection are sometimes combined.

Townships will often have a building inspector available to be sure any new buildings are safely built according to township specifications.

They may also build sidewalks, install street lights, and even have para-medics. Townships may have a solid waste disposal site, and they may also regulate some businesses for the health and safety of the residents, usually establishments selling liquor. They can also regulate the hours of pool halls and establish curfews.

Human Services

Some townships have a *housing commission* which can buy, build, and maintain housing facilities for those in need. They may assist some property owners in improving their homes, possibly installing insulation for the elderly or poor. This is often done with state or federal funds. Townships may provide water and sewer service, probably through a water and sewer authority. Some townships, anxious to encourage development in the township, may organize an economic development corporation, as discussed earlier, to provide financial assistance and incentives to developers.

Townships will occasionally fund local libraries, sometimes in cooperation with the county or a neighboring city. They may purchase and maintain parks. They may assist the elderly in filling out their tax forms, or help with certain personal problems.

Townships are a unique form of democracy in Michigan and provide benefits for those living outside a city which they might otherwise never have. Some groups suggest they be abolished and have their responsibilities assumed by county government. Although there is room for improvement in both township and county government, they are both an essential part of our state's local system of governments and are not likely to ever disappear from the scene.

The Problem of Losing Land to a City

Sometimes townships near growing cities face a challenge to their authority when the city wishes to take over part of the township and include it as a section of the city. This is known as *annexation*. Annexation is a legal means for one *municipality* to acquire land in another municipality. *A municipality is an area having the powers of local self government such as a city, village, or township.* Lansing Township, for example, has been annexed into four separate parts over the years by Michigan's capital city. What remains is now only about five square miles in size which is divided into four non-contiguous parts.

T. Deeter © HEP

The process for annexation is not automatic. The township does have the opportunity to defend itself, though the city often wins in the long run. The State Boundary Commission hears requests for annexations. This commission consists of three members appointed by the governor. Before the annexation becomes final, there is a vote among the affected residents.

Questions

1. Real life is full of many problems. George and Gracie love their new country home, but they never realized how much equipment it takes to keep up five acres of lawn. Now they want to build a new garage so they will finally have room for their two cars, a riding mower, a push mower, a gas grill, lawn spreader, and Rototiller. The contractor tells them the only place they can build is too close to the property line according to the township ordinance. Explain what groups they may need talk to and what they may have to do so they can build the much needed larger garage.

2. In your opinion do zoning laws make sense? Why or why not?

3. Why would a township want to adopt a charter under Michigan's 1947 Charter Township Act?

4. List some employees, not elected officials, a township may have.

5. What pressures cause rapidly growing townships to add new services? List examples of services and departments such townships may have.

10

CITY AND VILLAGE GOVERNMENT

Chapter 10   Section 1

Why They Formed and What They Are

Here are the key concepts in this section:

1. Cities offer many benefits to their residents and one is more government services, but such services always require money and manpower, adding to the complexity of city government.

2. A key difference between village and city government is that villages are still a part of their township while cities are separate from any township.

3. Becoming a city or village is a rather complex process which follows rules set up by the state government.

4. Forming a city or village in Michigan was once even more difficult because the early state constitutions did not provide any plan to follow. This led to much interference from the state legislature until the 1908 constitution.

A majority of Michigan residents live in cities or villages. If people don't actually live in a city, they usually live near one— in its *metropolitan area. A metropolitan area includes the smaller cities and towns which are close to the major city. These other cities or suburbs are not under the political control of the major city but they operate in its shadow.* Throughout Michigan, over 5 million residents live in cities or their metropolitan areas.

Detroit is the only really large city in Michigan the other bigger cities are much farther down in the national rankings. Detroit is huge, of course, with about one million people. According to the 1990 census Detroit is the ninth largest U.S. city— it once was 6th but its population has decreased considerably. Meanwhile, Grand Rapids (189,000) is the 78th largest city in the United States. Warren (145,000), Flint (141,000), and Lansing (123,000) are three other large cities in the state. All cities are not large and Michigan has many smaller ones. Alma (9,034), Gaylord (3,256), Grand Haven (11,951), and Marquette (21,977) are but a few of Michigan's 271 cities.

Franklin (2,626), Lake Orion (3,057), Ravenna (919), and Wolverine (283) are four of 263 villages in Michigan.

How are these cities and villages organized? What services do they provide? These are some of the questions answered in this chapter.

ORIGINS OF CITIES

Benefits of Living Together

History books tell of many great cities existing hundreds, even thousands, of years ago. Such cities as Athens, Alexandria, Rome and the more modern cities of Europe and the United States became the models for others to follow. They all rose out of a need of people to be more secure, to be provided the services needed to work, learn, and live, and the desire to have a voice in their local destiny. Throughout history people have moved to cities because they offered the economic benefits of higher paying jobs, more efficient delivery of essential services, and the cultural benefits that resulted from many people living close to one another. Michigan cities were settled for the same reasons.

Michigan's First Cities

The first *incorporated* city in Michigan was Detroit in 1815. Following closely behind was Monroe in 1820. No new cities incorporated in Michigan for the next 30 years. This was somewhat due to the first Michigan constitution failing to even mention local government. The second constitution in 1850 mentioned local governments in more detail, but it gave the state legislature almost total control of local governments.

Twice after 1850 the people of Michigan tried to rewrite the state constitution. Finally, the electorate succeeded and approved a new constitution in 1908. One of the motivating factors in accepting the new constitution was the frustration of citizens and local leaders over the lack of any real voice in how their local governments were organized. The new constitution gave the legislature the power to create a new category of city government called "home rule cities." The home rule concept lets the people of an area decide for themselves how their city government should be organized. Michigan was the seventh state to adopt this type of city government.

Michigan's Urban Growth

Population growth in Michigan and the United States since 1800 has been nothing short of remarkable. In that year, when the American population was about 6 million and the Michigan non-Indian population only a thousand or so, 96 percent of Americans lived in the "country." In 1790, there were only six cities in the U.S. with populations over 2,500— New York City, Philadelphia, Baltimore, Boston, Norfolk, and Richmond.

The westward migration of people from New England and foreign immigrants looking for a new home in America brought more people into Michigan.

The population exploded during the mid 1800s. It jumped from 31,639 in 1830 to 212,267 in 1840, and almost double that figure by 1850! Changing technology helped build our cities. At first, most people earned a living as farmers and their neighbors might be far away, but as manufacturing developed in the late 1800s many moved into the cities to find work in the factories.

WHAT IS A VILLAGE ?

As communities grew, two kinds of local government organization were possible— village or city. Many of the cities Michigan has today started out as villages which later changed their form of government as they grew larger.

Let's discover exactly what the village form of government is. A group of citizens living in close proximity may choose to organize their area into a village if they desire. The population of the area must be at least 150 residents, with a density of 100 residents per square mile. A village remains a part of the township in which it exists, so the township still does certain services for it. The township continues to assess property; collect taxes for the schools, the township, and the county; and conduct county, state, and national elections for villages.

People meeting the requirements for a village would likely consider starting fire and police protection or developing local laws regarding individual behavior or land use. The residents of an area often need some compelling situation to cause them to consider taking the formal steps to form an organized village or city. Such a move might be started because the sheriff took too long to reach the scene of a crime, or it could be that a house burned to the ground because of inadequate fire protection.

Village government and city government are much the same except that a village remains a part of the township and the township will continue to provide the services it did in the past unless the village decides to do some of them itself. The county also has a more important role in a village than it does in a city because the county may continue to provide the village with services through contracts between the two. The village may pay the county for such things as protection by the sheriff's department or road and street maintenance through the county road commission.

Both a city and village have an elected council; however, the village council members are known as trustees. Instead of a mayor a village has a president. This official has powers similar to a mayor except he or she also has the powers of a sheriff to stop disorder within the village limits. A few villages have law officers known as village marshalls. Village voters have to do a little extra work because they must register twice, once for village elections and another time for all other elections.

WHAT IS A CITY ?

Residents can choose to become a city if their population exceeds 750 or 2,000, depending on the kind of city they wish to establish. A city, unlike a village, withdraws from its township. It no longer takes part in any township activities. City residents pay no township taxes and elect no township officials.

A city must provide for all the services it no longer receives from the township. It must register voters, conduct elections, assess property, and collect property taxes. A city will also provide some services otherwise provided by the county. The county sheriff generally does not assume responsibilities inside city boundaries, so a city must establish its own police force. It has its own fire department, provides water and sewer services, does road construction and repair, and even generates electricity sometimes.

The great advantage of having the legal status of a city is self-determination. The residents of a city can determine themselves how they wish to be governed. City residents determine what services they desire, what they will pay in taxes, how the city will be planned, and much more. The laws of Michigan allow city residents to tax themselves to a greater extent than villages or townships. This extra funding capability allows the city to provide more services.

Detroit's Renaissance Center and People Mover. Larger cities face more complex problems which often require costly solutions, such as the People Mover. Photo courtesy Metropolitan Detroit Convention & Vistors Bureau.

BECOMING A CITY OR VILLAGE

When the public thinks of cities, the focus is often on the unpleasant aspects of city life. I remember when my township was considering becoming a city a few years ago. Many residents opposed the idea because they thought the township would automatically have slum housing, busy, noisy streets, and higher taxes. The vote to incorporate as a city failed and my township is still a township. The years have gone by and the streets are much busier and noisier anyway. Taxes have gone up about 400% regardless of the vote! A city, as opposed to a village or a township, is for the most part only a difference in the organization of the government. Becoming a city does not automatically change the people, their needs, the environment, the roads, the schools, or even the taxes. All these things are dependent on how the public deals with them— not on the form of government.

MANY STEPS TO BE FOLLOWED

When residents want to become a village or a city they must ask permission to do this. *The legal or formal process of becoming a village or city is called incorporation.* The process to become a city or village is a complex one and can have as many as 73 separate steps. Below is a simplified outline of what happens. Citizens wishing to incorporate a village, or villages hoping to become cities, must first seek approval from the State Boundary Commission.

Step 1— A Petition

At least one percent of the voters in the area to become a city must sign a petition which goes to the State Boundary Commission.

Step 2— A Hearing

The commission hears the arguments for the change, then holds a public hearing in the area after notifying interested parties.

The State Boundary Commission

The State Boundary Commission is composed of three individuals appointed by the governor. When they consider incorporation within a particular county, the senior probate judge within the county appoints two additional members to make a total of five people. One of the new appointees must be from a city. The other must be from a township.

The commission considers such criteria as population, density, land area, valuation, urban growth factors, and additional information that would help them determine if it is reasonable to consider village or city incorporation for the area.

Step 3— Vote to Write a Charter

If the commission concludes that incorporation is appropriate, they accept the petition. A referendum vote on the matter is then held for the approval of the residents involved.

Step 4-- A Charter Commission

If successful, the residents must establish a charter commission which produces a charter for the city or village. The completed charter must be presented to the governor.

Step 5— The Governor Approves the Charter

If the governor approves the charter, it is presented to the people of the area for their approval in another referendum vote.

Step 6 — People Give Final Approval

If that vote is successful, the new government is formed, officials are elected and appointed, and the new government begins its operation

TYPES OF CITY AND VILLAGE INCORPORATION

GENERAL LAW CITY GOVERNMENT

The first Michigan cities were created under special legislation by the territorial government and later by the state legislature. Because of that creation by the legislature, such cities were known as "General Law Cities." Since the legislature made the rules, the cities had very little control in how they were governed. Over the years all general law cities have changed to other options but some villages continue to operate under the general law provisions.

State Legislative Control

Since the first constitution in 1835 neglected to mention local governments, the state legislature was left with the question of how they should be established and organized. The legislators were delighted to assume this power. The result was the state legislature not only decided under what circumstances to allow a city to form but it also meddled with its daily affairs.

The state legislature often spent more time on local matters than on state matters. Early city charters were printed with the minutes of the state legislature in the *Public and Local Acts of Michigan*.

Problems with State Control

Needless to say, the residents of Michigan cities did not appreciate the politicians in Lansing telling them how to run their cities. They fought state control and even took the matter to the Michigan supreme court. In one important case, Elliott v. City of Detroit, in 1899, the court said cities were given no right to frame their own charters, according to the 1850 state constitution. The court added that the legislature was not able to allow cities to draft their own charters, even if the legislature wanted to do so.

Often the legislators weren't all that interested in writing and editing and rewriting numerous city and village charters. In 1867 one man gave his impression of the legislator's attitudes about reading city charters:

> "Because some one person interested in this matter sits down, writes out a charter, sends it to a member of the Legislature who presents it, and it is referred to the Committee on corporations. That committee does not read it or examine it; they ask the member who presents it, if it is all right? If he says it is, they report it and recommend its passage; nobody reads it, it passes and goes to the Governor for his approval, and very likely he never reads it; if he does, he is a very persevering man.... The result is often that great injustice and wrong is done to many interests."

One city had its ward (district) boundaries changed by the legislature without the citizens knowing the legislature was even considering such a move. The city leaders were furious. There are many more examples of early legislative meddling in city affairs.

HOME RULE CITY AND VILLAGE GOVERNMENT

The 1908 constitution didn't provide home rule by itself. The constitution gave the legislature the power to write a home rule law. The following year the legislature passed the Home Rule Act for Cities and the Home Rule Act for Villages. Villages and cities quickly took advantage of the new law. The new law was so popular that as of this writing every one of Michigan's cities has drafted a charter under the authority of the 1909 law and nearly fifty of its villages have as well.

Each local municipality that chooses the home rule charter procedure has the task of establishing a charter commission and developing a charter following one of several options.

For starters, they may choose a strong mayor form of government, meaning a mayor given substantial powers of appointment, budget preparation, veto, and a small council.

They may prefer to have an elected executive (mayor) with few powers (a weak mayor form), but aided by an appointed professional manager. Or they may have a <u>council-manager form</u> where the council hires a manager, and a mayor with limited powers is elected.

A charter commission has a task similar to the drafting of the United States Constitution. The possibilities are wide open. The completed charter must receive the approval of the governor, however, along with the approval of the people it affects.

Questions

1. Name the first two places in Michigan to legally become organized as cities.

2. What omission caused problems in the formation of Michigan's early cities and villages? What corrected this problem and when did it take place?

3. Make a list of all the differences between village government and city government.

4. What are the basic steps needed to become a city?

5. Explain what the phrase "Home Rule City" means?

Chapter 10   Section 2

Types of Organization for City Government
City Officials and What They Do

Here are the key concepts in this section:

1. There are four basic types of organization for city government in Michigan and three of them are still in use.

2. When a city is formed it takes on some responsibilities previously done by the county and townships.

3. The mayor is the chief executive officer of a city, but depending on the form of city government, some mayors have many powers while others have very few.

4. Often the city manager is the most powerful city official, even though this is not an elected position.

5. In Michigan it is the law that all meetings of government officials be open to the public, though there are some minor exceptions.

6. Both state and local governments have the right to obtain private land at a fair price for public use, even if the owner does not want to sell it.

CITY GOVERNMENT ORGANIZATION

While there are many different considerations for charter commissions to debate, there are only four basic structures used by cities and villages. Simply speaking, each of these four types relates to which official or officials have the most power.

COUNCIL—MANAGER

The most professional approach in organizing is the council-manager form of city government. This plan is characterized by a *city council*, which selects a professional *city manager* to run the city on a day-to-day basis and make recommendations to the council. The city must have a mayor, but the position is mostly honorary. These mayors may be elected by the voters or selected by the council. About 175 of Michigan's 271 cities use this form. The organizational chart shows who controls what areas. You can see that the manager is the one person who oversees the work of nearly every department in city government.

Organizational Chart for Council-Manager Form
of City Government

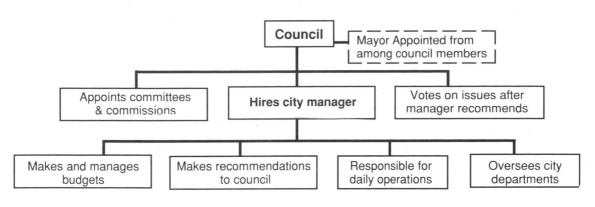

MAYOR-COUNCIL

The mayor-council form of city organization is the second most often used in Michigan. It is also the oldest in use in the country. Most large cities use this form. There are two types of mayor-council government: the "strong" mayor-council and the "weak" mayor-council.

Strong Mayor-Council

The *strong mayor-council* form of city government provides a city organization with a city council which is accompanied by a mayor who has considerable power. The mayor is referred to as "strong" because the position is provided a number of powers in the charter that a "weak" mayor is not given. A powerful mayor, for instance, is given broad appointive powers, a veto over measures passed by the council, and budget-drafting  responsibilities. The mayor may also preside over council meetings, be able to vote in case of a tie council vote, and be able to recommend legislation.

The mayor is elected separately and can gather significant political clout in city matters. He or she is the chief executive of the city. Mayors of larger cities are often found lobbying in Lansing or Washington for more benefits back home. The mayor of Detroit is an example of a "strong" mayor.

Weak Mayor-Council

In the *weak mayor-council* form, the city council is given most of the powers and the mayor is given very few. The council has the power to make most appointments. The mayor may not even be given veto power. The council prepares the budget with only recommendations from the mayor. Departments are often run by commissions appointed by the council.

Organizational Chart for Mayor-Council Form of City Government

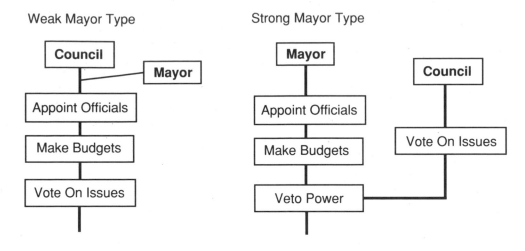

The weak-mayor form is not a popular choice for a number of reasons. One big problem is that there is no strong leader in the city. Power is too decentralized and spread out among the council members, the mayor, and various elected or appointed commissions and boards. At election time, voters are sometimes confused by the long list of candidates on the ballot. The advantages are that it provides for more citizen input and gives the council more control over the operation of the city. Often this form of city government is confused with the council-manager form because *both* types may hire a city manager.

COMMISSION

The *commission* form looked great on paper, but it did not work well. The last Michigan city to use it was Highland Park, which changed in 1968. There are no Michigan cities using the commission form today.

CITY FUNCTIONS

Services Increased

One reason people came to cities in the first place was to receive better services in a more efficient manner. No longer does each family need to take care of its own water, sewage, and garbage. In a city there is easy access to libraries, municipal swimming pools, tennis courts and other conveniences.

One of the first services to be provided was protection. Where large numbers of people gather, violence, crime, and the risk of fire become serious threats to the public welfare. Police and fire departments are basic city services. Cities also provide street lights, parks, and other conveniences to city dwellers, all to meet the needs, demands, and wishes of their residents.

Since people live closer together in a city than in the country it is easier to provide many services in a city. Less ground has to be covered. So it is more efficient to build sewers, pipelines, electric lines, have police patrols, drive to the scene of a fire, and maintain roads. It is usually less costly to connect city residents to a water system than to have each household dig its own well. The city can more inexpensively add fluoride and soften, purify, and pressurize the water. Similarly, municipal treatment of sewage is more efficient than having each family build and maintain a septic tank and drain field. It would be hard for the people in a sparsely settled township to pay for a park or library, and even if they could, it might be too far away to be usable.

Depending on the size and needs of the city, it may also have garbage pick-up, public transportation, land-use planning and zoning laws, parks, libraries, museums, zoos, cemeteries, and many other services. The extent of the services and regulations is left to the voters of the city to decide. The residents of Grand Rapids desire to spend some of their tax dollars on such items as John Ball Park and outdoor art in addition to their other needs. Residents in Lansing are provided electricity and water through a separate authority called the Board of Water and Light. These decisions are made through the selection of various elected officials and through ballot issues presented to the voter.

Local government is a creation of the state constitution so the legislature can require cities and villages to do various jobs too. For example, cities are required to conduct national, state, and local elections.

When an area becomes a city, it must take on many responsibilities previously handled by the township and some of the responsibilities of the county. The county is responsible for the construction and maintenance of roads, for example, except within city boundaries. The city must assume those responsibilities.

CITY AND VILLAGE OFFICIALS

Cities and villages may choose to provide a variety of services to residents, but the major elected and appointed officials are generally the same in any city or village.

THE MAYOR

The chief executive of the city is the mayor. The mayor is generally elected directly by the people in mayor-council city organizations. In council-manager forms, the mayor may be elected by the people or may be chosen by the council from among its own members. Qualifications for mayor and all other city and village offices are minimal and allow the voters the greatest opportunity of choosing among a large number of candidates. Mayors usually serve for terms of four years.

CITY MANAGER

A city manager is a trained specialist with preparation in the various phases of city government including city law, accounting and budgeting, problems of heath and sanitation, personnel matters, and traffic management. The duties of the city manager are to take care of the daily operation of the city. He or she supervises all city departments from police to garbage collection. The manager usually attends city council meetings and answers questions from the public about city programs.

Many aspects of the job require a political sensitivity and yet the manager is not elected but is instead hired by the city council. While this person may be an expert in all areas of city government, he or she may not be in touch with the residents of the city. The manager is usually an outsider who may not sense the direction of the general public. This may be a drawback in some cases.

CITY COUNCIL

The city council is the legislative body for the city. Unlike state and national legislatures, city councils are unicameral (have only one group), as are village, township, and county boards. Their numbers are also quite small in comparison. City councils usually consist of five to nine members. Terms of office are either two or four years and may be staggered so the entire council is not up for re-election at the same time. Most council members are elected by the voters from the entire city. In larger cities, some of the council members are elected from *wards. Wards are geographical divisions of the city used to elect the council. Usually one member of the council is elected from each ward.* This allows the residents of each ward to have closer contact with their representative on the council.

CITY MAP

City councils pass *ordinances* (city laws), make some appointments, and approve the budget. Depending on the city government's organization, the council may be very powerful. This is especially true in the council-manager and weak mayor-council forms.

CITY CLERK

The city clerk has responsibilities similar to a township clerk. He or she keeps a record of the council meetings and of the finances of the city. The clerk is also responsible for issuing permits for a variety of activities, including parades, use of city buildings, and many others. It is the clerk who registers voters and conducts elections.

CITY TREASURER

The city treasurer is responsible for the finances of the city. He or she will receive taxes, especially property taxes, pay the bills of the city on the order of the council, and report to the council at appropriate times on the financial status of the city.

OTHER OFFICES

Occasionally, other officers are elected, but a city usually has most officials and employees appointed to their positions. The personnel department will be chiefly responsible for finding the most qualified individuals for various positions. Although the county will elect offices like the sheriff, prosecutor, and drain commissioner, most cities appoint their police chief, city attorney, building inspector and so forth. They also have departments concerned with assessing, finance, public works, fire, and planning. The number of offices and employees in a city is usually related to its size.

PROBLEMS OF AGING CITIES

Many large cities have been around for decades. Buildings, water pipes, and roads were not necessarily meant to last that long. As the *infrastructure* ages (*Infrastructure is the roads, bridges, water and sewer lines, and so forth, required for a city to function efficiently and safely.*), and as more people leave for the suburbs, many cities have fallen into disrepair. It becomes a vicious cycle, property values decline and little new construction takes place, there is less money available in the budget for improvements and repairs and as the city deteriorates more people move away. Shopping malls draw customers away from downtowns and businesses in the city centers close or decay.

Some Michigan cities are organizing to respond to this situation. There are numerous state and federal programs to assist them in this effort. Many efforts are from the private sector, as well. Detroit's Renaissance Center and Grand Rapids' Amway Plaza are just two examples of private projects designed to give a boost to the inner city.

POWERS AND RESPONSIBILITIES

State and local governments have some special powers and responsibilities. One of these powers and one of the responsibilities apply to all levels of government in Michigan. They are explained as follows.

EMINENT DOMAIN— *The Right of Government to Take Land*

As cities increase in population more services are needed and sometimes this means local government needs more land. This is true with state government activities as well.

One obvious example is the need for roads. This was most apparent during the construction of the interstate highway system that began in Michigan in the 1950s and continues today. When the plans were still "on the drawing

184

board," it was determined where the roads should be built. Part of this project was to construct an interstate from Detroit to Muskegon called I-96. As the highway engineers decided where the highway should be laid, one consideration was the interruption of businesses and family life. The highway department sent agents to all the residents along the route to tell them of their plans to buy their land and build a highway on it. This was not welcome news for most and some fought the plans. In such cases, the land is usually *condemned*, which means the government buys needed property whether or not the owner wants to sell. The argument may end up in court. The government still gets the needed land but the court decides fair payment.

Government has the right to do this through the power of *eminent domain*. This is the power of government to take private property for public use. The concept of eminent domain goes back hundreds of years and has roots in the idea that the king owns everything, that what we consider "ownership" is a limited right to use the property. Government could never build a highway, or many other important structures, without this power. Eminent domain is not very popular with those it directly affects, but it is essential.

Occasionally, it is used for purposes that barely resemble government activity. The most dramatic recent example of this was the takeover of the Polish community in Detroit called Poletown by the city of Detroit. Wrecking balls smashed 1,362 homes, 143 businesses, 16 churches and 1 hospital. This entire community was condemned so General Motors could build a large automobile plant there. The only relationship to government activity was that the plant would provide jobs and pay taxes. Of course this use of eminent domain was hotly contested and it led to over $100 million in lawsuits which were still being resolved years after the event.

OPEN MEETINGS ACT— *the Public's Right to Know*

If government is to truly be "of the people, by the people, and for the people," it is essential for the people to know what is going on and to have the opportunity to tell government what they desire. There seems to be a powerful tendency for many government officials to forget that their role in a representative democracy is to represent the interests of the people. Their job should not be to advance the interests of powerful lobbyists, unions, or businesses, or worse yet, themselves. When government activities take place behind closed doors this is exactly what can happen. In the early 1970s there was a move by citizen groups in Michigan to force all levels of government to do their business in the open. Because of this the state legislature passed the *Open Meetings Act* in 1976.

T. Deeter © HEP

The Open Meetings Act requires open meetings of all legislative, city, village, township, and county governing boards. It requires open meetings of all local and intermediate school boards, state colleges, universities, community colleges, zoning boards, road commissions, public hospitals and others.

The Open Meetings Act requires that, before a meeting is held, notice of the time, place, and subject matter of the meeting must be provided to the public. Any person has the right to peaceably address a meeting of any body. To accommodate this, most government bodies have a time on the agenda for "public comment".

A meeting can be closed to the press and the public only when the body is discussing specific kinds of sensitive matters where more potential harm than good would likely occur from a public discussion. Examples are: labor negotiations, employee or student discipline, an option to purchase property, or a pending legal action. To close a meeting to the public, a two-thirds majority of the body must vote to do so by a roll call vote (so the public knows who was responsible). Only the stated agenda item can be discussed.

The Act also guarantees the availability of the minutes of open meetings at a reasonable cost of printing and copying.

It is still possible for some to try to work out of sight of the public. Groups that prefer the public not know how their decisions were reached might try to find ways to keep their discussions private by violating the "spirit of the law." The law's requirement for openness goes into effect whenever and wherever a majority of the group is present. For example, a seven member group which would have to meet in the open if four members are present, might meet in groups of two or three. Some might meet in a member's home causing the public to feel they are intruding. Some groups have met in sections of restaurants too small to accommodate any additional people. These situations are violations of the intent ("spirit") of the law. They occur more frequently than they should, but Michigan citizens now have much greater access to the decision-making process of government than they had even a few years ago.

Questions

1. Outline the type of government organization your city has or that of a city nearby. Name each of the major elected officials. Is the mayor elected or appointed by the council? How many members does the council have and are they elected from the entire city or by wards?

2. Let us suppose you are interested in running for city council. Under which type of basic city government organization would you prefer to work? Explain your reasoning.

3. Explain why it is more efficient for government services, such as water, sewer, police, fire protection, and libraries, to be provided in a city than in a rural township.

4. Make a list of city services which were once done by the township, county or individual before the city was formed.

5. Explain what eminent domain is and tell if you believe this procedure is fair. If you could change the way this procedure is used what changes would you make?

6. Frank Fox is a member of the city council. He finds most council meetings to be much too long— often delayed by arguments among the council members and the amount of time required for public comments. Frank has found it speeds up the meeting if he and some of his friends on the council meet at a restaurant over supper and decide on their positions before the meeting. This way they are ready to vote when the issues come up later.

Is Frank doing anything wrong? Does his action and the actions of his friends on the council shortchange the public in any way? Should these council members change their practice of getting together before public meetings? What do you think and why?

11

SCHOOL DISTRICTS AND RELATED ISSUES

Chapter 11   Section 1

School Districts Are a Form of Local Government

Here are the key concepts in this section:

1. School districts are a form of local government headed by elected boards of education.

2. There are six types of school districts. Student enrollment is the factor which basically determines the type of school district.

3. Superintendents are hired by the school districts to manage day-to-day affairs. In some ways they are like city managers.

SCHOOL DISTRICTS

Importance

Most students would consider the *school district* to be the unit of local government closest to them. It probably affects your daily life more than any other right now. Currently Michigan has about 1,640,000 students attending classes in grades kindergarten thru twelve in some 4,400 public schools. All of the state's public schools are in one or the other of our 560 school districts. Obviously what happens in these districts is very important to a large number of people.

History and Background

Michigan has a long history of leadership in the field of education. Michigan's 1835 constitution was the first of any state to mention the office of superintendent of public instruction. So, even though each school district is locally controlled, the state government has been involved in education from the very beginning.

The federal government has been involved in Michigan schools from an even earlier date. It helped provide the money to build the first schools through the Land Ordinance of 1785. This law set aside one section, or 640 acres, of land from each township. Land from section 16 was sold and the proceeds used to support schools in each township. Federal support for education continues to be significant. Nearly $500 million in federal aid reaches Michigan's education system each year.

Development

The state's public school system started with 98 teachers instructing 2,377 students in 1836. That year the average number of days of school was a mere 70. Today, the minimum number of days schools must be in session is set by state law at 180 per year. For many years most education took place in thousands of one-room school houses scattered across the state. One of the reasons for so many small schools was poor transportation. It was not practical to go more than two or three miles to a school. For this reason there were once over 7,000 school districts, but beginning in the 1950s the number declined rapidly as districts combined. Combination of school districts still takes place sometimes, usually to offer a wider variety of courses and keep overhead costs under control.

Once Michigan had a large number of school districts made up of one-room schools. Often one teacher taught all of the students in the school. This photo was taken in Montague in 1912. Photo courtesy Michigan State Archives.

How School Districts Combine

School districts become larger through three methods: consolidation, annexation and transfer of territory. Two or more districts can vote to consolidate and a new board may be elected. To annex a district, the larger board passes a resolution and the voters of the smaller district vote to approve. Two-thirds of the property owners in an area of land can petition the intermediate school district for the land to be transferred to an adjoining district.

Boundaries

Unlike townships, which are almost always uniform in size and shape, Michigan is a patchwork quilt of school districts. Where the population is low, Michigan has districts nearly as large as a county; and where it is high, there are a few counties with over a dozen school districts in each. Most districts are formed around the largest city in the area and they spread out in irregular shapes until they reach the border of the next district.

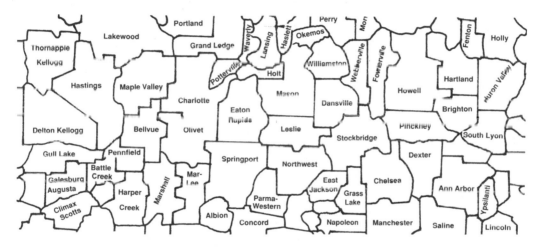

This map shows a small selection of the school districts in Michigan. Notice the irregular boundaries and sizes.

School district boundaries are important to some people. Often when individuals move into a new area they want to know which school district they are moving to and whether it has good schools. Good schools mean different things to different people. Most, however, are interested in knowing that the district's buildings are new and well maintained and that the teachers have the best credentials.

Types of School Districts

State law authorizes six types of school districts and basically these are set up by the district's population, though today it is rare to actually hear these designations used. Each type has a different number of board members. Detroit is the only first class school district in Michigan. It operates with a central board of education and is allowed to have 7 to 11 regional districts as well. Most school districts in Michigan are third or fourth class. Smaller districts are not always in rural areas; several heavily populated counties have districts with less than 2,500 students. There are still over 30 districts in Michigan which do not offer all the grades K thru 12.

TYPE OF SCHOOL DISTRICT
NUMBER OF BOARD MEMBERS
NUMBER OF STUDENTS/comments

First Class		120,000 students or more
Central Board	13	Detroit is the only 1st class district in Michigan.
Regional Board	5	
Second Class	9	30,000 to 119,999 students (Only a very few districts)
Third Class	7	2,400 to 29,999 students (Roughly 130 districts)
Fourth Class	5 or 7	75 to 2,399 students (Roughly 420 districts)
Primary	3	Rare- usually less than 75 students. Grades K-8 only

The Elected Board

The governing body of a school district is the elected *board of education*. Most boards of education have seven or nine members— which depends on the formal type of district. Usually the board members are elected in the school election on the second Monday of June each year though the dates for elections are not uniform and they are sometimes held at the same times as elections for city officials. Individuals nominated for school boards do not run on a party platform. There is a wide variety of term lengths for school board members. Third class district board members serve for four or six years, and fourth class districts usually have board members in office for three or four years.

In some ways a school district can be compared to a city government using a hired city manager. But in the case of the school district the superintendent serves the role of the city manager.

The board takes charge of general supervision of the district's schools and votes to set policies, raise money through taxation and so forth. They also hire all personnel— including a superintendent, principals, teachers, and custodians. They build and maintain buildings, pay all expenses, have the final say over what courses are offered, approve which textbooks are used, set the dates of the school year, provide for the transportation of students, and take the school census.

School boards can find themselves in the middle of controversy when they feel the need to raise more money by increasing the property tax rates or when they must cut programs because there is a shortage of money.

The Superintendent— The Hired Manager

The superintendent is hired by the board of education to manage the affairs of all the schools in the district. In addition to a superintendent, districts usually have assistant superintendents who may handle specialized areas such as business, finance or instructional services. Superintendents often spend much time in the area of public relations so the schools are seen in a positive light.

Principals are hired by the board of education to oversee individual school buildings. They have more contact with students and teachers than most superintendents and are involved with student discipline and other problems at the building level.

Questions

1. Find out what class your school district is. How many members does your board of education have and how long are their terms of office? When are elections held for the board? Who is currently the head of your board of education?

2. What are the three ways school districts can combine? Has your district ever considered combining with another in recent years and why was this being considered?

3. Discover what the boundaries of your school district are and describe them.

4. Find out how many students your district has and tell how many elementary, middle (or junior high), and high schools it has. Does your district operate a vocational-technical center?

Chapter 11 Section 2

Schools and Their Relationship With State Government

Here are the key concepts in this section:

1. School districts obtain their power from state government and are supervised by the State Board of Education.

2. Districts receive significant amounts of aid for each student from the state and there are some strings attached to this aid.

3. Besides regular public school districts for grades K-12, there are also separate intermediate school districts and community college districts. Both of these can also raise money through property taxes.

4. Private schools and home schools are governed by the state in some respects.

School Census

Because state aid to schools is based on the number of students in each district, an annual school census is made on the fourth Friday in September. An average school district receives about $3,500 from the state for each student. Since so much money is riding on the results, this head count is very important. Each student's name and address is collected and forwarded to the State Superintendent of Public Instruction. Besides the census, each district keeps track of students who move in or out of the district during the school year.

Generally speaking the number of students in Michigan's public schools is declining. Over the past 20 years the total number of students has dropped about 25 percent. The decline is caused by parents having fewer children and people moving out of the state.

State Supervision

All public schools in this state operate under the general supervision of the State Board of Education and the State Superintendent of Public Instruction. Chapter 5 on the executive branch explains the role of the board in more detail. The state superintendent is appointed by the State Board of Education.

As would be expected, there are usually some political considerations involved with appointment of any official with such a high position in government.

There is often controversy about how involved the state board should be in guiding the activities of local school districts. Michigan's board of education does not have the strict control such boards have in some other states. Several states require all schools in that state to teach the same courses and use the same textbooks. There is more

flexibility in Michigan but recent trends seem to show this board is becoming more active in some types of involvement.

For example, Michigan now has a state program of assessment testing for reading, math, and science called M.E.A.P. (Michigan Education Assessment Program). This program tests students in grades five, eight, and eleven each fall to check their progress in these basic subjects. Some educators believe the state board wants to use these tests to establish a more uniform curriculum, something it probably could not accomplish in other ways. There have been plans to increase the number of subjects tested to include social studies.

In 1990 the Michigan legislature passed Public Act 25 which demands local school districts do several things if they are to continue receiving full state aid. Under this law each district must:

1.) Adopt a three to five year school improvement plan
2.) Develop a core curriculum
3.) Certify each school with the state
4.) Provide an annual report to its residents

These regulations seem new but looking back into history they are not so different than some of the past requirements.

Intermediate School Districts

In addition to the 560 or so regular school districts, Michigan also has 57 intermediate school districts, often known as ISDs. Usually each ISD covers a single county except in the northern part of the state where some counties have combined into one ISD. The intermediate school districts developed from the older county school districts which were renamed in 1962. In earlier years when there were many small school districts, they frequently found they could not offer some of the special services required by their students and teachers. The need for these services was one reason for the formation of the county school districts.

Today, ISDs provide all the schools in their districts with a variety of services. These include data processing, media centers, and consultants in a number of areas. They operate programs for students with special needs including learning disabilities, the emotionally disturbed, physically handicapped, mentally retarded, and home bound. Vocational-technical education programs may also be run by intermediate school districts for training students in practical fields such as construction and cosmetology.

ISDs are controlled by a board, much as are regular school districts. The board hires a superintendent. State law sets the number of people on an ISD board at five except for ISDs made up of more than one county. These ISD boards have seven members. Board members can be elected directly by the voters or selected by representatives of the school districts in the county. Board members, whether elected directly or selected by the school districts, serve for six-year terms which begin July 1st. Most ISDs use the selection process. Direct election of members takes place with the annual school election on the second Monday in June, while the school board selection process occurs on the first Monday in June.

Community Colleges

Community colleges are mentioned here because they also have their own districts which may raise operating revenue much as regular school districts through property taxes. At this time about 26 percent of the money needed to operate the average community college comes from property taxes. They do have the advantage of also collecting tuition from their students to help pay for their expenses— unlike public K-12 schools.

Students who attend a community college and live within the district set up for that college pay a lower tuition than students who live outside the district. About 6.5 million Michiganians live in one of the established community college districts. Today about 224,000 students attend one of the state's 29 public community colleges. (See the map on the next page.)

Raising Money to Pay for Schools

Chapter 12 discusses some of the issues connected with school financing. The Headlee constitutional amendment places several limits on school financing. Some authorities also believe it limits state government from imposing new regulations without providing the money to pay for them. This might be one reason the State Board of Education does not set a curriculum for all

Community College Districts in Michigan

1. Alpena Community College
2. Bay De Noc Community College
3. Delta College
4. Glen Oaks Community College
5. Gogebic Community College
6. Grand Rapids Junior College
7. Henry Ford Community College
8. Highland Park Community College
9. Jackson Community College
10. Kalamazoo Valley Community College
11. Kellogg Community College
12. Kirtland Community College
13. Lake Michigan College
14. Lansing Community College
15. Macomb Community College
16. Mid Michigan Community College
17. Monroe County Community College
18. Montcalm Community College
19. Mott Community College
20. Muskegon Community College
21. North Central Michigan College
22. Northwestern Michigan College
23. Oakland Community College
24. St. Clair County Community College
25. Schoolcraft College
26. Southwestern Michigan College
27. Washtenaw Community College
28. Wayne County Community College
29. West Shore Community College

schools. Eventually this question will probably be resolved by the state courts.

The proportion of taxes raised in Michigan through the property tax is quite a bit higher than in most states and there are certainly those who want to change the system— perhaps by increasing the sales tax as one possibility. However, a sales tax system may not grow as fast as the current property tax system.

Private Schools

Besides its public schools, Michigan has about 1,000 private schools with somewhat more than 200,000 students. The majority of these are for grades K-8. Most private schools are run by religious groups with the Catholics having the largest number. Parents usually send their children to a private school because they want their education to have a religious focus, though this is not always the case. Some people believe private schools have better discipline and encourage their students to achieve more. In some areas private schools are expanding and taking students away from public schools.

Even though these schools are private, they are still under some control by the state government. Teachers in private schools are required to have the same qualifications as public school teachers and the curriculums are approved by the Superintendent of Public Instruction, at least in theory. Furthermore, all private school buildings must meet the same general construction and safety requirements as public schools.

In 1970 the state constitution was amended by a vote of the people— 1,416,838 for and 1,078,740 against— to prohibit any and all public aid to private schools, except in the area of transportation. However, the wording of this amendment was so strict that part of it was overturned in court as violating the United States constitutional provisions concerning the free exercise of religion. At any rate, private schools receive very little state help. Private school students do get some benefits at public expense such as driver education, counseling, or participation in athletic programs.

PRIVATE SCHOOL TUITION   PUBLIC SCHOOL TAXES

Parents of many private school students feel they are paying a double tax. They must pay property and state taxes to support public schools which they do not want to use and then pay high tuition directly to the private school for its operation. As long ago as 1972 Congress considered allowing tax benefits for those who go to private schools. Any change which would allow some shifting of tax support for private schools could have a significantly negative impact on public schools.

Home Schooling

Another area linked to private schools is home schooling. This concept is becoming more popular. Often home schooling follows plans like the Home Based Education Program of the Clonlara organization while other parents take a more independent approach.

There are parents who believe their children will have better training at home than by attending the public schools. It is hard to make scientific comparisons to know who is right. Some of the strongest supporters of home schooling feel the public schools no longer offer the moral leadership students should have or they believe discipline is too lax.

Michigan children between the ages of 6 and 16 must attend a qualified school and there are disagreements over whether all home schools qualify under the law.

For detailed information refer to *Michigan Compiled Laws* 340.11-389End (Public Act 1976 #451) West Publishing Company.

Questions

1. Explain why the school census is so important to school districts.

2. Explain some ways the State Board of Education controls local school districts. Would you personally favor more or less control from the state level?

3. Where is your local ISD office located and what services does it offer schools in your area? How much property tax millage goes to your ISD?

4. Do you live in a community college district? If you do, what is the name of this college and how much property tax millage does it get? If you don't, name the nearest community college.

5. Do you believe private schools and home schooling have a place in our society? Explain the benefits or drawbacks they offer.

12

LOCAL BUDGETING: TAXES & SPENDING

Chapter 12   Section 1

The Property Tax— the Focus of Many Complaints

Here are the key concepts in this section:

1. Property tax is the biggest source of money for local government and it pays for a majority of school expenses.

2. Basically property tax is a tax on the value of homes, buildings, business equipment, and land.

3. Calculating property tax is somewhat complicated and there is an involved set of procedures for appealing the values decided on for each piece of property.

4. Every property owner's tax bill usually changes each year and most often increases with the increasing value of real estate.

Almost all families get together for holidays, and to me they are always enlightening experiences. I like seeing the relatives again and eating all the delicious food, but most of all I enjoy the conversations. One special Thanksgiving comes to mind when family members were discussing property taxes which had increased for almost everyone, including me. My cousin Jim was especially irritated and critical of his tax increase. The discussion was heated and somewhat lengthy. I finally asked Jim how much were his usual taxes and how much was the increase.

His response was, "I usually pay $400, and the increase was $50."

He was surprised when I told him, "Jim, my increase in property taxes this year was the same as your entire bill — $400. For just this year my total property taxes are $2,000."

Cousin Jim was more perturbed than I was about a vastly smaller tax increase. No one wants his taxes raised. No matter how high or low our taxes are compared to others, we always think they are too high. Criticizing politicians and taxes is practically an established American pastime. Any tax increase is usually blamed on some recently passed controversial issue enacted into law by insensitive, if not stupid, politicians.

Michigan communities have different amounts of taxes for specific services. The services are generally the same— education, police, fire, roads— but the amounts and type of service may be different. Many communities spend very little on police protection, for example, but are much more concerned about good roads or athletic programs in the schools. The average 1990 property tax in Michigan was about 57 mills (which will mean more to you soon), but individual communities varied remarkably.

How local governments raise their needed revenues and spend them is the topic of this chapter.

THE PROPERTY TAX —*The property tax is the greatest source of revenue for local government*—

THE PROPERTY TAX PROCESS

Nearly all local governments receive some, and usually most, of their income from this source. It is one of the most stable taxes: revenues seldom go down and usually increase somewhat above inflation every year. Almost every homeowner, farmer, landowner, and business pays property taxes.

Local governments determine how much money they need and attempt to collect or *levy* that amount. The people in that unit of local government vote to accept or reject the amount requested. The amount of millage passed is then paid by property owners according to the value of their property.

Property in this sense is usually thought of as real estate— buildings, homes, farms, etc. In actual practice most individuals are not taxed on the contents of the buildings and other possessions they own, but businesses are. For example, a factory building would be taxed and so would the machinery in the building.

Property tax bills are sent out near the end of the year and many property owners will pay them before January 1st, but they are not actually due until February. A number of communities divide the property tax bills into two payments— one made in summer and one in the winter.

Assessments

All taxable property has an *assessed value* attached to it. Each property owner pays taxes on his or her taxable property according to the assessed value. The higher the property value, the higher the tax. By mandate of the state constitution all property is to be assessed at 50 percent of its *true market value*— the price for which it would sell to a willing buyer by a willing seller. The value is determined as of the previous December 31.

T. Deeter © HEP

There are several classifications of property. Some are residential; some are commercial; and other properties are agricultural or industrial. All properties are broken down into these classes.

The assessments are made by individuals trained in such assessing procedures. They are, not surprisingly, called *assessors*. The local assessors— in the township or city— determine the assessed value of each individual property and then add them together to arrive at the *assessment roll*— the total of all the property value in the municipality. The assessments must be completed each year by early March. Notices are sent out to property owners so they are aware of their assessments and to give them an opportunity to question them.

The Board of Review

Anyone who feels their assessment is not accurate may appeal and attempt to have the assessment lowered. (Seldom do property owners argue for their assessment to be raised. That means a higher tax!) Property owners can get information about the value of their type of land and the value of their neighbor's land from the registrar of deeds or mapping department in their county courthouse. This information may help to show the property was incorrectly assessed.

Such questions are brought to a locally appointed three member *board of review*. This group meets in March to hear complaints and to change any or all of the assessments. After making any changes, the board of review approves the assessment roll and it is sent to the *county department of equalization*.

State Tax Tribunal

Property owners who protested their assessment at the local level, but feel they did not get a satisfactory hearing from the board of review, may appeal to the state for another consideration. It can be argued that the local municipality is prejudiced in favor of raising assessments because it will receive more taxes. To provide a property owner one last opportunity to prove his or her allegation of an over assessment, the state allows an appeal to the *state tax tribunal*. The tribunal has the final word on such appeals, unless the matter is taken to court.

County Equalization

All property is not the same. Your home may be much different than your neighbor's. Just because a house down the street sold for an increased amount does not mean all property on the block can be valued at the higher amount. It is the county's responsibility to equalize values for all property. They will do a check of various properties that have recently sold to find out the market value. This is one of the best ways to decide a property's value. The job of the county equalization office is to try to make certain that similar properties are assessed at the same value throughout the county.

Since the assessment is supposed to be 50 percent of the market value, the property should sell for approximately twice the assessed value. In other words, if your house is determined by the local assessor to have a market value of $80,000, it should sell for about $80,000. The assessor will then assess it at $40,000, or 50 percent of its real value.

Each year the county department of equalization reviews the work of all assessors in the county. If the county's analysis concludes a local assessor did not assess fairly and, for example, assessed your house at only $30,000 when it should have been assessed at $50,000, the county may be forced to correct the situation. If it is determined the local assessor made similar mistakes throughout the city, township, or village, the county must assign an *assessment factor* for that class of property throughout the entire area. The assessment factor acts as a multiplier to bring all property in the class up to what the county feels the total value should be. It is the county's responsibility to guarantee the fairness of the assessment process and to assure equity between classes and local units of government. Each county's work is reviewed by the state, so counties must be accurate.

Not only are no two homes exactly alike but there are thousands of different people making assessments throughout the state. Usually each township has its own assessor and the same is true for each city. For many people assessing has become a full-time job!

Equalization is an important part of the property tax system because there are so many variables involved. If a large number of people felt the system was not fair it could break down.

State Tax Commission

The state also plays a role in the property tax process, even though it does not receive money directly from the property tax. Counties must provide the state tax commission with their property assessment figures by May of each year. The state does the same analysis for equity among counties that the counties did for local municipalities. The state tax commission verifies the final figure for every county's property assessment. This figure is called the *state equalized value* or the *SEV*.

SETTING THE TAX RATE

What's a Mill?

A *mill* is a value equal to 1/1,000th of a dollar. In other words, one mill represents a dollar of tax due on $1,000 worth of assessed value. It is com-

202

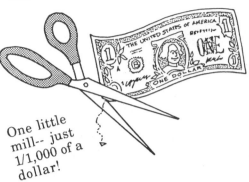

One little mill-- just 1/1,000 of a dollar!

monly used in calculating the rate of property taxation. If you own a home worth $2,000 and assessed at $1,000, which is very unlikely, and you had to pay a tax of 1 mill, which is also unlikely, your bill would be one dollar a year.

Figuring A Tax

There are two figures which must be multiplied together to get the final amount of tax that is owed. The first is the assessment and then there is the tax rate which is usually listed as a certain number of mills. The average property tax rate or millage paid in Michigan is about 57 mills (.057). A family living in a $50,000 home, assessed at $25,000, would be paying $1,425 a year in property taxes (.057 x $25,000). An individual living in a $100,000 home with this same average property tax rate would pay $2,850 (.057 x $50,000).

These are average figures; many communities have millage rates quite a bit higher and others have rates much lower. There are many people in expensive homes in communities with high millage rates who pay $8,000 and $10,000 or more a year in property taxes! The actual services provided by government seldom have to do with the value of a person's home. People in expensive homes get no more services (and often fewer) than someone living in a much less expensive home or in an apartment.

The value of property usually goes up every year and the millage rate in a community changes frequently, depending on voter approval of millage requests and other factors. So, the specific property tax an individual pays usually changes every year.

Deciding a Millage Level

The local unit of government must receive enough revenue from the property taxes to provide all the services expected of it. It may have other sources of income as well, but the property tax is usually the main source of money for all local governments.

Let's look at an example. A city needs an additional $1 million to pay for more police and fire protection. In order to have the needed money, it must look at the assessment roll of all property and decide how many mills will generate $1 million. This city has $2 billion worth of property and can collect taxes from $1 billion because of the 50 percent rule. It will be able to levy a tax of one mill annually and

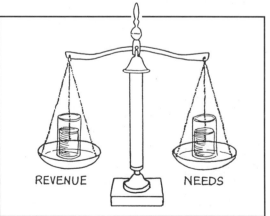

REVENUE   NEEDS

receive its needed $1 million of tax revenues because $1,000,000,000 of assessed value is multiplied by one mill (.001) to get this figure. What would be the increased tax for an individual in this city with a $100,000 home?

Then the city government will normally ask the voters to increase the millage on their property taxes by that amount. Though in some cases it may not need to get voter approval for the tax depending on the city charter and other circumstances.

Where Does the Money Go?

Regular townships are required to stay within one mill unless the voters approve a higher figure. Charter townships can have higher millages. Most other governments need much more than one mill to operate. Wherever you live, you have several different local governments, all of which need a certain number of mills of tax to do their business.

The school district is the largest consumer of property taxes. An average of 70 percent goes to schools. This revenue is used to pay the salaries of teachers, staff, buildings, books, athletics, and all the other programs for which a school is responsible. The school district may require 30, 40, or even more mills. There are also intermediate school districts (ISDs) as well as community colleges that are partially funded by property taxes .

Cities use the second largest share of property taxes. They receive an average of 14 to 15 percent of property taxes collected. Cities must have money to pay for their police forces, roads, sewers, fire protection, and perhaps to pay for airports, mass transit programs, etc.

Counties need considerable money to pay for their operations— courts, sheriff departments, health programs and more. Counties get about 11 percent of the total.

Townships are at the bottom of the list even though they collect a large share of the property taxes. They only get about three percent, which can be as low as a few dollars per resident to pay for any services provided.

Questions

1. Why are property tax revenues important to various local governments? Who gets most property tax money?

2. Write a short paragraph explaining how property taxes affect homeowners, renters, farmers, and businesses.

3. What is the difference between assessed value and market value of property?

4. What is the job of the office of county equalization? How does it go about its work and why does it do it?

(Questions continued)

5. If your home is worth $60,000 and you live in a district with a 50 mill property tax, what is your annual property tax bill? Explain how you arrived at your answer. When is this tax usually due?

Chapter 12   Section 2

Ways Property Taxes Are Limited
&
Other Means Used by Local Government to Raise Money

Here are the key concepts in this section:

1. In 1978 Michigan voters amended the state constitution with the Headlee amendment to slow down the rapid growth in property taxes and to give the people a greater voice in property tax increases. In 1992 and 1993 voters again tried to slow the growth in property taxes through ballot proposals named "A". The 1992 Proposal A passed. It holds increases to 5 percent or the rate of inflation, whichever is less. The 1993 Proposal A was more complex and included an increase in the state sales tax to 6 percent. It did not pass.

2. Compared with other states, Michigan has higher taxes on homes and other residential property. So, over the years it has passed several laws designed to help those who have extreme difficulty in paying their property taxes.

3. The purpose of these laws is to allow individuals to remain in their homes or on their farms regardless of their property tax bill; otherwise, they might need to move to a less valuable piece of property.

4. A number of Michigan cities have a city income tax paid by those who live in the city or work there.

PROPERTY TAX LIMITATIONS

The property tax is viewed by some as unfair for a variety of reasons. In fact, very few people— elected or otherwise— like the property tax, to hear them talk. School boards are often upset with the property tax system when real estate values are only rising slowly. But then property owners are upset when the values are rising rapidly. Frequently the rate of property tax increases in Michigan are above the rate of inflation and this has caused an outcry for change. Politicians hear these complaints and are attempting to do something, and in time the property tax system may be altered somewhat.

When the state income tax was passed many years ago, the legislature added a "circuit breaker" to make the property tax more tolerable. The circuit breaker set a maximum property tax amount based on income. Also, the Headlee Amendment provides limitations on the amount of the tax.

The Headlee Amendment— *A change made in Michigan's constitution to place certain limits on property taxes, primarily to protect homeowners—*

The tax limitation movement in Michigan has its origins in the "Proposition 13" issue in California. "Proposition 13" was a direct result of huge property tax increases in that state during the inflationary mid-1970s. When the proposition passed, it forced governments to decrease property taxes throughout the state.

In Michigan a similar movement resulted in the Headlee Amendment. It not only limits state government spending but also sets the maximum level of property taxes. The Headlee Amendment to the state constitution requires the following:

HEADLEE AMENDMENT

MUST VOTE FIRST

1. No new local taxes may be levied without a vote of the people, nor can any existing local government tax be increased without a vote.

2. Local property tax revenue is limited and it cannot be increased, on the average, any faster than the national rate of inflation. This does not include new construction.

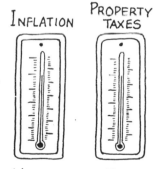

INFLATION   PROPERTY TAXES

HEADLEE'S IDEA

There is also a property tax limit for the schools and county government of 50 mills in total. This does not include other taxing units.

In 1991 a Macomb county commissioner, backed by an opinion from the Macomb county prosecutor, urged the county take legal action against the state concerning the Headlee Amendment. The basis of this action is the belief the state legislature did not follow the intent of the amendment when it wrote the regulations used to decide when property taxes can be increased. As the regulations are now written small increases can take place without voter approval. Richard Headlee himself agrees the legislature did not follow the intent of his amendment. For more information see "Property Tax Hikes Called Unconstitutional." *Michigan Assessor* (April 1991): pages 20-21.

Farmland and Open Space Preservation Act— *A law to help farmers by preventing them from being forced out of business due to increasing property taxes on their land—*

Another criticism that caused changes in the property tax law has to do with agricultural land. Farmers, particularly those near growing residential areas, were being driven out of farming because their land was rapidly increasing in value. Many were forced to sell land to developers because they could not afford more property taxes. Most farmland is worth $500 to $1000 per acre, but a developer might be willing to pay much more knowing he may get $30,000 to $50,000 for each lot in a new subdivision. This increase in the market value of the land causes property taxes to increase, sometimes substantially. To keep farmers from going out of business, the legislature passed the *Farmland and Open Space Preservation Act* which protects farmers and those owning "natural land" from high property tax assessments. Not only are the individual owners protected, but the community benefits by the land being kept in its natural state.

People wishing this protection may apply at their local assessor's office or at the Michigan Office of Land Use. Several restrictions must be agreed to, such as not selling any of the land for a certain number of years. It cannot be divided and only part of the land sold. Should any of the land be sold, all the exempted taxes must be paid. Because of such restrictions, people considering this option should carefully consider how they may want to use the land in the future. Nonetheless, many farmers, even those not so near development, have taken advantage of this legislation.

Other Reforms— Homestead Property Tax Credit— *A law designed to help those who have high property tax bills and a low income—*

Several other reforms have been passed to protect various individuals. We mentioned the Homestead Property Tax Credit in chapter 7 and explained how it operates like a circuit breaker to protect those whose incomes are low relative to their property taxes. This is intended especially for the poor and the elderly who may live in houses or communities where property taxes are quite high, yet their low incomes make paying these taxes a heavy burden. They could sell their houses, of course, and move into less expensive dwellings, but that doesn't seem fair to most of us.

This credit allows a deduction for property taxes on an individual's state income tax. About half the states have a similar arrangement. The Homestead

Property Tax Credit has helped ease the burden on those with low incomes and made both the property tax and the state income tax fairer.

A similar credit is also available to the deaf, blind, disabled, and some others. As of this printing, Michigan's property tax credits are the most liberal of all such programs in the nation. Approximately 1.5 million households, or roughly half the households in the state, receive some form of credit related to property tax.

This is how the Homestead Property Tax Credit works. If the property tax on an individual's principal residence exceeds 3.5 percent of household income, the state pays 60 percent of the excess back to the taxpayer as a credit. The maximum amount of the credit is $1,200. In the two examples below, both families live in the same neighborhood and have houses with the same assessed value.

Family #1
Household income $25,000
Property tax bill $2,500
Credit on income tax $975

Family #2
Household income $15,000
Property tax bill $2,500
Credit on income tax $1,185

[PROPERTY TAX – (INCOME x .035)] x .60 = Homestead Property Tax Credit
($1,200 maximum)

These credits were calculated like this: 3.5 percent of $25,000 is $875 and that figure from $2,500 is $1,625. Sixty percent of that figure is their tax credit of $975. If their income is only $15,000, they will receive a credit of $1,185.

The state believes that renters also pay property tax in an indirect way because the landlord eventually charges them more to cover property tax owed by the landlord. With this in mind, renters substitute 17 percent of their rent instead of property tax and use the same formula. The assumption, a very loose one, is that 17 percent of their rent is used by the landlord to pay property taxes.

LOCAL INCOME TAXES AND USER FEES

CITY INCOME TAX

The state passed the Uniform City Income Tax law in 1964 allowing cities to levy income taxes if approved by a vote of the people. This is done to either provide property tax relief or to generate new revenues. Since an income tax is based on ability to pay, this is sometimes a more popular way to increase revenue.

There are several requirements regarding amounts of taxes, but tax rates are the same, generally one percent. However the state law does allow exceptions and three are Saginaw, Highland Park and Detroit where the rates are higher. Since people who only work in the city but do not live there don't receive as many benefits from city government as resident, their city income rate is lower.

Examples of some Michigan cities with income taxes and their tax rates are shown below:

	CITY RESIDENT	CORPORATION	NONRESIDENT WORKING IN CITY
Detroit	3.0	2.0	1.5
Highland Park	2.0	2.0	1.0
Saginaw	1.5	1.5	0.75
Albion	1.0	1.0	0.5
Battle Creek	1.0	1.0	0.5
Big Rapids	1.0	1.0	0.5
Flint	1.0	1.0	0.5
Grand Rapids	1.0	1.0	0.5
Grayling	1.0	1.0	0.5
Hamtramck	1.0	1.0	0.5
Hudson	1.0	1.0	0.5
Jackson	1.0	1.0	0.5
Lansing	1.0	1.0	0.5
Lapeer	1.0	1.0	0.5
Muskegon Heights	1.0	1.0	0.5
Pontiac	1.0	1.0	0.5
Port Huron	1.0	1.0	0.5
Portland	1.0	1.0	0.5
Springfield	1.0	1.0	0.5
Walker	1.0	1.0	0.5

All of these cities collect a total of about $400,000,000 with over half the amount going to Detroit.

The Detroit public schools are also allowed to have an income tax of up to one percent with certain restrictions.

USER FEES

Cities and other units of government provide certain services to their residents and charge them according to the amount used. Common examples are water, sewer, electricity, and garbage disposal. Not all cities provide each of these. Only a few cities generate their own electricity. Residents feel the only fair way to pay for these types of services is based on the amount used. People use city water in widely varying amounts. Some people use the water to fill swimming pools; some have large families, and others water two acres of lawn. The charges for these services are known as user fees. Other user fees may be charged for visiting parks and zoos, tree trimming, etc. In Michigan local governments receive about 18 to 20 percent of their revenue from user fees and the trend is increasing due to the reluctance of voters to increase taxes to pay for many services.

As mentioned in chapter 7, some user fees go to the state government. Examples in this area are vehicle registration, hunting and fishing licenses, etc.

SPECIAL ASSESSMENTS

Local governments also may charge property owners a *special assessment*. This is owed to the government for a special service to improve the property. Common examples are for the construction of sidewalks, curbs, gutters, paving streets, and city water and sewer connections done by the city. Usually these charges are calculated on the number of feet installed or the number of feet a lot has on the street. Many people do not realize the city does not normally pay the complete cost for such services and they may be surprised by a special assessment bill. But this type of fee does make sense because it benefits the property owner, probably making the property more valuable.

STATE-GENERATED FUNDS

A huge portion of state funds goes to local governments. The Headlee Amendment requires the state not reduce the portion of its budget that is spent for local needs. This portion is approximately 42 percent, excluding federal aid to the state.

STATE REVENUE SHARING

The state shares some of its funds with local governments in much the same way the federal government shares with state and local governments. Both began this generosity during the inflationary 1970s when income taxes were bringing in additional revenues. Michigan started sharing revenue with local governments in 1971. The amounts involved change based on many factors, as does the state's enthusiasm for providing these funds to local governments.

State money that is used to provide revenue-sharing include the sales tax and the income tax. Thirty five percent of state income tax revenue is given to the counties and divided according to their populations.

HIGHWAYS   SCHOOLS   SOCIAL SERVICES

TRANSPORTATION FUNDS

The state receives considerable income from various transportation taxes—gasoline tax, vehicle registration, and others. Most of these revenues are put in the state transportation fund but it does find its way to help local governments. Ten percent of the fund is used for local mass transit programs, about 40 percent for state roads, another 40 percent for county road commissions, and 20 percent goes to cities and villages for their road needs. The amount each area receives is based on such factors as local road mileage, population, and weight taxes paid by tractor-trailers in a particular area.

STATE AID TO EDUCATION

Money spent on education in Michigan comes from several sources. Locally, as we mentioned earlier, much money is received through property taxes. This is a high percentage compared to other places— only 5 states get a greater percentage of school funding from local sources! As for the state, a portion of the taxes from cigarettes and liquor, nearly all "profits" from the lottery, and 60 percent of sales tax collected, plus funds from other sources allocated to the general fund are all used for education.

Even though huge sums of money go to the school districts from property taxes, money provided by the state is very important. Over time the percentage coming from the state varies. In the 1960s it was about 50 percent but currently it runs between 30-40 percent.

One of the purposes behind this state aid to schools is to even out the amount of money available between rich districts and poorer ones. Some wealthy districts have nearly ten times as much property tax base per student as the poorest districts! The state government tries to see that each district gets a minimum amount per student from a combination of property taxes and state aid. Currently this is in the neighborhood of $3,000 for most districts. About 25 percent of Michigan's school districts are well enough off to not receive any aid from the state. Many of these districts have such large property tax bases that the state will probably never be able to see that students in poor districts receive as much money as those in wealthy districts.

Education funds from the state generally fall into two categories— state aid and grants. Most money is provided to schools through the *school aid formula*— about two-thirds of the total. This is a formula which determines how much state aid school districts will receive. It includes such factors as the number of students in grades K-12, the local property tax base, millage rate, and other similar considerations.

The state also includes what it calls *categorical grants* which is state money set aside for special purposes, such as transportation of students, driver education, and bilingual education.

FEDERAL MONEY

Federal assistance to state governments (described in Chapter 7) amounts to about $100 billion a year. Some of that money finds its way into local treasuries via the state, but local governments also receive their own aid directly from the federal government. Washington does this with two major types of assistance— grants in aid and block grants.

Nearly all local governments receive some kind of federal aid. School districts receive money for lunch programs and many other items. General purpose governments, like counties and cities, receive assistance for law enforcement programs, mass transit, community development, alcohol and drug abuse, maternal and child care, social services, and job training.

Some of these dollars go through the state government first and are thus called "pass through" monies, but other programs are directly tied to Washington. Funds may come into local units based on such factors as population and need, but grant applications are often required for other federal programs.

FROM OUR FEDERAL GOVERNMENT

It amounts to an infusion of billions of dollars into the local government and is a way for Washington to both assist them and control their activities.

Questions

1. Why does Michigan have a number of laws to limit property taxes or to help those who might have trouble paying these tax bills?

2. Write a brief explanation for each of the following: The Headlee Amendment, Farmland and Open Space Preservation Act, Homestead Property Tax Credit.

3. Explain Michigan's city income tax system. What is the normal tax rate? Why are there different rates for people who live in these cities and those who work there but live elsewhere?

4. Give two examples of user fees collected by local government in Michigan.

5. In this example your home is on an unpaved street in a small town. The city decides to improve the area and paves the street, and puts in a sidewalk and curb. Will you have to pay for part of this work and if you do, what is this type of charge called?

6. Find out how much money is spent to educate each student per year in your school district.

7. What is your opinion about how the cost of Michigan schools should be paid? Is it right or wrong that some school districts collect much more property tax per student than others? Should the state government guarantee an equal amount of money for all students in Michigan regardless of where they live?

13

VOTING & ELECTIONS IN MICHIGAN

Chapter 13   Section 1

Becoming and Remaining a Voter

Here are the key concepts in this section:

1. If you don't vote you are letting someone else decide important issues which affect you!

2. State and local government does much to encourage people to register to vote. The registration process is NOT meant to stop people from voting but you must register at least 30 days ahead of time.

3. You must change your registration each time you move, even if it is within the same city.

4. Michigan's voter registration procedure is considered permanent, but if you do not vote for a long time— four years or more— you can lose your registration status.

　　The most direct way to participate in your state's political system is by voting. Wherever you live in Michigan you are in a state representative's district and a state senator's district. If eligible, you may vote for each of these and many other officials, not to mention the important issues which are placed on the ballot. These issues include tax increases and limitations, constitutional amendments, questions about building new prisons, and whether or not a public official should be recalled, to name only a few.

　　Although voting is an important privilege, many Americans fail to exercise it. Even in elections for president only about 55 percent bother to vote. In state and local elections lower voter turnout is common— often under 40 percent. Much of the time the percentage for young people is even lower. In one recent election only 16.6 percent of those between the ages of 18-24 voted!

　　What happens when you do not vote? The most important consequence is you allow someone else to say how government should be run. You allow those who do vote to have an even bigger say in what happens. If you don't bother to vote, you really should not expect to be able to complain about the outcome!

Michigan Voter Qualifications

Michigan has always been quite liberal in its qualifications for voting. Its laws encourage voter activity. The first constitution even allowed non-citizens to vote if they had resided in Michigan for over one year. Michigan women were allowed to vote in 1918-- two years ahead of the 19th amendment. The state has never used poll taxes or literacy tests.

Becoming a voter in Michigan is not hard. If you are an American citizen, have lived in Michigan and your precinct for 30 days by the time of the election, and will be at least 18 years of age by the next election, you may register to vote.

It is important to realize you must register at least 30 days before the actual election. If the election is on November 4, for example, and your 18th birthday is October 25, don't wait until your birthday to register. You will not be meeting the 30-day requirement and you won't be able to vote in the next election. An individual moving into Michigan may register and vote in the next election, assuming the qualifications are met and the election is at least 30 days away.

QUALIFICATIONS FOR VOTING

1. A citizen of the state and nation
2. Eighteen years of age by election
3. Lived in your community 30 days
4. Registered at least 30 days
   before next election

Where Do You Live ?

In these modern times it can be hard to tell where some people have their official residence. Normally this means the place where a person sleeps and keeps personal belongings— the place where they spend the greatest part of their time. The confusion results because some people have summer cottages or spend several months each year in Florida, etc. College students and members of the armed forces may choose to keep their official residence in their hometowns, or they can change it to where they actually live— but they can't be registered in both places.

Registering To Vote

Registration usually takes place at the local city or township clerk's office during regular business hours. Registration can also take place in any of the Secretary of State offices throughout the state. It involves filling out a short form or two, identifying yourself, your date of birth and current address, and swearing that "the information you have given is accurate to the best of your knowledge and belief."

Within a few weeks you will receive a voter's identification card that should be brought with you to your voting place. It contains identification information and indicates where you vote in your *precinct* (the smallest voting unit, usually containing 700-1000 adults).

Remember those who live in villages face the extra challenge of registering in two places— once with the village clerk for village elections and once with the township clerk for all other elections.

One of the excuses sometimes given for the failure of people to vote is that registration is too bothersome. It is possible a few clerks don't go out of their way to provide convenient registration, but this is the exception rather than the rule.

Some clerks take on the task of registering voters with a passion. Meridian Township Clerk Virginia White is such a person. It is quite difficult to be missed by her or her deputy registrars. She announces registration deadlines in the newspapers and on cable television. She keeps the office open for last minute registrants on the weekend and late in the evening as the 30-day requirement approaches.

She attempts to get young people in the high schools registered as they reach 18 by deputizing high school government teachers or counselors who are then empowered to register students. Occasionally, she and other clerks will deputize responsible individuals who go to shopping centers and set up registration booths, or go door to door asking if residents have registered. Many clerks who have college campuses in their jurisdictions register students to vote at the same time students are registering for classes, especially in the fall. With dedicated officials like Mrs. White doing all this work to register voters, how can someone say it is too much trouble to register?

Once people are registered to vote, they do not have to register again unless they move or stop voting for four years. (In some larger cities the limit is two years.)

The good news is Michigan outranks all other states in having the largest percentage of citizens registered to vote, but the bad news is voter turnout is still a problem.

Illegal Practices

It is illegal to be registered in more than one location. However, this often happens, usually by mistake, when a person moves. A voter registering in a new location is usually asked to fill out a form cancelling the old registration. This is then sent to the clerk in the previous location. It helps in correcting the problem of double registration.

The real difficulty comes when voters attempt to vote more than once. This is not a mistake and not forgivable. It is also very rare. Voting more than once, or voting in another district, is a felony. If it involves a national election, it also violates federal law. The reason we have a registration process is to eliminate the possibility for an unscrupulous person to vote more than once. Of course if someone is registered in more than one place, it is still conceivable to vote once in each location— though it is illegal.

Other examples of illegal activities are campaigning within a certain distance of the polling place during the time of the election, paying people to vote, threatening voters, lying about your qualifications to vote, trying to change the total on a voting machine, etc.

Voting After You Move (within the state)

To assist voters who have recently moved, certain allowances are made. The goal of voter registration is not to make it difficult to vote, but rather to provide assurances of honesty and accuracy in elections. If a person moves within the same community, voting is allowed in the previous *polling place* until the new voter registration takes effect. If a person moves to another community within Michigan, the voter may vote in the previous polling location in any election held within a 60-day period after the move. *(The polling place is the building where you vote— often a school or township office. Poll comes from an old Dutch word meaning head. So polling came to mean a head count and the polling place where the head count was made.)*

Questions

1. List the qualifications to vote in Michigan. List three excuses you have heard why people do not take the time to register or to vote.

2. If you move within Michigan, do you need to change your voter registration?

3. If you live in a city where do you go to register to vote? If you live in the country where would you register? Is there any other place to register you have not yet mentioned?

4. Ellen registered to vote through the encouragement of her high school government teacher. Many years passed and it wasn't until her family was nearly grown that she felt she had time to study the issues and actually vote. If Ellen expects to vote in the next election what does she need to check?

5. What illegal practice might an unscrupulous person try if he or she was registered in two or more places at the same time?

6. If you move from Benton Harbor to Harbor Springs, can you vote in Benton Harbor 50 days later since you had to spend election day there to pack your belongings for the mover?

Chapter 13   Section 2

Placing Your Vote

Here are the key concepts in this section:

1. The honesty and accuracy of voting procedures have improved tremendously over the years.

2. The hours voting places are open is the same throughout the state and for all elections. Elections are held on standard dates time after time.

3. There are several methods used to count votes. These include the voting machine, punch card ballots, and written paper ballots. In the future there may be new methods using computers or the telephone.

4. If you cannot get to your voting place on election day, special ballots are available from your city, township, or village clerk.

VOTING PROCEDURES— HOW IT WORKS

A Bit of History

When voting took place in the early years of our nation's history, it was often done verbally. Michigan's first American election was held in the winter of 1798. It was quite different than elections by modern standards. To begin with, it was held in a Detroit tavern. Each voter had to publicly announce his choice. James May ran against Solomon Sibley for territorial representative. Mr. May protested because Sibley gave out free drinks to voters and had soldiers with clubs threaten anyone who didn't vote for him! The people in far away places like Mackinac Island didn't even get a chance to vote at all!

Obviously this wasn't the most appropriate way to run an election. Improved procedures soon followed, including the paper ballot. At first, providing paper ballots was not an official function of the government. It was more commonly a convenience offered by political parties who were encouraging voters to support their candidates. Some political parties furnished ballots with all the names of the party's candidates on it. Competition being what it is in politics, some parties even furnished colored paper ballots so they could see who was voting the "right" way.

There was little privacy in voting at that time and ballots were not efficiently organized. This all changed when the *Australian ballot* was introduced to the United States.

The Australian ballot is a single secret ballot containing the names of all candidates from all the political parties represented. It is provided to voters at their polling places at government expense. It was first used in 1886 in Australia and caught on in the U.S. within a few years.

When to Vote

The hours to vote are always the same. The polls open at 7a.m. and close at 8 p.m. Anyone standing in line at 8 p.m. is allowed to vote.

Different elections are held on various dates but they are consistent from election to election.

VOTING HOURS

Primaries (for state officials)— First Tuesday after the first Monday in August of even numbered years (1994, 1996, 1998, etc.). Many nonpartisan primaries occur on the same date in odd-numbered years.

General Elections— First Tuesday after the first Monday in November of even-numbered years (1994, 1996, 1998, etc.) The regular fall general election is far and away the most popular election.

In the years the President is elected the following state officials are voted on: sometimes one U.S. senator (6 year terms), all U.S. representatives, all state representatives, some judges and justices for state courts, two members of the state board of education, two members for the governing boards of M.S.U., U of M, and Wayne State, (public universities), county and township officers and commissioners, etc.

In the non-Presidential years these officials are elected: governor and lieutenant governor, attorney general, secretary of state, all state senators and all state representatives, also sometimes one U.S. Senator (6 year terms), all U.S. representatives and county commissioners, some judges and justices for state courts, two members of the state board of education, and two members of the governing boards of M.S.U., U. of M., and Wayne State, (public universities), etc.

City Elections (mostly nonpartisan elections)— First Tuesday after the first Monday in November of odd-numbered years (1993, 1995, 1997), with a few exceptions. At this time most city officials are voted on as well as any city-wide issues. Some cities hold these elections in June. Some cities hold primary elections in September.

School Board Elections— Generally held every year in June. This also includes millage and bond proposals. Special elections can be used for millage and bonds too, especially when they do not pass on the first attempt.

Village Elections— March, with primaries in February, if necessary.

Special Elections— The voters can call for special elections almost anytime for many public policy questions. This includes recall elections, elections to fill vacancies, city charter questions, and many other issues.

All elections are announced ahead of time, usually in local newspapers or on the radio.

Going to the Polls (the place where you vote)

What happens when you go to vote? First you need to know where you should vote. This is often a school or township hall which is usually within a few miles of your residence. When you enter the polling place one of the things you will see is a sample ballot which looks just like the ballot in the voting booth. By looking over this ballot ahead of time you can be sure you understand the layout and wording before you make your selections. After voting, nothing can be worse than to discover you actually voted yes for a proposal or person you really wanted to vote against!

You will also see some tables and voting officials or clerks. On these tables are *poll books* which contain information about each voter. Usually you will be asked to fill out a slip of paper giving your name, address, and signature. The voting officials compare this information to what is in their books so they are certain you are voting in the correct precinct. After giving the paper to the clerks, you wait for a paper ballot or your turn in the voting machine.

If there is anything you do not understand, be sure to ask these people. They are there to assist you. If you are blind or disabled the clerks will help you vote. What happens if you want to vote but are out of town or sick when the election is held? In that case read about absentee voting below.

Absentee Voting

It is occasionally difficult or impossible for voters to get to their voting places. Voters who are handicapped, elderly (over 60 years of age), or ill may find it difficult to vote on election day. Also, voters who work outside their voting precinct or who expect to be absent from the precinct on election day are eligible for an absentee ballot. In addition, voters who are unable to go to the polls because of religious beliefs or because they are in jail awaiting arraignment or trial can get an absentee ballot (Convicted persons are not allowed to use absentee ballots.)

To accommodate all potential voters, election officials provide the opportunity to vote by *absentee ballot*. This is a ballot provided prior to the election day. If any of the above criteria are met, the voter need only contact the clerk's office and ask for an application for an absentee ballot. The application is filled out and returned. Several days before the election, the voter is sent a packet of materials including the ballot, which is completed and returned, usually by mail, before the closing of the polls on election day.

More and more voters are choosing to vote by absentee ballot. Some clerks even encourage it because it means fewer people at the polls on election day. That means shorter waiting lines and fewer complaints.

Marking Paper Ballots

Anyone using a paper ballot, which may include an absentee ballot, should take special care to be sure it is marked correctly. It is possible to mark a ballot so that it cannot be counted. If the ballot asks the voter to us an "X" to mark each selection then an "X" must be used. A check mark ($\sqrt{}$) or writing the word "yes" will not count.

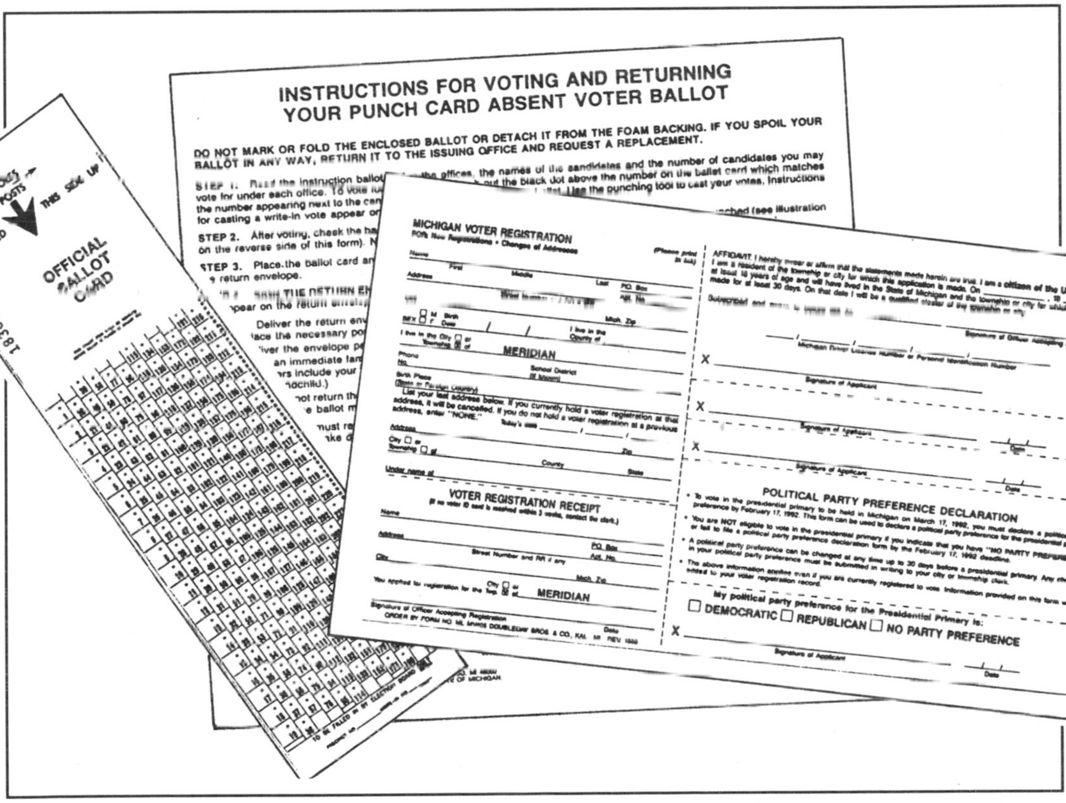

This picture shows samples of voting materials. On the left is a computer punch card which is used instead of a voting machine in many polling places. Behind it are instructions for absentee voters and in the forground is a application for voter registration which now includes a section on political party preference.

Questions

1. List and explain all of the incorrect facts in the following statement. "It was November 23, 1993 (the 4th Tuesday of the month). Jackson wanted to visit the polls early so he could vote for governor before he went to work. He reached the voting place at fifteen minutes to seven (a.m.) and walked directly to a voting machine and pulled the level to select the Democratic ticket. He was glad Michigan allowed split ticket voting because he felt the Republican nominee was the better candidate, since she was a woman."

2. Would someone in Michigan ever vote for a United States Senator, city mayor, and a school millage issue at the same time? Explain your reasoning.

3. List three criteria which would allow a Michigan citizen to receive an absentee ballot.

Chapter 13   Section 3

Who Runs the Elections?

Here are the key concepts in this section:

1. Many people are required to put a great deal of work into operating the state's elections.

2. The secretary of state oversees elections throughout the state and enforces the election laws.

3. County, city, village, and township clerks and secretaries of local school boards are responsible for conducting elections held within their jurisdictions.

4. Each polling place has a group of election inspectors working during the voting hours.

5. The board of canvassers certifies all election results.

CONDUCTING ELECTIONS

Voting may only take just a few minutes but for those involved in the conducting of elections it takes many months of work before and after election day.

The Secretary of State

The secretary of state oversees elections throughout the state. That doesn't mean the office is responsible for every election in Michigan. It means the secretary of state's office enforces the election laws, provides instructions and training for local election officials, and issues many of the forms candidates must use. All statewide ballot issues are handled by this office. It also keeps records of nominating petitions and various reports turned in by candidates and officeholders.

Local Clerks

County, city, village, and township clerks and secretaries of local school boards are responsible for conducting elections held within their jurisdictions. City and township election commissions, of which the clerk is the chair, devise the voting districts, or precincts. They aim to keep them reasonably sized allowing for short lines at the voting places. They select voting sites that are centrally located and accessible. They decide what machinery will be used by voters when casting their ballots: computerized ballots, paper ballots, or voting machines. Many dates are set by law for certain elections and it is the responsibility of the local clerks to be sure the elections run smoothly on those dates. The county election commissions establish dates for other elections as required.

Election Inspectors

Several individuals and groups assist with the election process. One such group is the *election inspectors*. These are the workers required at each polling place.

ELECTION INSPECTORS

They stay in the voting location all election day; they may not leave until the ballots have been safely transferred to another location. They make sure the equipment is all working properly, get all the forms and files of registered voters organized, and open the polls promptly at 7 a.m. It is their responsibility to assure that only properly registered voters vote and they see that ballots are placed securely in the ballot box. If any voter needs assistance, they provide help according to strictly enforced rules. Each group of election inspectors has a Republican and a Democrat to assure neither party receives favored treatment. They make sure the polls are closed promptly at 8 p.m. and that anyone standing in line at that time is allowed to vote. They have a very important responsibility in providing the honesty and integrity the election process requires for a democracy to survive. Many other governments throughout the world have faltered in this critical area.

Board of Canvassers

After the vote is complete, paper ballots and machine voting results are tabulated at the voting place. Punch card ballots are taken, often under police guard, to the location where the cards are run through the computer and counted. This may be a computer center or the county clerk's office. The votes are then totalled and announced to the public. They are still unofficial, however. Another group of individuals, called the *board of canvassers*, must first acknowledge, or certify, the accuracy of the vote.

The board of canvassers is a four-member group equally divided between the two major parties. They review the election results and the conduct of the election. Anyone concerned about the election process brings that concern to them. Each governmental unit responsible for elections has its own board of canvassers, except in cases where the township or city has fewer than five precincts. In this case, the county board of canvassers does the work. Questions about elections of state officials are brought to the state board of canvassers.

Most of the work of the local clerks and election inspectors is carefully done and few questions of impropriety ever arise. Typically issues brought to the boards of canvassers have to do with close votes or, occasionally, tie votes. If a candidate has lost an election by a very close margin, he or she may ask for a recount. The candidate making the request pays a

token fee of ten dollars per precinct counted. This fee does not cover costs, but it discourages frivolous recounts. Few results change with recounts, but they probably assure losing candidates they really did all they could to win. If a vote ends in a tie, the matter is settled by drawing pieces of paper at the county clerk's office. One says "elected." The other says "not elected."

Questions

1. If you live in a city, who is directly responsible for conducting all elections in your jurisdiction?

2. Who are the men and women who open the polls at 7 a.m. and stay there all day until the ballots have been collected after 8 p.m.?

3. What is the name of the four-member group which is responsible for reviewing election results and certifying them?

4. What procedure is used if there is a tie vote after a recount and who is in charge of carrying it out?

Chapter 13   Section 4

Voting Patterns in Michigan

Here are the key concepts in this section:

1. Once Michigan was a stronghold of the Republican party.

2. Today Michigan has more Democrats than Republicans but still the state has had several Republican governors recently.

3. Michigan has some interesting voting patterns. Most of the Democrats are concentrated in the large cities, though the western Upper Peninsula also favors that party.

4. Michigan voters often divide or split their ticket and vote for some Republicans and some Democrats.

VOTING PATTERNS

Republicans and Democrats
Today studies show Michigan has more Democrats than Republicans. But this was not always true. In July, 1854 the Republican Party had its beginnings at a large meeting in Jackson. Consequently Michigan was a strong Republican state for many years. Starting in 1855 it had Republican governors for the next 78 years except for three terms! In many ways Michigan is still solidly Republican. This is especially evident if you look at a map showing the majority party by township. A large number of townships vote Republican, but while Republicans make a big show geographically they lose out on a population basis. This is true because so much of the state's population lives in a small area.

Democrats are concentrated in the same areas as the state's population in general. The counties of Wayne, Oakland and Macomb containing about 43 percent of the total population, also have the largest number of Democrats. Obviously the political desires from these three Detroit metro counties have a major impact on what happens in Michigan!

Within Michigan, the city of Detroit is solidly Democratic, as are many of Michigan's larger urban areas, as is the Upper Peninsula, especially the western part.

Democrats gained in popularity during the troubled times of the Great Depression during the 1930s. The strong labor union movement in Michigan's auto industry helped promote the Democrats.

Surveys indicate business people and employers tend to vote Republican, while employees and union members vote mostly Democratic. People who are liberal vote Democratic, as do minority groups, especially blacks, while people who are conservative vote Republican. Older voters have tended to vote Republican, but recently this group has been voting more Democratic.

... But Elections Are Competitive

In spite of the fact that Michigan has a majority of Democrats, it has had several Republican governors in recent years. They include George Romney (1963-1969), William Milliken (1969-1982) and John Engler (1990 -). William Milliken served longer than any other governor to date. The Democrats have had their share as well. Especially well-known was G. Mennen Williams (1949-1960) who was elected more times than any other governor, but the terms were only two years long then. Many Michigan voters *split their ticket* and vote for both Republicans and Democrats. Ticket splitting and independent voting— preferring neither party – allow members of either party to win elections even though there is an overall Democratic majority.

Michigan's most successful governors seemed to owe their success to being flexible and building friendships with members of both parties.

Straight Party Voting

Some people tend to vote a straight party ticket; they either vote for all the Democrats or all the Republicans on the ballot. It is usually easy to do this. In order to cast a straight party vote, just one lever in the voting booth must be pulled. This one vote selects all the candidates on the ballot from the favored party. Cynics suggest many vote a straight party ticket because it is much easier. More likely, though, a party member feels that *any* candidate from his or her political party is much better than the *very best* candidate from the competing political party. It usually makes sense for voters, who identify themselves with a political party, to support all of that party's candidates.

Split Ticket Voters

However, fewer voters are now voting a straight party ticket in general elections. More voters split their ticket voting for candidates of both political parties. This is one reason Michigan, now with a majority of Democrats, has had Republican governors serve for so many years. It sounds thoughtful to say "I don't vote a straight party ticket, I vote for the best candidate."

T. Deeter © HEP

Nonpartisan Voting

After the *partisan* section of the ballot in general elections there is a *non-partisan* section which includes all the candidates running for offices that do not require party affiliation. *(Partisan means to be affiliated with one political party or another.)* In Michigan, this includes judges and many candidates for city and village positions. Most city elections are entirely non-partisan.

Questions

1. Give a reason why Michigan was so strongly Republican in the late 1800s and early 1900s. Give a reason why the Democrats became a major political force in Michigan during the 1930s and after.

2. Explain how it is possible for Michigan to have a majority of voters preferring the Democratic party and yet the state has had several Republican governors in recent years.

3. Tell where the state's Democratic and Republican voters are concentrated.

14

POLITICAL PARTIES, NOMINATIONS & PRIMARIES

Chapter 14   Section 1

How Political Parties Affect Government

Here are the key concepts in this section:

1. Sometimes sharp divisions develop between the two major parties and this can affect what happens in government and how it is accomplished or not accomplished.

2. Even though political parties are a collection of individuals, the members usually pull together and try to accomplish the same goals.

3. The underlying goal of any political party is to control enough of government to achieve its policies. In order to do this it must get its nominees elected to office and much of the party's time and energy go into these efforts.

4. Government is strengthened by having at least two political parties as they continually watch what the other is doing and report what they see to the public. Each serves as a watchdog over any poor practices which may take place.

5. The Democrats and Republicans are Michigan's two major parties but other parties play an important role from time to time.

Political Parties in Michigan

Political parties are a great influence in defining what happens at most levels of government. In recent years there have been many times when the governor's office and the legislature were controlled by different parties. Look at some examples.

Governor William G. Milliken "retired" from office in 1982 after serving for a record 14 years as the most important political figure in Michigan. He appointed hundreds of individuals to important positions in state government and proposed considerable legislation. But the legislature was controlled by the Democrats during much of his time in office and Governor Milliken was a Republican. So, many of his programs were never accomplished, since generally the goals of the Democrats and Republicans are not the same. The governor had to abandon or compromise many of his ideas, not so much because they were bad but because his ideas were Republican.

When Democratic Governor James Blanchard took office in January of 1983, he had his set of goals. For a while it looked as though he would have his way on most issues. The house and senate were controlled by the Democrats and they were quite willing to please the first Democratic governor since 1962. The house had 16 more Democrats than Republicans; whereas the senate had 20 Democrats and 18 Republicans. And the entire government was controlled by the same political party: the Democrats.

Governor Blanchard went about successfully getting his programs through the legislature. One of his concerns was Michigan's economy. It was in bad shape— welfare payments and other government costs were increasing dramatically and rising unemployment was causing tax revenues to be very low. Cuts were made, but the governor was convinced a tax increase was necessary. The legislature had to be convinced. The Democrats were willing while the Republicans were not. It became a completely partisan argument and both parties were divided or polarized over the issue.

The Democrats in the legislature were told they had to support the governor or they weren't being "team players." Republicans opposed it because they thought more spending cuts should be made. They also wanted to see the governor and the Democrats held responsible for increasing taxes. All but one of the Democrats supported the increase. All the Republicans opposed it. The governor finally got one Republican to vote for the increase and the measure passed the senate on a 20-18 vote. The vote was equally partisan in the house. The merits of the bill played only a minor role in the passage of the tax increase. The most important factor seemed to be party affiliation. The bill became law and the 38 percent plus income tax increase was paid by the citizens.

But the public was not happy. Two Democratic senators were recalled and replaced by two Republicans. This was one of the most dramatic turnarounds in Michigan political history and it gave control of the senate in 1984 to the Republicans who continued their 20-18 control after the 1986 elections. Democratic Governor Blanchard now had to deal with the Republicans. Democrats had lost the opportunity for complete control of the government. This meant a more difficult time getting programs passed. Much of this drama was due to the existence of political parties.

BASICS OF POLITICAL PARTIES

Political parties have become very important in America, despite George Washington telling the congress in his farewell address that he thought political parties would be bad for America and that he hoped they would never gain in popularity. President Washington did not get his wish. They are here to stay now and some would say they have not been that bad for our political system.

Definition

A *political party* is an organized group of individuals with broad common goals, seeking to influence public policy through the election of its candidates to public office.

Really a Collection of Smaller Groups

We tend to think of our country and our state having only two major political parties, which is true, to a degree. However, we actually have a Republican and Democratic party organization in each county. In addition there are party organizations in some of the cities, townships, and at the state level. Each of these party organizations has its own leaders and members with their own ideas. In a conservative county the Democrats may be more like the Republicans in a liberal county. But when the need arises, all the factions within each party throughout the state will combine their efforts to provide a united front against the other party. In the end, they realize party unity is in their best interests.

FUNCTIONS OF POLITICAL PARTIES

Most of us think we know what political parties are and what they do. Actually, they are more active in the political process than is understood. The following are only some of their more major functions.

Nomination of Candidates

The underlying goal of any political party is to control the government. That doesn't mean parties are planning evil things; rather, they must control enough of government to achieve their policy goals. To get their members elected, they must first nominate them. Parties attempt to find the best people they can to serve as their nominees in every office possible at all levels of government.

Financing Candidates

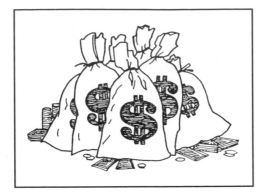

Once parties have good candidates they usually assist in the campaign to assure a victory. This assistance takes many forms including organizational help and volunteers. But the most important is money. The campaign has an excellent chance of victory if candidates have money to pay for brochures, yard signs, television and radio advertisements, billboards, and all the other necessities of a successful campaign.

Continuing Criticism

Usually, one party has control and is the "in" party or the *majority party*. The other party is the *minority party*. When a particular political party has control of the legislature or the governor's office, it isn't so important for them to get public support. Depending on the issue, they may or may not feel it necessary to hold press conferences. When this happens, the minority party will often hold its own press conferences to let the public know what the majority party is doing.

This is a very important responsibility for the party out of power. This continuous criticism is done at all levels of government in America and in other democracies as well. They attempt to rally support for their own policy positions and make the majority party look bad. This is one of the few ways to hold the majority party back. This is what the Republican party did to combat the Democrats' 1983 income tax proposal. A tax increase was inevitable, but their continuous criticism of the bill caused the public to feel it was unnecessary.

Providing Public Policy Proposals

Public policy proposals are the plans for changes each party wants to make— things they believe will be good for the public. Each party has different plans. These can range from the provision of free child care to a reduction in taxes on small businesses to the legalization of all drugs. Political parties want to influence government and they do it through public policy proposals. It is the purpose of political parties and the reason they exist. The members of each party want their ideas adopted because they think society will be better because of them.

Education of the Public

A party attempts to convince the public its proposals are desirable. Its candidates are more likely to win if more voters agree with their positions.

Party leaders and others often have news conferences and provide press releases in order to reach the public with their proposals and counterproposals on a variety of policy matters.

MICHIGAN'S PARTIES

Two Major Political Parties

Like most of the rest of the United States, Michigan is a two-party state. That means most of the time the only parties that really have a chance to win are the Democrats and the Republicans. One or the other has controlled the legislature during all of the 1900s. Republicans or Democrats have controlled the governor's office during Michigan's entire history with the exception of 1840-1841. William Woodbridge, a Whig, was elected for that term. At that time the Whigs were one of the major parties but it died out and was replaced by the Republican party, which did not exist in 1840.

Minor or Third Parties

There are exceptions to the two-party state. Occasionally, a third or *minor party* will be of some importance. *A minor party is one operating over a period of time in addition to two major political parties in an area where only the two-party system usually exists.* This happens infrequently and usually lasts for only an election or two. The strength of minor parties depends on the attitudes of the voters and how the major parties respond to their concerns. If one of the major parties responds to the needs of those who supported the minor party, it will probably soon melt away.

Minor parties have seldom been of importance in Michigan history. The last time a minor or third party elected a member to the legislature was back in 1912 when the National Progressives elected six of 32 senators and 11 of 100 house members. Michigan has had legislators from other minor parties elected further back in history. Their names— Populists, Silverites, Patrons of Industry, Fusionists, and Greenbacks— mean less to us now.

Though minor parties have seldom elected anyone to office in recent history, they have left an impact on Michigan. George Wallace's American Independence Party was a significant force in 1968. Wallace couldn't get on the ballot in Michigan as a candidate for his party, so he ran as a Democrat. Zolton Ferency was the leader of the Democratic Party in Michigan during much of the 1960s, but in a disagreement over the Democrats' position on the Vietnam War, he formed his own Human Rights Party. On The Human Rights Party ticket, Ferency ran for governor in 1978 and supreme court in 1986. He lost both times, but did well for a minor party candidate. One Michiganian, Robert Tisch, was so upset about taxes and government spending that he organized his own party in the state— the Tisch Independent Citizen's party. Other minor parties seen on the Michigan ballot are the Libertarian party, Socialist Workers party, Communist party, and Workers' League.

One-Party Control

Sometimes one political party gains control in a state and holds it for an extended period of time. This is fairly common. The "deep South" is a region that generally elects only Democrats to state and local offices. This region is also very conservative and, interestingly, voters fairly consistently cast their ballots for Republican presidential candidates. Other states, like Maine, Vermont, Connecticut, Utah, Wyoming, and Montana elect few Democrats.

In these states, the majority party seldom has to consider the views and wishes of minority party legislators. Then the real contest is not in the general election, but in the primary.

Michigan has gone through periods when it has been predominantly Republican or Democrat, especially the years between 1855 and 1930 when there were 18 Republican governors.

Getting a New Party on the Ballot

The national government affects state party politics particularly through legislation like the Voting Rights Acts and Supreme Court decisions. Otherwise, the states are left to make most decisions of when and how to allow minor parties on the ballot.

It would seem to be the constitutional right for any group to form a political party. But allowing every group to be placed on the ballot, when most would have little likelihood of winning, becomes a burden to voters who must muddle through an additional *party slate* (a party's entire list of candidates) and pay for the extra costs involved.

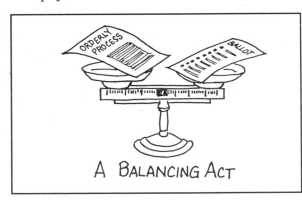

A BALANCING ACT

The final decision as to who can be on the ballot is a balancing act between providing for the rights of those seeking to start a third party and the need for an orderly election process. Different states take different approaches. Michigan's laws make it reasonably easy to get on the ballot.

To appear on the November ballot a party must acquire the signatures of one percent or more of the number of votes cast for the winning secretary of state candidate in the last election. The signatures must come from several areas of the state. To remain on the ballot the party must also receive one percent or more of the total votes cast for the winning secretary of state candidate in the previous election.

Meeting these requirements suggests the minor party has adequate support in the state to warrant placing its candidates on the ballot.

Recently, such parties have included the Libertarian party, Socialist Workers party, Communist party, Workers' League, the Human Rights party, the Tisch Independent Citizen's party, and others.

Questions

1. Give an example from Michigan politics which shows how the two major political parties became divided over an issue and this polarization had a certain affect on Michigan government afterwards.

2. What is the ultimate goal of a political party and what is done to achieve this goal?

3. List five functions of a political party.

4. Name a minor party found on the Michigan ballot and very briefly explain the goal of this party.

5. Which level of government has the most control over allowing new political parties on the ballot? In Michigan what must a new political party do so its slate of candidates can be placed on the ballot?

Chapter 14   Section 2

**Political Parties —
How They Are Organized and Operate**

Here are the key concepts in this section:

1. Political parties are organized at practically every level where people are elected to office— from township all the way to statewide and national.

2. Political primaries are used to select the single best and strongest candidate among all those from each party who are interested in the position.

3. After the primary has selected one individual from each party for each office, these people run against each other in the November general election.

4. In some situations and for some offices the nominees are selected at a party convention or by a meeting known as a party caucus.

5. The cost of campaigning for office can be very expensive, especially for the major offices such as governor. Candidates search for money from many sources including the political parties, special interest groups, and individuals.

ORGANIZATION OF POLITICAL PARTIES
Since there are candidates to elect at all levels of government, there are party organizations at all levels to see to it their men and women win. There are candidates running for office at the township, county, state, and national levels. There is a corresponding party organization at each of these levels to assist in these campaigns.

Most of the work of campaigns is done at the local level—at the grass roots. Because so much work is accomplished here, it is said parties are organized in a *decentralized* manner. *Decentralized means the work is done and decisions are made by many individuals locally rather than being concentrated in the hands of a few at the state level.*

National
To assist at the national level, each state sends two individuals, a male and a female, called the *national committeeman and national committeewoman*. They meet frequently and are responsible for running the national party organization. They vote for national party leaders and assist in cam-

paigns for president and for United States House and Senate seats. Their money, expertise, and prestige are very helpful.

State

The state level is often the most important political unit of the party. Each congressional district selects representatives to the *state central committee*. It is this committee which runs the party in the two years between conventions. State party conventions, held in February after the general election, select the chairperson of the party and many others who help run the organization.

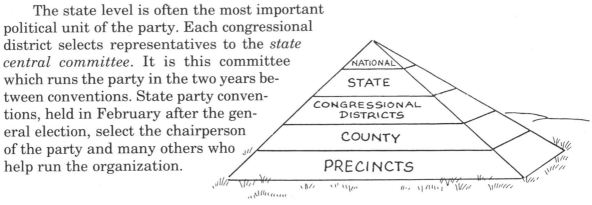

Congressional Districts

Each of the 16 congressional districts has a congressional campaign committee responsible for electing party members to those seats. Partially because they have only the one office to pursue, this level of party organization is not usually as important as the others, although as regional leaders they do have influence on general party business.

County

One of the most potent levels of party power is at the county level. The *county chairperson* is one of the most powerful positions in party politics. This office is chosen by one of the strongest grass roots units in politics— the *county executive committee. The county executive committee consists of all the party's nominees for state, county, and congressional offices and an equal number of individuals (who are not party nominees) from various parts of the county depending on the party's strength in the last election. The county executive committee is a group numbering from several individuals to over 100 in the more populous counties.*

The county party assumes much of the responsibility for finding good candidates for office and for assisting in the running and financing of various campaigns.

Occasionally, larger cities and townships will also have a party organization. Most cities, however, have nonpartisan elections for city positions and the parties often (but not always) stay out of these elections.

Precincts

The bottom rung in the ladder of political organizations is the precinct. Every municipality, no matter how small, has at least one precinct. Many cities and townships have dozens. Detroit has approximately 900. The precinct is the smallest political unit for election purposes. Usually a precinct contains from 700 to 1,000 people which makes it a very convenient grass roots unit for party organization. Political parties have precinct organizations which normally include leaders, *precinct delegates* (elected organizers of local party activities), and many others who do basic campaign work— handing out literature, telephoning, placing yard signs, and *poll watching. Poll watchers check on who has voted and try to evaluate how they think the election is going for their party's candidates.*

Money, many volunteers, and good organization are important for campaign victories. The more volunteers and money, the more likely a victory, and the more likely the party will be successful in promoting its programs. Precinct organization is where success begins.

Informal Organization

The party organization we just explained is the formal organization. It emphasizes how the parties are officially and legally organized to pursue victories. Both parties are similarly organized; most of which is required by state law. But there is much the law doesn't cover. This is the informal organization.

For example, it is not unusual for someone who does not have a high position in the party to still have considerable influence. These people might be community leaders. They may be wealthy, politically active members of the community or they may be local officeholders, like a county sheriff or clerk.

Besides political parties there are special groups and clubs which focus on party activities. High schools occasionally have such groups. Many college campuses have College Democratic or Republican clubs. Young men and women in their twenties and thirties may join the Young Republicans or Young Democrats.

NOMINATING CANDIDATES

The best way for a political party to be effective is to get its members elected to office. To do this, a party's candidates must first be nominated. There are several ways to do this.

PRIMARIES

There are two kinds of primaries: 1. Partisan for candidates associated with a political party, and 2. nonpartisan where candidates run with no outward affiliation to a political party.

Partisan Primaries

Partisan primaries narrow the number of party candidates to one for each available position. The governor's race is a good example. Only one person can serve as governor of Michigan. Each party must take all their possible candidates and pick the best one to run against the other party's best nominee. The

Democrats in 1986 had no need for a primary because their powerful incumbent governor, James Blanchard, was willing to run for reelection. Other Democrats could have run in the primary, but their chances of winning would have been slim.

The Republicans, on the other hand, had three candidates willing to challenge the incumbent governor. It made no sense for all three to run as this would divide the vote and all would lose. The purpose of the primary election is to let the people vote and narrow the choices down to the strongest candidate from each party. The three Republicans— Dan Murphy, Colleen Engler, and William Lucas— fought it out in the August primary and Lucas won. Lucas then challenged Governor Blanchard but lost.

In any August primary, candidates for many different offices do the same thing.

PARTISAN ELECTION PROCESS

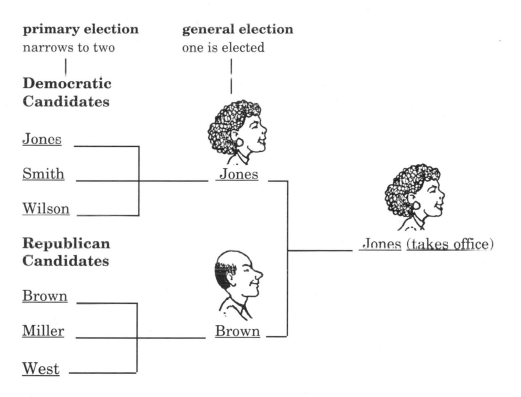

primary election
narrows to two

general election
one is elected

Democratic Candidates

Jones

Smith

Wilson

Jones

Republican Candidates

Brown

Miller

West

Brown

Jones (takes office)

240

Nonpartisan Primaries

Most city and village elections and all local school board and judicial elections are held on a nonpartisan basis. Candidates do not run on a political party slate. In fact, voters would likely be offended in many of these elections if candidates announced their party associations.

These offices are nonpartisan for many reasons, not the least of which is the hope that the nonpartisan nature will keep the race above party politics. That happens in many cases, but there is still much politicking not associated with parties.

The purpose of these nonpartisian primary elections— like any primary— is to narrow the number of choices for each position available so the winner will receive a majority of the votes cast in the fall election. Let us suppose Traverse City is electing two city council members. Seven people decided to run, so there would be a primary to narrow the choices to four individuals. The top four vote-getters would run against each other in the fall. The two candidates with the most votes would become the winners.

Closed and Open Primaries

If the task of a partisan primary is to choose a party's best candidates, then shouldn't only members of that party vote? In fact, that is exactly the argument in many states. These states have *closed primaries* for state and local elections. Only voters who are registered Democrats may vote in the Democrat primary. The same is true for the Republican primary and any other party that has a primary. Voters must declare which party they are associated with and they are given a ballot which lists only the candidates of that party.

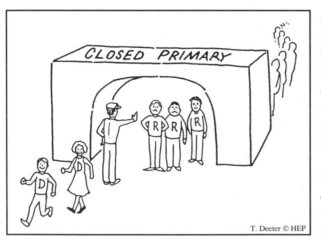

T. Deeter © HEP

But there are difficulties with closed primaries. Two problems are especially apparent. Closed primaries exclude huge numbers of people who don't consider themselves members of any political party. They also force voters to make public their party affiliation.

To get away from these problems, Michigan has adopted the *open primary* (except for presidential elections). An open primary allows any registered voter to vote and they do not declare their party affiliation. Voters are given ballots which have different sections for each party. The only limiting factor in open primaries is the voter may vote only for the candidates of one party. Generally that is considered a reasonable limitation.

Many voters will even look at which party has the most interesting contests and vote in that primary, regardless of their real party preference. It is felt Republicans did this in the 1968 Democratic presidential primary and voted for George Wallace. Wallace won the Michigan Democratic presidential primary.

Some criticize open primaries, especially when members of one party cast votes for the worst candidate in the other party in the hopes he or she will lose later when running against the voter's preferred candidate. Often, though, it is simply done because the other primary has more contests of importance to the voter.

To allow voters the most flexibility in choosing candidates and getting involved in the elective process, some states have *blanket primaries. In this kind of primary, voters are given lists of candidates from all parties and they may vote for nominees from any party they choose. They are limited only in that they may not vote for candidates of different parties running for the same office.* For example, if they vote from among the Republican candidates for sheriff they may not also vote for the Democratic sheriff candidates. Using such a primary is more generous than most state parties are willing to allow, including Michigan's.

CONVENTIONS

A few candidates in Michigan are chosen by conventions. The nominees for lieutenant governor are examples. The state parties meet in conventions once or twice each year for a variety of reasons. In September of years in which the governor is chosen (1994, 1998, etc.), the two major parties meet to choose several nominees who are then placed on the statewide November ballot. The party's nominee for governor would have just been chosen in August, but there is no "running mate" until the convention in September. Other nominees selected during the September convention are candidates for the following offices:

CANDIDATES CHOSEN AT PARTY CONVENTIONS

ONE CANDIDATE FOR FOUR-YEAR TERMS

Secretary of State
Attorney General

chart continued

**ONE OR TWO CANDIDATES CHOSEN EVERY
TWO YEARS FOR EIGHT-YEAR TERMS**

State Board of Education   (2 of the 8 members)
Michigan State University Board of Trustees (2 of 8)
University of Michigan Board of Regents   (2 of 8)
Wayne State University Board of Governors (2 of 8)
Supreme Court   (1 or 2 of 7)

PARTY CAUCUS

On occasion, a *party caucus* meets to choose candidates for the party. This is done only for certain offices AND only if the party's nominee dies between the primary and the general election or pulls out of the race. Sometimes the caucus has been used for the selection of a party's delegates to the national presidential nominating convention. *A caucus is any meeting of top-level party leaders to decide an issue impor-*
tant to the party.

In the past county and state conventions were held to select a party's delegates to the national presidential nominating convention. Once party caucuses accomplished the same thing. However, beginning with the 1992 presidential election, Michigan used the closed primary system to select their delegates. This change came about because of what happened in 1988.

In that year's Michigan presidential delegate contests, Jesse Jackson received the most Democratic delegates and Pat Robertson received the most Republican delegates. These two candidates won the majority of delegates because of their grass roots organizations, but they both basically ignored party regulars. Because Michigan's major parties did not want to allow this to happen again, they pushed the Michigan legislature to pass a law allowing a closed primary selection of delegates for the next presidential nomination.

BECOMING A CANDIDATE

Most people agree there must be restrictions on becoming candidates for office. If there were no rules, there would be literally hundreds of candidates on the ballot. But the rules should not be so restrictive that good, qualified and electable candidates find it too frustrating to get their names on the ballot. Most elective offices require potential candidates submit a number of petitions to the local clerk or the secretary of state. It is usually required that petitions contain registered voter signatures equal to between one and four percent of that party's votes cast for secretary of state in the last election for the area or district involved. This requirement assures only those who are serious will pursue their candidacy.

CAMPAIGN FINANCING

Many campaigns require very little money. Dozens of village, township, and city officials often have no opponents or only "token" opponents. They may spend nothing on their campaigns. Many more, such as county clerks, spend only a few hundred dollars every two or four years. There are expenses, even in the smaller races, for yard signs, billboards, pamphlets, stamps and envelopes, and computer-generated information.

However, in those races that involve larger municipalities, state house and senate seats, and congressional seats, campaigns have become increasingly expensive. Statewide races for governor and United States Senate each cost over one million dollars. In larger races, radio and television ads increase the cost. Salaries for several staff people may be added to that list. The cost for a state house seat ranges from a few thousand dollars to as much as $150,000 for each candidate. A state senate seat can cost as much as $250,000 to $500,000 while congressional races are often in the half million dollar range. These campaigns are expensive and the cost is increasing dramatically with every election.

Sources of Campaign Money

Since campaigns are expensive, there must be a source for these needed dollars. In less expensive local level campaigns, money will usually come from the candidate, friends, neighbors, and some interested individuals giving $10 or $20, and occasionally $50 to $100. The expensive campaigns require more creative fund raising. Special fund raisers are common, as are mailed requests for contributions.

When campaigns start costing several thousand dollars, campaign treasurers look to another large source of money: *political action committees or PACs. A PAC is an organization formed to further the political interests of its founder or members by raising and distributing campaign contributions.* Many organizations including the United Auto Workers and most other unions, issue-oriented groups, business groups, physicians, teachers, Realtors, chambers of commerce and others form political action committees. PACs formed by national groups may also get involved in Michigan political contests. Because they often represent large numbers of people, PACs can provide tremendous sums of money to campaigns and their support is eagerly sought by many candidates. It is not unusual for at least half of the money raised for a campaign to come from PACs!

Since the election of candidates is such an important matter, political parties provide funding for many campaigns themselves. The promise of financial assistance is frequently used to encourage candidates to run for offices the party is especially seeking. Like many other funding sources, they often promise more money than they provide.

Money in a campaign should be put in its proper perspective. A candidate is not guaranteed victory simply by having more money, but defeat is more likely without it. Wisely spent money is better than huge quantities of money. A large supply of dedicated, energetic campaign workers is preferred by the astute candidate over a large supply of dollars, and many successful campaigns have proven this point.

Campaign Finance Laws

When so much money is devoted to elections there is always the opportunity for problems. Candidates need to have the money and there are many people happy to give it— often with invisible strings attached. There is the potential for public officials to vote according to the wishes of those who give them money. It is readily apparent how problems of ethics and propriety may arise. It is a credit to the people in public office and those hoping to influence government that so few examples of improper activity take place.

Because of the potential for difficulties, the state has passed laws controlling campaign donations and requiring the reporting of campaign expenditures. Anyone giving more than $20 must publicly disclose his or her identity. Businesses may not donate money directly to candidates (although unions may). Businesses can give money for or against questions on the ballot and they may form PACs which then give money to individual candidates. Individuals and PACs are limited in the amount they are allowed to contribute. The maximum for an individual to give to any one statewide campaign is $3,400 and this drops to $1,000 for a state senate candidate and $500 for someone running for a state house seat. All contributions and expenses above a certain level must be reported to the appropriate person or place at different points in the campaign.

The governor's race is usually the most expensive among state campaigns. To lessen the likelihood of campaign funds being mishandled, and to somewhat limit expenditures, the state provides public funding for this election. To qualify, candidates in the primary must show broad support by acquiring donations of at least $50,000 in individual contributions of $100 or less. If a candidate accepts these public funds, they are required to keep expenses within certain limits, currently $1.5 million. If the public money is not accepted, then there is no limit on spending but the $3,400 maximum from any one contributor still applies. The candidate can spend an unlimited amount of his or her own money though.

Once elected to office, candidates decide which of their campaign promises are most important, organize their offices, and try to get comfortable in their new role. They must decide how they are going to vote on a variety of issues. They are familiar with some of these issues but there are many more with which they are probably unfamiliar. They receive input to help in making these decisions from you and all the other residents of their districts.

Questions

1. Why do the Democrats and Republicans have party organizations at the precinct, city, county, and state levels? Which of these groups is considered to be one of the most powerful?

2. What is the purpose of a primary election? What kind of primary does Michigan use for presidential elections and why was this type chosen?

3. If you live in a county where 85 percent of the registered voters are Republican, why is the primary election probably more important for a local office than the general election?

4. What is a PAC and why have they become important in helping candidates become elected to office?

5. About how much money does it cost a candidate to run for the following offices in Michigan: governor, U.S. Senator, state senator, state representative, and county clerk? What is this money spent for?

6. What limitations does the state put on collecting money for campaigns and campaign spending?

15

POLITICAL ACTIVISM

Chapter 15   Section 1

How to Tell Government Officials Your Opinions
&
Special Interest Groups in Michigan

Here are the key concepts in this section:

1. In order to expect your opinion to count, you need to understand the basics of how government works and to know what is happening in the political world around you.

2. The best way to do this is by watching the news, reading newspapers and magazines, and talking with others.

3. There are several basic guidelines to remember if you try to contact any government official.

4. Where politics is concerned there is always strength in numbers. Many groups of people have banded together to form special interest groups which keep an eye on political events and contact officials when necessary.

State and local government responds to the demands made on it by people. Sometimes these demands are quite obvious but there are times when the needs are not so apparent. Possibly a concern is only felt by a small group. The initial size of the group is not the most important thing, but it is the depth of their concern which really counts.

Issues that have affected only a handful in the entire state have still caused the legislature and governor to spend much of their time discussing remedies. This often occurs when the groups are persistent and, especially, if the media decides to provide coverage of the issue. This was true with surrogate mothering and doctor-assisted suicide legislation, for example, which directly affected only a few Michigan citizens. The depth of emotion surrounding such issues causes greater statewide concern than the actual number involved would suggest.

Dozens of types of issues come up before state and local officials each year. Because people differ, including legislators, government often isn't sure how to resolve these issues. People try to convince officials of the merits of their viewpoints; they try to "influence" government. Influencing government occurs every day. It is a major factor in shaping the final product— the laws of the state and local government. This chapter explains how you can make yourself heard . . . how you can influence government yourself.

Understanding Politics and Paying Attention

Before you can be active and expect your views to be listened to, you must understand how the political system works. That is what this book has tried to help you do! Next, you must be aware what the issues are. The easiest way to do this is to watch the state and local news on television. Discussing the news with friends and relatives should come next. There is always an issue about which you can talk. By talking with others and learn-

ing their thoughts on a variety of issues, you are able to better formulate your own ideas. Others have probably considered some aspect of the issue that you haven't. As you discuss issues more, and watch news shows more, you become better able to talk about issues which you seldom considered previously.

To really understand the news, it is essential to read about items of interest in newspapers and magazines, or watch in depth programs on television. Nearly every television station has a local version of a discussion show like "Off The Record," produced at Michigan State University and shown on several publicly funded television networks. The newspapers generally do an excellent job of discussing issues. Their regular coverage is usually more thorough than the evening news can provide in its short time slot. Additionally, they have editorials written by various staff personnel giving their thoughts on a variety of issues.

MAKING DECISION-MAKERS AWARE OF YOUR VIEWS
Public Meetings

Most groups deciding important issues have meetings where the public may speak. This is required by the Open Meetings Act. Even state legislative committee meetings are open to the public and arrangements can be made to present statements at

many of these. Sessions of the legislature are open to the public, but it is very unusual for members of the public to have the chance to speak before the state house or senate.

Writing Public Officials

Letters can be written to virtually any group. Few people bother to write, resulting in government officials actually giving quite a bit of consideration to any comments they do receive, assuming the letters are done well. There are effective and ineffective ways to write letters to government officials. Below is a list of guidelines, some suggested by the Michigan state legislature itself in its publication, *Citizen Guide to State Government*, published every two years. Whether contacting a state or a local official, the same basic rules apply.

GUIDELINES TO WRITING GOVERNMENT OFFICIALS

1. WRITE A PERSONAL LETTER for the greatest impact. Write it in your own words, with your own thoughts. Government officials don't like computer-generated letters any more than you do.

2. KEEP IT BRIEF (about a page) and well organized. Stick to your key points.

3. ADDRESS IT CORRECTLY. Get the proper title, address, and spelling. Send it to the right individuals or the correct committees. Include your name and address on the letter.

4. SOUND KNOWLEDGEABLE. Refer to the specific bill, ordinance, rezoning, etc. Make sure you have read it and your thoughts are not based on second-hand information. Mention specific examples of how the issue affects you, your family, or friends.

5. BE POSITIVE. Don't just criticize; suggest alternatives. Don't threaten.

6. FOLLOW THE ISSUE. Know when your contact will be most effective. Don't send your letter so early before the issue is being considered that it's forgotten. And don't send it after the final compromise is complete.

7. DON'T FORGET ANYONE. Write your own representative, but also write committee members and other members who have a hand in the decision. Write to those who already support your view to show your appreciation. They need your encouragement, too, and may be able to use your points in their discussions.

Calling Public Officials

Another fast way to let government officials know your opinions about things is to call them directly on the telephone. Call their offices if they have one and if it is possible to make contact this way. If it is not possible, however, try calling the individual at home. Many of the same rules apply when phoning. Use notes. Know what points you want to make and state your case concisely.

Letters to the Editor

An alternative to writing government officials is to send your letter to "the editor" of the local paper. Newspapers commonly have a large section on their editorial page devoted to letters from citizens about various issues. A letter to the editor may influence pubic opinion in addition to influencing elected officials. There may be times you may wish to say something directly to an official which you do not want to be stated publicly. In this case a letter to the editor is not a good idea.

Look at the newspaper to get an idea of the letters usually written. Many of the rules in the guidelines are also appropriate for letters to newspapers. Just remember, unlike a letter to someone in government that only a few people may see, letters to the editor are read by hundreds or even thousands of community members. You want to be sure it states your position in ways you can defend later.

Depending on the type of issue, you may want to send it to a newspaper with a large readership in addition to your local newspaper. The *Detroit Free Press* and *Detroit News* are read throughout the state. Rearrange your thoughts a bit so the letters aren't carbon copies of one another.

STRENGTH IN NUMBERS

Making your opinion known to government officials is effective in causing government to act in a particular way. If one person contacting government can be effective, however, it is much more powerful to have several people doing the same thing at the same time. The phrase "strength in numbers," surely applies to influencing government.

GROUP ACTIVISM

If you know others who are as concerned as you about something government is doing, contact them and discuss ways you can accomplish more working together. Discuss ways you can get additional people and groups involved. Draft a petition and get as many to sign it as possible. Those indicating particularly strong support while signing the petition can be asked to further help. One group of local students recently petitioned the county road commission to cut fewer trees during road improvement. It worked! Instead of 21 large, beautiful oaks and maples being cut down, a compromise with the group was made and only three were lost!

Groups of concerned individuals organized into permanent groups to influence (lobby) the government are called *interest groups*, or *pressure groups*. An individual registered to influence government is called a lobbyist. Lobbyists may work alone, but most work for one or more interest groups.

Interest groups and Lobbying

Often the expression "interest group" is associated with various powerful groups putting pressure on legislators in inappropriate ways. The widely held belief is that the goal of interest groups is to get the government to do things beneficial to the group, but not necessarily beneficial to anyone else. Less of this occurs than is believed, but such actions are widely talked about when they do happen.

KINDS OF INTEREST GROUPS

There are many kinds of interest groups. They represent unions, businesses, physicians, gun enthusiasts, religious organizations, local governments, and many other groups of people. They can usually be divided into the following categories.

Cause Groups

These are organizations of individuals who have joined to influence public policy concerning the social, political, moral, economic, or environmental health of the community or state. Groups form to support or stop millage requests, recall elections, rezonings, humane treatment of animals, save the earth, and many more issues. Some of the more active cause or public interest groups in Michigan are the following:

Common Cause of Michigan
Michigan Citizen Lobby
Mothers Against Drunk Driving
National Organization of Women
Planned Parenthood
Public Interest Research Group in Michigan
Right to Life of Michigan
Sierra Club

Many politically active groups have a cause they are working for or against.

Economic Groups

The interest groups that are often the most powerful are those associated with economic issues. It seems people get most excited about an issue that affects their pocketbook.

Banks want to be sure they don't lose profits because of legislation favorable to savings and loans or credit unions so they formed the Michigan Bankers Association. The Road Builders Association wants to be sure the state builds and repairs as many roads as possible. Farmers want to be sure land use ordinances don't curtail their plans drastically so they formed the Michigan Farm Bureau. Each of these groups is out to protect their members; they must because no one else will do it for them. Dozens of such groups looking out for their own economic interests are active at the local level. A few of the groups active at the state level include the following:

Automobile Club of Michigan
Michigan Bankers Association
Michigan Farm Bureau
Michigan Manufacturers Association
Michigan Petroleum Association
Michigan Retailers Association
Michigan State Chamber of Commerce

Professional and Occupational Groups

The state regulates many of the professions through the Department of Licensing and Regulation and other departments. The state also puts millions of dollars a year into many professional and occupational areas and assists in the negotiation of contracts and the resolution of work-related problems. Because of this, it is in the best interests of groups affected by these laws to follow the actions of state and local government. They do! Some active groups in Michigan are the following:

AFL-CIO (labor union)
American Federation of State and Community Municipal Employees (AFSCME)
Fraternal Order of Police
Michigan Association of Realtors
Michigan Education Association
Michigan Funeral Directors Association
Michigan Nurses Association
State Bar of Michigan (attorneys)
United Auto Workers

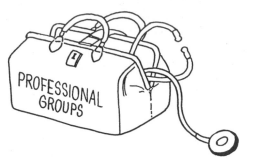

Government Groups

It may seem odd that government would be listed as a group that lobbies government, but it is true. State and local governments get a sizeable portion of their revenues from the units of government "above" them. They can influence the amount of that money by lobbying the state government. The city of Detroit could never have afforded the People Mover transportation system out of their own local dollars. The final cost was some $200 million and only about $3 million was local money! Detroit successfully lobbied the state and national governments to come up with the other 98.5 percent of the funds.

There are many grants available from the state and from Washington for a variety of programs. They especially have programs in the areas of health, mental health, public safety, child support, and economic development. There is lobbying to build new post offices, improve Amtrak railroad facilities, approve defense contracts, and complete highway projects. Governments can provide more services with fewer of their own dollars if they can convince other governments to assist them. The state of Michigan and the City of Detroit have full-time lobbying efforts based in Washington. Some of the government groups involved in lobbying are the following:

City of Detroit and several other municipalities
Michigan Association of Counties
Michigan Association of School Boards
Michigan Municipal League (supports city government)
Michigan Sheriffs Association

Michigan Townships Association
State of Michigan
Wayne and many other counties

Questions

1. Is it ever possible to speak your opinion before a government meeting in Michigan? Please explain your response.

2. Tad Brown's father flew into a rage when he learned the Michigan university Tad planned on attending next fall was raising its tuition. He quickly scribbled a note to his state representative sending it to "The Capital—Lansing." He told her, the representative, that all politicians should "jump in the lake." He did not explain why the increase would hurt his family nor did he contact anyone else about the matter. Explain what things Tad's father could have done to improve his chances of writing a productive letter.

3. If you are interested in expressing your opinion on a political matter, what are the pros and cons of writing a letter to the editor of a newspaper versus a letter directly to a state or local official?

4. A saying goes "There is strength in numbers." Explain how this quote can be related to the formation of special interest groups in Michigan.

5. Each of the following is an example of one of the four main types of special interest groups: Michigan Farm Bureau, Common Cause of Michigan, Michigan Townships Association, and Michigan Education Association. List each group and tell which type it is.

Chapter 15   Section 2

Goals and Methods of Interest Groups
&
Becoming Involved with a Political Party

Here are the key concepts in this section

1. One of the main goals of special interest groups is to make certain state or local government does not do something which will hurt its members. Since government has become so complex, this can easily happen.

2. Special interest groups provide lawmakers with information which tells the group's side of the story. They also keep in friendly contact with legislators and give them favors or gifts when appropriate.

3. Sometimes the ties between special interest groups and legislators can cross the boundary into the unethical and illegal if money is exchanged directly for votes, but this is rare.

4. Joining a political party is one of the best ways to become politically active. Being a precinct delegate will allow you to help the party and its candidates.

GOALS OF INTEREST GROUPS
   Goals of lobbying groups can probably be divided into three categories.

Watching Out for Number One
   The most important goal of lobbying efforts is to assure the government is not doing something that would harm the group. Sometimes different groups have competing interests and if one group isn't alert, the other might attempt to get public policy passed that benefits it. This is as true locally as it is at the state level. When government spends billions of dollars and makes hundreds of policy changes every year, groups affected by a particular policy must be active in the political process or they will lose out.

Informational

Often government officials act in certain ways because they are unaware of needed information. One job of lobbyists is to provide policy makers with information. It is likely to be slanted, but so is the information provided from the "other side." Policy makers know this and judge the material with this in mind. This role of interest groups is actually quite helpful to busy officials and assists them in presenting their position at appropriate times in the political process.

Watching Out for Others

While most lobbying efforts are of self-interest, more and more are by groups which hope to assist others. The "cause" groups have as their goal to make Michigan a better place environmentally, and to help people in need such as the homeless. The handicapped, for example, have a lobbying group, as do disabled veterans of foreign wars, several groups trying to find cures for various diseases, and groups hoping to clean the streams, lakes, and air. Their goals are not necessarily for their own self-interest, but for others in our society too.

METHODS OF INTEREST GROUPS

The methods used by lobbying groups have been tried and tested over time. They have not changed much in many years except that they have probably become more honest and sophisticated.

Friendly Contacts

One of the first things a newly elected legislator learns in Lansing is that he or she has gained about 250 new friends. Within a short time of taking office, legislators receive visits from many of the registered and full-time lobbyists. The interest groups want to contact policy makers as soon as possible. It is hard to vote against a friend, or even a pleasant person. Lobbyists are, therefore, very pleasant, very complimentary, and indicate their willingness to be as helpful as possible. They visit with officials, leave their business cards, and continue to keep in touch with those officials they feel will have an impact on legislation or other matters of interest to the group they represent.

Providing Information

As mentioned earlier, a major method of getting public policy favorable to an interest group is to be sure the policy makers know the group's position on issues, the group's reasons for being favorable or unfavorable toward a particular issue, and their suggestions for any changes. This is the essence of the lobbying effort.

Watchdog

Interest groups must always be diligent in pursuit of their goals. While there are many part-time lobbying efforts, more groups are pursuing the effort on a full-time basis. Government usually doesn't make public announcements of their plans; groups who care what government does should always be on the watch. To assist in this task, there are broad-based informational services that keep lobbyists aware of policy changes that may affect the group. One of the fastest growing is Public Sector Consultants which employs over 35 people who watch state politics and economic matters. They publish a newsletter to members who pay annually for the service. Two of several other sources of information are Gongwer's Information Service and Hannah Information Service.

Provide Favors

Policy makers are no different than others and lobbyists occasionally try to "win them over" by providing them with favors. We're not talking about anything illegal; these are simply favors that a good friend might provide. Michigan and many other states restrict this sort of lobbying to assure illegal activities do not take place. Favors may include weekends for the family at a lakeside condominium. It may be a round of golf, an expensive dinner at a nice restaurant, holiday gifts, or rides in company aircraft. The favor may be something more subtle, like a summer job for the legislator's daughter, or acceptance into a prestigious university program, tickets to college football games (in the college president's special box seating), or special attention at functions.

Financial Gifts

Lobbyists can't just give money to office holders. Nor can they say, "I'll give you $2,000 if you vote favorably on our bill." They can provide money in various ways, however, to legislators supportive of their positions.

Legislators are not paid all that much when you consider they control a state budget of several billion dollars. They have power equal to business executives making many times their income. They are also put in an environment where they associate with some of the wealthier individuals in the state.

The expensive lifestyle can be very tempting and once in a while someone will accept money to pass laws. The fact that so very few examples of improper exchanges of money occur is an indication of the integrity of Michigan's legislators and other state and local officials, as well as the integrity of Michigan's lobbyists.

There are ways, however, that lobbying groups can legally give money to public officials. Their intentions are rather apparent: they hope to influence public policy. Probably the most obvious method is through donations to campaigns and *officeholder accounts*. A few individuals give money to public officials, but the largest sums come from interest group political action committees(PACs). For example, such groups may give up to $5,000 to each state legislator for the primary and again for the general election. Individuals are limited to one tenth of what a PAC can give, or $500. Some wealthier groups find ways to form more than one PAC providing themselves with the opportunity to heavily "reward" officials who vote favorably on legislation of importance to the group.

The "officeholder accounts" are at least as controversial as campaign contributions. These are financial accounts used by elected officials for expenses "incidental to the operation of their offices." The funds are not to be used for campaign expenses. While most officials use the money to pay for office expenses, the funds have been used in questionable ways as well. House payments, automobile purchases, and donations to a variety of groups and organizations are probably not considered "normal" office expenses. Some abuses have resulted in reforms in the law.

Those officials in the most important government positions are the ones who receive the most money: committee chairpersons, majority and minority leaders, and the governor. Need does not play an important role... power does. Elected officials are usually willing to take the donations. Fund raisers occur frequently in Lansing and elsewhere for every reason imaginable.

POLITICAL PARTY INVOLVEMENT

Interest groups are not the only folks hoping to influence public policy. Political parties have the same goal. If an individual is interested in affecting policy, then he or she might consider party membership.

Political Party Membership

Membership in one of the political parties is a good way to get involved in politics. Either major political party, or one of the "minor" parties, would welcome your interest and your assistance. Party membership can start by simply calling the local or state party listed in the phone book.

Membership is not expensive; usually $5-$10. There are more expensive memberships for those with larger incomes or motivation, but parties prefer your involvement more than your money. If you aren't sure which party to join, talk to officials and others who share your political interests and ideas.

Precinct Delegate

The most important activity of political parties is the election of individuals to public office. Most party activities occur with that goal in mind. There are many ways you can become involved. One very official way is to run for the office of precinct delegate. The precinct delegate is one of several persons (usually two to five) elected in each voting precinct from each party. They assist in a variety of political party functions, especially at the local level.

How to Become a Precinct Delegate

Registered voters interested in being precinct delegates must merely get a few signatures from friends and neighbors in the precinct. The signed petitions must be turned in to the local clerk by a specified date. Call your city or township clerk to get details. If you miss the deadline it is still possible to be elected to the position. If there are more positions available than candidates on the ballot, persons receiving the most "write-in" votes will win (but there must be three or more voters who write in your name). The voters from a precinct select these individuals in the August primary of even-numbered years.

Role of the Precinct Delegate

Precinct delegates are expected to assist in organizing the precinct in the hopes of getting as many votes as possible for the party's candidates. They also help with fund raisers and assist candidates during the campaign season. In reality, many precinct delegates do very little; often others work much harder for the party. You don't have to be a precinct delegate to do party work or assist candidates. If you want to work for a party, just call their headquarters. If you want to work for a particular individual, call the individual and make your support known. The candidate will probably be flattered and you may be able to start your political activities immediately.

County Executive Committee

Precinct delegates may run for the county party *executive committee*, which heads the local party for the next two years. The executive committee includes all the nominees for state, national, and county elected offices and an equal number of members selected from among the precinct delegates and others. The executive committee selects the county party's officers including chairperson, vice-chair, secretary, finance chairperson, and treasurer.

Conventions and Presidential Primaries

Precinct delegates play a major part in the selection of their party's nominee for president of the United States. The Michigan Democratic and Republican parties have changed the process nearly every presidential elec-

tion season in the last few elections. Until recently, precinct delegates went to county conventions, where they selected state convention delegates. Parties still hold their state conventions where they, among other things, choose their delegates to the national nominating conventions. There, delegates are involved in deciding two important matters. They help determine the party's national *party platform*, their position on the important issues of the day. They also choose the party's presidential and vice-presidential nominees.

More recently, statewide presidential selection primaries, allowing all voters to indicate their favorites, have taken some of the power away from delegates. Delegates in many states, including Michigan, are forced to vote along the same percentages as the public voted in the primary election. For example, if 72 percent of the state's population voted for candidate Baker in the primary, then 72 percent of the state's delegates must vote for Baker at the convention.

If you feel strongly about a matter with which the government is involved, don't assume others will resolve the problem for you. Get active yourself, and get others to help too.

Questions

1. You are a political science major in college. For the summer you have been hired to help form a special interest group to stop drinking among high school students. Of the three types of goals special interest groups have, which type is this organization using? Give an example of at least one new law your group would like to see passed. What methods would you suggest the group use to influence legislators to pass this new law? What types of interaction would you want to see between the group and Michigan's legislators? Are there any practices you would suggest the group avoid?

2. If you strongly believe in the goals of a political party, how will joining this party help you, the party, and society?

3. What do party precinct delegates do and how are they selected?

Absentee ballot. It is occasionally difficult or impossible for voters to get to their voting places. To accommodate these individuals, election officials provide absentee ballots. The voter contacts the clerk's office and asks for an application for an absentee ballot. The application is filled out and returned. Several days before the election, the voter is sent a ballot, which is completed and returned, usually by mail, before the closing of the polls on election day.

Acquittal. An acquittal is a dismissal of the charges in a criminal case.

Ad hoc committees. The expression "ad hoc" means "for a time"; therefore, ad hoc committees are temporary.

Adjourning. Adjourning is the official act of closing a legislative session.

Adjutant General. The adjutant general serves as the commanding officer of the Michigan National Guard.

Administrative tribunals. Administrative tribunals, although not actually courts, are set up in a similar style to hear and decide disputes.

Affirmative action programs. Affirmative action programs are designed to increase the number of women, minorities, and handicapped who are employed by business and government.

Agriculture Commission. The Agriculture Commission, composed of five members appointed by the governor for four-year terms, manages and directs the Department of Agriculture.

Annexation. Annexation is a legal means for one unit of government such as a city to acquire land in another unit of government such as an adjoining city or township.

Appeal. An appeal is a legal proceeding by which a case is brought from a lower to a higher court for rehearing. Usually there must be some valid reason for an appeal, such as an error in the way the first trial was held.

Appellate courts. Appellate courts are those where appeals are heard concerning decisions from the trial courts. The Michigan State Supreme Court is an appellate court.

Arraignment. An arraignment is a judicial proceeding where charges are brought against an individual who at that time enters a plea of guilty or not guilty.

Assessed value. By mandate of the state constitution all property is to be assessed at 50 percent of its true market value. This becomes the assessed value of the property for property tax purposes.

Assessment. Assessment is the determination of the value of all real estate as well as certain other property for purposes of developing the tax rolls.

Assessment factor. The assessment factor acts as a multiplier to correct errors or differences in technique among various assessors. It is used to keep all county property of the same class equally valued.

Assessment roll. The assessment roll is the list of all properties and their values located in a municipality.

Assessors. Assessors are individuals trained in assessing procedures. They visit property and use guidelines to decide on its true market value. They are aware of the sales of similar property to make comparisons.

"At-large" election. In an at-large election the city or township is not broken into districts or wards so the people running for office are elected by the whole municipality and represent the entire municipality.

Attorney general. The attorney general is the state's chief legal officer and its top law enforcement officer.

Bicameral. Bicameral means two chambers or meeting rooms— specifically a house of representatives and a senate.

Blanket primary. In a blanket primary, voters are given lists of candidates from all parties and they may vote for nominees from any party they choose. They are limited only in that they may not vote for candidates of different parties running for the same office.

Block grants. Block grants are federal funds which must be used for the specified purpose, but states are allowed to make some decisions about the actual spending of the money.

Blueback. The blueback is a copy of the bill with a larger blue sheet stapled to its back. This blue sheet has lines for the signatures of other sponsors.

Board of canvassers. The board of canvassers is a four-member group equally divided between the two major parties. They review the election results and the conduct of the election.

Board of education. The board of education is the governing body of a school district. Most boards of education have seven or nine members who are elected for terms varying from three to six years.

Board of review. The board of review is a locally appointed three member board which meets in March to hear complaints about property tax assessments.

Briefs. Briefs are written statements of each side's position in a legal case.

Budget Stabilization Fund. Sometimes called the "rainy day fund," it saves money from good financial years to help balance the budget when bad economic times hit the state. It acts as an emergency bank account if the state faces tough times.

Bureau of the State Lottery. The Bureau of the State Lottery, an agency within the Department of Management and Budget, regulates the state lottery.

Calendar. The calendar is the daily agenda of bills to be discussed in the house or senate.

Capital. Capital spelled with an "al" refers to the city of Lansing where the legislature meets.

Capitol. Capitol spelled with an "ol" refers to the domed <u>building</u> in Lansing where the house and senate meet.

Categorical grant (in education). A categorical grant is state money set aside for special purposes, such as transportation of students, driver education, or bilingual education.

Caucus. In general a caucus is a planning meeting for political party strategy. A caucus is held before a new legislative term begins. Legislators belonging to the same party within each house elect their officers and establish their goals during the caucus.

Censure. Censure is the expression of official disapproval.

Charter. A charter is a written plan of local government organization similar to a constitution.

Circuit breaker. Circuit breaker is the common name for the Homestead Property Tax Credit. The circuit breaker allows people who pay high property taxes but have relatively low incomes to receive a credit on their state income taxes. (The credit is equal to 60 percent of property taxes in excess of 3.5 percent of household income for most individuals.)

Circuit court. The circuit court is the trial court which handles the most serious criminal cases, divorce cases, and civil cases involving over $10,000.

City council. The city council is the legislative body for the city. Its members are elected by the voters of the city.

City manager. A professional manager to run the city on a day-to-day basis and make recommendations to the city council. In many cities it is the city manager, not the mayor, who has the real power of operating the city.

Civil Rights Commission. The Civil Rights Commission, an eight-member group appointed by the governor for four-year terms, oversees the Civil Rights Department and selects its director.

Civil Service Commission. The Civil Service Commission consists of four persons appointed by the governor for eight-year terms to oversee the Civil Service Department.

Civil suit. A civil suit is a lawsuit brought by one person against another. These suits involve errors of judgement or arguments over contracts and so forth, but not crimes.

Closed primaries. Only voters who are registered as a member of one of the political parties may vote in a closed primary and only then for candidates from that particular party.

Co-sponsor. A co-sponsor is one of several legislators who originally backs a bill and adds his or her name to it.

Commission form of city government. Under this structure of city government the functions are performed by "commissioners" who are elected individually and each serve as department heads with administrative roles. Together, this group forms a legislative body and makes decisions for the city.

Committee chairperson. The committee chairperson is in charge of his or her committee. This is a powerful position because the chair places pending bills on the agenda and if a bill is never placed on the agenda it will almost never be made into law.

Committee of the whole. Committee of the whole takes place when the entire membership of the senate sits as a committee and operates with its own chairman under informal and flexible rules for the purpose of considering a bill.

Commutation. Commutation is a reduction of a criminal penalty to one which is less severe.

Condemned. This term has two meanings. Condemned property may be property which the city or municipality says is unfit for use because it is not safe. It can also be land which the city has taken by right of eminent domain for city use, such as building a new highway. In this case the former owner must be given fair payment for the property.

Conference Committee. The conference committee consists of six members— two from the majority party and one from the minority party of the house and the senate. They try to work out a compromise between the house and senate versions of a bill.

Congressional townships. Congressional, geographic, and survey townships are the same thing. It was Congress who authorized the first survey work for townships.

Constituents. Constituents are the citizens of each district and they are the people each representative works for. This includes those who are too young to vote along with those who did not vote for the winner.

Constitution. The state constitution is the rule book which organizes Michigan government and says what it may or may not do.

Contiguous. Contiguous describes two areas of land whose boundaries touch.

Corrections Commission. The Corrections Commission, five members appointed by the governor for four-year terms, selects the director of the department and sets its policy.

County board of commissioners. The board of commissioners is the administrative board which oversees county government in all but three of Michigan's counties. The other three counties have county executives. This board is elected and has from 5 to 27 members, depending on the county.

County chairperson. The county chairperson is one of the most powerful positions in party politics. This person is chosen by the county executive committee.

County clerk. The county clerk is an elected official who keeps the important records concerning the residents of the county. This includes births, marriages, divorces, etc. Another important duty is to oversee the elections in the county.

County Department of Equalization. The County Department of Equalization reviews the work of all assessors in the county. If the county's analysis concludes a local assessor did not assess fairly it may correct the situation. It is the county's responsibility to guarantee the fairness of the assessment process. Equalization is an important part of the property tax system because there are so many variables involved.

County executive committee. The county executive committee consists of all the party's nominees for state, county, and congressional offices and an equal number of individuals from various parts of the county who are not running for office.

County seat. The county seat may be thought of as the capital of the county. This is where the county courthouse is located and can be considered the headquarters of county government.

Court of Appeals. The court of appeals is the final stop for all criminal and civil cases tried under state law with the rare exception of those heard by the Michigan Supreme Court.

Court of Claims. The court of claims is where cases against the state of Michigan are heard.

Criminal action. Criminal action is a case started by the government, often through the county prosecutor's office, against someone believed to have broken the law.

Decentralized. Decentralized means decisions are made by many individuals at a local level rather than being concentrated in the hands of a few at the state or national level.

Deed. A deed is an official document concerning property ownership and location. It provides an official description of the property.

Defendant. The defendant is the individual against whom the case is brought. The person alleged to have committed a crime or done something wrong is the defendant and so is the person being sued in a civil case.

Delinquent tax roll. The delinquent tax roll is a list of people who haven't paid their property taxes.

Department of Agriculture. The Department of Agriculture assists farmers in many ways, especially by helping to produce high-quality crops and promoting their sale.

Department of Civil Rights. This department works to protect people against many kinds of discrimination and prejudice concerning jobs, education, and housing.

Department of Civil Service. The Department of Civil Service works to find qualified workers for state government jobs and sets standards for the employees and jobs alike. It covers about 55,000 Michigan government workers.

Department of Commerce. The Department of Commerce oversees and encourages business and economic development in Michigan, including tourism.

Department of Corrections. The Department of Corrections operates the state prison system.

Department of Education. The Department of Education, headed by the State Board of Education, provides leadership and general supervision of all public education, except for four-year colleges and universities.

Department of Labor. The Department of Labor promotes full employment and the welfare and safety of the workers of the state.

Department of Licensing and Regulation. The Department of Licensing and Regulation oversees and licenses occupations where the public could be harmed by poor practices.

Department of Management and Budget (DMB). The Department of Management and Budget helps manage state government, keeps state financial records, and prepares the state budget each year.

Department of Mental Health. The Department of Mental Health is responsible for the treatment of mental illness, for the promotion of research into the causes and prevention of mental diseases.

Department of Military Affairs. The Department of Military Affairs manages the army and air national guard for Michigan.

Department of Natural Resources. The Department of Natural Resources is responsible for Michigan's state parks, regulates hunting and fishing, and monitors toxic waste and environmental problems.

Department of Public Health. The Department of Public Health is responsible for the prevention of dangerous diseases and for the promotion of the general good health of the citizens of Michigan.

Department of Social Services. The Department of Social Services provides aid, generally known as welfare, for needy people in the state.

Department of State Police. The Department of State Police operates over 60 state police posts whose troopers patrol state and county roads, investigate organized crime, and more.

Department of the Treasury. The Department of the Treasury takes care of the state's money and collects state taxes.

Department of Transportation. The Department of Transportation maintains and builds major highways in Michigan, as well as managing all other types of transportation including air travel.

Detroit Recorder's Court. The Detroit recorder's court is much like the circuit court in criminal matters and handles felony criminal cases within the Detroit city limits. It has been administratively merged with the 3rd Judicial Circuit Court, Wayne County.

Discharge. Discharge is a vote taken in the house or senate to move a bill out of its committee to the floor so the entire group can debate it.

District courts. District courts handle both civil and criminal cases which include traffic cases, minor criminal cases, civil suits of $10,000 or less, and preliminary work for serious criminal cases.

Double jeopardy. Double jeopardy is trying (or sentencing) an individual twice for the same crime.

Election inspectors. Election inspectors are the workers required at each polling place. They make sure the equipment is working properly, get all the forms and files of registered voters organized, and open and close the polls. It is their responsibility to assure that only properly registered voters vote and they see that ballots are placed securely in the ballot box. If any voter needs assistance, they provide help. Each group of election inspectors has a Republican and a Democrat to assure neither party receives favored treatment.

Emergency Powers Act. The Emergency Powers Act passed by congress in 1981 forced the governor to shorten or commute all sentences by 90 days for those prisoners convicted of non-violent crimes— if the prison population had been over capacity for ar least 30 days.

Eminent domain. This is the power of government to take private property for public use.

Extradition. Extradition means to send a person accused of a crime in another state or country back to that location for trial or to have someone living elsewhere brought back to Michigan for trial.

Farmland and Open Space Preservation Act. This is a law to help farmers by preventing them from being forced out of business due to increasing property taxes on their land, especially in areas with a rapid growth in housing development.

Felony. A felony is a criminal offense punishable by one year or more in the state prison system. Such a criminal offense will involve $100 or more and the case is heard in the circuit court.

Fiscal. The term fiscal relates to financial matters when talking about government programs.

Fiscal agencies. Fiscal agencies aid the house and senate in determining the fiscal impact of bills. This means they tell the legislators how much the bills will cost the government and tax payers directly and indirectly. They keep track of the expenses of programs and changes in the tax laws, etc.

Fiscal year. The fiscal year covers the 12-month period from October 1 to September 30. This means that for planning and spending purposes, the new year for state government does not start in January but in October.

Friend of the court. The friend of the court office is a support unit for domestic problems.

Gavel. A gavel is a presiding officer's mallet or hammer with a barrel-shaped head of wood used to command attention or confirm an act.

General orders. General orders is the term used for first general discussion of a bill by all the senators and it is roughly the same as the second reading in the house.

Geographic township. A geographic township is the same as a congressional township or survey township. The geographic township has the boundaries first surveyed long ago, perhaps before Michigan even became a state.

Gerrymandering. Gerrymandering is the drawing of political districts for the purpose of gaining more political power.

Grand jury. A grand jury is a group of citizens brought together by the county prosecutor or the state attorney general to determine if there is sufficient evidence against someone to bring charges.

Grants-in-aid. Grants-in-aid use federal money for specific purposes designated by federal law.

Headlee amendment. Passed in 1978 the Headlee amendment is a multifaceted amendment which among other things tries to control property tax increases and to force state government to pay for new programs it legislates.

Home rule. Home rule allows the people of a county to decide for themselves how they want to be "ruled" or organized politically. In order to have home rule the county must adopt a charter.

Housing commission (county or township). Housing commissions are responsible for buying, building, and maintaining housing facilities for the needy. They may assist some property owners in improving their homes, possibly installing insulation for the elderly or poor.

Immediate effect. By a two-thirds vote of each house a bill may be given immediate effect and it becomes law on an agreed-upon date; otherwise, a new law goes into effect 90 days after the end of the session. Sessions are usually adjourned in December.

Incorporation (municipal government). The legal or formal process of becoming a village or city is called incorporation.

Infrastructure. The word infrastructure refers to the physical framework of society including roads, bridges, schools, libraries, etc.

Initiative. An initiative is a proposed law written by a group of people which is placed on the statewide ballot.

Interest groups. Interest groups are permanent organizations of concerned persons who want to influenece government policies to meet their goals. They do this through lobbying and methods which focus on the news media.

Joint committee. A joint committee is one which includes members of both houses brought together to solve a specific problem.

Judicial Tenure Commission. The Judicial Tenure Commission has nine members and reviews complaints concerning judges. Its goal is to "promote the integrity of the judicial process and preserve public confidence in the courts. It strives to hold judges accountable for their misconduct...."

Junket. From a French term for pleasure trip, now a junket is a trip by a lawmaker to gather more information concerning new legislation.

Jurisdictional question. A jurisdictional question is a situation where it is hard to decide who is responsible for taking care of the problem.

Juvenile. A juvenile is anyone under the age of 17.

Legislative Apportionment Commission. The Legislative Apportionment Commission has four members from each of the two major political parties in Michigan. They must decide on and draw up a plan of legislative districts which are equal in population.

Legislative immunity. Legislative immunity means freedom from arrest or prosecution for a member of the house or senate.

Legislative Service Bureau. The Legislative Service Bureau (LSB) is the organization that actually writes the bills for the legislators. It is a professional organization of experts who put the bills in correct legal language so they can become laws.

Levy. A levy is the amount of money a government unit expects to raise through tax collection.

Liaison. Liaison means to form a close bond or connection— so a person assigned to legislative liaison is responsible to keep in close contact with the legislature.

Lieutenant governor. The lieutenant governor is a person elected to serve as deputy to the governor. This person also heads the senate where he or she is known as the president of the senate. The president of the senate presides over the meetings but votes only in case of ties.

Limited obligation indebtedness. Limited obligation indebtedness is a form of borrowing. In this case the debt is paid by money brought in by the project. The cost of a loan to build a college dorm paid for by fees from students living in that dorm is one example.

Line item veto. The line item veto allows the governor to pass the majority of the bill about which there is no argument, yet remove items considered disagreeable.

Lobbyists. Lobbyists are paid professionals who try to influence public officials and legislators through personal appeals.

Lottery. A plan for the distribution of prizes or money by lot or chance. The state operates several kinds of lottery to raise money for education.

Lower chamber. The larger and more representative legislative group is traditionally known as the lower chamber. In Michigan it is the house of representatives.

Majority floor leader. The majority floor leader maneuvers legislation and attempts to assure that the majority caucus goals are reached.

Majority leader. The majority leader is elected by the legislative party with the most members. This person is the spokesperson for the majority party, has power to appoint committees and assumes leadership in developing a party program. Majority leader is a title used only in the senate.

Majority party. The majority party is the political party that has at least one more than half of the votes in the house or senate.

Metropolitan area. A metropolitan area includes the smaller cities and towns which are close to the major city. These other cities or suburbs are not under the political control of the major city but they operate in its economic and political shadow.

Michigan Supreme Court. The Michigan Supreme Court is the highest court in the state. It is the final word in legal matters relating to Michigan law. This court chooses the cases it hears.

Mill. A mill is commonly used in calculating the rate of property taxation. It is a value equal to 1/1,000th of a dollar. One mill represents a dollar of tax due on $1,000 worth of assessed value.

Minor party. A minor party is one operating over a period of time in addition to two major political parties in an area where only the two-party system usually exists.

Minority floor leader. The minority floor leader is a legislative member chosen by the minority party caucus to have charge of its organization on the floor. This person makes formal motions, opens debate, allots time to other members, and generally directs the party strategy related to the bills on the floor.

Minority leader. The minority leader is chosen by the party with fewer members to serve as chief negotiator on matters of party interest, to lead in developing a party program, and to be the chief contact with the media on behalf of the party.

Minority whip. The minority whip is the individual whose job it is to make sure the party is unified on important issues. This person assists the party floor leader. In this use the word whip means to hold together for united action.

Misdemeanor. A misdemeanor is usually a criminal offense punishable by a sentence of up to one year in a county jail. Most sentences are for 90 days or less.

Missouri Plan. The Missouri Plan, based on merit, combines both the election and appointment processes in the selection of state judges.

Modified commission (county government). Under this approach county government is headed by a county executive. The regular commission form of county organization does not have the position of county executive. There are two types of modified commission organization, optional unified plan and the home rule option.

Mortgage. A mortgage is a legal document between a bank or savings and loan company and those who borrowed money to buy a house or other property. The mortgage says if the borrower does not pay back the money, the bank can sell the property to get its money back!,

Municipal courts. The 1963 Michigan constitution provided that district courts would replace municipal courts. However, six municipal courts still remain in East Detroit and the Grosse Pointes. Mostly traffic problems and minor crimes are dealt with in these courts.

Municipality. A municipality is an area having the powers of local self government such as a city, village, or township.

National committeeman/national committeewoman. The political parties of each state send two individuals, a male and a female, called the national committeeman and national committeewoman to assist in the operation of the national party. They vote for party leaders and assist in campaigns for president, etc.

Natural Resources Commission. The Natural Resources Commission, seven-members appointed by the governor for four-year terms, appoints a director who supervises the department and sees that its functions are carried out.

Nonpartisan. Nonpartisan means not affiliated or associated with any political party.

Officeholder's account. The officeholder's account is an expense account for holding donations by supporters and lobbyists which can be spent on expenses associated with the responsibilities of the office, such as mailing Christmas cards. The funds are not to be used for campaign expenses. While most officials use the money to pay for office expenses, the funds have been used in questionable ways as well.

Open Meetings Act. This law requires open meetings so the public can attend and learn what is happening for all forms of government in Michigan. This includes everything from legislative meetings to intermediate school district boards, state and community college boards, zoning boards, road commissions, public hospitals, and others.

Open primary. An open primary allows all registered voters to vote and they do not declare their party affiliation.

Optional Unified Plan (county government). This is a plan of county organization which calls for the use of an elected or appointed county executive who manages county government on a day-to-day basis— though the county board of commissioners still has much power.

Ordinances. Ordinances are laws passed by city councils.

Pages. Pages serve as messengers and run various errands for the members of the legislature.

Pardon. A pardon is the forgiving and releasing of a criminal from punishment.

Parole Board. The parole board with five full-time members determines when a prisoner may be released.

Parole. Parole is an early release from prison. The paroled person must report to a parole officer and may be under other restrictions.

Partisan. Partisan means to be affiliated with one political party or another.

Party caucus. A party caucus is any meeting of top-level party leaders to decide an issue important to the party.

Party platform. The party platform is the position the party takes on important issues.

Party slate. A party's entire list of candidates in an election.

Peremptory challenge. Peremptory challenge is a technique used by lawyers in which prospective jurors can be dismissed for no stated reason at all.

Petit jury. The petit jury is the trial jury. The number of trial jurors may vary. In circuit court criminal cases there are 12, and six in civil matters. District and probate courts have six-member petit juries for both criminal and civil cases.

Petition. A petition is a formal written request by the people to the government. It must follow a certain format and be signed by a minimum number of voters.

Pigeonhole. Pigeonhole means to put the bill aside in committee and let it sit there without taking any action on it. To pigeonhole a bill has the same effect as voting against it but legislators don't have to tell constituents how they voted.

Plaintiff. The plaintiff is the individual who starts a civil suit.

Planning commission. This commission plans land use and development for either a county, city, or township which usually results in specific zoning regulations.

Plat. A plat is a detailed map of property boundaries kept in the register of deeds office. Plats are often laid out by township.

Political action committee or PAC. A PAC is an organization formed to further the political interests of its members by raising and distributing campaign contributions.

Political party. A political party is an organized group of individuals with common goals, seeking to influence public policy through the election of its candidates to office.

Political township. A political township is the unit of government which provides general government organization and services such as fire and police protection for a township. Political townships may have the exact boundaries of geographic townships or they may be a part of one township or a combination of two or three geographic townships.

Poll books. Poll books contain information about each voter, such as name, address, and which elections each voter has attended. This information is kept so that officials at elections are certain each voter is voting at the correct precinct.

Poll watchers. Poll watchers check on who has voted and try to evaluate how they think the election is going for their party's candidates.

Polling place. The polling place is the building where you vote— often a school or township office. Poll comes from an old Dutch word meaning head. So polling came to mean a head count and the polling place where the head count was made.

Precinct delegates. Precinct delegates are elected organizers of local party activities.

Precinct. A precinct is the smallest voting unit, usually containing 700-1000 adults.

Preliminary examination. A preliminary examination is held for the purpose of determining two things - if a crime has been committed and if there is enough evidence (probable cause) to believe the person being held is responsible.

President of the Senate Pro Tempore. This person is also known as the president pro tem. The president pro tem is selected from the senate majority party to lead "temporarily" while the lieutenant governor is away.

Pressure groups. See interest groups.

Private bills. Private bills are those which have a definite effect on one person, company, or organization.

Probate court. The probate court is where hearings are held regarding juvenile delinquents, child abuse, adoptions, wills, estates, guardianships, and commitment of the mentally ill.

Probation. Probation is the granting of a suspended sentence to a convicted offender by giving freedom after a promise of good behavior and his or her agreement to supervision and specified conditions.

Progressive tax. A progressive tax is one which has higher rates for those with larger incomes. It is based on a graduated scale.

Public administrator. The public administrator, an assistant to the attorney general, investigates estate matters.

Public and Local Acts of Michigan. The Public and Local Acts of Michigan are the printed laws passed by the state legislature each session. A new volume is prepared after the end of the session once a year.

Public bills. Public bills are those passed for the entire state and affect everyone in the same way.

Public Service Commission. The Public Service Commission is a group of three individuals each appointed for a six-year term by the governor. The commission regulates all telephone, electric, and gas companies and sets the rates for these utilities.

Reapportionment. Reapportionment is the redrawing of legislative districts to equalize their populations. This is done after each census.

Recess. A recess is a temporary break in the legislative session.

Referendum. A referendum gives voters a chance to accept or reject a law proposed by the legislature. The state constitution reserves this right to the people except for bills which appropriate money for state institutions or for tax measures needed to balance the state budget.

Register of deeds. The person elected to the office where the sales and descriptions of all homes, buildings, land, etc are recorded and stored.

Regressive tax. A regressive tax is a term given to a tax where everyone pays the same rate; therefore those with low incomes pay a larger portion of their available money for the tax.

Reprieve. A reprieve is the delay of punishment.

Resolution. A resolution is a written expression of the legislature's sentiment. It is not a law but the legislature's opinion on a matter.

Sales tax. Sales tax is a state tax on most purchases. The voters eliminated the sales tax on food (groceries) and prescription drugs in 1974.

School aid formula. This formula determines how much state aid a school district will receive. It includes such factors as the number of students in grades K-12, the local property tax base, millage rate, and other similar considerations.

School district. All of the state's public schools are in one or the other of Michigan's 560 school districts. The school district is the unit of local government responsible for public education in grades K-12. It has the power to collect property taxes to pay for educational services in the district.

Secretary of state. The secretary of state heads the department in charge of supervising voting, issuing drivers' licenses and handling other matters relating to cars, trucks, and buses; and is also in charge of preserving the state's history.

Seniority. Seniority refers to the length of time the legislator is in office. The legislators with greatest seniority (from the majority party) serve as chairs of nearly every committee.

Sergeant-at-arms. The sergeant-at-arms keeps order, sees that unauthorized people are kept off the floor of the house and senate, They also serve official papers and control the heating and lighting in the chamber.

Session. A session is the time during which the legislature meets regularly for the transaction of business and usually lasts for a period of one year. Each term has two sessions.

Single business tax. The single business tax was created in 1975. The legislature eliminated 11 business taxes and replaced them with the single business tax, often referred to as a type of value added tax.

Small claims division. A small claims court, a division in the district court, is where claims up to $1500 may be brought. To keep costs down, there are no attorneys for either side and no jury. Also the decision of the judge cannot be appealed.

Social services board. The social services board is responsible for administering the state welfare programs within each county. The board has three members, two appointed by the county commissioners and the third appointed by the governor, all for three-year terms. They may also be given additional responsibilities, such as the administration of a county nursing home or other similar facilities.

Solicitor general. The solicitor general, an assistant to the attorney general, handles appeals in the State Supreme Court, the Federal Circuit Court of Appeals, and the U.S. Supreme Court.

Speaker of the house. The speaker is the presiding officer in the House of Representatives. Because of the vast powers of this position the speaker can control the passage of any bills introduced by either party. Under normal conditions this person is chosen from the majority party in the house.

Special assessment. A special assessment is a type of tax owed to local government for a special service done by the city for a property owner. Common examples are for the construction of sidewalks, curbs, gutters, paving streets, and city water and sewer connections.

Split ticket. A split ticket results when a person votes for candidates from more than one political party in the same election.

Staggered term. A staggered term is used to give continuity within a commission so not all members are replaced at the same time. If there are three members in a commission and the term of office is six years, under a staggered term a new member would be chosen every two years.

Standing committees. Standing committees are those that "stand" or continue throughout the term and for all practical purposes are permanent from term to term. The legislature has standing committees and so do other levels of government such as counties.

State Board of Education. The state board of education is an elected board of eight members who are responsible to oversee the schools and education in Michigan. Each member serves for a term of eight years.

State central committee. This committee runs the party at the state level for the two years between conventions. Each congressional district selects representatives to the state central committee.

State court administrator. The state court administrator works under the supervision of the Supreme Court in Lansing. It is the administrator's job to prepare budget estimates on the cost of running the courts, keep statistical information, examine the calendars of cases in the courts, and to make recommendations for improvements in the running of the court system.

State equalized value or SEV. The SEV numbers result from the state tax commission's analysis of every county's property assessment figures. The state may adjust the numbers supplied by a county in order to have equality on a statewide basis.

State of the State Message. The State of the State speech is similar to the president's annual State of the Union address. It is a blueprint of the governor's plans for the upcoming year.

State Officers Compensation Commission. The State Officers Compensation Commission is appointed by the governor and every two years determines the salaries of the governor, lieutenant governor, supreme court justices, court of appeals judges, and legislators.

State tax tribunal. Property owners who protested their property tax assessment at the local level, but feel they did not get a satisfactory hearing, may appeal to the state tax tribunal. The tribunal has the final word on such appeals unless the matter is taken to court.

State Treasurer. The state treasurer is an individual appointed by the governor to head the Department of the Treasury. He or she is responsible for collecting state taxes and investing state funds and so forth.

Strong mayor-council form of city government. This form of city government provides an organization having a city council with a powerful mayor. The mayor has substantial powers of appointment, budget preparation, and veto.

Superintendent of public instruction. The state superintendent of public instruction, appointed by the State Board of Education, is responsible for carrying out the policies of the board and other duties provided by law.

Survey township. See geographic township.

Tax credits. Tax credits are a direct deduction of a person's tax bill. Credits have included city income taxes, donations to Michigan public universities, colleges, and libraries. Home heating costs are also allowed as credits for certain individuals.

Tax liens (leens). A tax lien is a claim against the property by the government for payment of back taxes.

Tax roll. A tax roll is a list of all taxable property in the township. The assessor is the person given the task of determining these properties and their values.

Township board. This board is the township's legislative body. It has either five or seven officials who vote at board meetings and run the township government. It includes the supervisor, treasurer, and clerk, who serve along with two or four trustees.

Township superintendent. Many charter townships hire a professional to help the supervisor. This is the township superintendent or manager who has the education and experience to aid the supervisor and the board.

Township supervisor. The township supervisor serves much like a city mayor, except it is for the township. This is an elected position.

Township trustees. The township trustees are the "pure" legislators of the township board. Most smaller townships have two trustees. If the township has over 5,000 people or 3,000 registered voters, the township board can choose to increase the number of trustees to four. All charter townships have four trustees.

Transportation Commission. The Transportation Commission, a six-member committee appointed by the governor for three-year terms, is responsible for directing the Department of Transportation.

Trial courts. Trial courts are the lower courts where trials take place. A trial court is the first step in the court system. Decisions from the trial courts can be appealed to higher courts. Juries are only a part of the trial court process.

True market value. The true market value is the price for which a piece of property would be sold to a willing buyer by a willing seller. For property tax purposes all property is assessed at one half of its true market value.

Unicameral. Unicameral means one chamber or legislative house. In a unicameral government the house of representatives and senate are combined.

Upper chamber. The upper chamber, also known as the senate, is the smaller group of legislators. Traditionally the senate met on the upper floor of the legislature building.

Use tax. A use tax is one paid by the user, the person who gets the benefit. The state gasoline tax is a use tax.

Value added tax. A value added tax is a tax on the value a business adds to the product it makes. As an example, a tire maker does not pay a tax on the rubber it buys but would pay a tax on what it costs them to make its tires under this type of system.

Variance. A variance is the granting of an exception to the zoning laws so individuals can build something which would otherwise be against the regulations.

Veto. The word veto means "to stop". When the governor uses this power, a bill passed by the legislature is stopped and does not become law unless the legislature overrides the veto by a two-thirds margin.

Voice vote. A voice vote is a legislative vote taken by calling for ayes and nays,(yes and no) and estimating which response is stronger.

Wards. Wards are geographical divisions of a city used to elect the council; usually one member of the council is elected from each ward.

Weak mayor-council form of city government. In the weak mayor-council form of city government the city council is given most of the powers and the mayor is given very few. The council has the power to make most appointments. The mayor may not even have veto power. The council prepares the budget with only recommendations from the mayor. Departments are often run by commissions appointed by the council.

Zoning. Zoning is the division of a city or township into areas which can only be used for specific types of development— homes, businesses, industry, etc.

Zoning board of appeals. This board receives requests to allow exceptions to the zoning map or to zoning rules and ordinances. The board may allow a variance to the ordinance if it sees fit.

Zoning laws. Zoning laws are comprehensive plans indicating what kinds of businesses and housing are allowed in each part of the township or city.

278

Michigan's Constitution / Contents

Article   I   (1)   Declaration of Rights

Article   II   (2)   Elections

Article   III   (3)   General Government

Article   IV   (4)   Legislative Branch

Article   V   (5)   Executive Branch

Article   VI   (6)   Judicial Branch

Article   VII   (7)   Local Government

Article   VIII   (8)   Education

Article   IX   (9)   Finance and Taxation

Article   X   (10)   Property

Article   XI   (11)   Public Officers and Employment

Article   XII   (12)   Amendment and Revision

CONSTITUTION of the STATE of MICHIGAN

PREAMBLE

We, the people of the State of Michigan, grateful to Almighty God for the blessings of freedom, and earnestly desiring to secure these blessings undiminished to ourselves and our posterity, do ordain and establish this constitution.

ARTICLE I

DECLARATION OF RIGHTS

Political power.
Sec. 1. All political power is inherent in the people. Government is instituted for their equal benefit, security and protection.
History: Const. 1963, Art. I, § 1, Eff. Jan. 1, 1964. **Former Constitution:** See Const. 1908, Art. II, § 1.

Equal protection; discrimination.
Sec. 2. No person shall be denied the equal protection of the laws; nor shall any person be denied the enjoyment of his civil or political rights or be discriminated against in the exercise thereof because of religion, race, color or national origin. The legislature shall implement this section by appropriate legislation.
History: Const. 1963, Art. I, § 2, Eff. Jan. 1, 1964.

Assembly, consultation, instruction, petition.
Sec. 3. The people have the right peaceably to assemble, to consult for the common good, to instruct their representatives and to petition the government for redress of grievances.
History: Const. 1963, Art. I, § 3, Eff. Jan. 1, 1964. **Former Constitution:** See Const. 1908, Art. II, § 2.

Freedom of worship and religious belief; appropriations.
Sec. 4. Every person shall be at liberty to worship God according to the dictates of his own conscience. No person shall be compelled to attend, or, against his consent, to contribute to the erection or support of any place of religious worship, or to pay tithes, taxes or other rates for the support of any minister of the gospel or teacher of religion. No money shall be appropriated or drawn from the treasury for the benefit of any religious sect or society, theological or religious seminary; nor shall property belonging to the state be appropriated for any such purpose. The civil and political rights, privileges and capacities of no person shall be diminished or enlarged on account of his religious belief.
History: Const. 1963, Art. I, § 4, Eff. Jan. 1, 1964. **Former Constitution:** See Const. 1908, Art. II, § 3.

Freedom of speech and of press.
Sec. 5. Every person may freely speak, write, express and publish his views on all subjects, being responsible for the abuse of such right; and no law shall be enacted to restrain or abridge the liberty of speech or of the press.
History: Const. 1963, Art. I, § 5, Eff. Jan. 1, 1964. **Former Constitution:** See Const. 1908, Art. II, § 4.

Bearing of arms.
Sec. 6. Every person has a right to keep and bear arms for the defense of himself and the state.
History: Const. 1963, Art. I, § 6, Eff. Jan. 1, 1964. **Former Constitution:** See Const. 1908, Art. II, § 5.

Military power subordinate to civil power.
Sec. 7. The military shall in all cases and at all times be in strict subordination to the civil power.
History: Const. 1963, Art. I, § 7, Eff. Jan. 1, 1964. **Former Constitution:** See Const. 1908, Art. II, § 6.

Quartering of soldiers.
Sec. 8. No soldier shall, in time of peace, be quartered in any house without the consent of the owner or occupant, nor in time of war, except in a manner prescribed by law.
History: Const. 1963, Art. I, § 8, Eff. Jan. 1, 1964. **Former Constitution:** See Const. 1908, Art. II, § 7.

Slavery and involuntary servitude.
Sec. 9. Neither slavery, nor involuntary servitude unless for the punishment of crime, shall ever be tolerated in this state.
History: Const. 1963, Art. I, § 9, Eff. Jan. 1, 1964. **Former Constitution:** See Const. 1908, Art. II, § 8.

Attainder; ex post facto laws; impairment of contracts.

Sec. 10. No bill of attainder, ex post facto law or law impairing the obligation of contract shall be enacted.

History: Const. 1963, Art. I, § 10, Eff. Jan. 1, 1964. **Former Constitution:** See Const. 1908, Art. II, § 9.

Searches and seizures.

Sec. 11. The person, houses, papers and possessions of every person shall be secure from unreasonable searches and seizures. No warrant to search any place or to seize any person or things shall issue without describing them, nor without probable cause, supported by oath or affirmation. The provisions of this section shall not be construed to bar from evidence in any criminal proceeding any narcotic drug, firearm, bomb, explosive or any other dangerous weapon, seized by a peace officer outside the curtilage of any dwelling house in this state.

History: Const. 1963, Art. I, § 11, Eff. Jan. 1, 1964.
Constitutionality: The last sentence of this section was held invalid as in conflict with U.S. Const., Amend. IV. Lucas v. People, 420 F.2d 259 (C.A. Mich. 1970); Caver v. Kropp, 306 F.Supp. 1329 (D.C. Mich. 1969); People v. Pennington, 383 Mich. 611, 178 N.W. 2d 460 (1970); People v. Andrews, 21 Mich. App. 731, 176 N.W. 2d 460 (1970).
Former Constitution: See Const. 1908, Art. II, § 10.

Habeas corpus.

Sec. 12. The privilege of the writ of habeas corpus shall not be suspended unless in case of rebellion or invasion the public safety may require it.

History: Const. 1963, Art. I, § 12, Eff. Jan. 1, 1964. **Former Constitution:** See Const. 1908, Art. II, § 11.

Conduct of suits in person or by counsel.

Sec. 13. A suitor in any court of this state has the right to prosecute or defend his suit, either in his own proper person or by an attorney.

History: Const. 1963, Art. I, § 13, Eff. Jan. 1, 1964. **Former Constitution:** See Const. 1908, Art. II, § 12.

Jury trials.

Sec. 14. The right of trial by jury shall remain, but shall be waived in all civil cases unless demanded by one of the parties in the manner prescribed by law. In all civil cases tried by 12 jurors a verdict shall be received when 10 jurors agree.

History: Const. 1963, Art. I, § 14, Eff. Jan. 1, 1964. **Former Constitution:** See Const. 1908, Art. II, § 13.

Double jeopardy; bailable offenses; commencement of trial if bail denied; bail hearing; effective date.

Sec. 15. No person shall be subject for the same offense to be twice put in jeopardy. All persons shall, before conviction, be bailable by sufficient sureties, except that bail may be denied for the following persons when the proof is evident or the presumption great:

(a) A person who, within the 15 years immediately preceding a motion for bail pending the disposition of an indictment for a violent felony or of an arraignment on a warrant charging a violent felony, has been convicted of 2 or more violent felonies under the laws of this state or under substantially similar laws of the United States or another state, or a combination thereof, only if the prior felony convictions arose out of at least 2 separate incidents, events, or transactions.

(b) A person who is indicted for, or arraigned on a warrant charging, murder or treason.

(c) A person who is indicted for, or arraigned on a warrant charging, criminal sexual conduct in the first degree, armed robbery, or kidnapping with intent to extort money or other valuable thing thereby, unless the court finds by clear and convincing evidence that the defendant is not likely to flee or present a danger to any other person.

(d) A person who is indicted for, or arraigned on a warrant charging, a violent felony which is alleged to have been committed while the person was on bail, pending the disposition of a prior violent felony charge or while the person was on probation or parole as a result of a prior conviction for a violent felony.

If a person is denied admission to bail under this section, the trial of the person shall be commenced not more than 90 days after the date on which admission to bail is denied. If the trial is not commenced within 90 days after the date on which admission to bail is denied and the delay is not attributable to the defense, the court shall immediately schedule a bail hearing and shall set the amount of bail for the person.

As used in this section, "violent felony" means a felony, an element of which involves a violent act or threat of a violent act against any other person.

This section, as amended, shall not take effect until May 1, 1979.

History: Const. 1963, Art. I, § 15, Eff. Jan. 1, 1964;—Am. H.J.R. Q, approved Nov. 7, 1978, Eff. May 1, 1979.
Effective date: The language certified by the Board of Canvassers was identical to House Joint Resolution Q of 1978, except for the deletion of the last sentence which contained the proposed May 1, 1979, effective date.
The May 1, 1979, effective date provision of House Joint Resolution Q was not stated in the text of ballot Proposal K or in any of the material circulated by the Secretary of State, and was neither considered nor voted upon by the electors in the November 7, 1978, general election.
Therefore, the effective date of Proposal K is December 23, 1978, which was the date 45 days after the election as provided by Const. 1963, Art. XII, § 1. Op. Atty. Gen., No. 5533 (1979).
Former Constitution: See Const. 1908, Art. II, § 14.

Bail; fines; punishments; detention of witnesses.

Sec. 16. Excessive bail shall not be required; excessive fines shall not be imposed; cruel or unusual punishment shall not be inflicted; nor shall witnesses be unreasonably detained.

History: Const. 1963, Art. I, § 16, Eff. Jan. 1, 1964. **Former Constitution:** See Const. 1908, Art. II, § 15.

Self-incrimination; due process of law; fair treatment at investigations.

Sec. 17. No person shall be compelled in any criminal case to be a witness against himself, nor be deprived of life, liberty or property, without due process of law. The right of all individuals, firms, corporations and voluntary associations to fair and just treatment in the course of legislative and executive investigations and hearings shall not be infringed.

History: Const. 1963, Art. I, § 17, Eff. Jan. 1, 1964.   Former Constitution: See Const. 1908, Art. II, § 16.

Witnesses; competency, religious beliefs.

Sec. 18. No person shall be rendered incompetent to be a witness on account of his opinions on matters of religious belief.

History: Const. 1963, Art. I, § 18, Eff. Jan. 1, 1964.   Former Constitution: See Const. 1908, Art. II, § 17.

Libels, truth as defense.

Sec. 19. In all prosecutions for libels the truth may be given in evidence to the jury; and, if it appears to the jury that the matter charged as libelous is true and was published with good motives and for justifiable ends, the accused shall be acquitted.

History: Const. 1963, Art. I, § 19, Eff. Jan 1. 1964.   Former Constitution: See Const. 1908, Art. II, § 18.

Rights of accused in criminal prosecutions.

Sec. 20. In every criminal prosecution, the accused shall have the right to a speedy and public trial by an impartial jury, which may consist of less than 12 jurors in prosecutions for misdemeanors punishable by imprisonment for not more than 1 year; to be informed of the nature of the accusation; to be confronted with the witnesses against him; to have compulsory process for obtaining witnesses in his favor; to have the assistance of counsel for his defense; to have an appeal as a matter of right; and as provided by law, when the trial court so orders, to have such reasonable assistance as may be necessary to perfect and prosecute an appeal.

History: Const. 1963, Art. I, § 20, Eff. Jan. 1, 1964;—Am. H.J.R. M, approved Aug. 8, 1972, Eff. Sept. 23, 1972.
Former Constitution: See Const. 1908, Art. II, § 19.

Imprisonment for debt.

Sec. 21. No person shall be imprisoned for debt arising out of or founded on contract, express or implied, except in cases of fraud or breach of trust.

History: Const. 1963, Art. I, § 21, Eff. Jan. 1, 1964.   Former Constitution: See Const. 1908, Art. II, § 20.

Treason; definition, evidence.

Sec. 22. Treason against the state shall consist only in levying war against it or in adhering to its enemies, giving them aid and comfort. No person shall be convicted of treason unless upon the testimony of two witnesses to the same overt act or on confession in open court.

History: Const. 1963, Art. I, § 22, Eff. Jan. 1, 1964.   Former Constitution: See Const. 1908, Art. II, § 21.

Enumeration of rights not to deny others.

Sec. 23. The enumeration in this constitution of certain rights shall not be construed to deny or disparage others retained by the people.

History: Const. 1963, Art. I, § 23, Eff. Jan. 1, 1964.

Rights of crime victims; enforcement; assessment against convicted defendants.

Sec. 24. (1) Crime victims, as defined by law, shall have the following rights, as provided by law:

The right to be treated with fairness and respect for their dignity and privacy throughout the criminal justice process.

The right to timely disposition of the case following arrest of the accused.

The right to be reasonably protected from the accused throughout the criminal justice process.

The right to notification of court proceedings.

The right to attend trial and all other court proceedings the accused has the right to attend.

The right to confer with the prosecution.

The right to make a statement to the court at sentencing.

The right to restitution.

The right to information about the conviction, sentence, imprisonment, and release of the accused.

(2) The legislature may provide by law for the enforcement of this section.

(3) The legislature may provide for an assessment against convicted defendants to pay for crime victims' rights.

History: Add. H.J.R. P, approved Nov. 8, 1988, Eff. Dec. 24, 1988.

ARTICLE II

ELECTIONS

Qualifications of electors; residence.

Sec. 1. Every citizen of the United States who has attained the age of 21 years, who has resided in this state six months, and who meets the requirements of local residence provided by law, shall be an elector and qualified to vote in any election except as otherwise provided in this constitution. The legislature shall define residence for voting purposes.

History: Const. 1963, Art. II, § 1, Eff. Jan. 1, 1964.
Compiler's Note: U.S. Const., Amendment XXVI, § 1, provides: "The right of citizens of the United States, who are eighteen years of age or older, to vote shall not be denied or abridged by the United States or by any State on account of age."
Former Constitution: See Const. 1908, Art. III, §§ 1-3.

Mental incompetence; imprisonment.

Sec. 2. The legislature may by law exclude persons from voting because of mental incompetence or commitment to a jail or penal institution.

History: Const. 1963, Art. II, § 2; Eff. Jan. 1, 1964.

Presidential electors; residence.

Sec. 3. For purposes of voting in the election for president and vice-president of the United States only, the legislature may by law establish lesser residence requirements for citizens who have resided in this state for less than six months and may waive residence requirements for former citizens of this state who have removed herefrom. The legislature shall not permit voting by any person who meets the voting residence requirements of the state to which he has removed.

History: Const. 1963, Art. II, § 3, Eff. Jan. 1, 1964.

Place and manner of elections.

Sec. 4. The legislature shall enact laws to regulate the time, place and manner of all nominations and elections, except as otherwise provided in this constitution or in the constitution and laws of the United States. The legislature shall enact laws to preserve the purity of elections, to preserve the secrecy of the ballot, to guard against abuses of the elective franchise, and to provide for a system of voter registration and absentee voting. No law shall be enacted which permits a candidate in any partisan primary or partisan election to have a ballot designation except when required for identification of candidates for the same office who have the same or similar surnames.

History: Const. 1963, Art. II, § 4, Eff. Jan. 1, 1964. **Former Constitution:** See Const. 1908, Art. III, §§ 1, 8.

Time of elections.

Sec. 5. Except for special elections to fill vacancies, or as otherwise provided in this constitution, all elections for national, state, county and township offices shall be held on the first Tuesday after the first Monday in November in each even-numbered year or on such other date as members of the congress of the United States are regularly elected.

History: Const. 1963, Art. II, § 5, Eff. Jan. 1, 1964.

Voters on tax limit increases or bond issues.

Sec. 6. Whenever any question is required to be submitted by a political subdivision to the electors for the increase of the ad valorem tax rate limitation imposed by Section 6 of Article IX for a period of more than five years, or for the issue of bonds, only electors in, and who have property assessed for any ad valorem taxes in, any part of the district or territory to be affected by the result of such election or electors who are the lawful husbands or wives of such persons shall be entitled to vote thereon. All electors in the district or territory affected may vote on all other questions.

History: Const. 1963, Art. II, § 6, Eff. Jan. 1, 1964. **Former Constitution:** See Const. 1908, Art. III, § 4.

Boards of canvassers.

Sec. 7. A board of state canvassers of four members shall be established by law. No candidate for an office to be canvassed nor any inspector of elections shall be eligible to serve as a member of a board of canvassers. A majority of any board of canvassers shall not be composed of members of the same political party.

History: Const. 1963, Art. II, § 7, Eff. Jan. 1, 1964. **Former Constitution:** See Const. 1908, Art. III, § 9. **Transfer of powers:** See § 16.128.

Recalls.

Sec. 8. Laws shall be enacted to provide for the recall of all elective officers except judges of courts of record upon petition of electors equal in number to 25 percent of the number of persons voting in the last preceding election for the office of governor in the electoral district of the officer sought to be recalled. The sufficiency of any statement of reasons or grounds procedurally required shall be a political rather than a judicial question.

History: Const. 1963, Art. II, § 8, Eff. Jan. 1, 1964. **Former Constitution:** See Const. 1908, Art. III, § 8.

Initiative and referendum; limitations; appropriations; petitions.

Sec. 9. The people reserve to themselves the power to propose laws and to enact and reject laws, called the initiative, and the power to approve or reject laws enacted by the legislature, called the referendum. The power of initiative extends only to laws which the legislature may enact under this constitution. The power of referendum does not extend to acts making appropriations for state institutions or to meet deficiencies in state funds and must be invoked in the manner prescribed by law within 90 days following the final adjournment of the legislative session at which the law was enacted. To invoke the initiative or referendum, petitions signed by a number of registered electors, not less than eight percent for initiative and five percent for referendum of the total vote cast for all candidates for governor at the last preceding general election at which a governor was elected shall be required.

Referendum, approval.

No law as to which the power of referendum properly has been invoked shall be effective thereafter unless approved by a majority of the electors voting thereon at the next general election.

Initiative; duty of legislature, referendum.

Any law proposed by initiative petition shall be either enacted or rejected by the legislature without change or amendment within 40 session days from the time such petition is received by the legislature. If any law proposed by such petition shall be enacted by the legislature it shall be subject to referendum, as hereinafter provided.

Legislative rejection of initiated measure; different measure; submission to people.

If the law so proposed is not enacted by the legislature within the 40 days, the state officer authorized by law shall submit such proposed law to the people for approval or rejection at the next general election. The legislature may reject any measure so proposed by initiative petition and propose a different measure upon the same subject by a yea and nay vote upon separate roll calls, and in such event both measures shall be submitted by such state officer to the electors for approval or rejection at the next general election.

Initiative or referendum law; effective date, veto, amendment and repeal.

Any law submitted to the people by either initiative or referendum petition and approved by a majority of the votes cast thereon at any election shall take effect 10 days after the date of the official declaration of the vote. No law initiated or adopted by the people shall be subject to the veto power of the governor, and no law adopted by the people at the polls under the initiative provisions of this section shall be amended or repealed, except by a vote of the electors unless otherwise provided in the initiative measure or by three-fourths of the members elected to and serving in each house of the legislature. Laws approved by the people under the referendum provision of this section may be amended by the legislature at any subsequent session thereof. If two or more measures approved by the electors at the same election conflict, that receiving the highest affirmative vote shall prevail.

Legislative implementation.

The legislature shall implement the provisions of this section.

History: Const. 1963, Art. II, § 9, Eff. Jan. 1, 1964.

Constitutionality: A law proposed by initiative petition which is enacted by the Legislature without change or amendment within forty days of its reception takes effect ninety days after the end of the session in which it was enacted unless two-thirds of the members of each house of the Legislature vote to give it immediate effect. Frey v. Department of Management and Budget, 429 Mich. 315, 414 N.W.2d 873 (1987).

Former Constitution: See Const. 1908, Art. V, § 1.

ARTICLE III

GENERAL GOVERNMENT

Seat of government.

Sec. 1. The seat of government shall be at Lansing.

History: Const. 1963, Art. III, § 1, Eff. Jan. 1, 1964. **Former Constitution:** See Const. 1908, Art. I, § 2.

Separation of powers of government.

Sec. 2. The powers of government are divided into three branches; legislative, executive and judicial. No person exercising powers of one branch shall exercise powers properly belonging to another branch except as expressly provided in this constitution.

History: Const. 1963, Art. III, § 2, Eff. Jan. 1, 1964. **Former Constitution:** See Const. 1908, Art. IV, § 2.

Great seal.

Sec. 3. There shall be a great seal of the State of Michigan and its use shall be provided by law.

History: Const. 1963, Art. III, § 3, Eff. Jan. 1, 1964. **Former Constitution:** See Const. 1908, Art. VI, §§ 11, 12.

Militia.

Sec. 4. The militia shall be organized, equipped and disciplined as provided by law.

History: Const. 1963, Art. III, § 4, Eff. Jan. 1, 1964. **Former Constitution:** See Const. 1908, Art. XV, §§ 1-3.

Intergovernmental agreements; service by public officers and employees.

Sec. 5. Subject to provisions of general law, this state or any political subdivision thereof, any governmental authority or any combination thereof may enter into agreements for the performance, financing or execution of their respective functions, with any one or more of the other states, the United States, the Dominion of Canada, or any political subdivision thereof unless otherwise provided in this constitution. Any other provision of this constitution notwithstanding, an officer or employee of the state or of any such unit of government or subdivision or agency thereof may serve on or with any governmental body established for the purposes set forth in this section and shall not be required to relinquish his office or employment by reason of such service. The legislature may impose such restrictions, limitations or conditions on such service as it may deem appropriate.

History: Const. 1963, Art. III, § 5, Eff. Jan. 1, 1964.

Internal improvements.

Sec. 6. The state shall not be a party to, nor be financially interested in, any work of internal improvement, nor engage in carrying on any such work, except for public internal improvements provided by law.

History: Const. 1963, Art. III, § 6, Eff. Jan. 1, 1964. Former Constitution: See Const. 1908, Art. X, § 14.

Common law and statutes, continuance.

Sec. 7. The common law and the statute laws now in force, not repugnant to this constitution, shall remain in force until they expire by their own limitations, or are changed, amended or repealed.

History: Const. 1963, Art. III, § 7, Eff. Jan. 1, 1964. Former Constitution: See Const. 1908, Schedule, § 1.

Opinions on constitutionality by supreme court.

Sec. 8. Either house of the legislature or the governor may request the opinion of the supreme court on important questions of law upon solemn occasions as to the constitutionality of legislation after it has been enacted into law but before its effective date.

History: Const. 1963, Art. III, § 8, Eff. Jan. 1, 1964.

ARTICLE IV

LEGISLATIVE BRANCH

Legislative power.

Sec. 1. The legislative power of the State of Michigan is vested in a senate and a house of representatives.

History: Const. 1963, Art. IV, § 1, Eff. Jan. 1, 1964. Former Constitution: See Const. 1908, Art. V, § 1.

Senators, number, term.

Sec. 2. The senate shall consist of 38 members to be elected from single member districts at the same election as the governor for four-year terms concurrent with the term of office of the governor.

Senatorial districts, apportionment factors.

In districting the state for the purpose of electing senators after the official publication of the total population count of each federal decennial census, each county shall be assigned apportionment factors equal to the sum of its percentage of the state's population as shown by the last regular federal decennial census computed to the nearest one one hundredth of one percent multiplied by four and its percentage of the state's land area computed to the nearest one-one hundredth of one percent.

Apportionment rules.

In arranging the state into senatorial districts, the apportionment commission shall be governed by the following rules:

(1) Counties with 13 or more apportionment factors shall be entitled as a class to senators in the proportion that the total apportionment factors of such counties bear to the total apportionment factors of the state computed to the nearest whole number. After each such county has been allocated one senator, the remaining senators to which this class of counties is entitled shall be distributed among such counties by the method of equal proportions applied to the apportionment factors.

(2) Counties having less than 13 apportionment factors shall be entitled as a class to senators in the proportion that the total apportionment factors of such counties bear to the total apportionment factors of the state computed to the nearest whole number. Such counties shall thereafter be arranged into senatorial districts that are compact, convenient, and contiguous by land, as rectangular in shape as possible, and having as nearly as possible 13 apportionment factors, but in no event less than 10 or more than 16. Insofar as possible, existing senatorial districts at the time of reapportionment shall not be altered unless there is a failure to comply with the above standards.

(3) Counties entitled to two or more senators shall be divided into single member districts. The population of such districts shall be as nearly equal as possible but shall not be less than 75 percent nor more than 125 percent of a number determined by dividing the population of the county by the number of senators to which it is entitled. Each such district shall follow incorporated city or township boundary lines to the extent possible and shall be compact, contiguous, and as nearly uniform in shape as possible.

History: Const. 1963, Art. IV, § 2, Eff. Jan. 1, 1964. Former Constitution: See Const. 1908, Art. V, § 2.

Representatives, number, term; contiguity of districts.

Sec. 3. The house of representatives shall consist of 110 members elected for two-year terms from single member districts apportioned on a basis of population as provided in this article. The districts shall consist of compact and convenient territory contiguous by land.

Representative areas, single and multiple county.

Each county which has a population of not less than seven-tenths of one percent of the population of the state shall constitute a separate representative area. Each county having less than seven-tenths of one percent of the population of the state shall be combined with another county or counties to form a representative area of not less than seven-tenths of one percent of the population of the state. Any county which is isolated under the initial allocation as provided in this section shall be joined with that contiguous representative area having the smallest percentage of the state's population. Each such representative area shall be entitled initially to one representative.

Apportionment of representatives to areas.

After the assignment of one representative to each of the representative areas, the remaining house seats shall be apportioned among the representative areas on the basis of population by the method of equal proportions.

Districting of single county area entitled to 2 or more representatives.

Any county comprising a representative area entitled to two or more representatives shall be divided into single member representative districts as follows:

(1) The population of such districts shall be as nearly equal as possible but shall not be less than 75 percent nor more than 125 percent of a number determined by dividing the population of the representative area by the number of representatives to which it is entitled.

(2) Such single member districts shall follow city and township boundaries where applicable and shall be composed of compact and contiguous territory as nearly square in shape as possible.

Districting of multiple county representative areas.

Any representative area consisting of more than one county, entitled to more than one representative, shall be divided into single member districts as equal as possible in population, adhering to county lines.

History: Const. 1963, Art. IV, § 3, Eff. Jan. 1, 1964. **Former Constitution:** See Const. 1908, Art. V, § 3.

Annexation or merger with a city.

Sec. 4. In counties having more than one representative or senatorial district, the territory in the same county annexed to or merged with a city between apportionments shall become a part of a contiguous representative or senatorial district in the city with which it is combined, if provided by ordinance of the city. The district or districts with which the territory shall be combined shall be determined by such ordinance certified to the secretary of state. No such change in the boundaries of a representative or senatorial district shall have the effect of removing a legislator from office during his term.

History: Const. 1963, Art. IV, § 4, Eff. Jan. 1, 1964.

Island areas, contiguity.

Sec. 5. Island areas are considered to be contiguous by land to the county of which they are a part.

History: Const. 1963, Art. IV, § 5, Eff. Jan. 1, 1964.

Commission on legislative apportionment.

Sec. 6. A commission on legislative apportionment is hereby established consisting of eight electors, four of whom shall be selected by the state organizations of each of the two political parties whose candidates for governor received the highest vote at the last general election at which a governor was elected preceding each apportionment. If a candidate for governor of a third political party has received at such election more than 25 percent of such gubernatorial vote, the commission shall consist of 12 members, four of whom shall be selected by the state organization of the third political party. One resident of each of the following four regions shall be selected by each political party organization: (1) the upper peninsula; (2) the northern part of the lower peninsula, north of a line drawn along the northern boundaries of the counties of Bay, Midland, Isabella, Mecosta, Newaygo and Oceana; (3) southwestern Michigan, those counties south of region (2) and west of a line drawn along the western boundaries of the counties of Bay, Saginaw, Shiawassee, Ingham, Jackson and Hillsdale; (4) southeastern Michigan, the remaining counties of the state.

Eligibility to membership.

No officers or employees of the federal, state or local governments, excepting notaries public and members of the armed forces reserve, shall be eligible for membership on the commission. Members of the commission shall not be eligible for election to the legislature until two years after the apportionment in which they participated becomes effective.

Appointment, term, vacancies.

The commission shall be appointed immediately after the adoption of this constitution and whenever apportionment or districting of the legislature is required by the provisions of this constitution. Members of the commission shall hold office until each apportionment or districting plan becomes effective. Vacancies shall be filled in the same manner as for original appointment.

Officers, rules of procedure, compensation, appropriation.

The secretary of state shall be secretary of the commission without vote, and in that capacity shall furnish, under the direction of the commission, all necessary technical services. The commission shall elect its own chairman, shall make its own rules of procedure, and shall receive compensation provided by law. The legislature shall appropriate funds to enable the commission to carry out its activities.

Call to convene; apportionment; public hearings.

Within 30 days after the adoption of this constitution, and after the official total population count of each federal decennial census of the state and its political subdivisions is available, the secretary of state shall issue a call convening the commission not less than 30 nor more than 45 days thereafter. The commission shall complete its work within 180 days after all necessary census information is available. The commission shall proceed to district and apportion the senate and house of representatives according to the provisions of this constitution. All final decisions shall require the concurrence of a majority of the members of the commission. The commission shall hold public hearings as may be provided by law.

Apportionment plan, publication; record of proceedings.

Each final apportionment and districting plan shall be published as provided by law within 30 days from the date of its adoption and shall become law 60 days after publication. The secretary of state shall keep a public record of all the proceedings of the commission and shall be responsible for the publication and distribution of each plan.

Disagreement of commission; submission of plans to supreme court.

If a majority of the commission cannot agree on a plan, each member of the commission, individually or jointly with other members, may submit a proposed plan to the supreme court. The supreme court shall determine which plan complies most accurately with the constitutional requirements and shall direct that it be adopted by the commission and published as provided in this section.

Jurisdiction of supreme court on elector's application.

Upon the application of any elector filed not later than 60 days after final publication of the plan, the supreme court, in the exercise of original jurisdiction, shall direct the secretary of state or the commission to perform their duties, may review any final plan adopted by the commission, and shall remand such plan to the commission for further action if it fails to comply with the requirements of this constitution.

History: Const. 1963, Art. IV, § 6, Eff. Jan. 1, 1964. **Transfer of powers:** See § 16.132.

Legislators; qualifications, removal from district.

Sec. 7. Each senator and representative must be a citizen of the United States, at least 21 years of age, and an elector of the district he represents. The removal of his domicile from the district shall be deemed a vacation of the office. No person who has been convicted of subversion or who has within the preceding 20 years been convicted of a felony involving a breach of public trust shall be eligible for either house of the legislature.

History: Const. 1963, Art. IV, § 7, Eff. Jan. 1, 1964. **Former Constitution:** See Const. 1908, Art. V, § 5.

Ineligibility of government officers and employees.

Sec. 8. No person holding any office, employment or position under the United States or this state or a political subdivision thereof, except notaries public and members of the armed forces reserve, may be a member of either house of the legislature.

History: Const. 1963, Art. IV, § 8, Eff. Jan. 1, 1964. **Former Constitution:** See Const. 1908, Art. V, § 6.

Civil appointments, ineligibility of legislators.

Sec. 9. No person elected to the legislature shall receive any civil appointment within this state from the governor, except notaries public, from the legislature, or from any other state authority, during the term for which he is elected.

History: Const. 1963, Art. IV, § 9, Eff. Jan. 1, 1964. **Former Constitution:** See Const. 1908, Art. V, § 7.

Legislators and state officers, government contracts, conflict of interest.

Sec. 10. No member of the legislature nor any state officer shall be interested directly or indirectly in any contract with the state or any political subdivision thereof which shall cause a substantial conflict of interest. The legislature shall further implement this provision by appropriate legislation.

History: Const. 1963, Art. IV, § 10, Eff. Jan. 1, 1964. **Former Constitution:** See Const. 1908, Art. V, §§ 7, 25.

Legislators privileged from civil arrest and civil process; limitation; questioning for speech in either house prohibited.

Sec. 11. Except as provided by law, senators and representatives shall be privileged from civil arrest and civil process during sessions of the legislature and for five days next before the commencement and after the termination thereof. They shall not be questioned in any other place for any speech in either house.

History: Const. 1963, Art. IV, § 11, Eff. Jan. 1, 1964;—Am. S.J.R. A, approved Nov. 2, 1982, Eff. Dec. 18, 1982. **Former Constitution:** See Const. 1908, Art. V, § 8.

State officers compensation commission.

Sec. 12. The state officers compensation commission is created which shall determine the salaries and expense allowances of the members of the legislature, the governor, the lieutenant governor and the justices of the supreme court. The commission shall consist of 7 members appointed by the governor. The commission shall determine the salaries and expense allowances of the members of the legislature, the governor, the lieutenant governor and the justices of the supreme court which determinations shall be the salaries and expense allowances unless the legislature by concurrent resolution adopted by 2/3 of the members elected to and serving in each house of the legislature reject them. The commission shall meet each 2 years for no more than 15 session days. The legislature shall implement this section by law.

History: Const. 1963, Art. IV, § 12, Eff. Jan. 1, 1964;—-Am. H.J.R. AAA, approved Aug. 6, 1968, Eff. Sept. 21, 1968.

Legislature; time of convening, sine die adjournment, measures carried over.

Sec. 13. The legislature shall meet at the seat of government on the second Wednesday in January of each year at twelve o'clock noon. Each regular session shall adjourn without day, on a day determined by concurrent resolution, at twelve o'clock noon. Any business, bill or joint resolution pending at the final adjournment of a regular session held in an odd numbered year shall carry over with the same status to the next regular session.

History: Const. 1963, Art. IV, § 13, Eff. Jan. 1, 1964. **Former Constitution:** See Const. 1908, Art. V, § 13.

Quorum; powers of less than quorum.

Sec. 14. A majority of the members elected to and serving in each house shall constitute a quorum to do business. A smaller number in each house may adjourn from day to day, and may compel the attendance of absent members in the manner and with penalties as each house may prescribe.

History: Const. 1963, Art. IV, § 14, Eff. Jan. 1, 1964. **Former Constitution:** See Const. 1908, Art. V, § 14.

Legislative council.

Sec. 15. There shall be a bi-partisan legislative council consisting of legislators appointed in the manner prescribed by law. The legislature shall appropriate funds for the council's operations and provide for its staff which shall maintain bill drafting, research and other services for the members of the legislature. The council shall periodically examine and recommend to the legislature revision of the various laws of the state.

History: Const. 1963, Art. IV, § 15, Eff. Jan. 1, 1964.

Legislature; officers, rules of procedure, expulsion of members.

Sec. 16. Each house, except as otherwise provided in this constitution, shall choose its own officers and determine the rules of its proceedings, but shall not adopt any rule that will prevent a majority of the members elected thereto and serving therein from discharging a committee from the further consideration of any measure. Each house shall be the sole judge of the qualifications, elections and returns of its members, and may, with the concurrence of two-thirds of all the members elected thereto and serving therein, expel a member. The reasons for such expulsion shall be entered in the journal, with the votes and names of the members voting upon the question. No member shall be expelled a second time for the same cause.

History: Const. 1963, Art. IV, § 16, Eff. Jan. 1, 1964. **Former Constitution:** See Const. 1908, Art. V, § 15.

Committees; record of votes, public inspection, notice of hearings.

Sec. 17. Each house of the legislature may establish the committees necessary for the efficient conduct of its business and the legislature may create joint committees. On all actions on bills and resolutions in each committee, names and votes of members shall be recorded. Such vote shall be available for public inspection. Notice of all committee hearings and a clear statement of all subjects to be considered at each hearing shall be published in the journal in advance of the hearing.

History: Const. 1963, Art. IV, § 17, Eff. Jan. 1, 1964.

Journal of proceedings; record of votes, dissents.

Sec. 18. Each house shall keep a journal of its proceedings, and publish the same unless the public security otherwise requires. The record of the vote and name of the members of either house voting on any question shall be entered in the journal at the request of one-fifth of the members present. Any member of either house may dissent from and protest against any act, proceeding or resolution which he deems injurious to any person or the public, and have the reason for his dissent entered in the journal.

History: Const. 1963, Art. IV, § 18, Eff. Jan. 1, 1964. **Former Constitution:** See Const. 1908, Art. V, § 16.

Record of votes on elections and advice and consent.

Sec. 19. All elections in either house or in joint convention and all votes on appointments submitted to the senate for advice and consent shall be published by vote and name in the journal.

History: Const. 1963, Art. IV, § 19, Eff. Jan. 1, 1964. **Former Constitution:** See Const. 1908, Art. V, § 17.

Open meetings.

Sec. 20. The doors of each house shall be open unless the public security otherwise requires.

History: Const. 1963, Art. IV, § 20, Eff. Jan. 1, 1964. **Former Constitution:** See Const. 1908, Art. V, § 18.

Adjournments, limitations.

Sec. 21. Neither house shall, without the consent of the other, adjourn for more than two intervening calendar days, nor to any place other than where the legislature may then be in session.

History: Const. 1963, Art. IV, § 21, Eff. Jan. 1, 1964. **Former Constitution:** See Const. 1908, Art. V, § 18.

Bills.

Sec. 22. All legislation shall be by bill and may originate in either house.

History: Const. 1963, Art. IV, § 22, Eff. Jan. 1, 1964. **Former Constitution:** See Const. 1908, Art. V, § 19.

Style of laws.

Sec. 23. The style of the laws shall be: The People of the State of Michigan enact.

History: Const. 1963, Art. IV, § 23, Eff. Jan. 1, 1964. **Former Constitution:** See Const. 1908, Art. V, § 20.

Laws; object, title, amendments changing purpose.

Sec. 24. No law shall embrace more than one object, which shall be expressed in its title. No bill shall be altered or amended on its passage through either house so as to change its original purpose as determined by its total content and not alone by its title.

History: Const. 1963, Art. IV, § 24, Eff. Jan. 1, 1964. **Former Constitution:** See Const. 1908, Art. V, §§ 21, 22.

Revision and amendment of laws; title references, publication of entire sections.

Sec. 25. No law shall be revised, altered or amended by reference to its title only. The section or sections of the act altered or amended shall be re-enacted and published at length.

History: Const. 1963, Art. IV, § 25, Eff. Jan. 1, 1964. **Former Constitution:** See Const. 1908, Art. V, § 21.

Bills; printing, possession, reading, vote on passage.

Sec. 26. No bill shall be passed or become a law at any regular session of the legislature until it has been printed or reproduced and in the possession of each house for at least five days. Every bill shall be read three times in each house before the final passage thereof. No bill shall become a law without the concurrence of a majority of the members elected to and serving in each house. On the final passage of bills, the votes and names of the members voting thereon shall be entered in the journal.

History: Const. 1963, Art. IV, § 26, Eff. Jan. 1, 1964.

Compiler's note: In Advisory Opinion on Constitutionality of 1978 PA 426, 403 Mich. 631, 272 N.W.2d 495 (1978), the Michigan supreme court held that the lieutenant governor may cast a tie breaking vote during the final consideration of a bill when the senate is equally divided, and 1978 PA 426 was constitutionally enacted.

Former Constitution: See Const. 1908, Art. V, §§ 22, 23.

Laws, effective date.

Sec. 27. No act shall take effect until the expiration of 90 days from the end of the session at which it was passed, but the legislature may give immediate effect to acts by a two-thirds vote of the members elected to and serving in each house.

History: Const. 1963, Art. IV, § 27, Eff. Jan. 1, 1964.

Constitutionality: A law proposed by initiative petition which is enacted by the Legislature without change or amendment within forty days of its reception takes effect ninety days after the end of the session in which it was enacted unless two-thirds of the members of each house of the Legislature vote to give it immediate effect. Frey v. Department of Management and Budget, 429 Mich. 315, 414 N.W.2d 873 (1987).

Former Constitution: See Const. 1908, Art. V, § 21.

Bills, subjects at special session.

Sec. 28. When the legislature is convened on extraordinary occasions in special session no bill shall be passed on any subjects other than those expressly stated in the governor's proclamation or submitted by special message.

History: Const. 1963, Art. IV, § 28, Eff. Jan. 1, 1964. **Former Constitution:** See Const. 1908, Art. V, § 22.

Local or special acts.

Sec. 29. The legislature shall pass no local or special act in any case where a general act can be made applicable, and whether a general act can be made applicable shall be a judicial question. No local or special act shall take effect until approved by two-thirds of the members elected to and serving in each house and by a majority of the electors voting thereon in the district affected. Any act repealing local or special acts shall require only a majority of the members elected to and serving in each house and shall not require submission to the electors of such district.

History: Const. 1963, Art. IV, § 29, Eff. Jan. 1, 1964. **Former Constitution:** See Const. 1908, Art. V, § 30.

Appropriations; local or private purposes.

Sec. 30. The assent of two-thirds of the members elected to and serving in each house of the legislature shall be required for the appropriation of public money or property for local or private purposes.

History: Const. 1963, Art. IV, § 30, Eff. Jan. 1, 1964. **Former Constitution:** See Const. 1908, Art. V, § 24.

General appropriation bills; priority, statement of estimated revenue.

Sec. 31. The general appropriation bills for the succeeding fiscal period covering items set forth in the budget shall be passed or rejected in either house of the legislature before that house passes any appropriation bill for items not in the budget except bills supplementing appropriations for the current fiscal year's operation. Any bill requiring an appropriation to carry out its purpose shall be considered an appropriation bill. One of the general appropriation bills as passed by the legislature shall contain an itemized statement of estimated revenue by major source in each operating fund for the ensuing fiscal period, the total of which shall not be less than the total of all appropriations made from each fund in the general appropriation bills as passed.

History: Const. 1963, Art. IV, § 31, Eff. Jan. 1, 1964.

Laws imposing taxes.

Sec. 32. Every law which imposes, continues or revives a tax shall distinctly state the tax.

History: Const. 1963, Art. IV, § 32, Eff. Jan. 1, 1964. **Former Constitution:** See Const. 1908, Art. X, § 6.

Bills passed; approval by governor or veto, reconsideration by legislature.

Sec. 33. Every bill passed by the legislature shall be presented to the governor before it becomes law, and the governor shall have 14 days measured in hours and minutes from the time of presentation in which to consider it. If he approves, he shall within that time sign and file it with the secretary of state and it shall become law. If he does not approve, and the legislature has within that time finally adjourned the session at which the bill was passed, it shall not become law. If he disapproves, and the legislature continues the session at which the bill was passed, he shall return it within such 14-day period with his objections, to the house in which it originated. That house shall enter such objections in full in its journal and reconsider the bill. If two-thirds of the members elected to and serving in that house pass the bill notwithstanding the objections of the governor, it shall be sent with the objections to the other house for reconsideration. The bill shall become law if passed by two-thirds of the members elected to and serving in that house. The vote of each house shall be entered in the journal with the votes and names of the members voting thereon. If any bill is not returned by the governor within such 14-day period, the legislature continuing in session, it shall become law as if he had signed it.

History: Const. 1963, Art. IV, § 33, Eff. Jan. 1, 1964. **Former Constitution:** See Const. 1908, Art. V, § 36.

Bills, referendum.

Sec. 34. Any bill passed by the legislature and approved by the governor, except a bill appropriating money, may provide that it will not become law unless approved by a majority of the electors voting thereon.

History: Const. 1963, Art. IV, § 34, Eff. Jan. 1, 1964. **Former Constitution:** See Const. 1908, Art. V, § 38.

Publication and distribution of laws and judicial decisions.

Sec. 35. All laws enacted at any session of the legislature shall be published in book form within 60 days after final adjournment of the session, and shall be distributed in the manner provided by law. The prompt publication of judicial decisions shall be provided by law. All laws and judicial decisions shall be free for publication by any person.

History: Const. 1963, Art. IV, § 35, Eff. Jan. 1, 1964. **Former Constitution:** See Const. 1908, Art. V, § 39.

General revision of laws; compilation of laws.

Sec. 36. No general revision of the laws shall be made. The legislature may provide for a compilation of the laws in force, arranged without alteration, under appropriate heads and titles.

History: Const. 1963, Art. IV, § 36, Eff. Jan. 1, 1964. **Former Constitution:** See Const. 1908, Art. V, § 40.

Administrative rules, suspension by legislative committee.

Sec. 37. The legislature may by concurrent resolution empower a joint committee of the legislature, acting between sessions, to suspend any rule or regulation promulgated by an administrative agency subsequent to the adjournment of the last preceding regular legislative session. Such suspension shall continue no longer than the end of the next regular legislative session.

History: Const. 1963, Art. IV, § 37, Eff. Jan. 1, 1964.

Vacancies in office.

Sec. 38. The legislature may provide by law the cases in which any office shall be vacant and the manner of filling vacancies where no provision is made in this constitution.

History: Const. 1963, Art. IV, § 38, Eff. Jan. 1, 1964. **Former Constitution:** See Const. 1908, Art. XVI, § 5.

Continuity of government in emergencies.

Sec. 39. In order to insure continuity of state and local governmental operations in periods of emergency only, resulting from disasters occurring in this state caused by enemy attack on the United States, the legislature may provide by law for prompt and temporary succession to the powers and duties of public offices, of whatever nature and whether filled by election or appointment, the incumbents of which may become unavailable for carrying on the powers and duties of such offices; and enact other laws necessary and proper for insuring the continuity of governmental operations. Notwithstanding the power conferred by this section, elections shall always be called as soon as possible to fill any vacancies in elective offices temporarily occupied by operation of any legislation enacted pursuant to the provisions of this section.

History: Const. 1963, Art. IV, § 39, Eff. Jan. 1, 1964. **Former Constitution:** See Const. 1908, Art. XVI, § 5.

Alcoholic beverages; age requirement; liquor control commission; excise tax; local option.

Sec. 40. A person shall not sell or give any alcoholic beverage to any person who has not reached the age of 21 years. A person who has not reached the age of 21 years shall not possess any alcoholic beverage for the purpose of personal consumption. An alcoholic beverage is any beverage containing one-half of one percent or more alcohol by volume.

Except as prohibited by this section, (t)he legislature may by law establish a liquor control commission which, subject to statutory limitations, shall exercise complete control of the alcoholic beverage traffic within this state, including the retail sales thereof. The legislature may provide for an excise tax on such sales. Neither the legislature nor the commission may authorize the manufacture or sale of alcoholic beverages in any county in which a majority of the electors voting thereon shall prohibit the same.

History: Const. 1963, Art. IV, § 40, Eff. Jan. 1, 1964;—-Am. Initiated Law, approved Nov. 7, 1978, Eff. Dec. 23, 1978.
Former Constitution: See Const. 1908, Art. XVI, § 11.

Lotteries.

Sec. 41. The legislature may authorize lotteries and permit the sale of lottery tickets in the manner provided by law.

History: Const. 1963, Art. IV, § 41, Eff. Jan. 1, 1964;—-Am. H.J.R. V, approved May 16, 1972, Eff. July 1, 1972.
Former Constitution: See Const. 1908, Art. V, § 33.

Ports and port districts; incorporation, internal.

Sec. 42. The legislature may provide for the incorporation of ports and port districts, and confer power and authority upon them to engage in work of internal improvements in connection therewith.

History: Const. 1963, Art. IV, § 42, Eff. Jan. 1, 1964. **Former Constitution:** See Const. 1908, Art. VIII, § 30.

Bank and trust company laws.

Sec. 43. No general law providing for the incorporation of trust companies or corporations for banking purposes, or regulating the business thereof, shall be enacted, amended or repealed except by a vote of two-thirds of the members elected to and serving in each house.

History: Const. 1963, Art. IV, § 43, Eff. Jan. 1, 1964. **Former Constitution:** See Const. 1908, Art. XII, § 9.

Trial by jury in civil cases.

Sec. 44. The legislature may authorize a trial by a jury of less than 12 jurors in civil cases.

History: Const. 1963, Art. IV, § 44, Eff. Jan. 1, 1964. **Former Constitution:** See Const. 1908, Art. V, § 27.

Indeterminate sentences.

Sec. 45. The legislature may provide for indeterminate sentences as punishment for crime and for the detention and release of persons imprisoned or detained under such sentences.

History: Const. 1963, Art. IV, § 45, Eff. Jan. 1, 1964. **Former Constitution:** See Const. 1908, Art. V, § 28.

Death penalty.

Sec. 46. No law shall be enacted providing for the penalty of death.

History: Const. 1963, Art. IV, § 46, Eff. Jan. 1, 1964.

Chaplains in state institutions.

Sec. 47. The legislature may authorize the employment of chaplains in state institutions of detention or confinement.

History: Const. 1963, Art. IV, § 47, Eff. Jan. 1, 1964. **Former Constitution:** See Const. 1908, Art. V, § 26.

Disputes concerning public employees.

Sec. 48. The legislature may enact laws providing for the resolution of disputes concerning public employees, except those in the state classified civil service.

History: Const. 1963, Art. IV, § 48, Eff. Jan. 1, 1964. **Former Constitution:** See Const. 1908, Art. XVI, § 7.

Hours and conditions of employment.

Sec. 49. The legislature may enact laws relative to the hours and conditions of employment.

History: Const. 1963, Art. IV, § 49, Eff. Jan. 1, 1964. **Former Constitution:** See Const. 1908, Art. V, § 29.

Atomic and new forms of energy.

Sec. 50. The legislature may provide safety measures and regulate the use of atomic energy and forms of energy developed in the future, having in view the general welfare of the people of this state.

History: Const. 1963, Art. IV, § 50, Eff. Jan. 1, 1964.

Public health and general welfare.

Sec. 51. The public health and general welfare of the people of the state are hereby declared to be matters of primary public concern. The legislature shall pass suitable laws for the protection and promotion of the public health.

History: Const. 1963, Art. IV, § 51, Eff. Jan. 1, 1964.

Natural resources; conservation, pollution, impairment, destruction.

Sec. 52. The conservation and development of the natural resources of the state are hereby declared to be of paramount public concern in the interest of the health, safety and general welfare of the people. The legislature shall provide for the protection of the air, water and other natural resources of the state from pollution, impairment and destruction.

History: Const. 1963, Art. IV, § 52, Eff. Jan. 1, 1964.

Auditor general; appointment, qualifications, term, removal, post audits.
Sec. 53. The legislature by a majority vote of the members elected to and serving in each house, shall appoint an auditor general, who shall be a certified public accountant licensed to practice in this state, to serve for a term of eight years. He shall be ineligible for appointment or election to any other public office in this state from which compensation is derived while serving as auditor general and for two years following the termination of his service. He may be removed for cause at any time by a two-thirds vote of the members elected to and serving in each house. The auditor general shall conduct post audits of financial transactions and accounts of the state and of all branches, departments, offices, boards, commissions, agencies, authorities and institutions of the state established by this constitution or by law, and performance post audits thereof.

Independent investigations; reports.
The auditor general upon direction by the legislature may employ independent accounting firms or legal counsel and may make investigations pertinent to the conduct of audits. He shall report annually to the legislature and to the governor and at such other times as he deems necessary or as required by the legislature. He shall be assigned no duties other than those specified in this section.

Governing boards of institutions of higher education.
Nothing in this section shall be construed in any way to infringe the responsibility and constitutional authority of the governing boards of the institutions of higher education to be solely responsible for the control and direction of all expenditures from the institutions' funds.

Staff members, civil service.
The auditor general, his deputy and one other member of his staff shall be exempt from classified civil service. All other members of his staff shall have classified civil service status.
History: Const. 1963, Art. IV, § 53, Eff. Jan. 1, 1964.

ARTICLE V
EXECUTIVE BRANCH

Executive power.
Sec. 1. The executive power is vested in the governor.
History: Const. 1963, Art. V, § 1, Eff. Jan. 1, 1964. **Former Constitution:** See Const. 1908, Art. VI, § 2.

Principal departments.
Sec. 2. All executive and administrative offices, agencies and instrumentalities of the executive branch of state government and their respective functions, powers and duties, except for the office of governor and lieutenant governor and the governing bodies of institutions of higher education provided for in this constitution, shall be allocated by law among and within not more than 20 principal departments. They shall be grouped as far as practicable according to major purposes.

Organization of executive branch; assignment of functions; submission to legislature.
Subsequent to the initial allocation, the governor may make changes in the organization of the executive branch or in the assignment of functions among its units which he considers necessary for efficient administration. Where these changes require the force of law, they shall be set forth in executive orders and submitted to the legislature. Thereafter the legislature shall have 60 calendar days of a regular session, or a full regular session if of shorter duration, to disapprove each executive order. Unless disapproved in both houses by a resolution concurred in by a majority of the members elected to and serving in each house, each order shall become effective at a date thereafter to be designated by the governor.
History: Const. 1963, Art. V, § 2, Eff. Jan. 1, 1964.

Single heads of departments; appointment, term.
Sec. 3. The head of each principal department shall be a single executive unless otherwise provided in this constitution or by law. The single executives heading principal departments shall include a secretary of state, a state treasurer and an attorney general. When a single executive is the head of a principal department, unless elected or appointed as otherwise provided in this constitution, he shall be appointed by the governor by and with the advice and consent of the senate and he shall serve at the pleasure of the governor.

Boards heading departments; appointment, term, removal.
When a board or commission is at the head of a principal department, unless elected or appointed as otherwise provided in this constitution, the members thereof shall be appointed by the governor by and with the advice and consent of the senate. The term of office and procedure for removal of such members shall be as prescribed in this constitution or by law.

Boards and commissions, maximum term.
Terms of office of any board or commission created or enlarged after the effective date of this constitution shall not exceed four years except as otherwise authorized in this constitution. The terms of office of existing boards and commissions which are longer than four years shall not be further extended except as provided in this constitution.
History: Const. 1963, Art. V, § 3, Eff. Jan. 1, 1964.

Commissions or agencies for less than 2 years.
Sec. 4. Temporary commissions or agencies for special purposes with a life of no more than two years may be established by law and need not be allocated within a principal department.
History: Const. 1963, Art. V, § 4, Eff. Jan. 1, 1964.

Examining or licensing board members, qualifications.
Sec. 5. A majority of the members of an appointed examining or licensing board of a profession shall be members of that profession.
History: Const. 1963, Art. V, § 5, Eff. Jan. 1, 1964.

Advice and consent to appointments.
Sec. 6. Appointment by and with the advice and consent of the senate when used in this constitution or laws in effect or hereafter enacted means appointment subject to disapproval by a majority vote of the members elected to and serving in the senate if such action is taken within 60 session days after the date of such appointment. Any appointment not disapproved within such period shall stand confirmed.
History: Const. 1963, Art. V, § 6, Eff. Jan. 1, 1964.

Vacancies in office; filling, senatorial disapproval of appointees.
Sec. 7. Vacancies in any office, appointment to which requires advice and consent of the senate, shall be filled by the governor by and with the advice and consent of the senate. A person whose appointment has been disapproved by the senate shall not be eligible for an interim appointment to the same office.
History: Const. 1963, Art. V, § 7, Eff. Jan. 1, 1964. Former Constitution: See Const. 1908, Art. VI, § 10.

Principal departments, supervision of governor; information from state officers.
Sec. 8. Each principal department shall be under the supervision of the governor unless otherwise provided by this constitution. The governor shall take care that the laws be faithfully executed. He shall transact all necessary business with the officers of government and may require information in writing from all executive and administrative state officers, elective and appointive, upon any subject relating to the duties of their respective offices.

Court enforcement of constitutional or legislative mandate.
The governor may initiate court proceedings in the name of the state to enforce compliance with any constitutional or legislative mandate, or to restrain violations of any constitutional or legislative power, duty or right by any officer, department or agency of the state or any of its political subdivisions. This authority shall not be construed to authorize court proceedings against the legislature.
History: Const. 1963, Art. V, § 8, Eff. Jan. 1, 1964. Former Constitution: See Const. 1908, Art. VI, § 3.

Principal departments, location.
Sec. 9. Single executives heading principal departments and the chief executive officers of principal departments headed by boards or commissions shall keep their offices at the seat of government except as otherwise provided by law, superintend them in person and perform duties prescribed by law.
History: Const. 1963, Art. V, § 9, Eff. Jan. 1, 1964. Former Constitution: See Const. 1908, Art. VI, § 1.

Removal or suspension of officers; grounds, report.
Sec. 10. The governor shall have power and it shall be his duty to inquire into the condition and administration of any public office and the acts of any public officer, elective or appointive. He may remove or suspend from office for gross neglect of duty or for corrupt conduct in office, or for any other misfeasance or malfeasance therein, any elective or appointive state officer, except legislative or judicial, and shall report the reasons for such removal or suspension to the legislature.
History: Const. 1963, Art. V, § 10, Eff. Jan. 1, 1964. Former Constitution: See Const. 1908, Art. IX, § 7.

Provisional appointments to fill vacancies due to suspension.
Sec. 11. The governor may make a provisional appointment to fill a vacancy occasioned by the suspension of an appointed or elected officer, other than a legislative or judicial officer, until he is reinstated or until the vacancy is filled in the manner prescribed by law or this constitution.
History: Const. 1963, Art. V, § 11, Eff. Jan. 1, 1964. Former Constitution: See Const. 1908, Art. IX, § 5.

Military powers.
Sec. 12. The governor shall be commander-in-chief of the armed forces and may call them out to execute the laws, suppress insurrection and repel invasion.
History: Const. 1963, Art. V, § 12, Eff. Jan. 1, 1964. Former Constitution: See Const. 1908, Art. VI, § 4.

Elections to fill vacancies in legislature.
Sec. 13. The governor shall issue writs of election to fill vacancies in the senate or house of representatives. Any such election

shall be held in a manner prescribed by law.
History: Const. 1963, Art. V, § 13, Eff. Jan. 1, 1964. **Former Constitution:** See Const. 1908, Art. VI, § 6.

Reprieves, commutations and pardons.
Sec. 14. The governor shall have power to grant reprieves, commutations and pardons after convictions for all offenses, except cases of impeachment, upon such conditions and limitations as he may direct, subject to procedures and regulations prescribed by law. He shall inform the legislature annually of each reprieve, commutation and pardon granted, stating reasons therefor.
History: Const. 1963, Art. V, § 14, Eff. Jan. 1, 1964. **Former Constitution:** See Const. 1908, Art. VI, § 9.

Extra sessions of legislature.
Sec. 15. The governor may convene the legislature on extraordinary occasions.
History: Const. 1963, Art. V, § 15, Eff. Jan. 1, 1964. **Former Constitution:** See Const. 1908, Art. VI, § 7.

Legislature other than at seat of government.
Sec. 16. The governor may convene the legislature at some other place when the seat of government becomes dangerous from any cause.
History: Const. 1963, Art. V, § 16, Eff. Jan. 1, 1964. **Former Constitution:** See Const. 1908, Art. VI, § 8.

Messages and recommendations to legislature.
Sec. 17. The governor shall communicate by message to the legislature at the beginning of each session and may at other times present to the legislature information as to the affairs of the state and recommend measures he considers necessary or desirable.
History: Const. 1963, Art. V, § 17, Eff. Jan. 1, 1964. **Former Constitution:** See Const. 1908, Art. VI, § 5.

Budget; general and deficiency appropriation bills.
Sec. 18. The governor shall submit to the legislature at a time fixed by law, a budget for the ensuing fiscal period setting forth in detail, for all operating funds, the proposed expenditures and estimated revenue of the state. Proposed expenditures from any fund shall not exceed the estimated revenue thereof. On the same date, the governor shall submit to the legislature general appropriation bills to embody the proposed expenditures and any necessary bill or bills to provide new or additional revenues to meet proposed expenditures. The amount of any surplus created or deficit incurred in any fund during the last preceding fiscal period shall be entered as an item in the budget and in one of the appropriation bills. The governor may submit amendments to appropriation bills to be offered in either house during consideration of the bill by that house, and shall submit bills to meet deficiencies in current appropriations.
History: Const. 1963, Art. V, § 18, Eff. Jan. 1, 1964.

Disapproval of items in appropriation bills.
Sec. 19. The governor may disapprove any distinct item or items appropriating moneys in any appropriation bill. The part or parts approved shall become law, and the item or items disapproved shall be void unless re-passed according to the method prescribed for the passage of other bills over the executive veto.
History: Const. 1963, Art. V, § 19, Eff. Jan. 1, 1964. **Former Constitution:** See Const. 1908, Art. V, § 37.

Reductions in expenditures.
Sec. 20. No appropriation shall be a mandate to spend. The governor, with the approval of the appropriating committees of the house and senate, shall reduce expenditures authorized by appropriations whenever it appears that actual revenues for a fiscal period will fall below the revenue estimates on which appropriations for that period were based. Reductions in expenditures shall be made in accordance with procedures prescribed by law. The governor may not reduce expenditures of the legislative and judicial branches or from funds constitutionally dedicated for specific purposes.
History: Const. 1963, Art. V, § 20, Eff. Jan. 1, 1964.

State elective executive officers; term, election.
Sec. 21. The governor, lieutenant governor, secretary of state and attorney general shall be elected for four-year terms at the general election in each alternate even-numbered year.

Lieutenant governor, secretary of state and attorney general, nomination.
The lieutenant governor, secretary of state and attorney general shall be nominated by party conventions in a manner prescribed by law. In the general election one vote shall be cast jointly for the candidates for governor and lieutenant governor nominated by the same party.

Secretary of state and attorney general, vacancies in office.
Vacancies in the office of the secretary of state and attorney general shall be filled by appointment by the governor.
History: Const. 1963, Art. V, § 21, Eff. Jan. 1, 1964. **Former Constitution:** See Const. 1908, Art. VI, § 1.

Governor and lieutenant governor, qualifications.
Sec. 22. To be eligible for the office of governor or lieutenant governor a person must have attained the age of 30 years, and have been a registered elector in this state for four years next preceding his election.
History: Const. 1963, Art. V, § 22, Eff. Jan. 1, 1964. **Former Constitution:** See Const. 1908, Art. VI, § 13.

State elective executive officers, compensation.

Sec. 23. The governor, lieutenant governor, secretary of state and attorney general shall each receive the compensation provided by law in full payment for all services performed and expenses incurred during his term of office. Such compensation shall not be changed during the term of office except as otherwise provided in this constitution.

History: Const. 1963, Art. V, § 23, Eff. Jan. 1, 1964.
Former Constitution: See Const. 1908, Art. VI, § 21.

Executive residence.

Sec. 24. An executive residence suitably furnished shall be provided at the seat of government for the use of the governor. He shall receive an allowance for its maintenance as provided by law.

History: Const. 1963, Art. V, § 24, Eff. Jan. 1, 1964.

Lieutenant governor; president of senate, tie vote, duties.

Sec. 25. The lieutenant governor shall be president of the senate, but shall have no vote, unless they be equally divided. He may perform duties requested of him by the governor, but no power vested in the governor shall be delegated.

History: Const. 1963, Art. V, § 25, Eff. Jan. 1, 1964.
Compiler's note: In Advisory Opinion on Constitutionality of 1978 PA 426, 403 Mich. 631, 272 N.W.2d 495 (1978), the Michigan supreme court held that the lieutenant governor may cast a tie-breaking vote during the final consideration of a bill when the senate is equally divided, and 1978 PA 426 was constitutionally enacted.
Former Constitution: See Const. 1908, Art. VI, § 19.

Succession to governorship.

Sec. 26. In case of the conviction of the governor on impeachment, his removal from office, his resignation or his death, the lieutenant governor, the elected secretary of state, the elected attorney general and such other persons designated by law shall in that order be governor for the remainder of the governor's term.

Death of governor-elect.

In case of the death of the governor-elect, the lieutenant governor-elect, the secretary of state-elect, the attorney general-elect and such other persons designated by law shall become governor in that order at the commencement of the governor-elect's term.

Duration of successor's term as governor.

If the governor or the person in line of succession to serve as governor is absent from the state, or suffering under an inability, the powers and duties of the office of the governor shall devolve in order of precedence until the absence or inability giving rise to the devolution of powers ceases.

Determination of inability.

The inability of the governor or person acting as governor shall be determined by a majority of the supreme court on joint request of the president pro tempore of the senate and the speaker of the house of representatives. Such determination shall be final and conclusive. The supreme court shall upon its own initiative determine if and when the inability ceases.

History: Const. 1963, Art. V, § 26, Eff. Jan. 1, 1964.
Former Constitution: See Const. 1908, Art. VI, §§ 16, 17.

Salary of successor.

Sec. 27. The legislature shall provide that the salary of any state officer while acting as governor shall be equal to that of the governor.

History: Const. 1963, Art. V, § 27, Eff. Jan. 1, 1964   Former Constitution: See Const. 1908, Art. VI, § 18.

State transportation commission; establishment; purpose; appointment, qualifications, and terms of members; director of state transportation department.

Sec. 28. There is hereby established a state transportation commission, which shall establish policy for the state transportation department transportation programs and facilities, and such other public works of the state, as provided by law.

The state transportation commission shall consist of six members, not more than three of whom shall be members of the same political party. They shall be appointed by the governor by and with the advice and consent of the senate for three-year terms, no three of which shall expire in the same year, as provided by law.

The director of the state transportation department shall be appointed as provided by law and shall be the principal executive officer of the state transportation department and shall be responsible for executing the policy of the state transportation commission.

History: Const. 1963, Art. V, § 28, Eff. Jan. 1, 1964;—Am. H.J.R. F, approved Nov. 7, 1978, Eff. Dec. 23, 1978.

Civil rights commission; members, term, duties, appropriation.

Sec. 29. There is hereby established a civil rights commission which shall consist of eight persons, not more than four of whom shall be members of the same political party, who shall be appointed by the governor, by and with the advice and consent of the senate, for four-year terms not more than two of which shall expire in the same year. It shall be the duty of the commission in a manner which may be prescribed by law to investigate alleged discrimination against any person because of religion, race, color or national origin in the enjoyment of the civil rights guaranteed by law and by this constitution, and to secure the equal protection of such civil rights without such discrimination. The legislature shall provide an annual appropriation for the effective operation of the commission.

Rules and regulations; hearings, orders.

The commission shall have power, in accordance with the provisions of this constitution and of general laws governing administrative agencies, to promulgate rules and regulations for its own procedures, to hold hearings, administer oaths, through court authorization to require the attendance of witnesses and the submission of records, to take testimony, and to issue appropriate orders. The commission shall have other powers provided by law to carry out its purposes. Nothing contained in this section shall be construed to diminish the right of any party to direct and immediate legal or equitable remedies in the courts of this state.

Appeals.

Appeals from final orders of the commission, including cease and desist orders and refusals to issue complaints, shall be tried de novo before the circuit court having jurisdiction provided by law.

History: Const. 1963, Art. V, § 29, Eff. Jan. 1, 1964. Administrative rules: R~37.1 et seq. and R~37.101 of the Michigan Administrative Code.

ARTICLE VI

JUDICIAL BRANCH

Judicial power in court of justice; divisions.

Sec. 1. The judicial power of the state is vested exclusively in one court of justice which shall be divided into one supreme court, one court of appeals, one trial court of general jurisdiction known as the circuit court, one probate court, and courts of limited jurisdiction that the legislature may establish by a two-thirds vote of the members elected to and serving in each house.

History: Const. 1963, Art. VI, § 1, Eff. Jan. 1, 1964. Former Constitution: See Const. 1908, Art. VII, § 1.

Justices of the supreme court; number, term, nomination, election.

Sec. 2. The supreme court shall consist of seven justices elected at non-partisan elections as provided by law. The term of office shall be eight years and not more than two terms of office shall expire at the same time. Nominations for justices of the supreme court shall be in the manner prescribed by law. Any incumbent justice whose term is to expire may become a candidate for re-election by filing an affidavit of candidacy, in the form and manner prescribed by law, not less than 180 days prior to the expiration of his term.

History: Const. 1963, Art. VI, § 2, Eff. Jan. 1, 1964. Former Constitution: See Const. 1908, Art. VII, § 2.

Chief justice; court administrator; other assistants.

Sec. 3. One justice of the supreme court shall be selected by the court as its chief justice as provided by rules of the court. He shall perform duties required by the court. The supreme court shall appoint an administrator of the courts and other assistants of the supreme court as may be necessary to aid in the administration of the courts of this state. The administrator shall perform administrative duties assigned by the court.

History: Const. 1963, Art. VI, § 3, Eff. Jan. 1, 1964.

General superintending control over courts; writs; appellate jurisdiction.

Sec. 4. The supreme court shall have general superintending control over all courts; power to issue, hear and determine prerogative and remedial writs; and appellate jurisdiction as provided by rules of the supreme court. The supreme court shall not have the power to remove a judge.

History: Const. 1963, Art. VI, § 4, Eff. Jan. 1, 1964. Former Constitution: See Const. 1908, Art. VII, § 4.

Court rules; distinctions between law and equity; master in chancery.

Sec. 5. The supreme court shall by general rules establish, modify, amend and simplify the practice and procedure in all courts of this state. The distinctions between law and equity proceedings shall, as far as practicable, be abolished. The office of master in chancery is prohibited.

History: Const. 1963, Art VI, § 5, Eff. Jan. 1, 1964.
Constitutionality: The State of Michigan, through the combined actions of the Supreme Court, the Legislature, and the State Bar, may compulsorily exact dues, and require association of attorneys, to support only those duties and functions of the State Bar which serve a compelling state interest and which cannot be accomplished by means less intrusive upon the First Amendment rights of objecting attorneys. Falk v. State Bar, 418 Mich. 270, 342 N.W.2d 504 (1983).
The regulation of the practice of law, the maintenance of high standards in the legal profession, and the discharge of the profession's duty to protect and inform the public are purposes in which the State of Michigan has a compelling interest justifying unavoidable intrusions on the First Amendment rights of attorneys; on the other hand, political and legislative activities are impermissible intrusions, as are activities designed to further commercial and economic interests of the members of the bar. Falk v. State Bar, 418 Mich. 270, 342 N.W.2d 504 (1983).
Former Constitution: See Const. 1908, Art. VII, § 5.

Decisions and dissents; writing, contents.

Sec. 6. Decisions of the supreme court, including all decisions on prerogative writs, shall be in writing and shall contain a concise statement of the facts and reasons for each decision and reasons for each denial of leave to appeal. When a judge dissents in whole or in part he shall give in writing the reasons for his dissent.

History: Const. 1963, Art. VI, § 6, Eff. Jan. 1, 1964. Former Constitution: See Const. 1908, Art. VII, § 7.

Staff; budget; salaries of justices; fees.

Sec. 7. The supreme court may appoint, may remove, and shall have general supervision of its staff. It shall have control of the preparation of its budget recommendations and the expenditure of moneys appropriated for any purpose pertaining to the operation of the court or the performance of activities of its staff except that the salaries of the justices shall be established by law. All fees and perquisites collected by the court staff shall be turned over to the state treasury and credited to the general fund.

History: Const. 1963, Art. VI, § 7, Eff. Jan. 1, 1964. **Former Constitution:** See Const. 1908, Art. VII, § 6.

Court of appeals; election of judges, divisions.

Sec. 8. The court of appeals shall consist initially of nine judges who shall be nominated and elected at non-partisan elections from districts drawn on county lines in as nearly as possible of equal population, as provided by law. The supreme court may prescribe by rule that the court of appeals sit in divisions and for the terms of court and the times and places thereof. Each such division shall consist of not fewer than three judges. The number of judges comprising the court of appeals may be increased, and the districts from which they are elected may be changed by law.

History: Const. 1963, Art. VI, § 8, Eff. Jan. 1, 1964.

Judges of court of appeals, terms.

Sec. 9. Judges of the court of appeals shall hold office for a term of six years and until their successors are elected and qualified. The terms of office for the judges in each district shall be arranged by law to provide that not all terms will expire at the same time.

History: Const. 1963, Art. VI, § 9, Eff. Jan. 1, 1964.

Jurisdiction, practice and procedure of court of appeals.

Sec. 10. The jurisdiction of the court of appeals shall be provided by law and the practice and procedure therein shall be prescribed by rules of the supreme court.

History: Const. 1963, Art. VI, § 10, Eff. Jan. 1, 1964.

Circuit courts; judicial circuits, sessions, number of judges.

Sec. 11. The state shall be divided into judicial circuits along county lines in each of which there shall be elected one or more circuit judges as provided by law. Sessions of the circuit court shall be held at least four times in each year in every county organized for judicial purposes. Each circuit judge shall hold court in the county or counties within the circuit in which he is elected, and in other circuits as may be provided by rules of the supreme court. The number of judges may be changed and circuits may be created, altered and discontinued by law and the number of judges shall be changed and circuits shall be created, altered and discontinued on recommendation of the supreme court to reflect changes in judicial activity. No change in the number of judges or alteration or discontinuance of a circuit shall have the effect of removing a judge from office during his term.

History: Const. 1963, Art. VI, § 11, Eff. Jan. 1, 1964. **Former Constitution:** See Const. 1908, Art. VII, § 8.

Circuit judges; nomination, election, term.

Sec. 12. Circuit judges shall be nominated and elected at non-partisan elections in the circuit in which they reside, and shall hold office for a term of six years and until their successors are elected and qualified. In circuits having more than one circuit judge their terms of office shall be arranged by law to provide that not all terms will expire at the same time.

History: Const. 1963, Art. VI, § 12, Eff. Jan. 1, 1964. **Former Constitution:** See Const. 1908, Art. VII, § 9.

Circuit courts; jurisdiction, writs, supervisory control over inferior courts.

Sec. 13. The circuit court shall have original jurisdiction in all matters not prohibited by law; appellate jurisdiction from all inferior courts and tribunals except as otherwise provided by law; power to issue, hear and determine prerogative and remedial writs; supervisory and general control over inferior courts and tribunals within their respective jurisdictions in accordance with rules of the supreme court; and jurisdiction of other cases and matters as provided by rules of the supreme court.

History: Const. 1963, Art. VI, § 13, Eff. Jan. 1, 1964. **Former Constitution:** See Const. 1908, Art. VII, § 10.

County clerks; duties, vacancies; prosecuting attorneys, vacancies.

Sec. 14. The clerk of each county organized for judicial purposes or other officer performing the duties of such office as provided in a county charter shall be clerk of the circuit court for such county. The judges of the circuit court may fill a vacancy in an elective office of county clerk or prosecuting attorney within their respective jurisdictions.

History: Const. 1963, Art. VI, § 14, Eff. Jan. 1, 1964. **Former Constitution:** See Const. 1908, Art. VII, § 11.

Probate courts; districts, jurisdiction.

Sec. 15. In each county organized for judicial purposes there shall be a probate court. The legislature may create or alter probate court districts of more than one county if approved in each affected county by a majority of the electors voting on the question. The legislature may provide for the combination of the office of probate judge with any judicial office of limited jurisdiction within a county with supplemental salary as provided by law. The jurisdiction, powers and duties of the probate court and of the judges thereof shall be provided by law. They shall have original jurisdiction in all cases of juvenile delinquents and dependents, except as otherwise provided by law.

History: Const. 1963, Art. VI, § 15, Eff. Jan. 1, 1964.
Former Constitution: See Const. 1908, Art. VII, § 13.

Probate judges; nomination, election, terms.

Sec. 16. One or more judges of probate as provided by law shall be nominated and elected at non-partisan elections in the counties or the probate districts in which they reside and shall hold office for terms of six years and until their successors are elected and qualified. In counties or districts with more than one judge the terms of office shall be arranged by law to provide that not all terms will expire at the same time.

History: Const. 1963, Art. VI, § 16, Eff. Jan. 1, 1964. **Former Constitution:** See Const. 1908, Art. VII, § 14.

Judicial salaries and fees.

Sec. 17. No judge or justice of any court of this state shall be paid from the fees of his office nor shall the amount of his salary be measured by fees, other moneys received or the amount of judicial activity of his office.

History: Const. 1963, Art. VI, § 17, Eff. Jan. 1, 1964.

Salaries; uniformity, changes during term.

Sec. 18. Salaries of justices of the supreme court, of the judges of the court of appeals, of the circuit judges within a circuit, and of the probate judges within a county or district, shall be uniform, and may be increased but shall not be decreased during a term of office except and only to the extent of a general salary reduction in all other branches of government.

Circuit judges, additional salary from county.

Each of the judges of the circuit court shall receive an annual salary as provided by law. In addition to the salary received from the state, each circuit judge may receive from any county in which he regularly holds court an additional salary as determined from time to time by the board of supervisors of the county. In any county where an additional salary is granted, it shall be paid at the same rate to all circuit judges regularly holding court therein.

History: Const. 1963, Art. VI, § 18, Eff. Jan. 1, 1964. **Former Constitution:** See Const. 1908, Art. VII, § 12; Art. XVI, § 3.

Courts of record; seal, qualifications of judges.

Sec. 19. The supreme court, the court of appeals, the circuit court, the probate court and other courts designated as such by the legislature shall be courts of record and each shall have a common seal. Justices and judges of courts of record must be persons who are licensed to practice law in this state. No person shall be elected or appointed to a judicial office after reaching the age of 70 years.

History: Const. 1963, Art. VI, § 19, Eff. Jan. 1, 1964. **Former Constitution:** See Const. 1908, Art. VII, § 17.

Removal of domicile of judge.

Sec. 20. Whenever a justice or judge removes his domicile beyond the limits of the territory from which he was elected or appointed, he shall have vacated his office.

History: Const. 1963, Art. VI, § 20, Eff. Jan. 1, 1964;—Am. H.J.R. F, approved Aug. 6, 1968, Eff. Sept. 21, 1968.
Former Constitution: See Const. 1908, Art. VII, § 19.

Ineligibility for other office.

Sec. 21. Any justice or judge of a court of record shall be ineligible to be nominated for or elected to an elective office other than a judicial office during the period of his service and for one year thereafter.

History: Const. 1963, Art. VI, § 21, Eff. Jan. 1, 1964. **Former Constitution:** See Const. 1908, Art. VII, § 9.

Incumbent judges, affidavit of candidacy.

Sec. 22. Any judge of the court of appeals, circuit court or probate court may become a candidate in the primary election for the office of which he is the incumbent by filing an affidavit of candidacy in the form and manner prescribed by law.

History: Const. 1963, Art. VI, § 22, Eff. Jan. 1, 1964;—Am. H.J.R. F, approved Aug. 6, 1968, Eff. Sept. 21, 1968.

Judicial vacancies, filling; appointee, term; successor; new offices.

Sec. 23. A vacancy shall occur in the office of judge of any court of record or in the district court by death, removal, resignation or vacating of the office, and such vacancy shall be filled by appointment by the governor. The person appointed by the governor shall hold office until 12 noon of the first day of January next succeeding the first general election held after the vacancy occurs, at which election a successor shall be elected for the remainder of the unexpired term. Whenever a new office of judge in a court of record, or the district court, is created by law, it shall be filled by election as provided by law. The supreme court may authorize persons who have been elected and served as judges to perform judicial duties for limited periods or specific assignments.

History: Const. 1963, Art. VI, § 23, Eff. Jan. 1, 1964;—Am. H.J.R. F, approved Aug. 6, 1968, Eff. Sept. 21, 1968.
Former Constitution: See Const. 1908, Art. VII, § 20.

Incumbent judges, ballot designation.

Sec. 24. There shall be printed upon the ballot under the name of each incumbent justice or judge who is a candidate for nomination or election to the same office the designation of that office.

History: Const. 1963, Art. VI, § 24, Eff. Jan. 1, 1964;—Am. H.J.R. F, approved Aug. 6, 1968, Eff. Sept. 21, 1968.
Former Constitution: See Const. 1908, Art. VII, § 23.

Removal of judges from office.

Sec. 25. For reasonable cause, which is not sufficient ground for impeachment, the governor shall remove any judge on a concurrent resolution of two-thirds of the members elected to and serving in each house of the legislature. The cause for removal shall be stated at length in the resolution.

History: Const. 1963, Art. VI, § 25, Eff. Jan. 1, 1964. **Former Constitution:** See Const. 1908, Art. IX, § 6.

Circuit court commissioners and justices of the peace, abolition; courts of limited jurisdiction.

Sec. 26. The offices of circuit court commissioner and justice of the peace are abolished at the expiration of five years from the date this constitution becomes effective or may within this period be abolished by law. Their jurisdiction, compensation and powers within this period shall be as provided by law. Within this five-year period, the legislature shall establish a court or courts of limited jurisdiction with powers and jurisdiction defined by law. The location of such court or courts, and the qualifications, tenure, method of election and salary of the judges of such court or courts, and by what governmental units the judges shall be paid, shall be provided by law, subject to the limitations contained in this article.

Present statutory courts.

Statutory courts in existence at the time this constitution becomes effective shall retain their powers and jurisdiction, except as provided by law, until they are abolished by law.

History: Const. 1963, Art. VI, § 26, Eff. Jan. 1, 1964.

Power of appointment to public office.

Sec. 27. The supreme court, the court of appeals, the circuit court, or any justices or judges thereof, shall not exercise any power of appointment to public office except as provided in this constitution.

History: Const. 1963, Art. VI, § 27, Eff. Jan. 1, 1964.
Former Constitution: See Const. 1908, Art. VII, § 11.

Administrative action, review.

Sec. 28. All final decisions, findings, rulings and orders of any administrative officer or agency existing under the constitution or by law, which are judicial or quasi-judicial and affect private rights or licenses, shall be subject to direct review by the courts as provided by law. This review shall include, as a minimum, the determination whether such final decisions, findings, rulings and orders are authorized by law; and, in cases in which a hearing is required, whether the same are supported by competent, material and substantial evidence on the whole record. Findings of fact in workmen's compensation proceedings shall be conclusive in the absence of fraud unless otherwise provided by law.

Property tax valuation or allocation; review.

In the absence of fraud, error of law or the adoption of wrong principles, no appeal may be taken to any court from any final agency provided for the administration of property tax laws from any decision relating to valuation or allocation.

History: Const. 1963, Art. VI, § 28, Eff. Jan. 1, 1964.

Conservators of the peace.

Sec. 29. Justices of the supreme court, judges of the court of appeals, circuit judges and other judges as provided by law shall be conservators of the peace within their respective jurisdictions.

History: Const. 1963, Art. VI, § 29, Eff. Jan. 1, 1964. **Former Constitution:** See Const. 1908, Art. VII, § 18.

Judicial tenure commission; selection; terms; duties; power of supreme court.

Sec. 30. (1) A judicial tenure commission is established consisting of nine persons selected for three-year terms as follows: Four members shall be judges elected by the judges of the courts in which they serve; one shall be a court of appeals judge, one a circuit judge, one a probate judge and one a judge of a court of limited jurisdiction. Three shall be members of the state bar who shall be elected by the members of the state bar of whom one shall be a judge and two shall not be judges. Two shall be appointed by the governor; the members appointed by the governor shall not be judges, retired judges or members of the state bar. Terms shall be staggered as provided by rule of the supreme court. Vacancies shall be filled by the appointing power.

(2) On recommendation of the judicial tenure commission, the supreme court may censure, suspend with or without salary, retire or remove a judge for conviction of a felony, physical or mental disability which prevents the performance of judicial duties, misconduct in office, persistent failure to perform his duties, habitual intemperance or conduct that is clearly prejudicial to the administration of justice. The supreme court shall make rules implementing this section and providing for confidentiality and privilege of proceedings.

History: Add. H.J.R. PP, approved Aug. 6, 1968, Eff. Sept. 21, 1968.

ARTICLE VII

LOCAL GOVERNMENT

Counties; corporate character, powers and immunities.
Sec. 1. Each organized county shall be a body corporate with powers and immunities provided by law.
History: Const. 1963, Art. VII, § 1, Eff. Jan. 1, 1964.   **Former Constitution:** See Const. 1908, Art. VIII, § 1.

County charters.
Sec. 2. Any county may frame, adopt, amend or repeal a county charter in a manner and with powers and limitations to be provided by general law, which shall among other things provide for the election of a charter commission. The law may permit the organization of county government in form different from that set forth in this constitution and shall limit the rate of ad valorem property taxation for county purposes, and restrict the powers of charter counties to borrow money and contract debts. Each charter county is hereby granted power to levy other taxes for county purposes subject to limitations and prohibitions set forth in this constitution or law. Subject to law, a county charter may authorize the county through its regularly constituted authority to adopt resolutions and ordinances relating to its concerns.

Election of charter commissions.
The board of supervisors by a majority vote of its members may, and upon petition of five percent of the electors shall, place upon the ballot the question of electing a commission to frame a charter.

Approval of electors.
No county charter shall be adopted, amended or repealed until approved by a majority of electors voting on the question.
History: Const. 1963, Art. VII, § 2, Eff. Jan. 1, 1964.

Reduction of size of county.
Sec. 3. No organized county shall be reduced by the organization of new counties to less than 16 townships as surveyed by the United States, unless approved in the manner prescribed by law by a majority of electors voting thereon in each county to be affected.
History: Const. 1963, Art. VII, § 3, Eff. Jan. 1, 1964.   **Former Constitution:** See Const. 1908, Art. VIII, § 2.

County officers; terms, combination.
Sec. 4. There shall be elected for four-year terms in each organized county a sheriff, a county clerk, a county treasurer, a register of deeds and a prosecuting attorney, whose duties and powers shall be provided by law. The board of supervisors in any county may combine the offices of county clerk and register of deeds in one office or separate the same at pleasure.
History: Const. 1963, Art. VII, § 4, Eff. Jan. 1, 1964.   **Former Constitution:** See Const. 1908, Art. VIII, § 3.

Offices at county seat.
Sec. 5. The sheriff, county clerk, county treasurer and register of deeds shall hold their principal offices at the county seat.
History: Const. 1963, Art. VII, § 5, Eff. Jan. 1, 1964.   **Former Constitution:** See Const. 1908, Art. VIII, § 4.

Sheriffs; security, responsibility for acts, ineligibility for other office.
Sec. 6. The sheriff may be required by law to renew his security periodically and in default of giving such security, his office shall be vacant. The county shall never be responsible for his acts, except that the board of supervisors may protect him against claims by prisoners for unintentional injuries received while in his custody. He shall not hold any other office except in civil defense.
History: Const. 1963, Art. VII, § 6, Eff. Jan. 1, 1964.   **Former Constitution:** See Const. 1908, Art. VIII, § 5.

Boards of supervisors; members.
Sec. 7. A board of supervisors shall be established in each organized county consisting of one member from each organized township and such representation from cities as provided by law.
History: Const. 1963, Art. VII, § 7, Eff. Jan. 1, 1964.
Constitutionality: Section held invalid under federal constitution. Advisory Opinion re Constitutionality of P.A. 1966, No. 261, 380 Mich. 736, 158 N.W. 2d 497 (1968); In re Apportionment of Ontonagon County Board of Supervisors, 11 Mich. App. 348, 157 N.W. 2d 698 (1967).
Former Constitution: See Const. 1908, Art. VIII, § 7.

Legislative, administrative, and other powers and duties of boards.
Sec. 8. Boards of supervisors shall have legislative, administrative and such other powers and duties as provided by law.
History: Const. 1963, Art. VII, § 8, Eff. Jan. 1, 1964.   **Former Constitution:** See Const. 1908, Art. VIII, § 8.

Compensation of county officers.
Sec. 9. Boards of supervisors shall have exclusive power to fix the compensation of county officers not otherwise provided by law.
History: Const. 1963, Art. 7, § 9, Eff. Jan. 1, 1964.   **Former Constitution:** See Const. 1908, Art. VIII, § 9.

Removal of county seat.
Sec. 10. A county seat once established shall not be removed until the place to which it is proposed to be moved shall be designated by two-thirds of the members of the board of supervisors and a majority of the electors voting thereon shall have approved the proposed location in the manner prescribed by law.
History: Const. 1963, Art. VII, § 10, Eff. Jan. 1, 1964. Former Constitution: See Const. 1908, Art. VIII, § 13.

Indebtedness, limitation.
Sec. 11. No county shall incur any indebtedness which shall increase its total debt beyond 10 percent of its assessed valuation.
History: Const. 1963, Art. VII, § 11, Eff. Jan. 1, 1964. Former Constitution: See Const. 1908, Art. VIII, § 12.

Navigable streams, permission to bridge or dam.
Sec. 12. A navigable stream shall not be bridged or dammed without permission granted by the board of supervisors of the county as provided by law, which permission shall be subject to such reasonable compensation and other conditions as may seem best suited to safeguard the rights and interests of the county and political subdivisions therein.
History: Const. 1963, Art. VII, § 12, Eff. Jan. 1, 1964. Former Constitution: See Const. 1908, Art. VIII, § 14.

Consolidation of counties, approval by electors.
Sec. 13. Two or more contiguous counties may combine into a single county if approved in each affected county by a majority of the electors voting on the question.
History: Const. 1963, Art. VII, § 13, Eff. Jan. 1, 1964.

Organization and consolidation of townships.
Sec. 14. The board of supervisors of each organized county may organize and consolidate townships under restrictions and limitations provided by law.
History: Const. 1963, Art. VII, § 14, Eff. Jan. 1, 1964 Former Constitution: See Const. 1908, Art. VIII, § 15.

County intervention in public utility service and rate proceedings.
Sec. 15. Any county, when authorized by its board of supervisors shall have the authority to enter or to intervene in any action or certificate proceeding involving the services, charges or rates of any privately owned public utility furnishing services or commodities to rate payers within the county.
History: Const. 1963, Art. VII, § 15, Eff. Jan. 1, 1964.

Highways, bridges, culverts, airports; road tax limitation.
Sec. 16. The legislature may provide for the laying out, construction, improvement and maintenance of highways, bridges, culverts and airports by the state and by the counties and townships thereof; and may authorize counties to take charge and control of any highway within their limits for such purposes. The legislature may provide the powers and duties of counties in relation to highways, bridges, culverts and airports; may provide for county road commissioners to be appointed or elected, with powers and duties provided by law. The ad valorem property tax imposed for road purposes by any county shall not exceed in any year one-half of one percent of the assessed valuation for the preceding year.
History: Const. 1963, Art. VII, § 16, Eff. Jan. 1, 1964. Former Constitution: See Const. 1908, Art. VIII, § 26.

Townships; corporate character, powers and immunities.
Sec. 17. Each organized township shall be a body corporate with powers and immunities provided by law.
History: Const. 1963, Art. VII, § 17, Eff. Jan. 1, 1964. Former Constitution: See Const. 1908, Art. VIII, § 16.

Township officers; term, powers and duties.
Sec. 18. In each organized township there shall be elected for terms of not less than two nor more than four years as prescribed by law a supervisor, a clerk, a treasurer, and not to exceed four trustees, whose legislative and administrative powers and duties shall be provided by law.
History: Const. 1963, Art. VII, § 18, Eff. Jan. 1, 1964. Former Constitution: See Const. 1908, Art. VIII, § 18.

Township public utility franchises.
Sec. 19. No organized township shall grant any public utility franchise which is not subject to revocation at the will of the township, unless the proposition shall first have been approved by a majority of the electors of such township voting thereon at a regular or special election.
History: Const. 1963, Art. VII, § 19, Eff. Jan. 1, 1964. Former Constitution: See Const. 1908, Art. VIII, § 19.

Townships, dissolution; villages as cities.
Sec. 20. The legislature shall provide by law for the dissolution of township government whenever all the territory of an organized township is included within the boundaries of a village or villages notwithstanding that a village may include territory within another organized township and provide by law for the classification of such village or villages as cities.
History: Const. 1963, Art. VII, § 20, Eff. Jan. 1, 1964.

Cities and villages; incorporation, taxes, indebtedness.

Sec. 21. The legislature shall provide by general laws for the incorporation of cities and villages. Such laws shall limit their rate of ad valorem property taxation for municipal purposes, and restrict the powers of cities and villages to borrow money and contract debts. Each city and village is granted power to levy other taxes for public purposes, subject to limitations and prohibitions provided by this constitution or by law.

History: Const. 1963, Art. VII, § 21, Eff. Jan. 1, 1964. **Former Constitution:** See Const. 1908, Art. VIII, § 20.

Charters, resolutions, ordinances; enumeration of powers.

Sec. 22. Under general laws the electors of each city and village shall have the power and authority to frame, adopt and amend its charter, and to amend an existing charter of the city or village heretofore granted or enacted by the legislature for the government of the city or village. Each such city and village shall have power to adopt resolutions and ordinances relating to its municipal concerns, property and government, subject to the constitution and law. No enumeration of powers granted to cities and villages in this constitution shall limit or restrict the general grant of authority conferred by this section.

History: Const. 1963, Art. VII, § 22, Eff. Jan. 1, 1964. **Former Constitution:** See Const. 1908, Art. VIII, § 21.

Parks, boulevards, cemeteries, hospitals.

Sec. 23. Any city or village may acquire, own, establish and maintain, within or without its corporate limits, parks, boulevards, cemeteries, hospitals and all works which involve the public health or safety.

History: Const. 1963, Art. VII, § 23, Eff. Jan. 1, 1964. **Former Constitution:** See Const. 1908, Art. VIII, § 22.

Public service facilities.

Sec. 24. Subject to this constitution, any city or village may acquire, own or operate, within or without its corporate limits, public service facilities for supplying water, light, heat, power, sewage disposal and transportation to the municipality and the inhabitants thereof.

Services outside corporate limits.

Any city or village may sell and deliver heat, power or light without its corporate limits in an amount not exceeding 25 percent of that furnished by it within the corporate limits, except as greater amounts may be permitted by law; may sell and deliver water and provide sewage disposal services outside of its corporate limits in such amount as may be determined by the legislative body of the city or village; and may operate transportation lines outside the municipality within such limits as may be prescribed by law.

History: Const. 1963, Art. VII, § 24, Eff. Jan. 1, 1964. **Former Constitution:** See Const. 1908, Art. VIII, § 23.

Public utilities; acquisition, franchises, sale.

Sec. 25. No city or village shall acquire any public utility furnishing light, heat or power, or grant any public utility franchise which is not subject to revocation at the will of the city or village, unless the proposition shall first have been approved by three-fifths of the electors voting thereon. No city or village may sell any public utility unless the proposition shall first have been approved by a majority of the electors voting thereon, or a greater number if the charter shall so provide.

History: Const. 1963, Art. VII, § 25, Eff. Jan. 1, 1964. **Former Constitution:** See Const. 1908, Art. VIII, § 25.

Cities and villages, loan of credit.

Sec. 26. Except as otherwise provided in this constitution, no city or village shall have the power to loan its credit for any private purpose or, except as provided by law, for any public purpose.

History: Const. 1963, Art. VII, § 26, Eff. Jan. 1, 1964.

Metropolitan governments and authorities.

Sec. 27. Notwithstanding any other provision of this constitution the legislature may establish in metropolitan areas additional forms of government or authorities with powers, duties and jurisdictions as the legislature shall provide. Wherever possible, such additional forms of government or authorities shall be designed to perform multipurpose functions rather than a single function.

History: Const. 1963, Art. VII, § 27, Eff. Jan. 1, 1964. **Former Constitution:** See Const. 1908, Art. VIII, § 31.

Governmental functions and powers; joint administration, costs and credits, transfers.

Sec. 28. The legislature by general law shall authorize two or more counties, townships, cities, villages or districts, or any combination thereof among other things to: enter into contractual undertakings or agreements with one another or with the state or with any combination thereof for the joint administration of any of the functions or powers which each would have the power to perform separately; share the costs and responsibilities of functions and services with one another or with the state or with any combination thereof which each would have the power to perform separately; transfer functions or responsibilities to one another or any combination thereof upon the consent of each unit involved; cooperate with one another and with state government; lend their credit to one another or any combination thereof as provided by law in connection with any authorized publicly owned undertaking.

Officers, eligibility.

Any other provision of this constitution notwithstanding, an officer or employee of the state or any such unit of government or subdivision or agency thereof, except members of the legislature, may serve on or with any governmental body established for the purposes set forth in this section and shall not be required to relinquish his office or employment by reason of such service.

History: Const. 1963, Art. VII, § 28, Eff. Jan. 1, 1964.

Highways, streets, alleys, public places; control, use by public utilities.

Sec. 29. No person, partnership, association or corporation, public or private, operating a public utility shall have the right to the use of the highways, streets, alleys or other public places of any county, township, city or village for wires, poles, pipes, tracks, conduits or other utility facilities, without the consent of the duly constituted authority of the county, township, city or village; or to transact local business therein without first obtaining a franchise from the township, city or village. Except as otherwise provided in this constitution the right of all counties, townships, cities and villages to the reasonable control of their highways, streets, alleys and public places is hereby reserved to such local units of government.

History: Const. 1963, Art. VII, § 29, Eff. Jan. 1, 1964. **Former Constitution:** See Const. 1908, Art. VIII, § 28.

Franchises and licenses, duration.

Sec. 30. No franchise or license shall be granted by any township, city or village for a period longer than 30 years.

History: Const. 1963, Art. VII, § 30, Eff. Jan. 1, 1964. **Former Constitution:** See Const. 1908, Art. VIII, § 29.

Vacation or alteration of roads, streets, alleys, public places.

Sec. 31. The legislature shall not vacate or alter any road, street, alley or public place under the jurisdiction of any county, township, city or village.

History: Const. 1963, Art. VII, § 31, Eff. Jan. 1, 1964. **Former Constitution:** See Const. 1908, Art. VIII, § 27.

Budgets, public hearing.

Sec. 32. Any county, township, city, village, authority or school district empowered by the legislature or by this constitution to prepare budgets of estimated expenditures and revenues shall adopt such budgets only after a public hearing in a manner prescribed by law.

History: Const. 1963, Art. VII, § 32, Eff. Jan. 1, 1964.

Removal of elected officers.

Sec. 33. Any elected officer of a political subdivision may be removed from office in the manner and for the causes provided by law.

History: Const. 1963, Art. VII, § 33, Eff. Jan. 1, 1964. **Former Constitution:** See Const. 1908, Art. IX, § 8.

Construction of constitution and law concerning counties, townships, cities, villages.

Sec. 34. The provisions of this constitution and law concerning counties, townships, cities and villages shall be liberally construed in their favor. Powers granted to counties and townships by this constitution and by law shall include those fairly implied and not prohibited by this constitution.

History: Const. 1963, Art. VII, § 34, Eff. Jan. 1, 1964.

ARTICLE VIII

EDUCATION

Encouragement of education.

Sec. 1. Religion, morality and knowledge being necessary to good government and the happiness of mankind, schools and the means of education shall forever be encouraged.

History: Const. 1963, Art. VIII, § 1, Eff. Jan. 1, 1964. **Former Constitution:** See Const. 1908, Art. XI, § 1.

Free public elementary and secondary schools; discrimination.

Sec. 2. The legislature shall maintain and support a system of free public elementary and secondary schools as defined by law. Every school district shall provide for the education of its pupils without discrimination as to religion, creed, race, color or national origin.

Nonpublic schools, prohibited aid.

No public monies or property shall be appropriated or paid or any public credit utilized, by the legislature or any other political subdivision or agency of the state directly or indirectly to aid or maintain any private, denominational or other nonpublic, pre-elementary, elementary, or secondary school. No payment, credit, tax benefit, exemption or deductions, tuition voucher, subsidy, grant or loan of public monies or property shall be provided, directly or indirectly, to support the attendance of any student or the employment of any person at any such nonpublic school or at any location or institution where instruction is offered in whole or in part to such nonpublic school students. The legislature may provide for the transportation of students to and from any school.

History: Const. 1963, Art. VIII, § 2, Eff. Jan. 1, 1964;—Am. Initiated Law, approved Nov. 3, 1970, Eff. Dec. 19, 1970.

Constitutionality: That portion of second sentence of second paragraph of this section, prohibiting use of public money to support attendance of any student or

employment of any person at any location or institution where instruction is offered in whole or in part to nonpublic students, was held unconstitutional, void, and unenforceable because it contravened free exercise of religion guaranteed by the United States Constitution and was violative of equal protection of laws provisions of United States Constitution. Traverse City School District v. Attorney General, 384 Mich. 390, 185 N.W. 2d 9 (1971).
Former Constitution: See Const. 1908, Art. XI, § 9.

State board of education; duties.

Sec. 3. Leadership and general supervision over all public education, including adult education and instructional programs in state institutions, except as to institutions of higher education granting baccalaureate degrees, is vested in a state board of education. It shall serve as the general planning and coordinating body for all public education, including higher education, and shall advise the legislature as to the financial requirements in connection therewith.

Superintendent of public instruction; appointment, powers, duties.

The state board of education shall appoint a superintendent of public instruction whose term of office shall be determined by the board. He shall be the chairman of the board without the right to vote, and shall be responsible for the execution of its policies. He shall be the principal executive officer of a state department of education which shall have powers and duties provided by law.

State board of education; members, nomination, election, term.

The state board of education shall consist of eight members who shall be nominated by party conventions and elected at large for terms of eight years as prescribed by law. The governor shall fill any vacancy by appointment for the unexpired term. The governor shall be ex-officio a member of the state board of education without the right to vote.

Boards of institutions of higher education, limitation.

The power of the boards of institutions of higher education provided in this constitution to supervise their respective institutions and control and direct the expenditure of the institutions' funds shall not be limited by this section.
History: Const. 1963, Art. VIII, § 3, Eff. Jan. 1, 1964.
Former Constitution: See Const. 1908, Art. XI, §§ 2, 6.

Higher education institutions; appropriations, accounting, public sessions of boards.

Sec. 4. The legislature shall appropriate moneys to maintain the University of Michigan, Michigan State University, Wayne State University, Eastern Michigan University, Michigan College of Science and Technology, Central Michigan University, Northern Michigan University, Western Michigan University, Ferris Institute, Grand Valley State College, by whatever names such institutions may hereafter be known, and other institutions of higher education established by law. The legislature shall be given an annual accounting of all income and expenditures by each of these educational institutions. Formal sessions of governing boards of such institutions shall be open to the public.
History: Const. 1963, Art. VIII, § 4, Eff. Jan. 1, 1964. **Former Constitution:** See Const. 1908, Art. XI, § 10.

University of Michigan, Michigan State University, Wayne State University; controlling boards.

Sec. 5. The regents of the University of Michigan and their successors in office shall constitute a body corporate known as the Regents of the University of Michigan; the trustees of Michigan State University and their successors in office shall constitute a body corporate known as the Board of Trustees of Michigan State University; the governors of Wayne State University and their successors in office shall constitute a body corporate known as the Board of Governors of Wayne State University. Each board shall have general supervision of its institution and the control and direction of all expenditures from the institution's funds. Each board shall, as often as necessary, elect a president of the institution under its supervision. He shall be the principal executive officer of the institution, be ex-officio a member of the board without the right to vote and preside at meetings of the board. The board of each institution shall consist of eight members who shall hold office for terms of eight years and who shall be elected as provided by law. The governor shall fill board vacancies by appointment. Each appointee shall hold office until a successor has been nominated and elected as provided by law.
History: Const. 1963, Art. VIII, § 5, Eff. Jan. 1, 1964. **Former Constitution:** See Const. 1908, Art. XI, §§ 3, 4, 5, 7, 8, 16.

Other institutions of higher education, controlling boards.

Sec. 6. Other institutions of higher education established by law having authority to grant baccalaureate degrees shall each be governed by a board of control which shall be a body corporate. The board shall have general supervision of the institution and the control and direction of all expenditures from the institution's funds. It shall, as often as necessary, elect a president of the institution under its supervision. He shall be the principal executive officer of the institution and be ex-officio a member of the board without the right to vote. The board may elect one of its members or may designate the president, to preside at board meetings. Each board of control shall consist of eight members who shall hold office for terms of eight years, not more than two of which shall expire in the same year, and who shall be appointed by the governor by and with the advice and consent of the senate. Vacancies shall be filled in like manner.
History: Const. 1963, Art. VIII, § 6, Eff. Jan. 1, 1964.

Community and junior colleges; state board, members, terms, vacancies.

Sec. 7. The legislature shall provide by law for the establishment and financial support of public community and junior colleges which shall be supervised and controlled by locally elected boards. The legislature shall provide by law for a state board for public community and junior colleges which shall advise the state board of education concerning general supervision and planning for such colleges and requests for annual appropriations for their support. The board shall consist of eight members who shall hold office for terms of eight years, not more than two of which shall expire in the same year, and who shall be appointed by the state board of education. Vacancies shall be filled in like manner. The superintendent of public instruction shall be ex-officio a member of this board without the right to vote.

History: Const. 1963, Art. VIII, § 7, Eff. Jan. 1, 1964.

Services for handicapped persons.

Sec. 8. Institutions, programs and services for the care, treatment, education or rehabilitation of those inhabitants who are physically, mentally or otherwise seriously handicapped shall always be fostered and supported.

History: Const. 1963, Art. VIII, § 8, Eff. Jan. 1, 1964. **Former Constitution:** See Const. 1908, Art. XI, § 15.

Public libraries, fines.

Sec. 9. The legislature shall provide by law for the establishment and support of public libraries which shall be available to all residents of the state under regulations adopted by the governing bodies thereof. All fines assessed and collected in the several counties, townships and cities for any breach of the penal laws shall be exclusively applied to the support of such public libraries, and county law libraries as provided by law.

History: Const. 1963, Art. VIII, § 9, Eff. Jan. 1, 1964. **Former Constitution:** See Const. 1908, Art. XI, § 14.

ARTICLE IX

FINANCE AND TAXATION

Taxes for state expenses.

Sec. 1. The legislature shall impose taxes sufficient with other resources to pay the expenses of state government.

History: Const. 1963, Art. IX, § 1, Eff. Jan. 1, 1964. **Former Constitution:** See Const. 1908, Art. X, § 2.

Power of taxation, relinquishment.

Sec. 2. The power of taxation shall never be surrendered, suspended or contracted away.

History: Const. 1963, Art. IX, § 2, Eff. Jan. 1, 1964. **Former Constitution:** See Const. 1908, Art. X, § 9.

Property taxation; uniformity, assessments, classes.

Sec. 3. The legislature shall provide for the uniform general ad valorem taxation of real and tangible personal property not exempt by law. The legislature shall provide for the determination of true cash value of such property; the proportion of true cash value at which such property shall be uniformly assessed, which shall not, after January 1, 1966, exceed 50 percent; and for a system of equalization of assessments. The legislature may provide for alternative means of taxation of designated real and tangible personal property in lieu of general ad valorem taxation. Every tax other than the general ad valorem property tax shall be uniform upon the class or classes on which it operates.

History: Const. 1963, Art. IX, § 3, Eff. Jan. 1, 1964. **Former Constitution:** See Const. 1908, Art. X, §§ 3, 4, 7, 8.

Exemption of religious or educational nonprofit organizations.

Sec. 4. Property owned and occupied by non-profit religious or educational organizations and used exclusively for religious or educational purposes, as defined by law, shall be exempt from real and personal property taxes.

History: Const. 1963, Art. IX, § 4, Eff. Jan. 1, 1964.

Assessment of property of public service businesses.

Sec. 5. The legislature shall provide for the assessment by the state of the property of those public service businesses assessed by the state at the date this constitution becomes effective, and of other property as designated by the legislature, and for the imposition and collection of taxes thereon. Property assessed by the state shall be assessed at the same proportion of its true cash value as the legislature shall specify for property subject to general ad valorem taxation. The rate of taxation on such property shall be the average rate levied upon other property in this state under the general ad valorem tax law, or, if the legislature provides, the rate of tax applicable to the property of each business enterprise assessed by the state shall be the average rate of ad valorem taxation levied upon other property in all counties in which any of such property is situated.

History: Const. 1963, Art. IX, § 5, Eff. Jan. 1, 1964.

Real and tangible personal property; limitation on general ad valorem taxes; adoption and alteration of separate tax limitations; exceptions to limitations; property tax on school district extending into 2 or more counties.

Section 6. Except as otherwise provided in this constitution, the total amount of general ad valorem taxes imposed upon real and tangible personal property for all purposes in any one year shall not exceed 15 mills on each dollar of the assessed valuation of property as finally equalized. Under procedures provided by law, which shall guarantee the right of initiative, separate tax limitations for any county and for the townships and for school districts therein, the aggregate of which shall not exceed 18 mills on each dollar of such valuation, may be adopted and thereafter altered by the vote of a majority of the qualified electors of such county voting thereon, in lieu of the limitation hereinbefore established. These limitations may be increased to an aggregate of not to exceed 50 mills on each dollar of valuation, for a period of not to exceed 20 years at any one time, if approved by a majority of the electors, qualified under Section 6 of Article II of this constitution, voting on the question.

The foregoing limitations shall not apply to taxes imposed for the payment of principal and interest on bonds approved by the electors or other evidences of indebtedness approved by the electors or for the payment of assessments or contract obligations in anticipation of which bonds are issued approved by the electors, which taxes may be imposed without limitation as to rate or amount; or, subject to the provisions of Section 25 through 34 of this article, to taxes imposed for any other purpose by any city, village, charter county, charter township, charter authority or other authority, the tax limitations of which are provided by charter or by general law.

In any school district which extends into two or more counties, property taxes at the highest rate available in the county which contains the greatest part of the area of the district may be imposed and collected for school purposes throughout the district.

History: Const. 1963, Art. IX, § 6, Eff. Jan. 1, 1964;——Am. Initiated Law, approved Nov. 7, 1978, Eff. Dec. 23, 1978.
Former Constitution: See Const. 1908, Art. X, § 21.

Income tax.

Sec. 7. No income tax graduated as to rate or base shall be imposed by the state or any of its subdivisions.

History: Const. 1963, Art. IX, § 7, Eff. Jan. 1, 1964.

Sales and use taxes.

Sec. 8. The Legislature shall not impose a sales tax on retailers at a rate of more than 4% of their gross taxable sales of tangible personal property.

No sales tax or use tax shall be charged or collected from and after January 1, 1975 on the sale or use of prescription drugs for human use, or on the sale or use of food for human consumption except in the case of prepared food intended for immediate consumption as defined by law.

This provision shall not apply to alcoholic beverages.

To compensate units of government other than the state for loss of revenue resulting from repeal of the sales tax on food and prescription drugs, each present allocation of sales tax revenue to such units shall be increased by 1/5.

History: Const. 1963, Art. IX, § 8, Eff. Jan. 1, 1964;——Am. Initiated Law, approved Nov. 5, 1974, Eff. Dec. 21, 1974.
Former Constitution: See Const. 1908, Art. X, § 23.

Use of specific taxes on fuels for transportation purposes; authorization of indebtedness and issuance of obligations.

Sec. 9. All specific taxes, except general sales and use taxes and regulatory fees, imposed directly or indirectly on fuels sold or used to propel motor vehicles upon highways and to propel aircraft and on registered motor vehicles and aircraft shall, after the payment of necessary collection expenses, be used exclusively for transportation purposes as set forth in this section.

Not less than 90 percent of the specific taxes, except general sales and use taxes and regulatory fees, imposed directly or indirectly on fuels sold or used to propel motor vehicles upon highways and on registered motor vehicles shall, after the payment of necessary collection expenses, be used exclusively for the transportation purposes of planning, administering, constructing, reconstructing, financing, and maintaining state, county, city, and village roads, streets, and bridges designed primarily for the use of motor vehicles using tires, and reasonable appurtenances to those state, county, city, and village roads, streets, and bridges.

The balance, if any, of the specific taxes, except general sales and use taxes and regulatory fees, imposed directly or indirectly on fuels sold or used to propel motor vehicles upon highways and on registered motor vehicles, after the payment of necessary collection expenses; 100 percent of the specific taxes, except general sales and use taxes and regulatory fees, imposed directly or indirectly on fuels sold or used to propel aircraft and on registered aircraft, after the payment of necessary collection expenses; and not more than 25 percent of the general sales taxes, imposed directly or indirectly on fuels sold to propel motor vehicles upon highways, on the sale of motor vehicles, and on the sale of the parts and accessories of motor vehicles, after the payment of necessary collection expenses; shall be used exclusively for the transportation purposes of comprehensive transportation purposes as defined by law.

The legislature may authorize the incurrence of indebtedness and the issuance of obligations pledging the taxes allocated or authorized to be allocated by this section, which obligations shall not be construed to be evidences of state indebtedness under this constitution.

History: Const. 1963, Art. IX, § 9, Eff. Jan. 1, 1964;——Am. H.J.R. F, approved Nov. 7, 1978, Eff. Dec. 23, 1978.
Former Constitution: See Const. 1908, Art. X, § 22.

Sales tax, distribution to local governments.

Sec. 10. One-eighth of all taxes imposed on retailers on taxable sales at retail of tangible personal property shall be used exclusively for assistance to townships, cities and villages, on a population basis as provided by law. In determining population the legislature may exclude any portion of the total number of persons who are wards, patients or convicts in any tax supported institution.

History: Const. 1963, Art. IX, § 10, Eff. Jan. 1, 1964. **Former Constitution:** See Const. 1908, Art. X, § 23.

State school aid fund, source and distribution.

Sec. 11. There shall be established a state school aid fund which shall be used exclusively for aid to school districts, higher education and school employees' retirement systems, as provided by law. One-half of all taxes imposed on retailers on taxable sales at retail of tangible personal property, and other tax revenues provided by law, shall be dedicated to this fund. Payments from this fund shall be made in full on a scheduled basis, as provided by law.

History: Const. 1963, Art. IX, § 11, Eff. Jan. 1, 1964.

Evidence of state indebtedness.

Sec. 12. No evidence of state indebtedness shall be issued except for debts authorized pursuant to this constitution.

History: Const. 1963, Art. IX, § 12, Eff. Jan. 1, 1964. **Former Constitution:** See Const. 1908, Art. X, § 11.

Public bodies, borrowing power.

Sec. 13. Public bodies corporate shall have power to borrow money and to issue their securities evidencing debt, subject to this constitution and law.

History: Const. 1963, Art. IX, § 13, Eff. Jan. 1, 1964.

State borrowing; short term.

Sec. 14. To meet obligations incurred pursuant to appropriations for any fiscal year, the legislature may by law authorize the state to issue its full faith and credit notes in which case it shall pledge undedicated revenues to be received within the same fiscal year for the repayment thereof. Such indebtedness in any fiscal year shall not exceed 15 percent of undedicated revenues received by the state during the preceding fiscal year and such debts shall be repaid at the time the revenues so pledged are received, but not later than the end of the same fiscal year.

History: Const. 1963, Art. IX, § 14, Eff. Jan. 1, 1964.

Long term borrowing by state.

Sec. 15. The state may borrow money for specific purposes in amounts as may be provided by acts of the legislature adopted by a vote of two-thirds of the members elected to and serving in each house, and approved by a majority of the electors voting thereon at any general election. The question submitted to the electors shall state the amount to be borrowed, the specific purpose to which the funds shall be devoted, and the method of repayment.

History: Const. 1963, Art. IX, § 15, Eff. Jan. 1, 1964.

State loans to school districts.

Sec. 16. The state, in addition to any other borrowing power, may borrow from time to time such amounts as shall be required, pledge its faith and credit and issue its notes or bonds therefor, for the purpose of making loans to school districts as provided in this section.

Amount of loans.

If the minimum amount which would otherwise be necessary for a school district to levy in any year to pay principal and interest on its qualified bonds, including any necessary allowances for estimated tax delinquencies, exceeds 13 mills on each dollar of its assessed valuation as finally equalized, or such lower millage as the legislature may prescribe, then the school district may elect to borrow all or any part of the excess from the state. In that event the state shall lend the excess amount to the school district for the payment of principal and interest. If for any reason any school district will be or is unable to pay the principal and interest on its qualified bonds when due, then the school district shall borrow and the state shall lend to it an amount sufficient to enable the school district to make the payment.

Qualified bonds.

The term "qualified bonds" means general obligation bonds of school districts issued for capital expenditures, including refunding bonds, issued prior to May 4, 1955, or issued thereafter and qualified as provided by law pursuant to Section 27 or Section 28 of Article X of the Constitution of 1908 or pursuant to this section.

Repayment of loans, tax levy by school district.

After a school district has received loans from the state, each year thereafter it shall levy for debt service, exclusive of levies for nonqualified bonds, not less than 13 mills or such lower millage as the legislature may prescribe, until the amount loaned has been repaid, and any tax collections therefrom in any year over and above the minimum requirements for principal and interest on qualified bonds shall be used toward the repayment of state loans. In any year when such levy would produce an amount in excess of the requirements and the amount due to the state, the levy may be reduced by the amount of the excess.

Bonds, state loans, repayment.

Subject to the foregoing provisions, the legislature shall have the power to prescribe and to limit the procedure, terms and conditions for the qualification of bonds, for obtaining and making state loans, and for the repayment of loans.

Power to tax unlimited.

The power to tax for the payment of principal and interest on bonds hereafter issued which are the general obligations of any school district, including refunding bonds, and for repayment of any state loans made to school districts, shall be without limitation as to rate or amount.

Rights and obligations to remain unimpaired.

All rights acquired under Sections 27 and 28 of Article X of the Constitution of 1908, by holders of bonds heretofore issued,

and all obligations assumed by the state or any school district under these sections, shall remain unimpaired.
History: Const. 1963, Art. IX, § 16, Eff. Jan. 1, 1964.   Former Constitution: See Const. 1908, Art. X, §§ 27, 28.

Payments from state treasury.
Sec. 17. No money shall be paid out of the state treasury except in pursuance of appropriations made by law.
History: Const. 1963, Art. IX, § 17, Eff. Jan. 1, 1964.   Former Constitution: See Const. 1908, Art. X, § 16.

State credit.
Sec. 18. The credit of the state shall not be granted to, nor in aid of any person, association or corporation, public or private, except as authorized in this constitution.

Investment of public funds.
This section shall not be construed to prohibit the investment of public funds until needed for current requirements or the investment of funds accumulated to provide retirement or pension benefits for public officials and employees, as provided by law.
History: Const. 1963, Art. IX, § 18, Eff. Jan. 1, 1964.   Former Constitution: See Const. 1908, Art. X, § 12.

Subscription to or interest in stock by state prohibited; exceptions.
Sec. 19. The state shall not subscribe to, nor be interested in the stock of any company, association or corporation, except that funds accumulated to provide retirement or pension benefits for public officials and employees may be invested as provided by law; and endowment funds created for charitable or educational purposes may be invested as provided by law governing the investment of funds held in trust by trustees and other state funds or money may be invested in accounts of a bank, savings and loan association, or credit union organized under the laws of this state or federal law, as provided by law.
History: Const. 1963, Art. IX, § 19, Eff. Jan. 1, 1964;—Am. H.J.R. GG, approved Nov. 7, 1978, Eff. Dec. 23, 1978.
Former Constitution: See Const. 1908, Art. X, § 13.

Deposit of state money in certain financial institutions; requirements.
Sec. 20. No state money shall be deposited in banks, savings and loans associations, or credit unions, other than those organized under the law of this state or federal law. No state money shall be deposited in any bank, savings and loan association, or credit union, in excess of 50 percent of the net worth of the bank, savings and loan association, or credit union. Any bank, savings and loan association, or credit union, receiving deposits of state money shall show the amount of state money so deposited as a separate item in all published statements.
History: Const. 1963, Art. IX, § 20, Eff. Jan. 1, 1964;—Am. H.J.R. GG, approved Nov. 7, 1978, Eff. Dec. 23, 1978.
Former Constitution: See Const. 1908, Art. X, § 15.

Accounting for public moneys.
Sec. 21. The legislature shall provide by law for the annual accounting for all public moneys, state and local, and may provide by law for interim accounting.

Accounting and auditing for local governments.
The legislature shall provide by law for the maintenance of uniform accounting systems by units of local government and the auditing of county accounts by competent state authority and other units of government as provided by law.
History: Const. 1963, Art. IX, § 21, Eff. Jan. 1, 1964.   Former Constitution: See Const. 1908, Art. X, § 18.

Examination and adjustment of claims against state.
Sec. 22. Procedures for the examination and adjustment of claims against the state shall be prescribed by law.
History: Const. 1963, Art. IX, § 22, Eff. Jan. 1, 1964.   Former Constitution: See Const. 1908, Art. VI, § 20.

Financial records; statement of revenues and expenditures.
Sec. 23. All financial records, accountings, audit reports and other reports of public moneys shall be public records and open to inspection. A statement of all revenues and expenditures of public moneys shall be published and distributed annually, as provided by law.
History: Const. 1963, Art. IX, § 23, Eff. Jan. 1, 1964.   Former Constitution: See Const. 1908, Art. X, § 17.

Public pension plans and retirement systems, obligation.
Sec. 24. The accrued financial benefits of each pension plan and retirement system of the state and its political subdivisions shall be a contractual obligation thereof which shall not be diminished or impaired thereby.

Financial benefits, annual funding.
Financial benefits arising on account of service rendered in each fiscal year shall be funded during that year and such funding shall not be used for financing unfunded accrued liabilities.
History: Const. 1963, Art. IX, § 24, Eff. Jan. 1, 1964.

Voter approval of increased local taxes; prohibitions; emergency conditions; repayment of bonded indebtedness guaranteed; implementation of section.

Sec. 25. Property taxes and other local taxes and state taxation and spending may not be increased above the limitations specified herein without direct voter approval. The state is prohibited from requiring any new or expanded activities by local governments without full state financing, from reducing the proportion of state spending in the form of aid to local governments, or from shifting the tax burden to local government. A provision for emergency conditions is established and the repayment of voter approved bonded indebtedness is guaranteed. Implementation of this section is specified in Sections 26 through 34, inclusive, of this Article.

History: Add. Initiated Law, approved Nov. 7, 1978, Eff. Dec. 23, 1978.

Limitation on taxes; revenue limit; refunding or transferring excess revenues; exceptions to revenue limitation; adjustment of state revenue and spending limits.

Sec. 26. There is hereby established a limit on the total amount of taxes which may be imposed by the legislature in any fiscal year on the taxpayers of this state. This limit shall not be changed without approval of the majority of the qualified electors voting thereon, as provided for in Article 12 of the Constitution. Effective with fiscal year 1979-1980, and for each fiscal year thereafter, the legislature shall not impose taxes of any kind which, together with all other revenues of the state, federal aid excluded, exceed the revenue limit established in this section. The revenue limit shall be equal to the product of the ratio of Total State Revenues in fiscal year 1978-79 divided by the Personal Income of Michigan in calendar year 1977 multiplied by the Personal Income of Michigan in either the prior calendar year or the average of Personal Income of Michigan in the previous three calendar years, whichever is greater.

For any fiscal year in the event that Total State Revenues exceed the revenue limit established in this section by 1% or more, the excess revenues shall be refunded pro rata based on the liability reported on the Michigan income tax and single business tax (or its successor tax or taxes) annual returns filed following the close of such fiscal year. If the excess is less than 1%, this excess may be transferred to the State Budget Stabilization Fund.

The revenue limitation established in this section shall not apply to taxes imposed for the payment of principal and interest on bonds, approved by the voters and authorized under Section 15 of this Article, and loans to school districts authorized under Section 16 of this Article.

If responsibility for funding a program or programs is transferred from one level of government to another, as a consequence of constitutional amendment, the state revenue and spending limits may be adjusted to accommodate such change, provided that the total revenue authorized for collection by both state and local governments does not exceed that amount which would have been authorized without such change.

History: Add. Initiated Law, approved Nov. 7, 1978, Eff. Dec. 23, 1978.

Exceeding revenue limit; conditions.

Sec. 27. The revenue limit of Section 26 of this Article may be exceeded only if all of the following conditions are met: (1) The governor requests the legislature to declare an emergency; (2) the request is specific as to the nature of the emergency, the dollar amount of the emergency, and the method by which the emergency will be funded; and (3) the legislature thereafter declares an emergency in accordance with the specific of the governor's request by a two-thirds vote of the members elected to and serving in each house. The emergency must be declared in accordance with this section prior to incurring any of the expenses which constitute the emergency request. The revenue limit may be exceeded only during the fiscal year for which the emergency is declared. In no event shall any part of the amount representing a refund under Section 26 of this Article be the subject of an emergency request.

History: Add. Initiated Law, approved Nov. 7, 1978, Eff. Dec. 23, 1978.

Limitation on expenses of state government.

Sec. 28. No expenses of state government shall be incurred in any fiscal year which exceed the sum of the revenue limit established in Sections 26 and 27 of this Article plus federal aid and any surplus from a previous fiscal year.

History: Add. Initiated Law, approved Nov. 7, 1978, Eff. Dec. 23, 1978.

State financing of activities or services required of local government by state law.

Sec. 29. The state is hereby prohibited from reducing the state financed proportion of the necessary costs of any existing activity or service required of units of Local Government by state law. A new activity or service or an increase in the level of any activity or service beyond that required by existing law shall not be required by the legislature or any state agency of units of Local Government, unless a state appropriation is made and disbursed to pay the unit of Local Government for any necessary increased costs. The provision of this section shall not apply to costs incurred pursuant to Article VI, Section 18.

History: Add. Initiated Law, approved Nov. 7, 1978, Eff. Dec. 23, 1978.

Reduction of state spending paid to units of local government.

Sec. 30. The proportion of total state spending paid to all units of Local Government, taken as a group, shall not be reduced below that proportion in effect in fiscal year 1978-79.

History: Add. Initiated Law, approved Nov. 7, 1978, Eff. Dec. 23, 1978.

Levying tax or increasing rate of existing tax; maximum tax rate on new base; increase in assessed valuation of property; exceptions to limitations.

310

Sec. 31. Units of Local Government are hereby prohibited from levying any tax not authorized by law or charter when this section is ratified or from increasing the rate of an existing tax above that rate authorized by law or charter when this section is ratified, without the approval of a majority of the qualified electors of that unit of Local Government voting thereon. If the definition of the base of an existing tax is broadened, the maximum authorized rate of taxation on the new base in each unit of Local Government shall be reduced to yield the same estimated gross revenue as on the prior base. If the assessed valuation of property as finally equalized, excluding the value of new construction and improvements, increases by a larger percentage than the increase in the General Price Level from the previous year, the maximum authorized rate applied thereto in each unit of Local Government shall be reduced to yield the same gross revenue from existing property, adjusted for changes in the General Price Level, as could have been collected at the existing authorized rate on the prior assessed value.

The limitations of this section shall not apply to taxes imposed for the payment of principal and interest on bonds or other evidence of indebtedness or for the payment of assessments on contract obligations in anticipation of which bonds are issued which were authorized prior to the effective date of this amendment.

History: Add. Initiated Law, approved Nov. 7, 1978, Eff. Dec. 23, 1978.

Suit to enforce sections 25 to 31.

Sec. 32. Any taxpayer of the state shall have standing to bring suit in the Michigan State Court of Appeals to enforce the provisions of Sections 25 through 31, inclusive, of this Article and, if the suit is sustained, shall receive from the applicable unit of government his costs incurred in maintaining such suit.

History: Add. Initiated Law, approved Nov. 7, 1978, Eff. Dec. 23, 1978.

Definitions applicable to sections 25 to 32.

Sec. 33. Definitions. The definitions of this section shall apply to Section 25 through 32 of Article IX, inclusive.

"Total State Revenues" includes all general and special revenues, excluding federal aid, as defined in the budget message of the governor for fiscal year 1978-1979. Total State Revenues shall exclude the amount of any credits based on actual tax liabilities or the imputed tax components of rental payments, but shall include the amount of any credits not related to actual tax liabilities. "Personal Income of Michigan" is the total income received by persons in Michigan from all sources, as defined and officially reported by the United States Department of Commerce or its successor agency. "Local Government" means any political subdivision of the state, including, but not restricted to, school districts, cities, villages, townships, charter townships, counties, charter counties, authorities created by the state, and authorities created by other units of local government. "General Price Level" means the Consumer Price Index for the United States as defined and officially reported by the United States Department of Labor or its successor agency.

History: Add. Initiated Law, approved Nov. 7, 1978, Eff. Dec. 23, 1978.

Implementation of sections 25 to 33.

Sec. 34. The Legislature shall implement the provisions of Sections 25 through 33, inclusive, of this Article.

History: Add. Initiated Law, approved Nov. 7, 1978, Eff. Dec. 23, 1978.

Michigan natural resources trust fund.

Sec. 35. There is hereby established the Michigan natural resources trust fund. The trust fund shall consist of all bonuses, rentals, delayed rentals, and royalties collected or reserved by the state under provisions of leases for the extraction of nonrenewable resources from state owned lands, except such revenues accruing under leases of state owned lands acquired with money from state or federal game and fish protection funds or revenues accruing from lands purchased with such revenues. The trust fund may receive appropriations, money, or other things of value.

All money in the state recreational land acquisition trust and the heritage trust shall be transferred to the trust fund. The legislature may provide by law that revenues otherwise dedicated to the trust fund be distributed to the Michigan economic development authority under the terms and in amounts not to exceed the distributions allowed by law on March 30, 1984. The legislature shall provide by law that all rights acquired by holders of bonds heretofore issued by the Michigan economic development authority shall remain unimpaired.

The amount accumulated in the trust fund in any state fiscal year shall not exceed $200,000,000.00, exclusive of interest and earnings, except that this limitation may be increased by law.

The interest and earnings of the trust fund shall be expended for the acquisition of land or rights in land for recreational uses or protection of the land because of its environmental importance or its scenic beauty, for the development of public recreation facilities, and for the administration of the trust fund, which may include payments in lieu of taxes on state owned land purchased through the trust fund. The trust fund may provide grants to units of local government or public authorities which shall be used for the purposes of this section. The legislature shall provide that a portion of the cost of a project funded by such grants be provided by the local unit of government or public authority.

The legislature may provide that a portion, not to exceed 33-1/3 percent, of the revenues received by the trust fund during a fiscal year may be expended during the following fiscal year for the purposes of this section. Not less than 25 percent of the total expenditures from the trust fund in any fiscal year shall be expended for acquisition of land and rights in land and not more than 25 percent of the total expenditures from the trust fund in any fiscal year shall be expended for development of public recreation facilities.

The legislature shall provide by law for the establishment of a trust fund board within the department of natural resources. The trust fund board shall recommend the projects to be funded. The board shall submit its recommendations to the governor who shall submit the board's recommendations to the legislature in an appropriations bill.

The legislature shall provide by law for the implementation of this section.

History: Add. H.J.R. M, approved Nov. 6, 1984, Eff. Dec. 22, 1984.

ARTICLE X

PROPERTY

Disabilities of coverture abolished; separate property of wife; dower.

Sec. 1. The disabilities of coverture as to property are abolished. The real and personal estate of every woman acquired before marriage and all real and personal property to which she may afterwards become entitled shall be and remain the estate and property of such woman, and shall not be liable for the debts, obligations or engagements of her husband, and may be dealt with and disposed of by her as if she were unmarried. Dower may be relinquished or conveyed as provided by law.

History: Const. 1963, Art. X, § 1, Eff. Jan. 1, 1964. **Former Constitution:** See Const. 1908, Art. XVI, § 8.

Eminent domain; compensation.

Sec. 2. Private property shall not be taken for public use without just compensation therefor being first made or secured in a manner prescribed by law. Compensation shall be determined in proceedings in a court of record.

History: Const. 1963, Art. X, § 2, Eff. Jan. 1, 1964. **Former Constitution:** See Const. 1908, Art. XIII, §§ 1-5.

Homestead and personalty, exemption from process.

Sec. 3. A homestead in the amount of not less than $3,500 and personal property of every resident of this state in the amount of not less than $750, as defined by law, shall be exempt from forced sale on execution or other process of any court. Such exemptions shall not extend to any lien thereon excluded from exemption by law.

History: Const. 1963, Art. X, § 3, Eff. Jan. 1, 1964. **Former Constitution:** See Const. 1908, Art. XIV, §§ 1-4.

Escheats.

Sec. 4. Procedures relating to escheats and to the custody and disposition of escheated property shall be prescribed by law.

History: Const. 1963, Art. X, § 4, Eff. Jan. 1, 1964. **Former Constitution:** See Const. 1908, Art. VI, § 20.

State lands.

Sec. 5. The legislature shall have general supervisory jurisdiction over all state owned lands useful for forest preserves, game areas and recreational purposes; shall require annual reports as to such lands from all departments having supervision or control thereof; and shall by general law provide for the sale, lease or other disposition of such lands.

State land reserve.

The legislature by an act adopted by two-thirds of the members elected to and serving in each house may designate any part of such lands as a state land reserve. No lands in the state land reserve may be removed from the reserve, sold, leased or otherwise disposed of except by an act of the legislature.

History: Const. 1963, Art. X § 5, Eff. Jan. 1, 1964.

Resident aliens, property rights.

Sec. 6. Aliens who are residents of this state shall enjoy the same rights and privileges in property as citizens of this state.

History: Const. 1963, Art. X, § 6, Eff. Jan. 1, 1964. **Former Constitution:** See Const. 1908, Art. XVI, § 9.

ARTICLE XI

PUBLIC OFFICERS AND EMPLOYMENT

Oath of public officers.

Sec. 1. All officers, legislative, executive and judicial, before entering upon the duties of their respective offices, shall take and subscribe the following oath or affirmation: I do solemnly swear (or affirm) that I will support the Constitution of the United States and the constitution of this state, and that I will faithfully discharge the duties of the office of .... according to the best of my ability. No other oath, affirmation, or any religious test shall be required as a qualification for any office or public trust.

History: Const. 1963, Art. XI, § 1, Eff. Jan. 1, 1964. **Former Constitution:** See Const. 1908, Art. XVI, § 2.

Terms of office of state and county officers.

Sec. 2. The terms of office of elective state officers, members of the legislature and justices and judges of courts of record shall begin at twelve o'clock noon on the first day of January next succeeding their election, except as otherwise provided in this constitution. The terms of office of county officers shall begin on the first day of January next succeeding their election, except as otherwise provided by law.

History: Const. 1963, Art. XI, § 2, Eff. Jan. 1, 1964. **Former Constitution:** See Const. 1908, Art. XVI, § 1.

Extra compensation.

Sec. 3. Neither the legislature nor any political subdivision of this state shall grant or authorize extra compensation to any public officer, agent or contractor after the service has been rendered or the contract entered into.

History: Const. 1963, Art. XI, § 3, Eff. Jan. 1, 1964. **Former Constitution:** See Const. 1908, Art. XVI, § 3.

Custodian of public moneys; eligibility to office, accounting.

Sec. 4. No person having custody or control of public moneys shall be a member of the legislature, or be eligible to any office of trust or profit under this state, until he shall have made an accounting, as provided by law, of all sums for which he may be liable.

History: Const. 1963, Art. XI, § 4, Eff. Jan. 1, 1964. **Former Constitution:** See Const. 1908, Art. X, § 19.

Classified state civil service; scope; exempted positions; appointment and terms of members of state civil service commission; state personnel director; duties of commission; collective bargaining for state police troopers and sergeants;gf appointments, promotions, demotions, or removals; increases or reductions in compensation; creating or abolishing positions; recommending compensation for unclassified service; appropriation; reports of expenditures; annual audit; payment for personal services; violation; injunctive or mandamus proceedings.

Sec. 5. The classified state civil service shall consist of all positions in the state service except those filled by popular election, heads of principal departments, members of boards and commissions, the principal executive officer of boards and commissions heading principal departments, employees of courts of record, employees of the legislature, employees of the state institutions of higher education, all persons in the armed forces of the state, eight exempt positions in the office of the governor, and within each principal department, when requested by the department head, two other exempt positions, one of which shall be policy-making. The civil service commission may exempt three additional positions of a policy-making nature within each principal department.

The civil service commission shall be non-salaried and shall consist of four persons, not more than two of whom shall be members of the same political party, appointed by the governor for terms of eight years, no two of which shall expire in the same year.

The administration of the commission's powers shall be vested in a state personnel director who shall be a member of the classified service and who shall be responsible to and selected by the commission after open competitive examination.

The commission shall classify all positions in the classified service according to their respective duties and responsibilities, fix rates of compensation for all classes of positions, approve or disapprove disbursements for all personal services, determine by competitive examination and performance exclusively on the basis of merit, efficiency and fitness the qualifications of all candidates for positions in the classified service, make rules and regulations covering all personnel transactions, and regulate all conditions of employment in the classified service.

State Police Troopers and Sergeants shall, through their elected representative designated by 50% of such troopers and sergeants, have the right to bargain collectively with their employer concerning conditions of their employment, compensation, hours, working conditions, retirement, pensions, and other aspects of employment except promotions which will be determined by competitive examination and performance on the basis of merit, efficiency and fitness; and they shall have the right 30 days after commencement of such bargaining to submit any unresolved disputes to binding arbitration for the resolution thereof the same as now provided by law for Public Police and Fire Departments.

No person shall be appointed to or promoted in the classified service who has not been certified by the commission as qualified for such appointment or promotion. No appointments, promotions, demotions or removals in the classified service shall be made for religious, racial or partisan considerations.

Increases in rates of compensation authorized by the commission may be effective only at the start of a fiscal year and shall require prior notice to the governor, who shall transmit such increases to the legislature as part of his budget. The legislature may, by a majority vote of the members elected to and serving in each house, waive the notice and permit increases in rates of compensation to be effective at a time other than the start of a fiscal year. Within 60 calendar days following such transmission, the legislature may, by a two-thirds vote of the members elected to and serving in each house, reject or reduce increases in rates of compensation authorized by the commission. Any reduction ordered by the legislature shall apply uniformly to all classes of employees affected by the increases and shall not adjust pay differentials already established by the civil service commission. The legislature may not reduce rates of compensation below those in effect at the time of the transmission of increases authorized by the commission.

The appointing authorities may create or abolish positions for reasons of administrative efficiency without the approval of the commission. Positions shall not be created nor abolished except for reasons of administrative efficiency. Any employee considering himself aggrieved by the abolition or creation of a position shall have a right of appeal to the commission through established grievance procedures.

The civil service commission shall recommend to the governor and to the legislature rates of compensation for all appointed positions within the executive department not a part of the classified service.

To enable the commission to exercise its powers, the legislature shall appropriate to the commission for the ensuing fiscal year a sum not less than one percent of the aggregate payroll of the classified service for the preceding fiscal year, as certified by the commission. Within six months after the conclusion of each fiscal year the commission shall return to the state treasury all moneys unexpended for that fiscal year.

The commission shall furnish reports of expenditures, at least annually, to the governor and the legislature and shall be subject to annual audit as provided by law.

No payment for personal services shall be made or authorized until the provisions of this constitution pertaining to civil service have been complied with in every particular. Violation of any of the provisions hereof may be restrained or observance compelled by injunctive or mandamus proceedings brought by any citizen of the state.

History: Const. 1963, Art XI, § 5, Eff. Jan. 1, 1964;—Am. Initiated Law, approved Nov. 7, 1978, Eff. Dec. 23, 1978.
Former Constitution: See Const. 1908, Art. VI, § 22.

Merit systems for local governments.

Sec. 6. By ordinance or resolution of its governing body which shall not take effect until approved by a majority of the electors voting thereon, unless otherwise provided by charter, each county, township, city, village, school district and other governmental unit or authority may establish, modify or discontinue a merit system for its employees other than teachers under contract or tenure. The state civil service commission may on request furnish technical services to any such unit on a reimbursable basis.

History: Const. 1963, Art. XI, § 6, Eff. Jan. 1, 1964.

Impeachment of civil officers.

Sec. 7. The house of representatives shall have the sole power of impeaching civil officers for corrupt conduct in office or for crimes or misdemeanors, but a majority of the members elected thereto and serving therein shall be necessary to direct an impeachment.

Prosecution by 3 members of house of representatives.

When an impeachment is directed, the house of representatives shall elect three of its members to prosecute the impeachment.

Trial by senate; oath, presiding officer.

Every impeachment shall be tried by the senate immediately after the final adjournment of the legislature. The senators shall take an oath or affirmation truly and impartially to try and determine the impeachment according to the evidence. When the governor or lieutenant governor is tried, the chief justice of the supreme court shall preside.

Conviction; vote, penalty.

No person shall be convicted without the concurrence of two-thirds of the senators elected and serving. Judgment in case of conviction shall not extend further than removal from office, but the person convicted shall be liable to punishment according to law.

Judicial officers, functions after impeachment.

No judicial officer shall exercise any of the functions of his office after an impeachment is directed until he is acquitted.

History: Const. 1963, Art. XI, § 7, Eff. Jan. 1, 1964. **Former Constitution:** See Const. 1908, Art. IX, §§ 1-4.

ARTICLE XII

AMENDMENT AND REVISION

Amendment by legislative proposal and vote of electors.

Sec. 1. Amendments to this constitution may be proposed in the senate or house of representatives. Proposed amendments agreed to by two-thirds of the members elected to and serving in each house on a vote with the names and vote of those voting entered in the respective journals shall be submitted, not less than 60 days thereafter, to the electors at the next general election or special election as the legislature shall direct. If a majority of electors voting on a proposed amendment approve the same, it shall become part of the constitution and shall abrogate or amend existing provisions of the constitution at the end of 45 days after the date of the election at which it was approved.

History: Const. 1963, Art. XII, § 1, Eff. Jan. 1, 1964. **Former Constitution:** See Const. 1908, Art. XVII, § 1.

Amendment by petition and vote of electors.

Sec. 2. Amendments may be proposed to this constitution by petition of the registered electors of this state. Every petition shall include the full text of the proposed amendment, and be signed by registered electors of the state equal in number to at least 10 percent of the total vote cast for all candidates for governor at the last preceding general election at which a governor was elected. Such petitions shall be filed with the person authorized by law to receive the same at least 120 days before the election at which the proposed amendment is to be voted upon. Any such petition shall be in the form, and shall be signed and circulated in such manner, as prescribed by law. The person authorized by law to receive such petition shall upon its receipt determine, as provided by law, the validity and sufficiency of the signatures on the petition, and make an official announcement thereof at least 60 days prior to the election at which the proposed amendment is to be voted upon.

Submission of proposal; publication.

Any amendment proposed by such petition shall be submitted, not less than 120 days after it was filed, to the electors at the next general election. Such proposed amendment, existing provisions of the constitution which would be altered or abrogated thereby, and the question as it shall appear on the ballot shall be published in full as provided by law. Copies of such publication shall be posted in each polling place and furnished to news media as provided by law.

Ballot, statement of purpose.

The ballot to be used in such election shall contain a statement of the purpose of the proposed amendment, expressed in not more than 100 words, exclusive of caption. Such statement of purpose and caption shall be prepared by the person authorized by law, and shall consist of a true and impartial statement of the purpose of the amendment in such language as shall create no prejudice for or against the proposed amendment.

314

Approval of proposal, effective date; conflicting amendments.

If the proposed amendment is approved by a majority of the electors voting on the question, it shall become part of the constitution, and shall abrogate or amend existing provisions of the constitution at the end of 45 days after the date of the election at which it was approved. If two or more amendments approved by the electors at the same election conflict, that amendment receiving the highest affirmative vote shall prevail.

History: Const. 1963, Art. XII, § 2, Eff. Jan. 1, 1964. **Former Constitution:** See Const. 1908, Art. XVII, §§ 2, 3.

General revision of constitution; submission of question, convention delegates and meeting.

Sec. 3. At the general election to be held in the year 1978, and in each 16th year thereafter and at such times as may be provided by law, the question of a general revision of the constitution shall be submitted to the electors of the state. If a majority of the electors voting on the question decide in favor of a convention for such purpose, at an election to be held not later than six months after the proposal was certified as approved, the electors of each representative district as then organized shall elect one delegate and the electors of each senatorial district as then organized shall elect one delegate at a partisan election. The delegates so elected shall convene at the seat of government on the first Tuesday in October next succeeding such election or at an earlier date if provided by law.

Convention officers, rules, membership, personnel, publications.

The convention shall choose its own officers, determine the rules of its proceedings and judge the qualifications, elections and returns of its members. To fill a vacancy in the office of any delegate, the governor shall appoint a qualified resident of the same district who shall be a member of the same party as the delegate vacating the office. The convention shall have power to appoint such officers, employees and assistants as it deems necessary and to fix their compensation; to provide for the printing and distribution of its documents, journals and proceedings; to explain and disseminate information about the proposed constitution and to complete the business of the convention in an orderly manner. Each delegate shall receive for his services compensation provided by law.

Submission of proposed constitution or amendment.

No proposed constitution or amendment adopted by such convention shall be submitted to the electors for approval as hereinafter provided unless by the assent of a majority of all the delegates elected to and serving in the convention, with the names and vote of those voting entered in the journal. Any proposed constitution or amendments adopted by such convention shall be submitted to the qualified electors in the manner and at the time provided by such convention not less than 90 days after final adjournment of the convention. Upon the approval of such constitution or amendments by a majority of the qualified electors voting thereon the constitution or amendments shall take effect as provided by the convention.

History: Const. 1963, Art. XII, § 3, Eff. Jan. 1, 1964. **Former Constitution:** See Const. 1908, Art. XVII, § 4.

SCHEDULE AND TEMPORARY PROVISIONS

To insure the orderly transition from the constitution of 1908 to this constitution the following schedule and temporary provisions are set forth to be effective for such period as are thereby required.

Recommendations by attorney general for changes in laws.

Sec. 1. The attorney general shall recommend to the legislature as soon as practicable such changes as may be necessary to adapt existing laws to this constitution.

History: Const. 1963, Schedule, § 1, Eff. Jan. 1, 1964. **Former Constitution:** See Const. 1908, Schedule, § 8.

Existing public and private rights, continuance.

Sec. 2. All writs, actions, suits, proceedings, civil or criminal liabilities, prosecutions, judgments, sentences, orders, decrees, appeals, causes of action, contracts, claims, demands, titles and rights existing on the effective date of this constitution shall continue unaffected except as modified in accordance with the provisions of this constitution.

History: Const. 1963, Schedule, § 2, Eff. Jan. 1, 1964. **Former Constitution:** See Const. 1908, Schedule, § 2.

Officers, continuance in office.

Sec. 3. Except as otherwise provided in this constitution, all officers filling any office by election or appointment shall continue to exercise their powers and duties until their offices shall have been abolished or their successors selected and qualified in accordance with this constitution or the laws enacted pursuant thereto.

Terms of office.

No provision of this constitution, or of law or of executive order authorized by this constitution shall shorten the term of any person elected to state office at a statewide election on or prior to the date on which this constitution is submitted to a vote. In the event the duties of any such officers shall not have been abolished or incorporated into one or more of the principal departments at the expiration of his term, such officer shall continue to serve until his duties are so incorporated or abolished.

History: Const. 1963, Schedule, § 3, Eff. Jan. 1, 1964. **Former Constitution:** See Const. 1908, Schedule, § 5.

Officers elected in spring of 1963, term.

Sec. 4. All officers elected at the same election that this constitution is submitted to the people for adoption shall take office and complete the term to which they were elected under the 1908 constitution and existing laws and continue to serve until their successors are elected and qualified pursuant to this constitution or law.

History: Const. 1963, Schedule, § 4, Eff. Jan. 1, 1964. **Former Constitution:** See Const. 1908, Schedule, § 6.

State elective executive officers and senators, 2 and 4 year terms.
Sec. 5. Notwithstanding any other provision in this constitution, the governor, the lieutenant governor, the secretary of state, the attorney general and state senators shall be elected at the general election in 1964 to serve for two-year terms beginning on the first day of January next succeeding their election. The first election of such officers for four-year terms under this constitution shall be held at the general election in 1966.
History: Const. 1963, Schedule, § 5, Eff. Jan. 1, 1964.

Supreme court, reduction to 7 justices.
Sec. 6. Notwithstanding the provisions of this constitution that the supreme court shall consist of seven justices it shall consist of eight justices until the time that a vacancy occurs as a result of death, retirement or resignation of a justice. The first such vacancy shall not be filled.
History: Const. 1963, Schedule, § 6, Eff. Jan. 1, 1964.

Judges of probate, eligibility for re-election.
Sec. 7. Any judge of probate serving on the effective date of this constitution may serve the remainder of the term and be eligible to succeed himself for election regardless of other provisions in this constitution requiring him to be licensed to practice law in this state.
History: Const. 1963, Schedule, § 7, Eff. Jan. 1, 1964.

Judicial officers, staggered terms.
Sec. 8. The provisions of Article VI providing that terms of judicial offices shall not all expire at the same time, shall be implemented by law providing that at the next election for such offices judges shall be elected for terms of varying length, none of which shall be shorter than the regular term provided for the office.
History: Const. 1963, Schedule, § 8, Eff. Jan. 1, 1964.

State board of education; first election, terms.
Sec. 9. The members of the state board of education provided for in Section 3 of Article VIII of this constitution shall first be elected at the first general election after the effective date of this constitution for the following terms: two shall be elected for two years, two for four years, two for six years, and two for eight years as prescribed by law.

Abolition of existing state board of education.
The state board of education provided for in the constitution of 1908 is abolished at twelve o'clock noon January 1 of the year following the first general election under this constitution and the terms of members thereof shall then expire.
History: Const. 1963, Schedule, § 9, Eff. Jan. 1, 1964.

Boards controlling higher education institutions and state board of public community and junior colleges, terms.
Sec. 10. The provisions of this constitution providing for members of boards of control of institutions of higher education and the state board of public community and junior colleges shall be implemented by law. The law may provide that the term of each member in office on the date of the vote on this constitution may be extended, and may further provide that the initial terms of office of members may be less than eight years.
History: Const. 1963, Schedule, § 10, Eff. Jan. 1, 1964.

Michigan State University trustees and Wayne State University governors, terms.
Sec. 11. The provisions of this constitution increasing the number of members of the Board of Trustees of Michigan State University and the Board of Governors of Wayne State University to eight, and of their term of office to eight years, shall be implemented by law. The law may provide that the term of each member in office on the date of the vote on this constitution may be extended one year, and may further provide that the initial terms of office of the additional members may be less than eight years.
History: Const. 1963, Schedule, § 11, Eff. Jan. 1, 1964.

Initial allocation of departments by law or executive order.
Sec. 12. The initial allocation of departments by law pursuant to Section 2 of Article V of this constitution, shall be completed within two years after the effective date of this constitution. If such allocation shall not have been completed within such period, the governor, within one year thereafter, by executive order, shall make the initial allocation.
History: Const. 1963, Schedule, § 12, Eff. Jan. 1, 1964.

State contracts, continuance.
Sec. 13. Contractual obligations of the state incurred pursuant to the constitution of 1908 shall continue to be obligations of the state.

Korean service bonus bonds, appropriation.
For the retirement of notes and bonds issued under Section 26 of Article X of the 1908 constitution, there is hereby appropriated from the general fund each year during their life a sum equal to the amount of principal and interest payments due and payable in each year.
History: Const. 1963, Schedule, § 13, Eff. Jan. 1, 1964.

Mackinac Bridge Authority; refunding of bonds, transfer of functions to highway department.
Sec. 14. The legislature by a vote of two-thirds of the members elected to and serving in each house may provide that the state may borrow money and may pledge its full faith and credit for refunding any bonds issued by the Mackinac Bridge Authority and at the time of refunding the Mackinac Bridge Authority shall be abolished and the operation of the bridge shall be assumed by the state highway department. The legislature may implement this section by law.
History: Const. 1963, Schedule, § 14, Eff. Jan. 1, 1964.

Submission of constitution; time, notice.
Sec. 15. This constitution shall be submitted to the people for their adoption or rejection at the general election to be held on the first Monday in April, 1963. It shall be the duty of the secretary of state forthwith to give notice of such submission to all other officers required to give or publish any notice in regard to a general election. He shall give notice that this constitution will be duly submitted to the electors at such election. The notice shall be given in the manner required for the election of governor.
History: Const. 1963, Schedule, § 15, Eff. Jan. 1, 1964. Former Constitution: See Const. 1908, Schedule, § 10.

Voters, ballots, effective date.
Sec. 16. Every registered elector may vote on the adoption of the constitution. The board of election commissioners in each county shall cause to be printed on a ballot separate from the ballot containing the names of the nominees for office, the words: Shall the revised constitution be adopted? ( ) Yes. ( ) No. All votes cast at the election shall be taken, counted, canvassed and returned as provided by law for the election of state officers. If the revised constitution so submitted receives more votes in its favor than were cast against it, it shall be the supreme law of the state on and after the first day of January of the year following its adoption.
History: Const. 1963, Schedule, § 16, Eff. Jan. 1, 1964. Former Constitution: See Const. 1908, Schedule, § 11.

Adopted by the Constitutional Convention of nineteen hundred sixty-one at Constitution Hall in Lansing on the first day of August, nineteen hundred sixty-two.

Stephen S. Nisbet, President
Fred I. Chase, Secretary

The vote on the Constitution of 1963, as certified by the Board of State Canvassers on June 20, 1963, was 810,860 to 803,436 in favor of adoption.

Index

Absentee Ballot	220
Acquittal	144
Ad Hoc Committee	45-46
Administrative Tribunals	100
Affirmative Action Programs	85
Agriculture Commission	83
Amendment of the State Constitution	
(See Michigan State Constitution, Article IX)	
Annexation	169
Appellate Courts	100
Appointment	52, 65
(See Michigan State Constitution,	
Article V, Sections 2, 6-7, 11)	
Appropriations Bills	44, 130-131
Appropriations Committee	45, 53
Arraignment	94
Assessments	199
Assessed Value	199
Board of Review	200
Market Value	199
State Equalized Value (SEV)	201
State Tax Commission	201
State Tax Tribunal	200
Assessor	165
Attorney General	66
Australian Ballot	218
Bail	105
Baker vs. Carr	16
Ballots	
Absentee	220
Getting a Party on the Ballot	234
Putting Names on the Ballot	146
Benzie County	137
Bicameral Legislature	11
(See Michigan State Constitution,	
Article IV, Section 1)	
Bills	9
Analysis	35
Blueback	35
Co-sponsoring	34
Drafting	31, 35
First Reading	36, 41
Numbering	35
Referral to Committee	36
Public	42
Private	42
Second Reading	38
Sources of	33
Sponsors of	34
Third Reading	38, 41
Three Readings Required	36
Block Grant	118
Board of County Commissioners	138
Compensation	140
Districts	139
Powers	141
Qualifications	139

Term of Office	139
Vacancies	140
Board of	
Canvassers	224
Education	68, 190
Election Inspectors	224
Borrowing	125
Bonds	125
Bound Over	95, 105
Branches of Government	3
Executive	48-89
(See Michigan State Constitution, Article V)	
Legislative	8-47
(See Michigan State Constitution, Article IV)	
Judicial	3, 90-115
(See Michigan State Constitution, Article VI)	
Briefs	102
Budget, State	128, 131
Process of making	130
Budget Stabilization Fund	132
Bureau of Occupational and Professional	
Regulation	2
See Department of Licensing and Regulation	
Bureau of the State Lottery	74
Calendar, Legislative	38
Calling Public Officials	259
Campaign Financing	243
Contribution Limits	244
Candidate, Becoming a	242
Capital, State	3
Capitol Building	3
Caucus	26, 242
Census (Federal)	15
Charter County	155
Circuit Court	98
City Council	5
City Government	5
Charters	176
Clerk	182
Commission Type	180
Council	182
Council-Manager Type	178
Elections	219
Federal Relations	129, 211
Finance	208
Home Rule	176
Incorporation	175-177
(See Michigan State Constitution,	
Article VII, Section 21)	
Kinds of City Government	178
Manager	182
Mayor	5, 179, 181
Police	180
Public Works	181
Recreation	181
Services	180
Wards	182
Water	181

318

Circuit Breaker	120	(See Michigan State Constitution, Article VI)	
Civil Cases	91	Administrator	108
Civil Rights	84	Case Load	104
Civil Rights Commission	84	Circuit Court	98
Civil Service Commission	85	Court of Appeals	93-94, 101
Clerk of the House	36	Court of Claims	104
Clinton Township	157	District Courts	94
Committees, Legislative	36	Juvenile Court	96, 104
Conference	41	Municipal Courts	104
Chairman	46	Probate Court	1, 96
Joint	46	Recorders Court	104
Number of in House	45	Relationship Federal / State	106
Number of in Senate	45	Special Court	103
Of the Whole	41	Trial Courts	93
Options with Bills	38	Supreme Court	102
Powers of	38	Civil Cases	91, 94, 98
House	46	Crime Statistics	87
Senate	41	Criminal Cases	91,94, 98, 104, 105
Standing	45	Crops, Ranking	84
Community Colleges	194		
Commutation	56	Deed	146
Compromise (in Legislative Process)	10, 131	Defendant	91
Conference Committee	34	Department of Agriculture	83
Congressional Township	159	Department of Civil Rights	84
Constituents	8	Department of Civil Service	53, 85
Constitutional Amendment	44	Department of Commerce	70
Coroner (See Medical Examiner)		Department of Corrections	86
Corrections Commission	86	Department of Education	68
County	134-155	Department of Labor	71
(See Michigan State Constitution, Article VII, Sections 1-16)		Department of Licensing and Regulation (Now Bureau of Occupational and Professional Regulation)	72
Animal Control	150		
Board of Commissioners	138, 139	Department of Management and Budget	73, 130
Clerk	145, 161	Department of Mental Health	74
Courts	151	Department of Military Affairs (National Guard)	75
Drain Commissioner	146, 147		
Election	144, 219	Department of Natural Resources	88
Emergency Services	151	Department of Public Health	77
County Executives	138	Department of Social Services	78
		Department of State	67
Government	4	Department of State Police	78
Home Rule	154	Department of Transportation	79
Managers	155	Department of the Treasury	81
Medical Examiners	150	Detroit	70, 171
Origins	135	Districts	
Register of Deeds	146	Community College	195
Road Commissioners	149	Court	95,99,101
Seat	134	House	14
Services	141	Public Schools	187,189
Sheriff	145, 168	Senate	13
Treasurer	145		
What Counties Are	135	Divorce	98
County Department Heads	143	Documents Room, State Legislature	23
Qualifications	144	Double Jeopardy	106
Terms	144		
Vacancies	144	Education	
County Department of Equalization	200	Annexation of Districts	189
County Executive Committee	258	Categorical Grants	211
Courts	90-115, 134	Census (Students)	192

Community Colleges	194
Compulsory Education	197
Consolidation of Districts	189
Department of Education	68
Districts	187
Federal Aid	188
Home Schooling	197
Minimum Number of Days	188
Private/Parochial Schools	196
State Board of	190
Superintendent	190
Superintendent of Public Instruction	187
Transfer of Territory	189
Election Commission	223
Election Inspectors	224
Elections	219-220, 223-225
City Officials	181-182, 219
County Officials	144, 219
Governor	48-50, 219
Michigan Representatives	22, 219
Michigan Senators	22, 219
Primaries	219, 240
Process (Chart)	239
Recount	225
School Board	190, 219
Township Officials	161, 219
U.S. Representatives	219
U.S. Senators	219
Eminent Domain	183
Ethnic Groups	64
Environmental Problems	88
Executive Branch	48-61, 62-89
(See Michigan State Constitution, Article V)	
Departments Headed by:	
Appointed Commissions	82-89
Appointed Department Heads	70-81
Elected Officials	65, 66-69
See each of the 18 departments under the heading of "Department of _____"	
Extradition	57
Farmland and Open Space Preservation Act	206
Federal Assistance	118
Cities	118, 211
Counties	150, 211
School Districts	188
State Government	129
Federal Government and State Government	
Relationship of 106-107, 117-119, 129, 211	
Felony	94
Finances	
Borrowing	125
Bonds	125
Financial Responsibility, State vs. Federal	129
Fines, Use of	108
First Reading, defined	36, 41
Fiscal Agencies	31
Flint	170

Friend of the Court Office	99
Gerrymandering	17
General Orders	41
Geographical Township	158-159
Governor	3, 41, 48
Appointing Directors	52-53
Duties and Powers	41, 52-58
Election of the	49
Judicial Powers	56
Legislative Powers	54
Military Powers	53
Qualifications	49
State of the State Speech	56
Succession of Power	60, 67
(See Michigan State Constitution, Article IV, Section 39 and Article V, Section 26.)	
Term of Office	49
Vacancy in Office	51
Grand Jury	114
Grand Rapids	170
Grants-in-Aid, Federal	118
Handicapped, Civil Rights	85
Headlee Tax Limitation Amendment	126
Highways, Trivia Facts	80
Highway Funds	118, 129
Home Rule Cities	171
Home Rule Option	154
Homestead Property Tax Credit	206-207
House of Representatives, Michigan	28
See Legislature	
Clerk of the House	30, 35
Districts	12, 14
Number of Members	11
Party Control	25, 29
Sergeant-at-Arms	30
Speaker of the House	29, 36
Speaker Pro Tem	27
Term	28
Vacancies	22
Immediate Effect	42
Impeachment	
(See Michigan State Constitution, Article XI, Section 7)	
Interest Groups	250
Goals of	254
Methods	255
Intermediate School Districts (ISD)	193
Board Member Terms	194
Income Tax	119
Infrastructure, City	183
Initiative	43
Journal of the House and Senate	23
Judges	
Censure	112

320

Judges (continued)
    Election of   111
    Removal   112
    Term   110
Judicial Branch   3, 90-115
Judicial Tenure Commission   112
Junkets   36
Jurisdictional Question   145
Juries   113-114
    Civil Cases   113
    Criminal Cases   113
    Grand Jury   114
    Petit Jury   113
    Selection Options   113
Juvenile Courts   96
Juvenile Delinquents   96

Keweenaw County   137

Lansing   170
Laws, Making of the   32-45
Laws, Publishing the   23
Laws, When Take Effect   42
Legislative Agents - See Lobbyists
Legislative Service Bureau   31, 35
Legislative Apportionment Commission   15, 16
Legislative Branch   3, 8-47
Legislative Staff   30
Legislators   20
    See House of Representatives and Senate
    Background   20
    Elections   22
    Immunity   23
    Qualifications   21
    Removal and Replacement   22
    Restrictions   22
    Salary and Benefits   22
    Travel   36
Legislature   8-47
    Adjournment   19
    Lower Chamber   15
    Meeting Times   20
    Reapportionment   15-17
    Recesses   19
    Sessions   19
    Seniority   46
    Special Sessions   19, 55
    Term   19
    Upper Chamber   15
Legislative Liaison   59
Letters to the Editor   249
Libraries, Public   108
    (See Michigan State Constitution,
    Article VIII, Section 9)
License Fees   122
Lieutenant Governor   26, 60
    Election   60
    Qualifications   60
    Term   60

Line Item Veto   42, 55
Lobbyists/Lobbying   33, 250
Lottery   1, 74, 124
Lower Chamber   15

Majority Party   26
Majority Floor Leader   28
Majority Leader   28
Majority Whip   27
Marquette   137
Mayor   5, 179, 181
Medical Examiner   150
Metropolitan Area   170
Michigan
    Background of State   62
    Population   63
Michigan Historical Museum   63
Millage Explained   201
Minority Floor Leader   27
Minority Leader   27, 30
Minority Party   233
Minority Whip   27
Misdemeanor   94
Missouri Plan   111
Municipal Courts   104

National Guard   75
Natural Resources Commission   88
Non-Tax Revenue   124
    Borrowing   125
    Bonds   125
    State Lottery   124
Northwest Ordinance   136

Office Holders Account   50
Open Meetings Act   184
Optional Unified Plan   154
Ordinance   142
Override Veto   42

PACs, Campaign Contributions   244
Pages in Legislature   30
Pardon   56
Parole   57
Parole Board   86
Peremptory Challenge   113
Petitions
    Annexation (school district)   189
    Constitutional Amendments   43
    Nominating   242
Plaintiff   91
Plat   146
Poll Books   220
Poll Watchers   238
Political Parties   230, 257
    Conventions   241
    Leadership   236-237, 258
    Make Up   231
    Membership   257

Political Parties (continued)

    Minor Parties 233

    Organization 236

    Platform 259

Political Township 158, 160

Precinct Delegates 258

Preliminary Examination 95

President of the Senate 27, 61

Presidential Primary 258

President of the Senate Pro Tempore 27

Primaries 238

    Blanket 241

    Closed 240

    Nonpartisan 240

    Open 240

    Presidential 240

Prisons 86-87, 94

Private Schools 196

Probate Courts 1, 96

Probation 86

Property Tax 198

    Assessments 199

    Uses 203

    School Districts 203

    Cities 203

    Counties 203

    Townships 203

    Limitations 204

    Headlee 205

    Homestead Tax Credit 206

    Farmland & Open Space Preservation 206

Prosecuting Attorney 91, 94, 105, 114, 144

Public Administrator 67

Public Service Commission 71

Publishing the Laws 23

Rainy Day Fund 132

Reapportionment 15-17

Recall 230

    (See Michigan State Constitution,

    Article II, Section 8)

Recorders Court (Detroit) 104

Recount 225

Redford Township 157

Referendum 44

Register of Deeds 4

Registration for Voting 215

Removal from Office (See Recall)

Representatives (Legislators)

    Election of 22, 219

    Number of 12

    Qualifications 21

    Removal 22

    (See Michigan State Constitution

    Article II, Section 8, Article IV,

    Section 16)

    Salary 22

    Term of office 25

    Vacancies 22

Reprieves 56

Resolutions 10, 142

Revenue for Local Governments 211

Revenue Sharing, State 210

Revenue Sources, State 119

Road Commissioners 149

Roll Call Vote 39

Salaries, Executive 50

Salaries, Legislative 22

School Aid Formula 211

School Boards 5

School Districts 187

    Boundaries 189

    Intermediate (ISD) 193

School Financing 194

    Public aid to private schools

    prohibited 196

Scholle vs. Hare 16

School Districts 5

Sales Tax 121, 210

Second Reading, defined 38

Secretary of State 223

Secretary of the Senate 35

Section of Land 159

Senate 13, 25-28, 40

    See Legislature

    Approval of Appointments 66

    Committees 45

    Districts 13

    Officers 27

    Party Control 25

    President 61

    President Pro Tempore 27

    Sergeant-at-Arms 30

    Secretary of the 35

    Term 25

    Tie Vote 25

Senators, State,

    See Senate

    Election of 22, 219

    Number of 12

    Qualifications 21

    Removal 22

    Salary 22

    Term of Office 25

    Vacancies 22

Seniority 46

Sheriff, See County 145, 219

Single Business Tax 122

Small Claims Court 96

Solicitor General 67

Speaker of the House 29, 36

Special Sessions of Legislature 19, 55

Standing Committees 140

State Aid to Education 210

State Board of Education 68, 193

State Boundary Commission 174

322

State Constitution 3
    Complete 280-316
State/Federal Government Relationship
    6, 106-107, 117-119, 129, 211
State Officers Compensation Commission 23
State Party Convention 241
State Spending 128
State Treasurer 81
Strong Mayor-Council 179
Subcommittee 45
Superintendent of Public Instruction 68, 187
Supreme Court, Justices 110
Survey, Land 136

Tax Allocation Board, County 203
Taxes 81, 119-123
    Assessment Roll 200
    Boats (watercraft) 122
    Business 122
    Cigarette 122
    Cities with Income Tax 208
    Equalization of 201
    Exemptions 120
    Figuring the Tax 202
    Headlee Tax Limitation 205
    Hotel and Motel 122
    Income Tax 119
    Inheritance Tax 123
    Lien 146
    Limitations of Taxing 204
    Mill Limitation 205
    Municipal Income Tax 208
    Oil and Gas 122
    Property Tax 120, 198, 199
    Real Estate 122
    Sales Tax 121
    Single Business 122
    Special Assessment 209
    State Tax Tribunal 200
    Timber (Stumpage) 122
    Transportation Taxes 210
    Use Tax 122, 209
    Value Added Tax 122
Township 156-169
    Annual Meeting 166, 167
    Average Population 160
    Assessor 165
    Board 160
    Charter Townships 160, 167
    Clerk 156, 160, 162
    Compensation 161
    Commissions 162
    Congressional Townships 159
    Election Commission 223
    Elections 161
    Geographical Townships 158-159
    Government 4, 156, 157
    Home Rule 176
    Housing Commission 168

    Planning Commission 165
    Political Townships 158, 160
    Property Assessment 162, 165
    Sales Tax Returned to 121
    Superintendent 162
    Supervisor 157, 160, 162
    Survey Township 159
    Treasurer 163
    Trustees 160
    Vacancies 161
    Zoning Board of Appeals 165
    Zoning Laws 165
Toxic Waste 88
Traffic Cases 94
Transportation Commission 80

Unicameral Legislature 11
Upper Chamber 15

Veto 42, 54
Villages 5, 172, 174-176
    Assessment of Property 172
    Charters 175
    Elections 173
    General Law 175
    Home Rule 171
    Incorporation 174-177
    Marshal 173
    President 173
    Relationship to Township 172
    Requirements 172
    Treasurer 173
    Trustees 173
    Voting 173
Voice Vote 38
Voting 213, 216, 219-221
    Absentee Voting 220
    Ballots 220
    Counting the Vote 224
    Illegal Practices 216
    Non-Partisan 228
    Patterns 226
    Place and Manner 219
    Poll Books 220
    Polls 216
    President and Vice President 219
    Qualifications for 214
    Registration 215
    Residence Requirements 215
    Split Ticket 227
    Straight Ticket 227
    Village Residences 215
    Write-in Candidates 258
Warren 170
Waterford Township 160
Wayne County 136, 137
Weak Mayor-Council 179
Welfare 128
Whip 27

Wills	1, 96
Writing Public Officials	248
Zoning	5, 165-166